D0554736

VOICES AND VISIONS

A STORY OF
CANADA

Daniel Francis

Contributing authors: Angus Scully and Jill Germain

OXFORD
UNIVERSITY PRESS

OXFORD
UNIVERSITY PRESS

70 Wynford Drive, Don Mills, Ontario M3C 1J9
www.oup.com/ca

Oxford University Press is a department of
the University of Oxford.

It furthers the University's objective of excellence
in research, scholarship, and education
by publishing worldwide in

Oxford   New York

Auckland   Cape Town   Dar es Salaam   Hong Kong
Karachi   Kuala Lumpur   Madrid   Melbourne   Mexico City
Nairobi   New Delhi   Shanghai   Taipei   Toronto

With offices in

Argentina   Austria   Brazil   Chile   Czech Republic
France   Greece   Guatemala   Hungary   Italy   Japan
Poland   Portugal   Singapore   South Korea   Switzerland
Thailand   Turkey   Ukraine   Vietnam

Oxford is a registered trade mark of Oxford University Press
in the UK and in certain other countries

Published in Canada
by Oxford University Press

Copyright © Oxford University Press Canada 2006

ISBN-13: 978-0-19-542169-9
ISBN-10: 0-19-542169-8

The moral rights of the author have been asserted

Database right Oxford University Press (maker)

First published 2006

All rights reserved. No part of this publication may be
reproduced, stored in a retrieval system, or transmitted, in any
form or by any means, without the prior permission in writing of
Oxford University Press, or as expressly permitted by law, or
under terms agreed with the appropriate reprographics rights
organization. Enquiries concerning reproduction outside the
scope of the above should be sent to the Rights Department,
Oxford University Press, at the address above.

You must not circulate this book in any other binding or cover
and you must impose this same condition on any acquirer.

Printed and bound in Canada
This book is printed on permanent (acid-free) paper ∞.

1 2 3 4 – 09 08 07 06

Managing editor: Monica Schwalbe
Co-Developmental editors: Margaret Hoogeveen, Tracey MacDonald
Production editor: Heather Kidd
Copyeditor/proofreader: Susan McNish
Photo research and permissions: Maria DeCambra
Cover design: Joan Dempsey
Text design, layout, and art: VISUTronX

Publisher's note: This resource is based on an instructional
design by Sharon Sterling.

Acknowledgements

The publisher would like to thank the following people who
have contributed to this resource throughout its development:
David Ball, F.E. Osborne Junior High School, Calgary Board of
Education; **Selena Frizzley**, Ascension of Our Lord School,
Calgary Roman Catholic Separate School District #1; **Norma
Jani**, Edmonton Catholic School District; **Barb Nagel**, Rimbey
Junior Senior High School, Wolf Creek School Division; **Laurie
Paddock**, Ernest Morrow Junior High School, Calgary Board of
Education; **Gary Smith**, T.D. Baker School, Edmonton Public
Schools; **Thomas A. Smith**, Monsignor J.S. Smith School,
Calgary Roman Catholic Separate School District #1; **Jackie
Underhill**, S. Bruce Smith School, Edmonton Public Schools;
Joanne Wheeler, St. Margaret School, Calgary Roman Catholic
Separate School District #1; **Shelley Williams**, Monsignor J.S.
Smith School, Calgary Roman Catholic Separate School
District #1; and **Brandy Yee**, Mitford Middle School, Rocky
View School Division.

Cover Images

Main/background image: Aurora borealis
Other images (clockwise from top right): Teresa Holloway, 15,
a member of the Red Thunder professional dance group,
prepares to perform at Buffalo Nations Day in Banff, 1993;
Shooting the Rapids by Frances Anne Hopkins, 1879; Polish
"Dozynki" celebration, Tide Lake, Alberta, 1915; fifty-three
new Canadians are sworn in during a citizenship ceremony at
the Museum of Civilization in Gatineau, Québec, on 1 July
2002; woman plowing a field in Manitoba (date unknown).

Since this page cannot accommodate all copyright notices, pages
345 and 346 are considered extensions of this page.

Every possible effort has been made to trace the original source
of text and photographic material contained in this book. Where
the attempt has been unsuccessful, the publisher would be
pleased to hear from copyright holders to rectify any errors or
omissions.

Contents

When you see this icon on pages of this book, go to the *Voices and Visions* Online Resource Centre at www.oup.com/ca/education/companion and click on the cover. You can also go to the site directly at www.oup.com/ca/education/companion/voicesandvisions.

Features

Skill Check

Biography

Case Study

Identity

Chapter Project

Part 1

Active citizenship means many things. It means learning about what's going on in your community, in your country, and in the world. It means working together with other people for a common goal. It means stepping up to support your community.

Pierre La Vérendrye—a Canadien—did just that. While farming the land near Trois-Rivières, in Québec, he began to yearn for adventure. So, in 1732, he set out for the West, a place virtually unknown to Canadiens or Europeans. Here La Vérendrye met new people, such as the Assiniboine, and began trading for fur.

One day, a Cree named Auchagah told La Vérendrye about a great "Western Sea." La Vérendrye devoted the rest of his life to exploring the West, searching in vain for a route to the Pacific Ocean. During those years, he built forts, created maps, and inspired many others to make their way west. In this way, he helped lay the foundations for the development of Western Canada.

In this unit, you will learn about the history of our country before Confederation in 1867. You will meet the First Nations, Canada's indigenous peoples, who lived throughout this land. You will meet travellers who bravely went to places that were completely unknown to them. You will see how people learned to work together. As well, you will learn how the diverse peoples of this land survived life in a harsh land, war, rebellion, and assimilation to create a country called Canada.

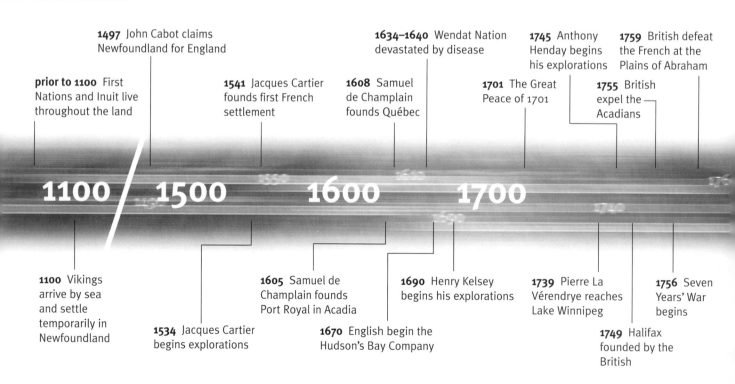

1497 John Cabot claims Newfoundland for England

prior to 1100 First Nations and Inuit live throughout the land

1541 Jacques Cartier founds first French settlement

1634–1640 Wendat Nation devastated by disease

1608 Samuel de Champlain founds Québec

1745 Anthony Henday begins his explorations

1759 British defeat the French at the Plains of Abraham

1701 The Great Peace of 1701

1755 British expel the Acadians

1100 / **1500** **1600** **1700**

1100 Vikings arrive by sea and settle temporarily in Newfoundland

1605 Samuel de Champlain founds Port Royal in Acadia

1690 Henry Kelsey begins his explorations

1739 Pierre La Vérendrye reaches Lake Winnipeg

1756 Seven Years' War begins

1534 Jacques Cartier begins explorations

1670 English begin the Hudson's Bay Company

1749 Halifax founded by the British

Active Citizenship Project One

Form a small group to research active citizenship in Canada today.

a) Explore ideas about citizenship. What does it mean to belong?

b) Brainstorm examples of ways in which individual people can be active citizens. Think of ways that individuals can make a difference. Think of people in business and politics. Also think of ways people help others by volunteering in their communities. Think of people who are leaders. Think of those who make our country a home for everyone.

c) Find examples of active citizenship in your community or in Canada. Listen to the radio, watch television, read the newspaper, or search the Internet. Take note of people's names. How is each making a difference?

d) In your group, compare notes. Create an oral report to present four examples of active citizenship in Canada today.

e) In what ways are you an active citizen?

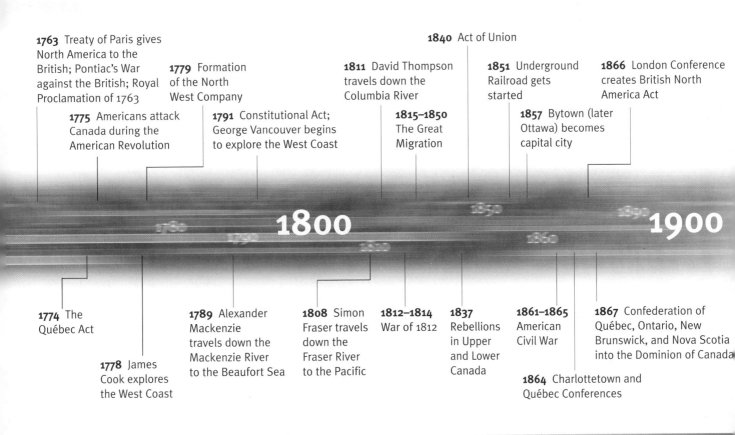

1763 Treaty of Paris gives North America to the British; Pontiac's War against the British; Royal Proclamation of 1763

1779 Formation of the North West Company

1811 David Thompson travels down the Columbia River

1840 Act of Union

1851 Underground Railroad gets started

1866 London Conference creates British North America Act

1775 Americans attack Canada during the American Revolution

1791 Constitutional Act; George Vancouver begins to explore the West Coast

1815–1850 The Great Migration

1857 Bytown (later Ottawa) becomes capital city

1800

1900

1774 The Québec Act

1789 Alexander Mackenzie travels down the Mackenzie River to the Beaufort Sea

1808 Simon Fraser travels down the Fraser River to the Pacific

1812–1814 War of 1812

1837 Rebellions in Upper and Lower Canada

1861–1865 American Civil War

1867 Confederation of Québec, Ontario, New Brunswick, and Nova Scotia into the Dominion of Canada

1778 James Cook explores the West Coast

1864 Charlottetown and Québec Conferences

Chapter 1 Aboriginal Societies

Chapter INQUIRY

Who are the diverse Aboriginal peoples who have contributed to the building of the country we now call Canada?

Key CONCEPT ▸ Culture

Culture is a way of life or a way of being that is shared by a group of people. Culture includes the knowledge, experiences, and values that a group shares and that shape the way its members see the world. Governments, relationships with nature, languages, and beliefs, for example, are all part of your culture. It can include the foods you eat, the clothes you wear, the sports you play, and the entertainment you enjoy.

Because culture is an active part of our lives and our identities, it changes to reflect changes in our society. However, even though a culture may change over time, it always stays associated with a particular group of people.

SKILLS

Honing Your Skills

You will encounter many different images throughout this textbook. Photographs, paintings, and other illustrations can be great ways to explore a people's history and culture—if you know how to analyze them. The Skill Check feature in this chapter will show you how to **Interpret Images**. At the end of the chapter, you will be asked to work with images as part of the project, in which you'll examine the importance of cross-cultural understanding.

Pluralistic Societies

Canada is a **pluralistic society**. This means that our history has helped us learn to value all cultures. We are a society made up of many groups of people. All these groups have unique identities, ideas, cultures, and ways of seeing the world. Individual members within each group have their own points of view and identity, which may be different from those of other members. *Pluralism* means that we respect and value the individual and collective opinions and identities of all people. This respect for diversity in Canada encourages the development of a vibrant, democratic society.

Long before Canada became the country we know today, the many First Nations and Inuit [IN-yoo-it] who lived here formed a pluralistic society. Each group had its own ideas, world view, language, spiritual beliefs, government, and way of life.

This chapter explores three of the groups: the Mi'kmaq [MIG-mah], Haudenosaunee [hah-duh-nuh-SAH-nee], and Anishinabe [a-nih-shih-NAH-bee]. They are the first three peoples to come in contact with the European explorers who travelled to North America in the 1400s and 1500s.

The Mi' kmaq people and other First
Nations believe that this land existed
before man's short stay on earth and it
will exist long after we have gone.
Therefore it is something to be
respected as it is a gift from the
Creator for us to use.

–John Joe Sark
(Mi'kmaq)

We Haida were surrounded by art. Art
was one with the culture. Art was our
only written language. Throughout our
history, it has been the art that has
kept our spirits alive.

–Robert Davidson
(Haida)

**Values and
Beliefs**

If the old
will remember, the very
young will listen.

–Chief Dan George
(Coast Salish)

Our responsibilities to
Mother Earth are the
foundation of our spirituality,
culture and traditions.

–Chief Harold Turner
(Swampy Cree)

The women have a very noble,
respectful place in our society. Women
are in the forefront of keeping our
traditions, of keeping our ways of life
that were given to us in the beginning
of our time. And this is the way we are
told that it should be.

–Audrey Shenandoah
(Onondaga)

In tribal customs, there was not a need
by individuals to beg to be needed,
wanted, or valued. It was simply a
given that each person brought her
special talent to the dance. Everyone and
every talent was celebrated, in other
words, because each person's contribution
helped balance the community.

–Shannon Thunderbird
(Mohawk)

**Think ▶
AHEAD**

Read aloud each of the quotations above. On the blackboard or on an overhead, record the
values you think are being expressed by each speaker. Then discuss this question: Do these
values exist in the broader Canadian society today?

SKILL CHECK: Interpret Images

There is a saying that a picture is worth a thousand words. It is true that images—photographs, paintings, and drawings—can give us a lot of information about history and culture. But can images always be trusted?

Points of View

All types of images are influenced by the photographer's or artist's **point of view**. This means that no matter how or when an image is made, it is affected by the views, values, and culture of the person who created it.

Critical Interpretation

When viewing an image, ask yourself the following questions in order to determine how **authentic**, or trustworthy and reliable, it is.

- What is the image about?
- Who made it, and when?
- What might be the point of view of the person who made the image?
- Is the image a primary or secondary source?
- Do other images of the same event show similar details? What does this suggest?
- Does the image maker show any **bias** toward the people or events being depicted? (A bias is a personal like or dislike of something or someone that is not necessarily based on fact. The statement "I do not trust teenaged male drivers" reflects a bias against a certain group of drivers.)
- Are there any details in the image that you know to be inaccurate?
- Is this image a reliable view of real events and people?

Primary and Secondary Source Images

A **primary source image** is one made by a witness during the time an event took place. A photograph of people signing a treaty is a primary source image. So is a sketch of a battle drawn by a reporter who is on the scene.

A **secondary source image** is one that is created from memory, imagination, or a pre-existing image. A sketch of a battle scene drawn by a soldier after a war is over is a secondary source image.

Further Research

What questions has the image raised? What are some sources you can use to find answers?

Try It!

This painting was done by a European. It is supposed to show a Haudenosaunee village before the society had had much contact with Europeans. Point out at least three historical inaccuracies in the painting. What biases does the artist show?

Values and Viewpoints

As mentioned at the beginning of the chapter, the First Nations in North America are diverse peoples. For example, the Mi'kmaq, Anishinabe, and Haudenosaunee, as well as all other First Nations, have different teachings about their history and origins. In this section, we will read about a few of these teachings. We will also examine some of the values and viewpoints that these three First Nations shared.

Focus

What were some of the shared values and ways of life of the Mi'kmaq, Anishinabe, and Haudenosaunee?

Reading
STRATEGY

Before you begin reading this chapter, skim through it to learn how it is organized. You will see that the text is presented in different ways: paragraphs, bulleted lists, and boxed features. There are also illustrations and photographs with caption text. How do they influence the way we read the text?

Diversity

First Nations peoples have lived in all parts of the land we now call Canada. They lived in the frozen lands of the Arctic. They lived in the mountains and on the islands of the west coast. They lived in the eastern woodlands, on the prairie grasslands, on the western plateau, and on the subarctic tundra. Each First Nation developed a unique culture suited to its surroundings in the natural world. **Natural world** means the land, water, mountains, forests, plants, wildlife, and climate. The peoples' cultures became as diverse as the Canadian landscape.

Figure 1.1 Location of Aboriginal language groups and peoples across Canada. Before contact with Europeans, there were 50 to 70 different languages spoken across the country. Some First Nations no longer exist (for example, the Beothuk [bay-AH-thuk]) or have been absorbed into other cultures. According to the map, which First Nations lived in the area where you now live? Do they still live there?

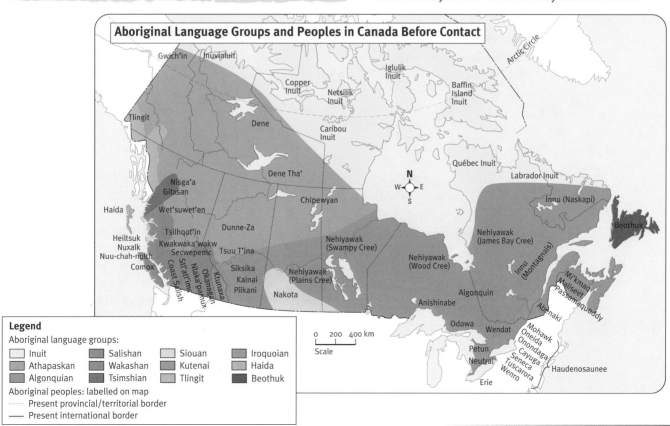

Aboriginal Language Groups and Peoples in Canada Before Contact

Gwich'in   Inuvialuit   Iglulik Inuit   Arctic Circle

Copper Inuit   Netsilik Inuit   Baffin Island Inuit

Tlingit   Dene   Caribou Inuit

Québec Inuit   Labrador Inuit

Dene Tha'   Innu (Naskapi)

Nisga'a Gitxsan   Chipewyan   Beothuk

Haida   Wet'suwet'en

Heiltsuk   Tsilhqot'in   Dunne-Za   Nehiyawak (James Bay Cree)

Nuxalk   Kwakwaka'wakw   Tsuu T'ina   Nehiyawak (Swampy Cree)   Innu (Montagnais)

Nuu-chah-nulth   Secwepemc   Nehiyawak (Wood Cree)

Comox   Okanagan   Nlaka'pamux   Stl'atl'imc   Coast Salish   Ktunaxa   Siksika Kainai Piikani   Nehiyawak (Plains Cree)   Mi'kmaq Maliseet Passamaquoddy

Nakota   Algonquin   Abenaki

Anishinabe   Odawa   Wendat

Mohawk Oneida Onondaga Cayuga Seneca Tuscarora Wenro

Petun Neutral   Haudenosaunee

Erie

0   200   400 km
Scale

Legend
Aboriginal language groups:
- Inuit
- Athapaskan
- Algonquian
- Salishan
- Wakashan
- Tsimshian
- Siouan
- Kutenai
- Tlingit
- Iroquoian
- Haida
- Beothuk

Aboriginal peoples: labelled on map
...... Present provincial/territorial border
—— Present international border

World Views

So far, you have learned that there were many unique First Nation cultures here. However, these diverse peoples also shared some **core values**. Core values are important ideas or beliefs about how people should live. Taken together, these values make up a **world view**. Many First Nations peoples, including the Mi'kmaq, Anishinabe, and Haudenosaunee, shared values relating to their relationships with the Creator, the natural world, other people, and themselves. For example, they believed the following:

Tech Link

Some First Nations call the drum "the heartbeat of the earth." Open Chapter 1 on your *Voices and Visions* CD-ROM to listen to a recording of a drumming piece.

- People are not separate from nature or from the non-living world. Everything on earth is connected to everything else.
- The wisdom and experience of the Elders is highly valued. Elders deserve the respect of all members of the community.

- A spiritual world exists. It plays a very important role in all that happens on earth.
- People must live in harmony with each other and in balance with nature.

Each of these values affected how these First Nations lived. However, different First Nations also held some values that were not shared by all nations. You will investigate the diversity of the Mi'kmaq, Anishinabe, and Haudenosaunee in the upcoming sections of this chapter.

Indigenous Peoples

First Nations peoples are **indigenous** to North America. This means that they are the original people of this land. Each First Nation has unique beliefs about how the earth was created and how people came to exist.

These beliefs are often passed from generation to generation through **traditional teachings**. Traditional teachings also help to explain the relationships among the plants, animals, land, people, and the spirit world. On the next page is an example from the Mi'kmaq people. It tells about the creation of the earth and the first human, a man named Kluskap.

Figure 1.2 This painting is called *Birth of the Earth* and was created by Haudenosaunee artist Arnold Jacobs. It shows the first human, a woman, falling from the Sky World onto the back of a sea turtle. With the help of the animals, they create a continent of land around the turtle's back. That is why some First Nations today call North America "Turtle Island."

Respond

This is an English translation of a teaching that was originally told in the language of the Mi'kmaq. What issues might there be with people using translations to try to understand another's culture?

On the other side of the Path of the Spirits, in ancient times, Kisúlk, the Creator, made a decision. Kisúlk created the first born, Niskam, the Sun, to be brought across the Milky Way to light the earth. Also sent across the sky was a bolt of lightning that created Sitqamúk, the Earth. And from the same bolt, Kluskap was also created out of the dry earth. Kluskap became a powerful teacher, whose gifts and allies were great.

In another bolt of lightning came the light of fire, and with it came the animals, the vegetation, and the birds. These other life forms gradually gave Kluskap a human form. Kluskap rose from the earth and gave thanks to Kisúlk as he honoured the six directions: the sun, the earth, and then the east, south, west, and north. The abilities within the human form made up the seventh direction.

Kluskap asked Kisúlk how he should live, and Kisúlk in response sent Nukumi, Kluskap's grandmother, to guide him in life. Created from a rock that was transformed into the body of an old woman through the power of Niskam, the Sun, Nukumi was an Elder whose knowledge and wisdom were enfolded in the Mi'kmaq language.

Source: Based on the ancient teachings of Mi'kmaq Elders and compiled by Kep'tin Stephen Augustine of Big Cove, NB, Evan Thomas Pritchard, comp., with annotations by Stephen Augustine, *Introductory Guide to Micmac Words and Phrases* (Rexton, NB: Resonance Communications, 1991).

Global Connections ■

Canada is not the only country in the world where indigenous peoples existed long before colonists arrived from other countries. The Aborigines of Australia, the Yanomami of Brazil and Venezuela, the Ainu of Japan, and the Maori of New Zealand are all examples of indigenous peoples around the world.

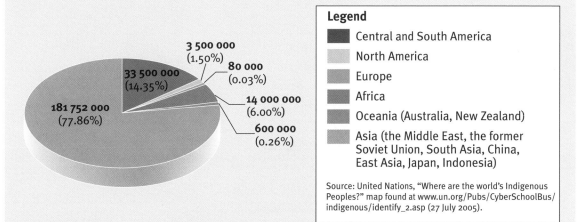

Legend

- Central and South America
- North America
- Europe
- Africa
- Oceania (Australia, New Zealand)
- Asia (the Middle East, the former Soviet Union, South Asia, China, East Asia, Japan, Indonesia)

3 500 000 (1.50%)
80 000 (0.03%)
33 500 000 (14.35%)
14 000 000 (6.00%)
181 752 000 (77.86%)
600 000 (0.26%)

Source: United Nations, "Where are the world's Indigenous Peoples?" map found at www.un.org/Pubs/CyberSchoolBus/indigenous/identify_2.asp (27 July 2005).

Figure 1.3 Indigenous peoples of the world, 2005. This graph shows the percentage of indigenous peoples living on the different continents. Investigate an indigenous people living outside of Canada to discover one of the traditional teachings on their origins.

Keepers of Knowledge

Traditional teachings, such as the one about Kluskap, have been passed down orally from generation to generation by **Elders**. Elders have traditionally been the most respected members of Aboriginal communities. They have used their experience and wisdom to help people in their communities make good decisions. Language, traditions, ceremonies, laws, skills, and histories are some of the things they have taught. Elders' teachings have been very important to the upbringing of every child.

Stories

One way Elders taught youngsters morals and values was by telling stories. Sometimes the stories were about the spiritual heroes of the First Nation. For example, the Siksika [sik-SIK-uh] told stories about Napi, and the Cree (Nehiyawak [nay-HI-uh-wuk]) told about Wisakecahk. These stories were used not only for teaching lessons but for entertaining listeners as well. Elders also told very old legends that had been passed down to them through the generations.

Reading
STRATEGY

Copy the following story outline into your notebook. As you are reading the Ehep Legend on the next page, fill in the outline. Compare your completed outline with that of a classmate. Do your outlines differ? Why?

This legend starts when two people ...
After that ...
Next ...
Then ...
The story ends when ...

Canada Today

Elders continue to play a very important role in their communities today. They do this by exploring the unique relationships that humans have with the land, places, and environment. Elders are helping young Aboriginal people reconnect with their culture by teaching them traditional activities. One example was a program run in the community of Bigstone Cree Nation in Alberta. Students were taught how to trace their ancestry. As part of the program, Elders held workshops to teach the students about the history of their band. They also took part in hunting and canoe trips. The Elders were positive role models for the students. The program also gave the youths and the Elders the chance to build rewarding relationships.

Figure 1.4 Emily Saganash (of the Waswanipi Cree First Nation in Québec) prepares a beaver as her granddaughter watches. She will remove the pelt for sale and cook the meat. Why is it important for Elders to continue to be teachers and role models in their communities today?

VOICES ■

Swampy Cree Elder Louis Bird is a well-known storyteller from Peawanuck, Ontario. He explains that legends are a very important part of his people's culture:

❝ The legends were very, very useful. And it was part of the education system. They were made for that—an education medium—for any age group. And it is used for the young people, who always look forward to hearing it again, no matter where they go, no matter how many times they hear the legends. The same one. There's always humour in it. Humour, humour— they always laugh. No matter if you have laughed at it before, another storyteller can create it in a different way that you still laugh at it. ❞

Here is an example of one of the legends that Louis remembers.

Ehep Legend

When the first human beings [two people, a man and woman] came to the earth, they were somewhere in the land—we don't know for sure exactly where, but they were there. And they noticed that there was a land down there, a land so beautiful, and they so wished to go and see that land. There was a giant spider who noticed that they were longing to go there.

So he says to them: "Do you wish to go and see and live in that land?"

So the people say: "Yes, I wish we could go there and see that land."

So Ehep, the giant spider, says: "I will help you if you do what I say. I will lower you down with my string. But you will have to sit in here, in this sort of basket, but it is actually like a nest." He says, "I will lower you down in this nest, but the thing you have to do is, you have to not look at the land even when you think you are getting closer. You must not look down until you touch down to this land. Because if you do that, if you look at it before you hit the ground, you will not be happy. You will have to suffer to live in that land, even though it's beautiful."

And so they got on and agreed not to look. So Ehep the giant spider lowered them with his nest. And so it went down and down—we don't know how far it was, but it seemed to be far away and it took some time to lower them into this land, which is more like the earth, sort of. They were so eager, they were so excited. And when they thought that they should be there, that they should see it, they wondered what it looked like close up. So they went down—they looked—they looked over the side and noticed the land.

And it was just at that moment that the string that held them up sort of let go and they landed on the ground forcefully. They didn't get hurt really. But what Ehep had said to them was that if they should look down they would not be happy on that land and that they would suffer in order to live there. And that was the end of the story.

Source: From a transcribed recording of Elder Louis Bird, 26 December 2002, www.ourvoices.ca.

Tech Link

Open Chapter 1 on your *Voices and Visions* CD-ROM to see petroglyphs created by First Nations people thousands of years ago. These were found at Writing-On-Stone in southern Alberta.

VOICES AND VISIONS

CASE STUDY

Oral and Written Histories

Right now, you are *reading* about First Nations' ways of life and events that took place in the past. Traditionally, young First Nations people learned about such things by *listening*. They listened to Elders and other people in their communities share their language, teachings, and traditional stories. The people recited histories, place names, family trees, laws, and events that took place locally and far away. The information was memorized and passed orally from one generation to the next. It did not need to be written down. In this way, the First Nations peoples developed a rich **oral culture**.

First Nations people had ways of making sure they remembered everything correctly.

- One method was to repeat the information often, so that they would not forget.
- Another method was to make visual reminders. One example is the wampum belts used by the Haudenosaunee. These belts were made from different-coloured pieces of seashells. The shells were woven into symbols and designs. A knowledgeable person would look at the symbols and "read" the belt.

When the European explorers came to North America, they recorded events in writing. For example, in the next chapter you will read the description of the explorer Jacques Cartier trading with the Mi'kmaq as he wrote about it in his journal (page 36). The Europeans also wrote down things that were done and said by First Nations. Some of these records have survived through the centuries. They can still be read today.

Respond

The First Nations did not record information in written documents. Therefore, many of the First Nations' quotes in this textbook were actually recorded by Europeans. What issues might there be with using documents written by Europeans to explain First Nations' histories?

Figure 1.5 Wampum belts were used to record treaties and agreements. Treaties allowed First Nations to share the land peaceably. In this way, the wampum symbolized harmony. These Haudenosaunee Chiefs from the Six Nations Reserve are reading wampum belts in the 1870s. Why might First Nations people consider this an important photo? SKILLS

What's in a Name?

When someone calls you by the wrong name, you may feel insulted. After all, your name is an important part of who you are. Few people like it when someone says their name incorrectly or mixes them up with someone else.

This is what happened to the First Nations when Europeans came to North America in the 1400s and 1500s. During that time, Europeans tended to be **ethnocentric**. This means that they judged other global cultures and ideas according to European values and standards. Generally they did not respect perspectives that differed from their own. For example, explorer Christopher Columbus sailed from Spain across the Atlantic Ocean in 1492. When he arrived in North America, he mistakenly thought he had reached India. He called the indigenous people he met "Indians" rather than asking them what they called themselves. Columbus brought the term back to Europe, where it was widely adopted even though it was known to be wrong. Today, the term *Indian* is still used, though many people feel this does not respect their identity.

As more Europeans came to North America, they renamed the First Nations peoples they met. Some examples are listed in the table that follows.

First Nations called themselves ...	But European explorers re-named them ...
Haudenosaunee	Iroquois
Nehiyawak [nay-HI-uh-wuk]	Cree
Wendat [WAH-n-dot]	Huron

Today, many First Nations people affirm their identity by using their original names.

Aboriginal peoples is a name for the indigenous peoples of North America and their descendants. The Canadian government recognizes three groups of Aboriginal peoples—First Nations, Inuit, and Métis [may-TEE].

First Nations	This term came into use in the 1970s in Canada to replace the words *band* and *Indian*. The First Nations are the original inhabitants of the land, along with the Inuit.
Inuit	The Inuit are several different peoples. They are the original inhabitants of the coastal regions of the Canadian Arctic and Greenland.
Métis	*Métis* is a French word meaning "mixed blood." The Métis are descendants of First Nations women and European explorers and fur traders. (You will learn more about the Métis in Chapter 8.)

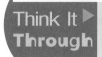

Think It Through

1. Why were the Elders so important to First Nations communities? How do they continue to make positive contributions to their communities today?

2. What can you learn about the culture of a First Nation using maps?
   a) Choose one of the First Nations from the map on page 7. Locate the region in which the nation lived on the climate map and physical relief map in your atlas.
   b) Using these and other atlas maps, list the characteristics of the environment in a web diagram. Consider landforms, bodies of water, vegetation, soils, and climate.
   c) Using your web diagram, explain how this physical environment might have influenced the First Nation's way of life.

The Mi'kmaq of the East Coast

The Mi'kmaq lived, and continue to live, in what is now Eastern Canada. They were one of the first peoples to make contact with explorers who sailed here from Europe hundreds of years ago. In this section, we will look at some aspects of the Mi'kmaq culture. You will read about how this coastal people lived and the different roles played by members of the society.

Focus

How did the Mi'kmaq people organize their societies?

Hunter-Gatherers

The Mi'kmaq lived in the woodlands and along the seacoasts of what are now the provinces of Nova Scotia, Prince Edward Island, and New Brunswick, and on the Gaspé Peninsula of Québec. They were hunters, fishers, and gatherers.

The Mi'kmaq lived in small villages of extended families, called **clans**. The clan system helped the people co-operate. It also allowed them to live together in harmony and organize the sharing of resources. For example, each clan had specific territories where they could hunt and fish. Because of their bountiful food supply and active lifestyle, the Mi'kmaq lived long and healthy lives. It was not unusual for people to reach 100 years of age!

Connection to Nature

Like all First Nations peoples who relied on hunting, fishing, and gathering, the Mi'kmaq had a close relationship with nature, which they called Mother Earth.

The Mi'kmaq believed that humans were put on earth by Kisúlk, the Creator. Kisúlk made the humans equal to everything else in nature. Humans were not separate from the mountains, plants, and animals, nor were they better than them. Due to this spiritual belief, the Mi'kmaq treated all living and non-living things in nature with respect. For example, it was a terrible wrong to destroy an animal for any reason other than need. The Mi'kmaq never wasted resources, nor did they ever take more from nature than they needed.

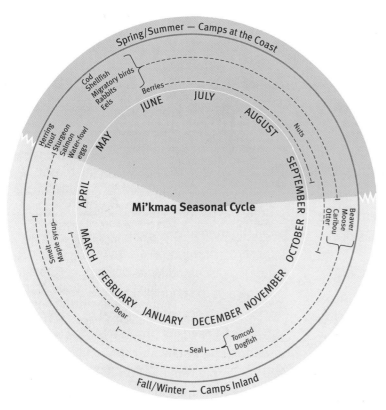

Figure 1.6 Every aspect of the Mi'kmaq culture was connected to nature. The people lived according to the seasons, as this diagram shows. How do you think Mi'kmaq people keep this connection to nature in their lives today?

Mi'kmaq Government

All cultures have some form of **government**. Government is the way people organize themselves to choose their leaders and make decisions. The Mi'kmaq government allowed the people to live in harmony, work together, and get things done.

Figure 1.7 A Mi'kmaq village in New Brunswick by Mi'kmaq artist Roger Simon about 1990. Europeans believed that land was something people owned. First Nations peoples believed that land was something people shared. They had rules and protocols governing how the people used the land and its resources, such as fish and game. How might these different values affect relations between First Nations peoples and Europeans after contact?

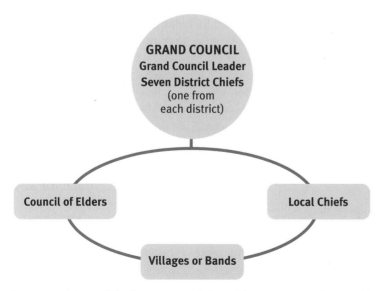

Figure 1.8 The political structure of the Mi'kmaq. A Grand Council Leader was elected from among the District Chiefs. The remaining District Chiefs formed the Council. The Grand Council united the seven districts and helped to resolve disputes between them.

Solving Problems

The way that First Nations chose their leaders depended on how they organized their societies. You have learned that the Mi'kmaq lived together in small family clans. Each clan had a local leader called a *sagamaw*. This was usually someone who was a good hunter and knew how to search for game.

The land of the Mi'kmaq was divided into seven districts. A district leader and a council governed each district. They had the power to make war or peace. They also settled disputes and divided hunting and fishing territories among family clans.

At some time long ago, the Mi'kmaq decided to create a *Sante Mawiomi* (Grand Council) to solve problems affecting the entire Mi'kmaq Nation. The diagram in Figure 1.8 shows how the Grand Council was set up.

Making Decisions

Mi'kmaq leaders did not tell the people what to do. In Mi'kmaq society, leaders were chosen for their ability to reach agreement among the people. The councils would listen to all the men and women who wanted to express an opinion on an issue. Then everyone discussed the issue until all members of the council agreed on what to do. This is called **decision making by consensus**.

The consensus process is a natural way of addressing issues and solving problems. You can apply this method in your own life. Suppose you and four friends are trying to decide on what topping to order on a pizza. To make this decision by consensus, the group would discuss the choices and try to persuade everyone to reach the same decision. Even if someone disagreed at first, the question could not be settled until a decision was made that everyone could live with. This method of decision making requires compromise from all members of the group.

The Role of Women

Mi'kmaq women played important roles in their communities. They were responsible for ensuring their families had all they needed to live a good life. They raised the children and took care of the homes. They collected and prepared the food and hunted small game for food and clothing.

Women also had an important role in the Mi'kmaq government. Although the leaders were usually men, women voiced their concerns in all matters.

There were many female Elders. Their opinions were valued on small, local matters and on major questions, such as whether or not to go to war.

Figure 1.9 This scene of a traditional Mi'kmaq summer camp was painted by Mi'kmaq artist Roger Simon in 1991. It shows women preparing blueberry cakes for the coming winter. Using the Skill Check on page 6, analyze this painting to decide how authentic you think it is. **SKILLS**

Tech Link

Open Chapter 1 on your *Voices and Visions* CD-ROM to view an image of a Mi'kmaq woman weaving a basket. What might the finished basket be used for?

Think It Through

1. Reaching a consensus requires respect and co-operation among people. Think about an issue in your class or school and try to solve the problem by reaching a consensus.
   - Begin by discussing the issue as a class to make sure everyone understands it. Then each student should express his or her opinion on the issue.
   - Once everyone has had a chance to speak, brainstorm possible solutions.
   - Choose one solution and check to see if there is a consensus. If there isn't, discuss changes the class would like to make. Then check for consensus again. The proposal can be adopted only if everyone agrees to accept it.

   What is your opinion of this method of decision making?

2. Museums and historic sites throughout Atlantic Canada display collections of Mi'kmaq artifacts. A **historic site** is a location of historical or cultural importance to a group of people or nation. Kejimkujik National Park in Nova Scotia is an example of a historic site because this area has old fishing sites, hunting territories, travel routes, and burial grounds that are significant to the Mi'kmaq people. Working in groups of three or four, answer these questions:
   - Why are museums and historic sites important?
   - Why would a place such as Kejimkujik be important to Mi'kmaq?
   - How can museums and historic sites foster pride in one's cultural heritage?
   - Should Mi'kmaq artifacts be kept in a museum or in the care of the community where they were found? What are the benefits and drawbacks of each choice?
   - How can museums ensure they are presenting Aboriginal cultural artifacts accurately and with respect?

   After your discussion, summarize your group's ideas and share them with the class.

3. **Democracy** is a system of government in which the people in a society are involved in the decision making. Usually, the people vote for representatives, who then make the people's concerns and wishes known to the government. Was the government of the Mi'kmaq democratic? Give reasons to support your answer.

The Haudenosaunee of the Northeastern Woodlands

The Haudenosaunee are a group that includes six different First Nations: Mohawk, Oneida [oh-NY-duh], Onondaga [on-on-DOG-uh], Cayuga [kay-OO-guh], Seneca [SEN-uh-kuh], and (later) Tuscarora [TUS-kuh-ror-ruh]. At different periods in their history, they lived either to the north or south of the St. Lawrence River. While they shared a similar language (Algonquin) and some traditions, each of these nations had a distinct culture. This section looks at some of the things that all Haudenosaunee had in common. It also examines the way they governed themselves and the role of women in the communities.

Focus

What were some of the characteristics of the Haudenosaunee way of life?

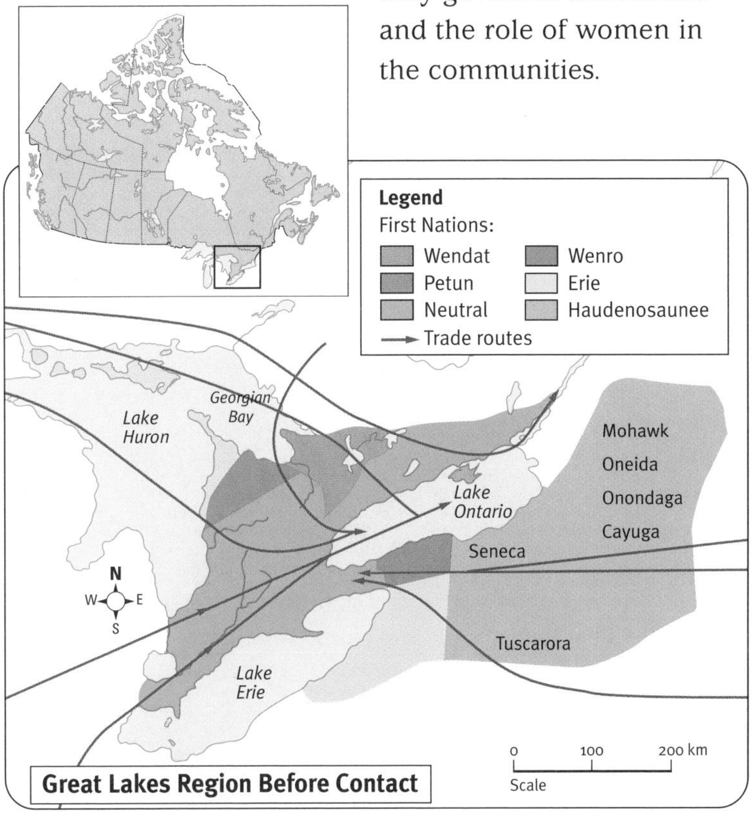

Legend
First Nations:
- Wendat
- Petun
- Neutral
- Wenro
- Erie
- Haudenosaunee
- → Trade routes

Georgian Bay
Lake Huron
Lake Ontario
Lake Erie
Mohawk
Oneida
Onondaga
Cayuga
Seneca
Tuscarora

N W E S

0   100   200 km
Scale

Great Lakes Region Before Contact

Figure 1.10 The First Nations of the Great Lakes region. At one time (no one is certain exactly when), the Haudenosaunee moved from the north side of the St. Lawrence River to south of Lake Ontario in what is now part of the Northeastern United States. What physical features in this region would allow trading to take place between nations?

Haudenosaunee World View

Although the Haudenosaunee held beliefs in common with other Aboriginal peoples, they also had their own set of values. These values formed their world view. It affected all aspects of their way of life, as you will see in this section. The following are some Haudenosaunee values, which are still an important part of their world view today:

- collective thinking and considering the future generations
- decision making by consensus; considering all points of view
- sharing labour and the benefits of that labour
- duty to family, clan, nation, and the Iroquois Confederacy
- equality; everyone is equal and is a full partner in the society, no matter what their age or gender

Source: Adapted from Haudenosaunee Home Page, http://sixnations.buffnet.net

The Original Farmers

The Haudenosaunee hunted and fished and gathered nuts, roots, and berries. The soil was fertile and the climate mild where the Haudenosaunee lived. This allowed them to become one of Canada's first farming peoples.

The Three Sisters

Corn, beans, and squash were the main crops. They were called the **Three Sisters** and they were always planted together to help each other grow. The corn stalks supported the climbing beans. The squash discouraged weeds from crowding the corn

Figure 1.11 A sculpture of the Three Sisters, by Gregg M. Thomas (Wolf clan, Onondaga, 1996). How does the story of the Three Sisters show a close connection between the Haudenosaunee and the land?

and beans. Also, the big squash leaves shaded the soil and kept it moist. Eaten together, these three vegetables made for a well-balanced diet.

The origins of the Three Sisters are linked to the creation of the Haudenosaunee people. Traditional Teachings say that the earth began when the first human, called Sky Woman, fell to earth. She was pregnant before she fell, and when she landed she gave birth to a daughter. Years later the daughter died while she was giving birth to twin boys. Sky Woman buried her daughter. In the grave, she placed the plants and leaves that she had clutched in her hands when she

Figure 1.12 A painting of a Haudenosaunee village behind a log stockade, by Lewis Parker about 1975. The Haudenosaunee lived in huge longhouses made of bark laid over a framework of poles. Several families, which could total as many as 100 people, lived in each longhouse. Each family had its own living space, with a cooking fire, a sleeping platform, and a storage area. Study this painting. What personal qualities do you think would be important to get along in a house where many families lived? SKILLS

fell from the Sky World. Soon after, corn, beans, and squash began to grow from her daughter's grave. These became the main foods of the Haudenosaunee people.

Sharing Work and Rewards

The Haudenosaunee also grew tobacco, cucumbers, melons, potatoes, turnips, and many other fruits and vegetables. It was one of the many roles of the women to care for the crops. The women worked together to do the planting. All the women were expected to share the work, just as they would share the harvest later.

The Haudenosaunee believed that all resources, such as land, crops, medicine, game, and housing, belonged to the entire community. So, when harvest time came, everyone shared the food. The women handed it out to each family according to need. The first to receive resources were the children, then the Elders, then the women, and finally the men.

Role of Women

The society of the Haudenosaunee was **matrilineal**. This means that the head of each longhouse was a woman. She was known as the **Clan Mother**. When a marriage took place, the husband went to live in his wife's longhouse. All the women and children living in a longhouse were of the same clan, or extended family. The women of the clan owned all the possessions in the house.

Each clan had its own animal symbol, such as a bear, wolf, turtle, snipe, deer, eel, or hawk. Members of a clan were family, so they could not marry one another. Instead, they married members of another clan.

Tech Link

All First Nations women tanned hides. Open Chapter 1 on your *Voices and Visions* CD-ROM to view a video of a Cree woman preparing a hide.

Before the men could go to war, it was the custom that the women would make them leather shoes, called moccasins, to wear. If the women did not want war, they would not make the moccasins.

Life Givers

Haudenosaunee women were well respected for their ability to create life. They gave birth to children and they grew food crops from the body of Mother Earth. For these reasons, women's role in the community was equal to men's. Some of their responsibilities included

- deciding on the location of a new village
- deciding what crops to plant, and where they should be planted
- deciding whether the men would go to war, as well as when to make peace
- controlling immigration and deciding whether their community would accept refugees or orphans
- playing a central role in ceremonies by making sure rituals were performed correctly
- helping troubled people and teaching the children

Canada Today

Today, many First Nations women continue to play important roles both in their communities and in Canadian society. For example, many become doctors, scientists, professors, writers, or lawyers. Such women are role models for the younger members of their communities.

One such role model is Brenda Chambers, a member of the Champagne and Aishihik [AY-zhak] First Nations. Chambers began her media career by attending Grant MacEwan College in Edmonton. She eventually created her own media company to produce shows such as *All My Relations* and *Venturing Forth*. She said, "You know what? I've got the talent. I've got the experience.... So, let's put together an Aboriginal crew and tell Aboriginal stories from our perspective with our authentic voice." She also teaches in the Aboriginal Film and Television Production Program at Capilano College in Vancouver.

Figure 1.13 Brenda Chambers, owner of Brenco Media.

Haudenosaunee Government

First Nations often formed alliances with each other. An **alliance** is a union in which groups agree to trade and help each other resolve disputes. One such alliance was the **Iroquois Confederacy**. It included the five Haudenosaunee nations living south of the Great Lakes: the Seneca, Cayuga, Onondaga, Oneida, and Mohawk.

According to oral tradition, long before the arrival of Europeans, the five nations were at war with one another. A peacemaker arrived in the land of the Haudenosaunee in a stone canoe. He brought a message of peace to the five nations and united them under the Iroquois Confederacy. In 1715, a sixth nation, the Tuscarora, joined the alliance. Then it became known as the Six Nations Confederacy.

The Peacemaker created the Great Law of Peace, called *Gawyehnehshehgowa* [gahn-YEH-neh-seh-go-wah]. It was a set of laws that explained how the government would work and how people should behave in society.

The Great Law of Peace

The Great Law of Peace was memorized. It would take several days to recite the laws orally. As you read the following excerpt, identify the message and its three parts. How does each part support the message?

The Word that I bring is that all people should love one another and live together in peace. This message has three parts: Righteousness, Health, and Power ....

Righteousness means justice practised between men and between nations. It also means the desire to see justice prevail.

Health means soundness of mind and body. It also means peace, for that is what comes when minds are sane and bodies are cared for.

Power means authority of law and custom, backed by such force as is necessary to make justice prevail ....

Making Decisions

Haudenosaunee women played an important role in government. Although the leaders were usually men, the Clan Mothers chose them. The women closely watched the actions of the men. They could veto any law the men passed. If the women thought that a leader was not doing a good job, they removed him from leadership. Then they appointed a new leader to take his place.

Each of the six nations that belonged to the Confederacy sent leaders to take part in a central council. The council consisted of 50 leaders chosen by the Clan Mothers. The council met at least once a year to discuss important issues, such as trade, disputes between nations, and treaties. Talks took place around a council fire. Ideas were passed back and forth across the fire until a consensus was reached. If there was no agreement, the matter was set aside for discussion later on.

The Seventh Generation

The Haudenosaunee believed they were responsible for the health of their environment. They knew that if they did not take care of Mother Earth, there would be no resources left for their future grandchildren and great-grandchildren. Therefore, whenever the Haudenosaunee made an important decision, they considered it very carefully. They tried to guess what impacts their actions would have seven generations into the future. If it looked like an action could bring harm to their descendants, they would reconsider it.

Canada Today

Today, some members of the Haudenosaunee do not accept being governed by Canada or the United States. They believe that the Haudenosaunee, whose land is divided by the Canada–US border, are a **sovereign** people. This means that they govern themselves and consider themselves independent of either country. They have their own police force to patrol their territories. Also, the Grand Council issues its own passport—the document people need to travel outside their country. The Iroquois Nationals lacrosse team, pictured at right, has travelled to countries around the world using Haudenosaunee passports. The passport declares that the Haudenosaunee are "a sovereign people."

Figure 1.14 The Iroquois Nationals lacrosse team is one of the few Aboriginal sports teams in Canada to compete internationally. As a result of their travels, they have raised global awareness of the Haudenosaunee people's quest for sovereignty—that is, independence. Why do you think it is important to the Haudenosaunee to be a sovereign people?

Think It Through

1. Working with a partner, create a Venn diagram to compare the roles of women in Mi'kmaq and Haudenosaunee societies. Start by putting the similarities in the middle. What do you notice about the similarities and differences between the two cultures?

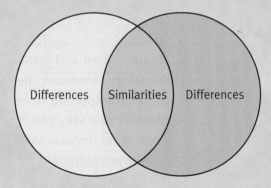

Differences | Similarities | Differences

2. Create a culture web for the Haudenosaunee based on what you have learned in this chapter so far. You can use the web diagram you made for Think It Through activity 2 on page 13 as a model. If some information is missing, use the Internet to research the facts you need.

3. Apply the "Seventh Generation" rule on page 20 to Canadian society today.
   a) Think of an activity that Canadians currently take part in that will affect future generations. Consider how the activity would affect various groups.
   b) Explain whether the effect will be positive or negative and how you feel about it.
   You may present your response to this question in writing, orally, or visually (using, for example, a drawing, cartoon, collage, organizer, timeline, or multimedia).

The Anishinabe

The Anishinabe lived in the wooded country of northern and central Ontario and in southern Manitoba. The Europeans called them the "Ojibway" or "Saulteaux," but the people called themselves Anishinabe, meaning "the people." Over time, some of the Anishinabe moved westward onto the Plains, where they still live today. This section describes the society of the Anishinabe and the way they governed themselves.

Focus

What were some of the characteristics of Anishinabe culture?

Anishinabe World View

In order to understand the Anishinabe culture, it is important to understand that they try to live their lives according to seven main values:

1. Wisdom: to cherish knowledge
2. Love: to know peace
3. Respect: to honour all of Creation
4. Bravery: to face your foes
5. Honesty: to face a situation
6. Humility: to know yourself
7. Truth: to know all these things

Cycle of Life

Like the Mi'kmaq, the Anishinabe were hunter-gatherers. However, they had an additional food source that set them apart from the other First Nations—wild rice. This grain, which the Anishinabe called mamomin, played a central role in their way of life (see figure below).

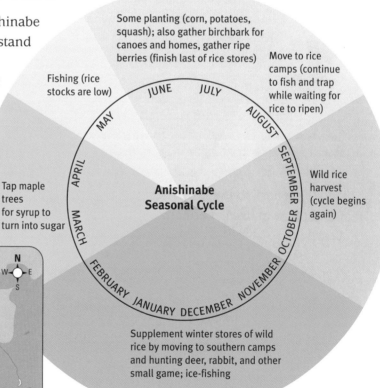

Some planting (corn, potatoes, squash); also gather birchbark for canoes and homes, gather ripe berries (finish last of rice stores)

Move to rice camps (continue to fish and trap while waiting for rice to ripen)

Fishing (rice stocks are low)

Wild rice harvest (cycle begins again)

Tap maple trees for syrup to turn into sugar

Anishinabe Seasonal Cycle

MAY JUNE JULY AUGUST SEPTEMBER OCTOBER NOVEMBER DECEMBER JANUARY FEBRUARY MARCH APRIL

Supplement winter stores of wild rice by moving to southern camps and hunting deer, rabbit, and other small game; ice-fishing

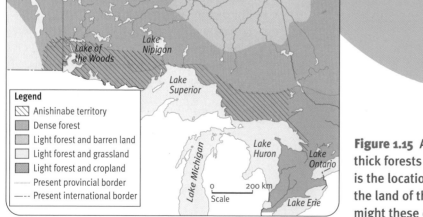

Anishinabe Territory Before Contact

James Bay

N
W — E
S

Lake Winnipeg

Lake of the Woods

Lake Nipigon

Lake Superior

Lake Michigan

Lake Huron

Lake Ontario

Lake Erie

Legend
- Anishinabe territory
- Dense forest
- Light forest and barren land
- Light forest and grassland
- Light forest and cropland
- Present provincial border
- Present international border

0   200 km
Scale

Figure 1.15 Anishinabe territory. The land is covered with thick forests and dotted with many lakes and rivers. How is the location of the Anishinabe territory different from the land of the Haudenosaunee and the Mi'kmaq? How might these differences affect the Anishinabe culture?

VOICES ■

Traditional teachings explain that "the Seven Grandfathers" gave these values to the Anishinabe as gifts long ago. Edward Benton-Banai is an Anishinabe Elder. He wrote down the traditional teaching "The Seven Grandfathers and the Little Boy" as it was told to him when he was young. In this teaching, Benton-Banai explains that before humans (called "the second people") received these gifts, they were weak in spirit and body. Here are some excerpts:

> " The second people of the Earth grew in number and their villages began to spread across the land. But, in their early years, the second people had a very hard time. At first, they were a weak people. Diseases took many lives each year. There were many times when people would be killed by just stumbling and falling down. …
>
> Ojibway tradition tells us that there were Seven Grandfathers who were given the responsibility by the Creator to watch over the Earth's people. They sent their Osh-ka-bay-wis (helper) to the Earth to walk among the people and bring back to them a person who could be taught how to live in harmony with the Creation. "

The helper took a baby boy from his family and brought him back to the Seven Grandfathers. The Grandfathers asked the helper to take the boy around the world and teach him how people should live. Seven years later, after their travels, the helper and the boy returned to the Seven Grandfathers. The Grandfathers saw that the boy had grown into a good and honest person. They showed him a vessel covered with cloths of four colours standing for the Four Directions: red (South), black (West), white (North), and yellow (East). Each grandfather reached into the vessel and brought out a "gift," which they gave to the boy.

Then they asked an otter to guide the boy back to his people so that he could share the gifts with them.

> " Along the way, they stopped seven times. At each stop a spirit came and told the boy the meaning of one of the seven gifts that were given to him out of the vessel of the Grandfathers. "

The journey back to his village took a long time, and the boy was an old man by the time he arrived. The old man found his parents, but they and the other villagers were hungry and weak.

> " The old man pulled a gift out of his bundle and said to his parents, "I give you this. It represents the power, love, and mercy of the Creator." He continued on the visit and talked with the rest of his people. To the middle of the village he went with his bundle and all the people followed. At the village's centre he stopped and put down his bundle. "

He shared the Grandfathers' lessons, to be physically strong and spiritually strong. Because of the gifts, the people became healthier. They began living in harmony with all of the Creation.

Source: Excerpts from Edward Benton-Banai, "The Seven Grandfathers and the Little Boy," in *The Mishomis Book: The Voice of the Ojibway* (Hayward, WI: Indian Country Communications, Inc., and Red School House Press, 1988), pp. 60–68.

The Role of Women

The Anishinabe believed in equality and balance. Men and women were equal partners in the annual cycle of work. Each had a specific set of jobs to do for the good of the community.

The work of the women was very important to the people's economy. Women looked after the children and maintained the lodge. They hunted smaller animals, such as rabbits, birds, and porcupines. Women also harvested a variety of wild fruits, berries, nuts, roots, and wild rice. Then they dried and stored them for the winter. Without the work of gathering and storing food, the community would not survive.

Figure 1.16 Winnowing wild rice at Rice Lake, Ontario, in 1921. The Anishinabe believed that if they were in harmony with nature, the rice crop would always return. They sowed just enough rice seed to meet the needs of the people. How is this different from the way commercial farmers plant crops?

Wild Rice Harvesters

Before the wild rice harvest began, the women would tie together sections of the tall stocks with different-coloured twine. This was a way for each family to claim a portion of the harvest. The Anishinabe also divided up the maple trees. Each family would use an axe to make a special mark in the trees they wished to tap when the sap started running. No one was allowed to touch the trees or the rice stocks that had been claimed by someone else.

Once the rice harvesting began, there were certain rules that everyone followed:

- Only women and children took part in the harvest. The men were hunting and trapping game.
- The harvest was **communal**. This meant that everyone was supposed to harvest the rice at the same time, in an organized way.
- Harvesters had to use traditional harvesting techniques. This ensured that unripe rice stocks were not damaged.
- Most important, harvesters had to leave enough rice unharvested to seed the next year's crop.

Figure 1.17 The Anishinabe word for wild rice is *mamomin*. This word comes from the word *Manitou*, meaning Great Spirit, and *meenun*, meaning delicacy. It is a very nutritious grain, which is also low in fat. In what ways was mamomin important to the Anishinabe?

Solving Problems

The Anishinabe lived in extended family clans in lodges made of birchbark. Each village usually looked after its own affairs, but they had contact with each other from time to time. They also co-operated in short-term alliances.

In order to meet their needs for protection, education, food, medicine, and leadership, the Anishinabe people created a clan system. In this system, the people organized themselves into seven clans named after animals. Each clan had duties to carry out for the good of the entire nation, as seen in the diagram at left.

Bird

Spiritual leaders; responsible for well-being and spiritual development of the community

Deer

Poets and pacifists; responsible for creating and maintaining shelter

Marten

Hunters, food gatherers, and warriors

Anishinabe Clan System

Bear

Strong and steady; responsible for patrolling and policing the community

Fish

Teachers and scholars; responsible for teaching young people and solving disputes

Loon and Crane

Leadership clans; responsible for providing governance

Making Decisions

Each of the clans had a leader, who was chosen because he displayed courage, good character, or skill in hunting. The leaders of the Crane and the Loon clans were responsible for making decisions that affected all the people of the community. Members of the Crane clan were leaders in matters outside the community. The Loon clan members were leaders in matters within the community. They worked together to create a balanced government. There could be times of conflict, though. In these cases, it was the role of the Fish clan to help settle disputes between the Cranes and the Loons.

Think It Through

1. Think about how leaders are chosen in your society.
   a) Complete a chart similar to the one shown below.
   b) Which method of choosing a leader do you think is the best? Give reasons for your answer.

2. In the Mi'kmaq, Haudenosaunee, and Anishinabe First Nations, women had many important roles and duties in the community, and their opinions were highly valued. Men and women were considered equals. Do you think this is true in Canadian society today? Express your opinion in a journal entry or editorial, or draw a political cartoon that shows your point of view. (Before beginning, you may want to refer to Skill Check: Analyze Political Cartoons on page 218 and Skill Check: Develop an Opinion on page 170.)

	WHO is the leader?	HOW is this leader chosen?
At home		
In the school classroom		
In a school sports team		
In your local government		

Economies and Resources

An important part of every culture is the **economy**. This is the way in which people meet their basic needs, such as food, clothing, and shelter. This section explains how First Nations' economies differed according to the resources available to them.

Focus

How did the economies of First Nations rely on the natural environment in which they lived?

Hunter-Gatherer Economies

The economies of the First Nations were based on the food supply. If resources were scarce, the people spent most of their time gathering food. If resources were plentiful, life was easier. The people had more time to spend on other things, such as creating art and taking part in recreation.

In hunter-gatherer societies, the people gathered plants, hunted, and fished according to the seasons. Most of the food was eaten fresh, but some of it was preserved and stored to eat during the winter. The people had to have an excellent knowledge of the land and climate and the cycles of nature in order for this economy to work.

Hunter-gatherers moved their camps as the seasons and food supply changed. They did not gather many extra goods for trading because they would have to abandon them each time they moved. Although they did some trading, they focused more on being in rhythm with the seasons and nature. The Piikani [bee-GUN-ee], Kainai [KY-ny], and Siksika First Nations who lived on the Western Plains are examples of hunter-gatherers.

Both *prairie* and *plains* refer to any large area of flat, usually treeless, grassland. The Plains refers to the prairie region in western North America.

Canada Today

Many First Nations peoples have adapted past economic activities into modern companies. The Anishinabe are no exception. For example, the Sucker Creek First Nation is located on Manitoulin Island in Ontario. This Anishinabe community runs the Wabuno Fish Farm. Operating since 1992, the fish farm has grown into a successful business. It uses computer technology and environmentally friendly practices to produce rainbow trout.

Figure 1.18 A photo of the Wabuno Fish Farm. What would happen if people did not adapt their economy to changes and advancements taking place in the broader society?

Chapter 1

CASE STUDY

Economy of a Plains People

Before the arrival of Europeans, the grassy plains of the prairies teemed with buffalo. The First Nations peoples who lived on the Plains relied on the buffalo for their existence. It was the basis of their economy.

The Plains peoples had an expert understanding of the land and buffalo behaviour. They used this knowledge to develop effective hunting methods. One method was the buffalo jump. The Piikani, Kainai, and Siksika peoples used the Head-Smashed-In Buffalo Jump for almost 6000 years.

Hunters frightened the buffalo into a stampede. They directed the herd toward a steep cliff, and some of the animals would plunge over the edge. The people set up camps at the base of the cliff to clean and prepare the meat of the fallen buffalo. Below, a Piikani Elder explains how all parts of the buffalo were used to meet the peoples' needs:

Respond

How did the Plains peoples and the Europeans differ in their use of natural resources such as the land and buffalo in the West? Can it be said that one of these ways of using the resources was better than the other way? Why or why not? What factors would need to be considered in determining the best use of resources?

> *My grandfather, he was the one who knew all about how the buffalo moved around and they (the people) followed and hunted the buffalo. The men would do the hunting and the women would take care of the kill.*
>
> *They used every part of the buffalo, there was nothing they spoiled or wasted. This is what my mother told me. For example, the hide was used and the meat was sliced and dried so that it would last long. The bones were pounded and crushed and boiled. They were boiled for a long time. It was then cooled and the marrow was taken and used for grease. … The hides they would scrape and stretch and the women would also do this work. This they used for blankets and flooring and many other uses. Those even further back (the first people) would use the hides to build homes.*

Source: Roxanne Warrior, "Case Study of the Economy of the Nation," 1993.

When the Europeans arrived on the Plains, they set up a great number of farms to grow crops and raise animals. Overhunting and the technology of the newcomers, such as barbed-wire fences, guns, and trains, helped drive the herds to near extinction.

Figure 1.19 Head-Smashed-In Buffalo Jump in southern Alberta. Today, the buffalo jump is preserved as a historic site. How did the economy of the Piikani show respect for the natural world in which they lived?

Farming Economies

In some regions of the country where soil and weather were ideal for growing crops, farming economies developed. Farming societies did not move around as hunter-gatherer societies did. They stayed in the same village year-round. Only when the soil was depleted would the village be moved to a new location, which was usually not very far away.

Farming societies were often able to grow more food than the people needed. This meant that less time had to be spent hunting and gathering. The people had more time for creating art, performing ceremonies, and recreation. They were able to produce and store extra food and many other goods. These extras could be used for trade with other groups, who had resources that did not exist in the farming region. As a result, farming nations were involved in a great deal of trade with other First Nations peoples.

Trading Networks

The First Nations traded goods with one another long before European traders arrived. The people travelled across well-used trade routes that stretched over long distances. For example, the Haudenosaunee traded corn, tobacco, and other crops with neighbouring nations that were unable to grow crops. In return, they received such things as copper from the Anishinabe, who lived around Lake Superior. They also obtained seashells and birchbark to make canoes from the Mi'kmaq on the eastern coast.

All across North America, First Nations traded with each other to obtain goods they did not have. When Europeans arrived, they joined this trading network.

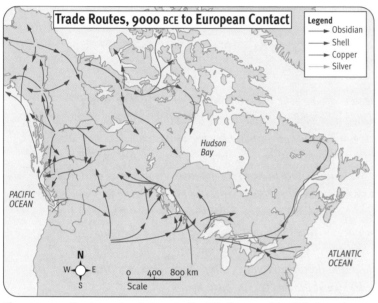

Figure 1.20 Trade routes between First Nations and Inuit before the arrival of the Europeans. Is it possible that shells from the East Coast could eventually end up with the First Nations on the northwest coast of the continent? Explain.

Think It Through

1. Think about what you have learned about the goods available to the Mi'kmaq, the Haudenosaunee, and the Anishinabe. Then complete a diagram similar to the one shown here to explain what goods might be exchanged among these three nations.

2. Make a chart in which you compare the economies, governments, and role of women in the Mi'kmaq, Haudenosaunee, and Anishinabe First Nations. From your chart, determine aspects of their cultures that were very similar. Review the section on world views on page 8. What core values might account for these similarities?

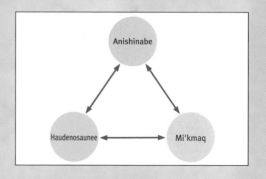

Chapter 1

Chapter 1 PROJECT
The Importance of Cross-Cultural Understanding

Canada has many cultures that contribute to our diversity. Understanding other cultures is important. You have seen in this chapter that there are many different First Nations cultures in Canada. The physical environment, experiences, history, and values of the people have shaped each of these cultures.

1. Complete the following statement: "It is important to understand other cultures because …."

2. Use examples from this chapter to create a web diagram to explain why it is important to understand First Nations cultures.

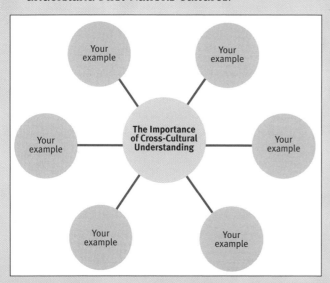

3. Demonstrate your understanding of the First Nations cultures discussed in this chapter by completing the following statement for each one: "From the [name of the First Nation], we can learn …."

Stereotypes

Hockey is a popular sport in Canada. But we know that many Canadians do not play hockey nor are they interested in watching it. So, to say that all Canadians love hockey would be untrue. It would be a **stereotype** about Canadians.

Stereotypes can be negative: for example, "Teens are troublemakers." Or, they may seem positive: for example, "All Canadians are polite." Either way, stereotypes should not be used, because they assume that a particular group of people are all the same. Stereotypes place a label on an entire group of people instead of considering the characteristics of each individual. This particularly applies to culture. People of a particular culture do *not* all have the same characteristics. While they may have some things in common, such as language, they are all individuals with many different qualities.

It is important to be aware of stereotypes in the media. Every day we see thousands of images. They appear in magazines and newspapers, on billboards and buses, and on television. Use the steps in Skill Check: Interpret Images on page 6 to help you recognize stereotypes wherever you see them.

4. Create a web diagram to show that you understand the dangers of stereotypes.

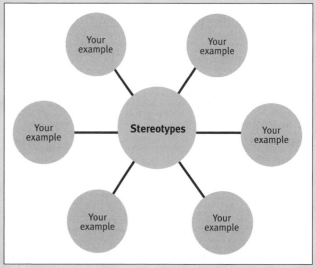

5. **Citizenship and Identity:** Discuss what you can do to promote cultural understanding in your community. Then, take one of your ideas and put it into action.

Chapter 2 — The French in North America

Chapter INQUIRY

What kind of society did the French colonists create in their North American colonies?

Key CONCEPT ▶ Imperialism

When Europeans first came to North America, they created new settlements called colonies. A **colony** is a territory of land that is controlled by another country. Up until the mid-1900s, many countries in Europe, Asia, and the Middle East claimed colonies around the globe. The earliest colonists in Canada came from France. They are the ancestors of most Francophone Canadians today.

Empires are networks of colonies controlled by a single country, sometimes called the home country. Colonies had no independence, meaning that the people living in a colony did not have control of their political or economic affairs. Decisions about their future were usually made by the home country. This system of countries extending their control over other nations is called **imperialism**. For centuries, much of the world was ruled by imperial powers. It was within this framework that Canada became a country.

The French were not the only imperialists during this era. The British, the Spanish, the Portuguese, and many other peoples also established empires around the world. This chapter focuses on the French because they were the first imperial power to have a lasting impact on the identity of Canada.

Honing Your Skills

Maps allow us to see and show many different types of information about a particular place. The Skill Check feature on the next page will take you through the steps to **Analyze Thematic Maps**. Wherever you see SKILLS in this chapter, it is an opportunity to practise your new skill.

New France

In this chapter, we will investigate why France was interested in building a colony in North America. We'll look at the journeys of some French explorers as they set out to claim new lands for France. In Chapter 1, you learned about the societies and economies of three different First Nations. In this chapter, you'll look at these same aspects of New France.

The flow chart below shows the relationship between a colony such as New France and its home country.

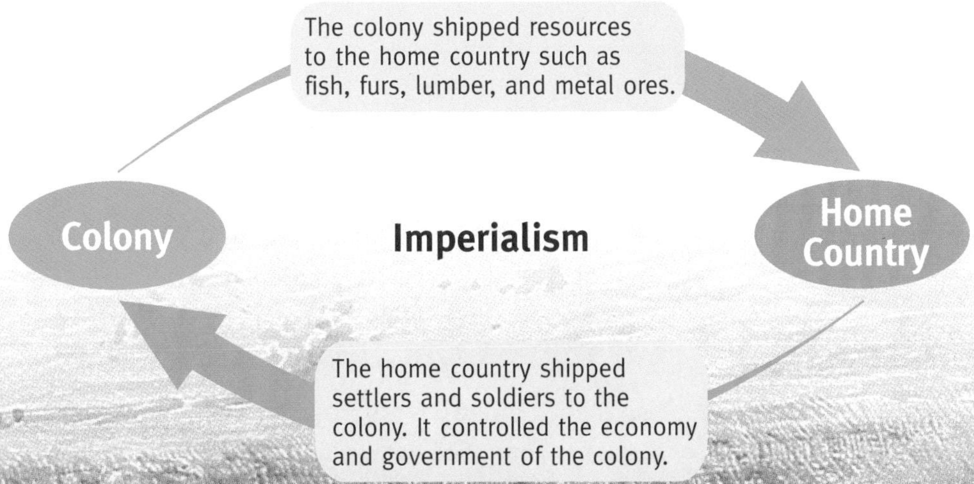

Colony

The colony shipped resources to the home country such as fish, furs, lumber, and metal ores.

Imperialism

Home Country

The home country shipped settlers and soldiers to the colony. It controlled the economy and government of the colony.

Think AHEAD

Think about what you already know about early French explorers, colonists, and the way of life in New France. Record your information in a chart like the one below. In the "Know" column, record everything you know, or think you know, about this topic. Then, in the "Wonder" column, record those things you would like to know. When you have finished this chapter, return to your chart. Check off the questions in the "Wonder" column that have been answered. Then summarize what you have learned in the "Learn" column.

New France		
Know	Wonder	Learn

SKILL CHECK: Analyze Thematic Maps

Thematic maps show specific types of detailed information (or themes) about a place. For example, a climate map might show precipitation patterns across a province. A historic map might use different colours or patterns to show the empires around the world in the past. Here are some guidelines for analyzing and interpreting thematic maps.

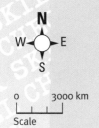

0   3000 km
Scale

Legend
---- Silk Road
—— Spice Route
······ Columbus (1492)

Legend
British
French
Dutch
Portuguese

Examine the Basics

Most maps contain a title, a directional symbol such as a compass rose, and a scale. The most important feature on a thematic map is the legend. Maps, especially thematic maps, contain different patterns, colours, and symbols. These are explained in the legend.

Interpret the Information

Use the legend to identify patterns on the map. Then ask yourself what the patterns mean. For example, the theme of the map in Figure 2.2 (page 35) is "empires around the world between the 1500s and the 1700s." By studying the colour-coded legend and applying it to the map, we can see the following:

- Britain and Spain were in control of most of North America.
- France, Spain, Portugal, and the Netherlands controlled South America.
- The Middle East and Northern Africa were mainly under the control of the Turkish empire, while China and Russia were dominant in Asia.
- The Dutch seemed to be mainly interested in coastal colonies in the Southern Hemisphere.
- Russia controlled the largest area of land, while Spain had the largest number of colonies spread around the globe.

Tech Link

You can see several historical maps of New France, including two by Samuel de Champlain. Just open Chapter 2 on your *Voices and Visions* CD-ROM.

Communicate Your Understanding

Use the information you have gathered to try to draw conclusions. Then think about the significance this information might have on the topic you are studying.

Try It!

Using GIS software or another online mapping program, create a thematic map of Canada. What are the two most important things a foreigner should know about Canada, in your opinion? Add two theme layers to your map to show this information as well as a legend to explain the colours or symbols used.

European Imperialism

Europeans began arriving in the land we call Canada 1000 years ago. They were the Norse, who sailed from Scandinavia. In the 1400s, long after the Norse had left North America, sailors from Spain, Portugal, and possibly England crossed the Atlantic to catch fish off the shores of present-day Newfoundland and Labrador.

Focus

Why did explorers and colonists from Europe come to North America?

These fishermen were followed by many other Europeans, who came across the ocean as explorers and colonists.

In this section, you'll examine the different reasons why the imperial countries of Europe decided to cross the ocean to North America. You'll see why they wanted to claim colonies here.

When we say the 1400s or the fifteenth century, we mean any year from 1400 to 1499. What years are included in the twenty-first century?

Looking for a New Silk Road

For centuries, the countries of Europe and Asia traded with one another. France, England, Spain, Portugal, and the Netherlands looked to India, China, Japan, and Indonesia to obtain spices, tea, silk, porcelain, and precious gems.

To bring these goods home, the Europeans travelled a route known as the Silk Road. This long overland route crossed through Asia and Eastern Europe. The route was dangerous because ambush parties would often attack the traders. They would either steal the traders' cargo or charge them a large payment, or "tax," to pass through the territory. By the 1400s, the Europeans were eager to find another route to Asia, preferably a water route.

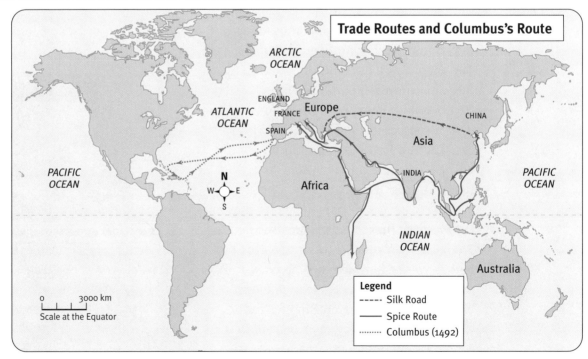

Figure 2.1 European explorers were looking for a water route to Asia. Do you see a possible route? What disadvantages and challenges might this route pose? SKILLS

Portugal led the search for a water route to the Far East, sending ships south around the tip of Africa as far as India. Soon after, Spain began looking for a route. In 1492, Queen Isabella sent Christopher Columbus west across the Atlantic.

More explorers followed in the wake of Columbus. Their voyages increased European knowledge of and interest in the land across the ocean.

Expanding Across the Ocean

Why did the imperial countries of Europe want to expand their empires?

- **Economics.** Europeans set up colonies so they could claim the resources of the land for themselves. In the country we now call Canada, the resource the Europeans valued most was fur. In Europe, there was a fashion craze for beaver hats and fur coats. Since the beaver had been hunted to extinction in Europe, the Europeans looked to North America for more.

- **Competition.** The countries of Europe were often at war with one another as they competed for land and resources. The more colonies a country controlled, the more power and prestige it had. Colonies supplied their home countries with resources such as timber and iron ore. These were used to build up European armies and navies.

- **Religion.** Most Europeans were Christians. Like the followers of many religions, they believed that theirs was the one true faith. There was competition within the Christian faith, however, between the Catholics and the Protestants. Most people in France were Catholic. Most people in England were Protestant. Both groups wanted to send missionaries around the world to spread their version of Christianity.

- **Curiosity.** The Europeans were also curious about what lay beyond the horizon. This played an important part in their expansion around the world. New technologies and improvements in navigation helped them to travel farther than they had ever been before.

Global Connections

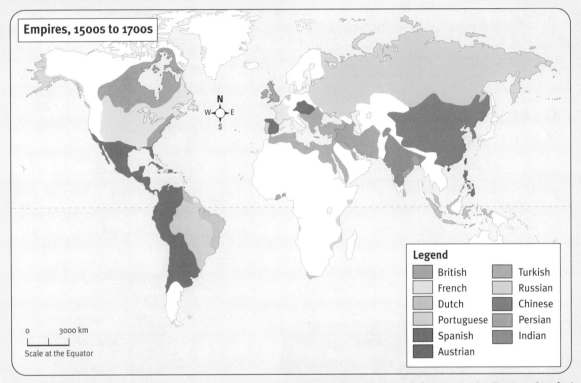

Empires, 1500s to 1700s

Legend

British		Turkish	
French		Russian	
Dutch		Chinese	
Portuguese		Persian	
Spanish		Indian	
Austrian			

0   3000 km
Scale at the Equator

Figure 2.2 Examples of empires around the world between the 1500s and the 1700s. **La Francophonie** is an organization of all the countries around the world today where French is the people's first language or is the official (or main) language. Do some research in an atlas or on the Internet to find all the current member countries. Then, on a tracing of this map, mark these countries with a symbol. How do the two maps compare?

Many imperial countries used to claim colonies around the world. Once a land was claimed, its resources and original inhabitants were controlled by the home country. How do you think the people who lived in the lands that were colonized felt about being told what to do by a foreign power? How would you feel if this happened in Canada today?

Think It Through

1. You are a French explorer in the 1500s. Write a diary entry in which you explain why you feel it is a good idea to sail to North America and set up a colony there. Point out the ways in which the colony will benefit the home country as well as the colonists who move there.

2. Think about what you learned in Chapter 1. In a chart, outline the arguments the First Nations might have made for and against the Europeans coming to North America.

France Takes an Interest in North America

France entered the race to find an ocean passage to Asia in the mid-1500s. The king, François I, was determined that his people should find a route before the other countries of Europe. The French decided to start their search by exploring North America.

This section looks at some of the reasons the French continued to come back to North America and eventually built colonies here.

Focus

Why did the French decide to explore North America and build colonies here?

Cartier Crosses the Atlantic

The king of France sent a French sea captain named Jacques Cartier to find a passage through North America to Asia. In 1534, Cartier set out across the Atlantic with two ships. After 20 days at sea, he arrived off the coast of Newfoundland. Sailing around the north end of the island, Cartier entered a broad inland sea—the Gulf of St. Lawrence.

One day, Cartier and his men were exploring along the shore. They came across a group of Mi'kmaq [MIG-mah] paddling in their canoes. Can you imagine how the Mi'kmaq reacted upon encountering Cartier and his crew? The boat would have been larger than any they had seen before. The style of clothing and the language of the men on board would have been unfamiliar to them as well. In his journal, Cartier wrote about what happened next from his point of view:

A large number of people ... set up a great clamour and made frequent signs to us to come on shore, holding up to us some skins on sticks....

We likewise made signs to them that we wished them no harm, and sent two men ashore to offer them some knives and other iron goods and a red hat to give to their chief....

They bartered all they had, to such an extent that all went back naked ... and they made signs to us that they would return on the morrow with more skins.

Source: Ramsay Cook, ed., *The Voyages of Jacques Cartier* (Toronto: University of Toronto Press, 1993), pp. 20–21. Translated from the French original.

This is the first known written account of trade between the Europeans and First Nations peoples. What things in this account suggest that the Mi'kmaq had traded before? With whom do you think they might have traded?

Figure 2.3 Mi'kmaq rock drawing showing sailors on board a European ship. The Mi'kmaq had a rich oral culture to pass along information. They also made drawings on rocks, called **petroglyphs**, to record events and information. Why do you think these old petroglyphs are considered so important today?

The Challenges of Settlement

In July 1534, Cartier landed at a place he called Gaspé. There, he met a First Nations people called the Haudenosaunee [hah-duh-nuh-SAH-nee] and their leader, a man named Donnacona. They had travelled from their home farther up the St. Lawrence River to fish in the region we know as the Gaspé Peninsula.

After this meeting, Cartier took two of Donnacona's sons, Taignoagny and Domagaya, on board his ship. He sailed with them back to France to prove to the king what he had found. In 1535, Cartier returned to North America with three ships and 110 men. He brought Donnacona's sons back with him. They guided the French up the St. Lawrence River, deeper into the continent. They went as far as Stadacona, where Donnacona and his people lived.

Cartier and his crew decided to stay the winter. They built a small log fort near Stadacona. However, they did not have enough fresh fruit and vegetables. Many of the crew became ill and died from scurvy, a disease brought on by a lack of vitamin C. But the Haudenosaunee had a cure for scurvy. They taught the French how to make the tea cure by boiling pieces of white cedar. Without their help, Cartier and the rest of his men may not have survived the winter.

Tech Link

Look in Chapter 2 on the *Voices and Visions* CD-ROM to compare two different paintings showing the meeting of Cartier and the Haudenosaunee.

Tech Link

Look under the Videos section of Chapter 2 on the *Voices and Visions* CD-ROM to see a First Nations person making cedar tea.

VOICES ■

The Haudenosaunee had lived in the Great Lakes–St. Lawrence Lowlands since time immemorial. They controlled travel along the river and governed the surrounding lands. However, when Cartier arrived at Gaspé, he and his men raised a large wooden cross. He wrote across the top, *Vive le Roi de France!*—Long Live the King of France!

In his journal, Cartier described how Donnacona reacted to the cross:

66 When we had returned to our ships, the captain [Donnacona], dressed in an old black bear skin, arrived in a canoe with three of his sons and his brother. ... Pointing to the cross, he made us a long harangue, making the sign of the cross with his two fingers; and then he pointed to the land all around, as if to say that all this region belonged to him, and that we ought not to have set up this cross without his permission. 99

Source: H.P. Biggar, ed., *The Voyages of Jacques Cartier* (Ottawa: Public Archives of Canada, 1924), p. 65.

Figure 2.4 A painting of Cartier raising the cross for France at Gaspé, by Charles Walter Simpson, 1927. In those days, it was typical for European explorers to claim lands they visited on their travels. Judging by this encounter, what issue do you predict may develop between the First Nations peoples and the Europeans who will eventually come to live in North America?

Land of Riches

The Haudenosaunee told Cartier about a land northeast of their village where there were fruit trees, metals, and gems. In the spring of 1536, Cartier forcibly took Donnacona and nine other villagers back to Europe. He did this so that they could tell the king about the riches in North America. Cartier hoped this information would convince the king to pay for another cross-Atlantic trip.

Cartier Visits Again

Cartier returned to North America in 1542. He planned to set up a colony along the St. Lawrence River. By this time, all but one of the Haudenosaunee Cartier had taken across the ocean had died in Europe. Cartier told the Haudenosaunee that the people he took were well and living in Europe. However, written historical accounts say they didn't believe him. As a result, the Haudenosaunee were hostile toward the French.

After another terrible winter, the French colonists decided to return to Europe. Cartier took samples of what he believed were gold and diamonds with him. But it turned out they were worthless pyrite (fool's gold) and quartz. Although he was not able to establish a permanent colony in North America, Cartier did succeed in gathering a great deal of important information about the land across the ocean.

Figure 2.5 A painting of Jacques Cartier, by Théophile Hamel, about 1844. No one knows for sure what Cartier looked like. A Québec artist made this painting many years after Cartier's death. He had to rely on other portraits handed down over the years. How might this affect the accuracy of this painting?

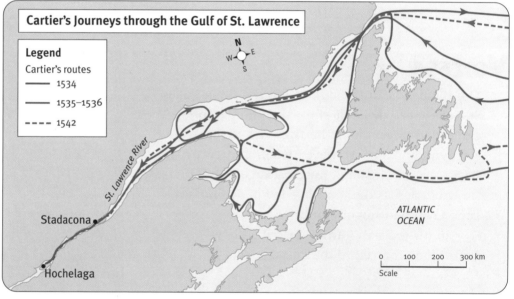

Cartier's Journeys through the Gulf of St. Lawrence

Legend
Cartier's routes
— 1534
— 1535–1536
- - - 1542

St. Lawrence River

Stadacona

Hochelaga

ATLANTIC OCEAN

0   100   200   300 km
Scale

Figure 2.6 The routes followed by Jacques Cartier on three of his trips to the St. Lawrence. How do historians know Cartier travelled these particular routes? Where might they have found supporting historical evidence? SKILLS

Think It ▶ Through

1. Think about why Cartier's explorations in North America were important for France. What did he accomplish? Create a web diagram to illustrate your answer.

2. With a partner, role-play the encounter between Cartier and Donnacona as Cartier raised the cross at Gaspé. Try to express why Cartier felt justified in raising the cross and why Donnacona felt justified in objecting. (You may want to refer to Skill Check: Research and Perform a Role Play on page 268 before beginning.)

France Expands Its Empire

Jacques Cartier's settlement on the St. Lawrence River had failed, but the French did not forget about North America completely. Fishing fleets still came to the North Atlantic each year. Fur traders still came to trade with First Nations trappers. In this section, you'll learn how France began to build North American colonies at Acadia and Québec. You'll see why the explorer Champlain and some First Nations forged alliances, and you'll investigate the impact these alliances had on the colonies.

Focus

How were the first permanent French colonies established in North America?

The French Return

By the early 1600s, the demand for furs in Europe was growing. The French king, Louis XIII, decided that France should build a colony in North America. Then they would have access to the abundant supply of furs.

Another reason the French returned to North America was that Louis XIII wanted to be the most powerful ruler in Europe. To reach his goal, he needed to expand France's colonial empire. Resources from the colonies would give France a military advantage over its imperial rivals.

The king knew that a colony so far from home would be expensive for him to build and support. So he decided to let someone else pay for it. The king granted a trade **monopoly** to a group of merchants. This meant that only the merchants within the group would be allowed to trade for furs in the colony. In return, the merchants agreed to build settlements in North America and find French citizens to live in them.

The French in Acadia

In 1604, a French noble named Pierre de Monts received a monopoly. He sailed to North America to set up a colony. He took a map-maker and explorer named Samuel de Champlain with him. In the spring of 1605, de Monts established a settlement at Port Royal on the Bay of Fundy. The French called the area Acadia. It was from the Greek word *Arcadia*, meaning "an earthly paradise."

At first, the Mi'kmaq who lived there did not object to the newcomers. The French did not interfere with their fishing and hunting activities, and the Mi'kmaq welcomed the chance to trade their furs for metal goods and blankets. The Mi'kmaq were willing to share the land as long as they had access to it.

In time, more and more French people came to Acadia. Although life was hard, it was no harder than it had been back in France. Acadia offered poor farmers from France an opportunity to make a new start.

Figure 2.7 A re-creation of Port Royal in Acadia. The early French colonists in North America built forts called *habitations*. What do you think it would have been like living in such a place at that time? What type of person do you think would have been willing to take on the challenge of colonization?

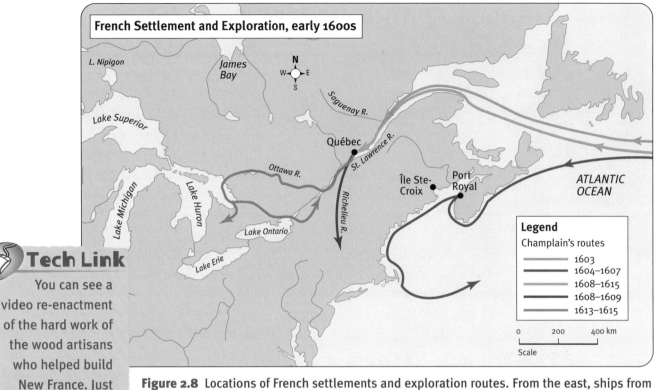

French Settlement and Exploration, early 1600s

Legend
Champlain's routes

	1603
	1604–1607
	1608–1615
	1608–1609
	1613–1615

0   200   400 km

Scale

Tech Link

You can see a video re-enactment of the hard work of the wood artisans who helped build New France. Just open Chapter 2 on your *Voices and Visions* CD-ROM.

Figure 2.8 Locations of French settlements and exploration routes. From the east, ships from France could bring supplies to Québec. From the west, canoes could travel from the interior, bringing furs. As a result of the fur trade, strong partnerships developed between the First Nations and the French. Why was water transportation so important in those days? **SKILLS**

The colonists spread out along the shores of the Bay of Fundy. They survived through farming, fishing, and hunting. These French pioneers formed a unique community and culture. They were the first **Acadians**.

The Founding of Québec

Port Royal was a long way from the centre of the fur trade, so de Monts and Champlain decided to move to the St. Lawrence River. They chose a site near Stadacona, where Jacques Cartier had built a fort many years earlier.

The French colonists called their settlement Québec. The name came from an Algonquin [al-GONG-kwin] word meaning "the place where the river narrows." It was an ideal place to trade furs, as

Tech Link

The *Voices and Visions* CD-ROM contains an image of the original plan for Québec. Look at the image, and explain how security issues influenced the plan.

Figure 2.8 shows. However, living conditions were far from ideal for the colonists. During their first winter, 20 of the 28 newcomers died due to the weather and lack of food.

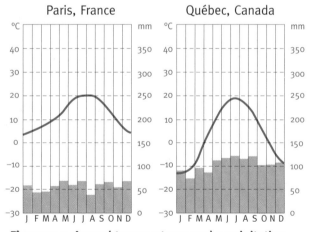

Figure 2.9 Annual temperatures and precipitation in Paris, France, and Québec. The lines show temperature while the bars show precipitation. Compare these two graphs. How do they explain one of the reasons why Champlain and his men had such a difficult time surviving in New France?

Biography

Samuel de Champlain (1567–1635)

Samuel de Champlain worked to build the colony at Québec and to develop the fur trade. He lived in Québec for 27 years. During that time, he returned to France eight times to persuade the king to send more French colonists and to provide greater support for the settlement.

At the same time, Champlain built alliances with the Montagnais [MON-tun-yay] and Algonquin First Nations. He travelled the rivers into the interior. When he reached the Great Lakes, he established a friendship with the Wendat [WAH-n-dot] (also known as Huron) who lived in what is now Central Ontario.

Champlain wanted to trade with the Wendat. He agreed to fight with them against their enemies, the Haudenosaunee. The French and the Haudenosaunee had been enemies since Jacques Cartier's encounter with them years before. The two First Nations raided one another to obtain furs and to take revenge for relatives who had died in earlier conflicts. By siding with the Wendat, Champlain fuelled a conflict that would last for another 100 years. It would make life insecure and unstable for all sides.

Champlain died at Québec on Christmas Day in 1635. At that time, Québec was still a struggling settlement with just a few dozen people. In time, though, the colony began to flourish. Champlain came to be known as the founder of New France.

Figure 2.10 A self-portrait by Champlain. This is the only picture of Champlain that dates from his lifetime. It shows him firing his gun at a group of Haudenosaunee during a battle. Is this a primary source image or a secondary source image? Give reasons for your choice.

Think It Through

1. Examine the painting at the beginning of this chapter (pages 30–31). It shows early Acadians. Describe the details of the scene to get a better idea of the Acadian way of life. Consider clothing, tools, farming techniques, roles of men/women, and so on.

2. a) Working in a small group, brainstorm a list of challenges the French faced as they tried to build the colonies. Prepare a list of arguments to justify France spending more money on the colony. Then prepare a list of arguments to justify France not spending more money.

b) Write one of the following letters:
   - Imagine you are Samuel de Champlain. Write a letter to the king of France asking him to send more colonists to Québec.
   - Imagine you are the king. Write a letter to Champlain explaining why you cannot fulfill his request.

3. Create a chart like the one below in which you outline both the positive and negative economic aspects of the colonies from the perspective of each of the people listed.

	Positive	Negative
The king		
A French colonist		
A First Nations person		

Exploring Deeper into the Continent

Aside from the official explorers, the first people to leave the settlements of New France and begin roaming the countryside were the *coureurs de bois* (in English, "runners of the woods").

In this section, you'll investigate how these adventurers and the First Nations built the fur trade. You'll see why they pushed farther west and south into the continent. As you read about their explorations, you'll analyze how European ideas of land ownership caused conflict between them and the First Nations peoples.

Focus

What did the early French explorers in New France achieve?

Figure 2.11 An artist's portrayal of a coureur de bois. Many of these adventurers married First Nations women and had families. Their children were the Métis. The Métis learned both French and First Nations languages from their parents. They also learned the customs and ways of life of both peoples. What effect do you think these families might have had on the fur trade?

The Coureurs de Bois

The coureurs de bois were a unique group of adventurers. They lived for long periods among the First Nations. In fact, many coureurs de bois married First Nations women, and these couples became parents to the first Métis [may-TEE]. The coureurs de bois learned to speak the First Nations' languages and how to build birchbark canoes. They also learned many of the other skills they needed to survive in the woods.

Many of the young French men who became coureurs de bois were lured into the fur trade by the promise of adventure, freedom, and money. Their main interest was fur trapping, but they also acted as guides and interpreters for the French traders. In this way, they were responsible for much of the early European exploration of the continent.

Cultural Exchange ... Even Then

A young French colonist named Étienne Brûlé was one of the first coureurs de bois. In 1610, the French and the Wendat agreed to a cultural exchange. Brûlé went to live with the Wendat. A young Wendat man named Savignon went to live in France.

Brûlé wanted to learn as much as possible about the Wendat. During his years living with them, he gained an appreciation for the Wendat way of life. He learned to speak their language. He practised their customs. Brûlé travelled with the Wendat hunters and came to know their territory. He was the first European to travel up the Ottawa River and into Georgian Bay.

Things did not go as well for Savignon in France. He learned to speak French, but he was eager to return to North America. When he did, Savignon described France as a place where children were treated badly. He described beggars living in the streets, arguing loudly with one another.

Expanding West

Two of the most adventurous coureurs de bois were Pierre Radisson and his brother-in-law, the Sieur des Groseilliers. Radisson came

Figure 2.12 A painting of Radisson and des Groseilliers (Radisson is standing), by Frederick Remington, 1905. Because the coureurs de bois lived with First Nations peoples, each side learned about the other's culture. How can this type of cultural exchange affect the relationship between peoples?

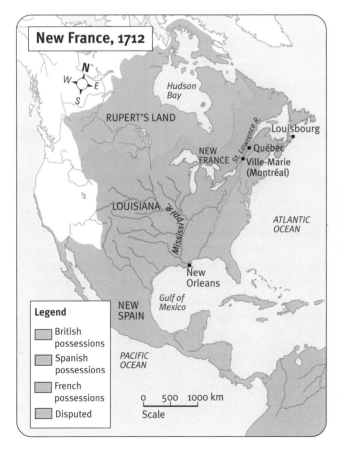

to New France in 1650 as a boy. When he was a teenager, a group of Mohawk took him to their home and adopted him into their family. For two years, Radisson lived among the Mohawk before deciding to return to Québec.

During the time he lived with the Mohawk, Radisson learned to speak their language and survive in the woods. It seemed only natural that he would become a coureur de bois. In 1659, he joined des Groseilliers on a trading trip. It took them deep inland to the far end of Lake Superior. No Europeans had ever been there before. Everywhere they went, the First Nations people welcomed them. Their knowledge of the fur country grew. As they travelled, they gave French names to some of the settlements, lakes, rivers, mountains, and other landforms they encountered. In this way, they claimed these lands for France.

In 1670, Radisson and des Groseilliers travelled to Hudson Bay because First Nations people had told them the land was rich in fur-bearing animals. Later the same year, a fur-trading business called the Hudson's Bay Company was founded as a result of the accomplishments of these two explorers.

Reading
STRATEGY

Visuals, such as photos, diagrams, and maps, often help us better understand the text we are reading. For the section of text on the next page titled "Expanding South," use the map in Figure 2.13 to see the route the explorers took and the land they claimed.

Figure 2.13 New France at its largest extent. Some people believe that New France grew too large too quickly and that this was a disadvantage to the French colony. Look at the map. What problems do you think the size of the colony posed? SKILLS

Expanding South

For many years, the French heard the First Nations talk about a mighty river beyond the Great Lakes that flowed into the south. In the Cree (Nehiyawak [nay-HI-uh-wuk]) language, the river was called the Mississippi—the "big river." In 1672, the king of France sent two explorers, Louis Jolliet and Jacques Marquette, to find out where this mysterious river flowed. Would it take them south to the Gulf of Mexico or west to the Pacific Ocean?

After several weeks of canoeing, they learned that there was a Spanish colony only a few days' journey away. Worried that the Spanish might take them hostage, Jolliet and Marquette turned back. They had travelled a long way and learned that the river emptied into the Gulf of Mexico. But they still had not reached the mouth of the mighty Mississippi.

In 1682, a French fur trader named René Robert Cavelier de la Salle finally reached the mouth of the Mississippi River at the Gulf of Mexico. Due to his expedition, France claimed ownership of all of the Mississippi country. They called it Louisiana, after the French king Louis XIV.

Different Perspectives about Land

Like people from the other imperial countries of Europe, the French claimed "ownership" of the territories they explored. They did not discuss land ownership with the First Nations or Inuit. They did not understand that the First Nations had a different idea about land. Although a First Nation granted certain bands or families the right to hunt and fish in a territory, no one owned land privately. First Nations believed land was to be shared by everyone.

While France claimed a vast territory, most colonists remained clustered along the St. Lawrence River. First Nations people lived in other parts of the colony. To gain control of the territory, France needed more colonists. It wasn't easy to persuade people to come to New France, though. The climate was much colder than it was in France. Also, it was hard to start a farm in the wilderness. As a result, the population in the colony grew slowly.

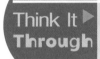

Think It Through

1. a) Make a colourful poster to show the accomplishments of a French explorer. Your poster should include
   - images of the explorer
   - a map(s) and/or photos showing the areas explored
   - an explanation of the challenges faced and the person's contributions to the growth of the colony
   - any other biographical information you can find at the library or online

   b) In your opinion, how important was this person's exploration to the future development of Canada?

2. The French claimed a great deal of land in North America, but there were not enough people to occupy it.

   a) Come up with at least two possible solutions to this problem. Create a table to show the advantages and disadvantages of each solution.

   b) Choose the solution you feel is the best one. Explain your choice.

3. Outline in writing, orally, or using a visual illustration the differing perspectives that the First Nations and the Europeans had on the idea of land ownership.

4. Why do you think the First Nations helped the French survive in the wilderness? Write a scenario predicting what might have happened if the First Nations had not helped the French.

Economy and Government in New France

In this section, you'll investigate how the king of France increased the population of the colony. You'll analyze the tensions between the French and some First Nations. You'll examine the role of religion and the Catholic Church in building the colony. Finally, you'll investigate the way of life that was evolving in New France.

Focus

How did the king of France and the Catholic Church influence the development of New France?

made France richer and more powerful, which were the aims of imperialism.

In the early days of New France, however, this system was not working well. To the merchants who ran it, New France was simply a place to trade for furs. They had little interest in building settlements. As a result, few people wanted to move there, and the colony failed to prosper.

The Royal Takeover

As a colony, New France depended on France for its survival. It relied on the home country for colonists, supplies, and military protection. In return, New France supplied resources such as furs and fish. The colony

Year	Population
1608	28
1641	240
1653	2 000
1667	3 918
1680	9 677
1685	10 725
1692	12 431
1698	15 355

Figure 2.15 The population of New France.

Figure 2.14 King Louis XIV of France. Louis was known as the Sun King because he was all-powerful. Louis was so forceful in acquiring colonies that the other countries of Europe united against him. Why would it have been important to the king for New France to thrive?

In 1663, King Louis XIV took control of the colony from the merchants. He set up a **Sovereign Council** to govern the colony. This council was made up of appointed councillors and three key officials.

- **Governor.** The most powerful member of the Sovereign Council was the governor. The governor, who was the King's personal representative, was usually an army officer and a noble. He took charge of the defence of the colony and of its relations with allies and enemies.
- **Intendant.** The second-most important official was the intendant. The intendant was in charge of the day-to-day affairs of the colony. For example, he supervised the courts, saw that roads were built and that settlers were looked after, and managed the economy.

The Government of New France

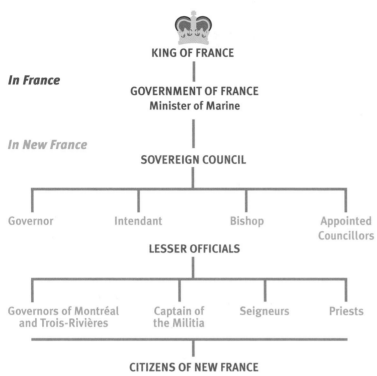

KING OF FRANCE

In France

GOVERNMENT OF FRANCE
Minister of Marine

In New France

SOVEREIGN COUNCIL

| Governor | Intendant | Bishop | Appointed Councillors |

LESSER OFFICIALS

| Governors of Montréal and Trois-Rivières | Captain of the Militia | Seigneurs | Priests |

CITIZENS OF NEW FRANCE

Reading
STRATEGY

What is a citizen? Brainstorm words and phrases that come to mind when you think of this word. Work together to come up with a definition.

The first intendant in New France was Jean Talon. On the king's orders, Talon brought newcomers from France to live in the colony. He talked with colonists to find out what they needed to improve their lives. He started shipbuilding and fishing industries, and built factories and roads.

- **Bishop.** The head of the church in the colony was the bishop. As a member of the Sovereign Council, he played a leading role in politics as well. The first bishop, François de Laval, opened a seminary in Québec to train priests; it later became Laval University.

The royal government paid the colony's expenses, so taxes were lower than they were in France. The government of New France was all-powerful, and the colonists had to follow the rules and laws established by the Sovereign Council. However, the courts heard complaints filed by the colonists. Overall, the people enjoyed greater freedom in New France than they had back in France.

A distinctive Francophone society developed. The colonists were expected to be responsible, contributing members. In this way, they became the **citizens** of New France.

Figure 2.16 A weekly session of the Sovereign Council, by Charles Huot, 1929. The governor is seated in the tall chair. The bishop is to the left. The intendant is to the right. Other members of the Council were appointed from among the most important merchants and nobles in the colony. Was this seventeenth-century government democratic? Explain.

CASE STUDY

Interactions with the First Nations

What impact did the First Nations have on the French newcomers? The *habitants* [a-bee-TAH(N)], who were the farmers of New France, admired many things in the First Nations' cultures. They adopted some of their skills and technologies. For example, they learned to line their winter coats and mittens with fur and to make boots out of moose hides to keep warm during the long, cold winters.

However, not all interaction between the First Nations and the habitants was peaceful. From the early days of the fur trade, the French and the Wendat were allies. Farther south, the British and the Haudenosaunee were allies. France and England were often at war in Europe. Sometimes, these conflicts spilled over into North America. For decades, the people of New France lived under the threat of attack by the British or the Haudenosaunee.

In the 1600s, the people of New France and the Haudenosaunee lived in the same territory in the St. Lawrence River Valley. Often, the habitants were afraid to venture beyond their villages. Their lives were at risk when they were simply working in the fields or hunting in the forests. For their safety, the habitants would often arm themselves when doing chores like gathering firewood. The hostilities between the people of New France and the Haudenosaunee convinced many people in France not to move to the colony.

The habitants needed help. Intendant Jean Talon wrote to the king asking for military protection. The king sent 1500 soldiers to New France. The soldiers burned down Haudenosaunee homes and villages. The Haudenosaunee seemed to be overpowered and agreed to sign a peace treaty with the French.

Respond

Why do you think the French decided to use military force against the Haudenosaunee? Would such a solution be acceptable in Canada today? Explain.

The Catholic Church in New France

Religion had an important place in the lives of the Europeans. In France, most people were Catholic. Therefore, almost all the colonists in New France were Catholic, too.

Priests, nuns, and missionaries who went to New France helped build the colony. They held religious services, taught school, ran hospitals, and cared for the poor. The colonists supported the Church and its activities by donating a portion of their income, called a tithe.

The most important goal of the Church was to spread the Catholic faith. The missionaries came to North America to convert First Nations peoples to their religion. The village of Ville-Marie was founded as a place where missionaries could do this. Today, we know this place as Montréal.

Many of the missionaries were adventurous. They pioneered canoe routes into the interior of the continent. As they travelled, they wrote accounts of their travels and life in the colony, which they sent to family and friends in France. Many of these writings have survived through the centuries and are an important source of historical information about that time. For example, a series of journals called the *Jesuit Relations* were written by a special order of missionaries. The **Jesuits**, who started arriving in New France in 1625, wrote mainly about their work and travels. They sent their journals back to France, where they were published. The following is an excerpt from the *Jesuit Relations*. In it, a Jesuit missionary described the conversion of some Wendat children and their parents to the Catholic faith.

In our Processions we had the little children march before the Cross, and perform some service, such as carrying the lights, or other things. Both they and their fathers take pleasure in this …. Thank God this much has already been accomplished, that they do not wish to die without baptism, believing that they will be forever miserable, if they pass away without it, or at least a strong desire for it, and without sorrow for their sins.

Source: *Jesuit Relations*, Vol. 4, "Acadia and Quebec 1633–34" (translation) (Cleveland: The Burrows Brothers Company, 1897), p. 89.

Populating the Colony

Aside from nuns, few French women were interested in living in New France. It was far from home, and life there was very harsh. But the colony needed women to marry the male colonists and raise families. Without them, New France would fail to grow and prosper.

The king had a solution. Between 1665 and 1673, he sent about 900 single young women and girls to New France to become wives. Some of the women were orphans. Others were poor. If they married, the king gave each couple an ox, a cow, two pigs, two chickens, some salt beef, and a purse of money. The women were known as the *filles du roi*—the "king's daughters."

Within 14 years, the population of New France grew from 3200 to 10 000. After 1680, there were few newcomers from France. These 10 000 colonists are therefore the ancestors of most Canadians of French descent—the original *Canadiens*.

Women in New France

The family was the centre of daily life in New France. Women worked very hard alongside their husbands in the fields. They also cared for their homes and children and helped manage the family finances.

Girls in New France received a better education than they did in France. The daughters of wealthier families went to boarding schools in the towns. Other families sent their daughters to schools

Figure 2.17 A statue of Marguerite Bourgeoys, by sculptor Jules LaSalle, 1988. When she arrived in Ville-Marie in 1653, there were only 200 inhabitants. There was no school, so Bourgeoys took over a stone stable and began to teach girls such things as cooking, sewing, reading, and writing. Why do you think this was important?

in the countryside. The nuns operated the schools and taught the children how to read and write as well as how to do domestic chores. Since there were more schools for girls than for boys in the colony, girls often received a better education.

Many children had a greater opportunity to attend school than children in France did. In France, many children were sent to the cities at a young age to learn a trade. Therefore, they never attended school. In New France, though, most children stayed with their families so they could help on the farm. This gave them the chance to go to school when planting and harvesting were finished.

Tech Link

Look on the *Voices and Visions* CD-ROM to see a map of the extent of the seigneuries in New France.

The Economy of New France

There was more to the economy of New France than the fur trade. Most of the French colonists were farmers.

The social structure of New France was based on the **seigneurial system**. In this system, the king gave large tracts of land along the St. Lawrence River to the nobles, called *seigneurs*. In return, each seigneur had to find colonists to settle the land. These colonists, known as habitants, rented strips of land from the seigneur and set up farms. The river was used for travel and irrigation. Both seigneurs and habitants had duties to each other that were protected by law. For example, each habitant had to give the seigneur a portion of each year's crop and pay other fees. The seigneur had to build a mill and a church on his land.

Voices ■

Pierre Boucher came to live in New France in 1635. For many years, he lived among the Wendat. Later, he settled on a farm near the village of Trois-Rivières. Boucher published a book about life in New France in 1664. In it, he described the kind of people who made the most successful settlers in the colony.

66 The people best fitted for this country are those who can work with their own hands in making clearings, putting up buildings and otherwise. ...

Poor people would be much better off here than they are in France, provided they are not lazy; they could not fail to get employment and could not say, as they do in France, that they are obliged to beg for their living because they cannot find anyone to give them work; in one word, no people are wanted, either men or women, who cannot turn their hands to some work, unless they are very rich. 99

Source: Pierre Boucher, *True and Genuine Description of New France*, 1664; reprinted in English in 1883 as *Canada in the Seventeenth Century* (Montréal: GE Desbarats, 1883).

Figure 2.18 The filles du roi arriving in New France, as painted by C.W. Jefferys about 1940. Girls were usually quite young when they married, anywhere from 12 to 16 years old. Imagine you were a young French person who was shipped across the ocean without any family. What would be your greatest fear about coming to New France? What would be your greatest hope?

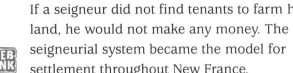

The king knew the seigneurial system would encourage settlement in New France. If a seigneur did not find tenants to farm his land, he would not make any money. The seigneurial system became the model for settlement throughout New France.

The French: Forging the Foundations of Canada

The citizens of New France had a much different life than they would have had if they had stayed in France. They had more food and better houses than people in the home country did. As well as being pioneers in the fur trade, they were explorers of the interior as far west as the plains and as far south as the Gulf of Mexico. The French colonists became a self-reliant people with a unique way of life that was distinct from that of France. Through hard work and perseverance, the citizens of New France laid the foundations of Canada.

Canada Today

Farming is still important in Québec today. About 7 per cent of the province's total land area is farmland. Most of this land is located along the St. Lawrence River where the first French colonists settled.

Figure 2.19 The seigneurial system was officially abolished in 1854, and tenants were able to start purchasing the farmland rather than rent it. This is a modern photo of the St. Lawrence River. Even though the system no longer exists, can you see its lasting impact on the landscape?

Think It Through

1. Create a chart to show all the ways in which life in New France was different from life in France. How do you think these differences influenced the colonists' views of their relationship to France?

2. Create a web diagram to show how each of the following contributed to the building of New France:
   - Louis XIV
   - Jean Talon
   - the First Nations
   - the Catholic Church
   - the Jesuits
   - the nuns
   - the filles du roi
   - the habitants

3. Return to the K-W-L chart you started at the beginning of this chapter.
   a) Check off the questions in the "Wonder" column that have been answered.
   b) Summarize what you have learned in the "Learn" column.

4. The French were the first permanent colonists here. As a class, discuss the impact of this fact on the development of the Canadian society we know today.

Chapter 2 PROJECT Drama and History

Dramas can help us to understand and appreciate a historical event and the motives of the people involved. A tableau is a type of drama that can both entertain and inform us.

Tableau is a French word meaning a painting. It is a scene created when actors dramatize an event without moving or speaking. Imagine watching a DVD movie and pressing the pause button during a scene. The image that is frozen on the screen is a tableau.

Tableaux can be performed in a series to show a sequence of events. To signal a new tableau, the stage lighting is dimmed to allow the actors to rearrange themselves for the next scene.

Selecting Scenes

In a small group, select an event from this chapter that would make good tableaux. Think about why this event is important and why it would make a good drama. For example, the first meeting of French explorers and First Nations peoples would make effective tableaux.

Once your group has decided what scene to present, think about how the event can be presented from different points of view. For example, how would the French have viewed the event? How would the First Nations have viewed it? Women? The king? Create a tableau for each point of view.

Designing the Tableaux

Once you have the characters for the tableaux, write a description of the scene from each character's point of view. Identify the props that will be needed. Keep these simple. For example, a paddle or a paper hat may be sufficient to

identify certain characters. Avoid stereotypes, and be respectful of the groups and cultures you represent. Include a rough sketch of each scene.

Rehearsing the Tableaux

- Decide who will play each character. Select one person to be the technician who controls the lights during your presentation.
- Practise each scene. Actors should have a frozen body position and facial expression.
- Take turns looking at the others in their frozen positions. Suggest changes that might improve the drama or express emotions more clearly.
- Practise changing from one tableau to the next until you are able to make these changes quickly and easily. Hold a final practice, turning out the lights to provide the transition from scene to scene.

The Audience's Role

While you are watching other groups' tableaux, write down the historic events you think they are presenting. Remember to be a polite and attentive audience. Don't interrupt the presentations, and applaud when a presentation is over.

As you watch the tableaux, think of any questions you have about the scene. Then raise your questions following the presentation.

Metacognition: Reflecting

Recall your original ideas and points of view on contact, imperialism, and colonization. Once all groups have presented their tableaux, discuss how the dramatization has affected your views. Have you changed your thinking on any of the topics presented? Explain.

Chapter **3** The British in North America

Key CONCEPT ▶ Mercantilism

Many imperial powers from Europe used the mercantile system to grow powerful. **Mercantilism** allowed an imperial country to become rich in gold and silver by selling the resources taken from its colonies.

Fish, furs, wood, and iron ore could bring the home country great wealth. With unlimited access to these resources, the home country no longer had to pay to get them from other countries. The imperial country could consume as many resources as it needed. Then it could make even more money by selling what it didn't need to other countries in exchange for gold and silver.

This chapter examines Britain as an example of one imperial power that used the mercantile system. Through its colonies in North America, Britain hoped to obtain everything it needed to become rich and powerful.

British Colonies

In Chapter 2, you learned how newcomers from France built colonies in North America. In this chapter, you'll discover the reasons why Britain wanted to do the same. You'll see how Britain's colonies differed from those of France. This chapter gives you a chance to analyze the impact of the newcomers on the First Nations. Finally, you will have the opportunity to learn about some early British explorers and their accomplishments in North America.

Perspectives on Mercantilism

Chapter 3

This chapter asks you to think further about the economic reasons behind the Europeans' desire to colonize North America.

Honing Your Skills

Comparing and contrasting two things means finding similarities and differences between them. The Skill Check feature on the next page will show you how to do this. The project at the end of this chapter will ask you to compare and contrast the societies of the First Nations, New France, and the British colonies.

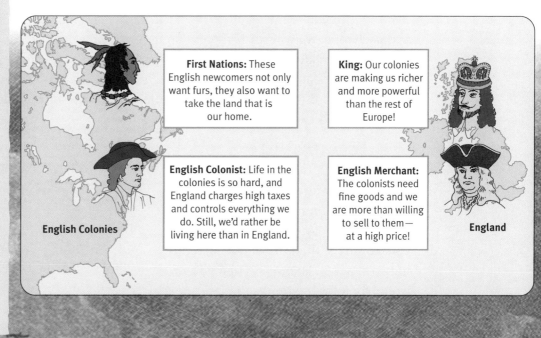

First Nations: These English newcomers not only want furs, they also want to take the land that is our home.

King: Our colonies are making us richer and more powerful than the rest of Europe!

English Colonist: Life in the colonies is so hard, and England charges high taxes and controls everything we do. Still, we'd rather be living here than in England.

English Merchant: The colonists need fine goods and we are more than willing to sell to them— at a high price!

English Colonies

England

Think ► AHEAD

Study the diagram and the painting of the British colony at Halifax.

a) Brainstorm a list of ways the mercantile system might benefit
  • the home country
  • the colonists
  • the First Nations

b) Can you think of any drawbacks of using this system? List those as well.

c) When you have finished this chapter, return to your list and revise it according to what you have learned.

SKILL CHECK: Compare and Contrast

In Chapter 1, we looked at the societies of three different First Nations. Chapter 2 introduced you to the ways of life of the early French colonists in North America. In this chapter, we will study the British in North America and explore the kind of society they created. By the end of Chapter 3, you may be able to see similarities and differences among all of these societies. This will help you begin to understand the relationships that developed among them. Here are some guidelines for comparing and contrasting information effectively.

Create a Graphic Organizer

A graphic organizer helps you compare and contrast information. To compare two European countries in the 1600s, you would list the facts about each one in two separate columns. Then you would look for the things that are similar and different.

of France and England in the 1600s, you could divide your chart into categories such as type of government, religion, language spoken, location of colonies, and so on. The categories you choose will depend on the question you are trying to answer. (You may have to do extra research—at the library or on the Internet—in order to find all the information needed for your chart.)

Decide on Categories for Comparison

Dividing your organizer into categories allows you to compare and contrast the most important characteristics. For example, if you are looking at the countries

Try It!

1. Fill in the chart below to make a very general comparison of France and England in the 1600s. Add two more categories of your own choosing and fill them in.
2. Create your own organizer to compare and contrast two things of your choice. You could look at two music groups, two different newspapers, or a couple of different clothing stores, for example.

Communicate Your Findings

Once you have completed your organizer and analyzed the results, you can communicate your findings in one of several ways:

- through an oral presentation, using your organizer to point out similarities and differences
- in a Venn diagram
- in a written summary that explains the information in paragraph form

Categories	France	England
Government	Monarchy – ruled by a king	Monarchy – ruled by a king
Religion		
Language		
Location of colonies in North America (Hint: See page 35.)		

The British Cross the Atlantic

France was not the only European country building an empire. All the imperial powers of Europe believed an empire was the path to wealth and power. In this section, you'll discover some of the different reasons why the British decided to expand their empire by building colonies in North America.

Focus

Why did the British build colonies in America?

Colonizing America

Walter Raleigh was the first English explorer to try to build a colony in North America. His first attempt was in 1585. It failed, so he tried again in 1587. This attempt failed, too. Raleigh failed because he and the colonists were not prepared for the harsh life of the North American wilderness. Still, the British wanted to try again. Why was it important for Britain to build colonies in America?

- **The economy.** France, Spain, and Portugal had made a lot of money from their colonies in the Americas. Britain hoped it could do the same.
- **Competition.** Spain and France were expanding their empires. Britain was in competition with them and wanted to prevent them from becoming more powerful.
- **Quality of life.** In Britain, the cities were overcrowded and there was little good farmland left. Colonies provided a place to resettle people.
- **Religious freedom.** Many religious groups in Britain (for example, the Puritans, Quakers, and Baptists) were treated badly because of their beliefs. They wanted to find a place where they could practise their faiths freely. Going to America seemed like a good opportunity.

King James I of England knew it would cost a great deal of money to set up the colonies. However, he did not want to risk losing the government's money. Instead, in 1607 he began granting permission to private groups who were interested in setting up colonies along the eastern coast of North America.

The Thirteen Colonies

Eventually, colonists from Britain established 13 separate colonies along the eastern coast of the present-day United States. Together the colonies became known as New

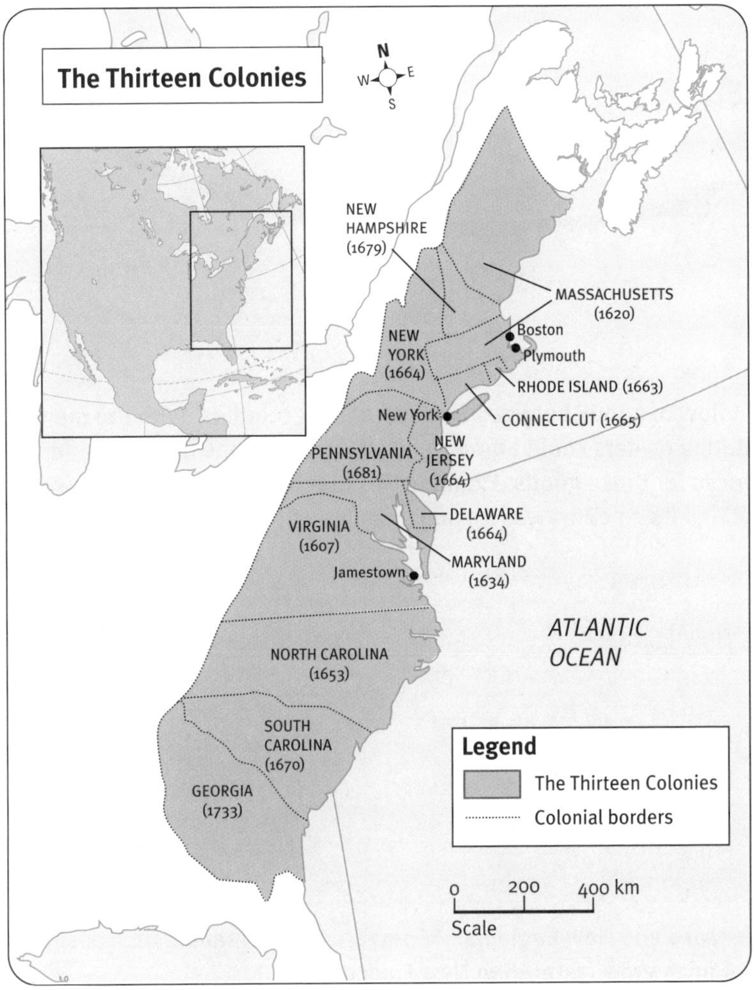

The Thirteen Colonies

NEW HAMPSHIRE (1679)

MASSACHUSETTS (1620)

Boston

Plymouth

NEW YORK (1664)

RHODE ISLAND (1663)

New York

CONNECTICUT (1665)

PENNSYLVANIA (1681)

NEW JERSEY (1664)

DELAWARE (1664)

VIRGINIA (1607)

MARYLAND (1634)

Jamestown

ATLANTIC OCEAN

NORTH CAROLINA (1653)

SOUTH CAROLINA (1670)

GEORGIA (1733)

Legend

    The Thirteen Colonies

.... Colonial borders

0   200   400 km

Scale

Figure 3.1 The Thirteen Colonies in North America. Compare this map to a modern map of the United States. What has changed? SKILLS

England. Each colony was unique. Each had its own social structure, religious groups, and type of government.

Their economies were based on producing various goods. For example, the colony called Virginia had a mild climate that was suited to growing tobacco. This product was very popular in Europe. The demand for tobacco played the same role in Virginia as the demand for furs played in New France. To the north of Virginia, a religious group called the Pilgrims founded a colony at Plymouth, Massachusetts. The Pilgrims came to America in search of a place where they could practise their religion freely. They were joined by other settlers who cleared farms, raised cattle, and fished for a living.

The Thirteen Colonies and New France Compared

New France and the first of the Thirteen Colonies were founded around the same time. Yet England's colonies grew much more quickly (see Figure 3.3). Why was this so?

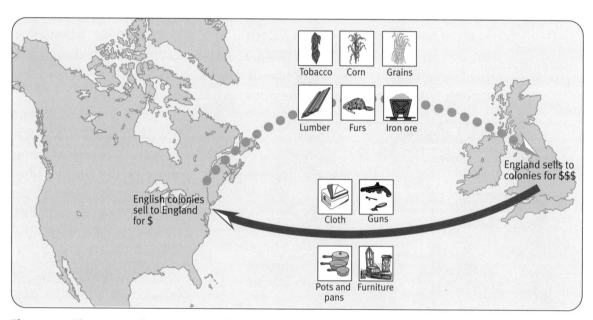

Figure 3.2 The mercantile system and flow of goods between England and its colonies. With the money they earned from tobacco, many plantation owners could afford to import luxury items from England. England charged the colonists high prices for these goods. Examine this diagram. How does it show that the relationship between England and its colonies was a good example of the mercantile system?

	New France	The Thirteen Colonies
1660	3 000	90 000
1710	18 000	331 711
1720	24 474	446 185
1730	34 118	629 445
1740	44 000	905 563
1750	53 000	1 170 760
1760	64 000	1 593 625

Figure 3.3 Population growth in New France and New England, 1660–1760. Before reading on, speculate about the reasons why the Thirteen Colonies grew faster than New France. SKILLS

Britain and France had different reasons for colonizing North America. In the beginning, they did not have the same goals or use the same systems to run their colonies. The following chart outlines some of the characteristics of each. These factors will help you understand why the population of the British colonies in America grew relatively quickly.

	New France	**The Thirteen Colonies**
Different Goals	France was not interested in spending heavily on its North American colonies. Its priority was collecting furs and other natural resources such as timber, fish, and metal ores from the land.	Britain invested a lot of money in its colonies overseas. The British wanted to establish large settlements to gain military and economic advantage over the other imperial countries.
The Climate	The climate of the St. Lawrence Valley and Acadia was extreme. Winters were long and cold. Most of the year, it was too cold for farming. This made it harder for people to earn a living. However, it was the best place to find thick furs, which is why France preferred it.	The climate was mild, especially in the southern colonies. In the south, farms flourished year-round. Overall, the climate made life more comfortable.
Employment	The early economy of New France was based mainly on the fur trade. First Nations trappers, the coureurs de bois, and the fur traders ran most of the fur trade. There were not as many opportunities for others to earn a living.	The economies of the British colonies were based mainly on farming, fishing, and logging. Therefore, there were many more opportunities for colonists to earn a living.
Religion	Only French Catholics were encouraged to come to New France.	The Thirteen Colonies allowed settlers from many faiths to settle there. They also permitted people from different countries to come, as opposed to just from Britain.
Trade	New France was allowed to trade only with France. All trade revolved around the fur trade, and one company had a monopoly on that trade.	The Thirteen Colonies were initially allowed to trade with other countries, not just Britain. The colonists were free to start businesses and grow a variety of crops for profit.

Canada Today

Since the 1700s, the population gap between Canada and the United States has continued to grow. In 2002, Canada's population was 32 million. The United States' population was 290 million. What impact do you think living beside a large and powerful neighbour has on Canada? As a class, discuss some of your ideas. Then work on your own to create a cartoon or slogan that illustrates your point of view.

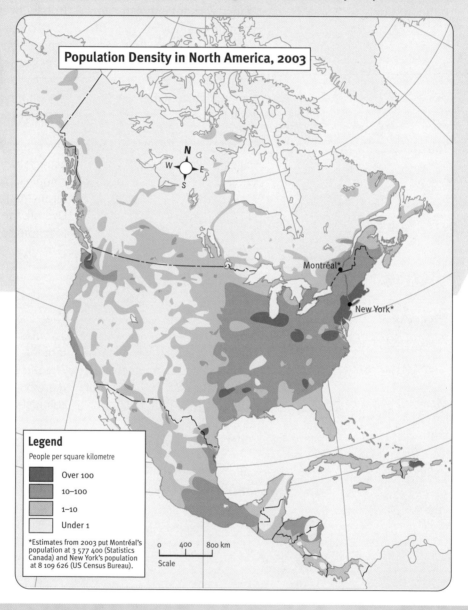

Population Density in North America, 2003

Montréal*

New York*

Legend

People per square kilometre

- Over 100
- 10–100
- 1–10
- Under 1

*Estimates from 2003 put Montréal's population at 3 577 400 (Statistics Canada) and New York's population at 8 109 626 (US Census Bureau).

0   400   800 km

Scale

Think It Through

1. In a group, discuss the importance of the British government's role in building the Thirteen Colonies.

2. How did the French and the British use the natural resources of North America differently to make money? You can respond to this question in writing, orally, or by creating an organizer or illustrations. SKILLS

The British Colonies in Atlantic Canada

Focus

What role did Britain play in colonizing the land we now call Canada?

In Chapter 2, you discovered that the French had built colonies in the country we now call Canada and explored the interior of the continent. As they did, they claimed all the lands they passed through for France, expanding the French Empire. In this section, you'll see how Britain also set out to build colonies here. You'll look at the issues surrounding the colonies in Newfoundland and Halifax. As you do, you'll discover one of the great tragedies of the early days of contact.

A New Found Land

John Cabot (called Giovanni Caboto in his native Italy) reached the waters off Newfoundland in 1497. When he returned to England, he reported seeing fish so plentiful they could be caught just by lowering a basket into the water.

News about the fish stocks spread quickly among the fishing fleets of Europe. Fish was an important food staple there. This was especially true in Catholic countries, where the Church prohibited people from eating meat on certain days of the week. Soon hundreds of ships were fishing in the waters off the coast of this "New Found Land."

Although Cabot claimed Newfoundland for Britain, the British didn't really want the island as a colony. They were not interested in building settlements there. The climate was too harsh and the soil wasn't good for farming. All they wanted was fish.

Most fishers stayed on board their ships. They went ashore only to dry the catch. They all returned home before the winter storms set in. As the fishery grew, however, there was competition among the fleets to secure the best harbours for drying stations. Some of the crew began staying behind in the winter to guard these sites.

Canada Today

People believed the abundant fish stocks Cabot found would last forever. For hundreds of years, fishers from around the world overfished the cod on the Atlantic coast. By 1992, almost all the codfish were gone! The Canadian government decided to shut down the fishery. It reopened it in 1999 but allowed only a limited number of boats to fish for cod. The stocks, however, continued to decline. In 2003, the government shut down the fishery again. The fishery that first lured Europeans to North America may never reopen.

Figure 3.4 Cod-fishing boats docked in St. John's, 2003. What lesson can we, as a society, learn from the collapse of the cod fishery on the East Coast? In your opinion, has Canada learned this lesson well? Give a recent example to support your answer.

Over time, the number of British newcomers in Newfoundland began to grow. The king, George II, granted the captains permission to build fishing villages on the coast. As the villages grew, Britain could no longer ignore the island. In 1729, the king appointed a governor. Newfoundland was evolving from a fishing station into a colony.

Figure 3.5 A fishing station in Newfoundland. The European fishers used salt to preserve their catch. The British didn't have much salt, though. They had to go ashore to clean and dry their fish on platforms in the sun. Draw a cause-and-effect diagram to illustrate how this led to the building of settlements in Newfoundland. (You may want to refer to the Skill Check on page 76.)

CASE STUDY

Extinction of a Nation

What happened to the First Nations people who once lived in Newfoundland? Long before the British came, the Beothuk [bay-AH-thuk] had lived on the island. In the summer, they lived along the coast, where they fished and gathered shellfish. In the winter, they moved inland to hunt caribou.

The arrival of the British fishers disrupted this way of life. The British fishing villages cut off the Beothuk's access to the sea. Now they had to compete with the British for the island's food resources.

The Beothuk were afraid of the newcomers. They tried to avoid them, even though this meant going hungry because they were unable to reach the fishing areas. Once the fishing season ended, the British would return home to Europe with their catch. While they were gone, the Beothuk would sometimes raid fishing stations and take steel hooks, ropes, and other supplies. When the British returned in the spring, hostilities between the two peoples grew more violent. Eventually, the British used guns to hunt down and kill many Beothuk men, women, and children. The British also unintentionally brought diseases to the island, which resulted in the deaths of many Beothuk.

By 1828, only one Beothuk remained. She was a young woman named Shanawdithit. She lived with an English family in St. John's (the capital of the island) during her last years. By this time there were people interested in

Tech Link

For a closer look at drawings by Shanawdithit, open Chapter 3 on your *Voices and Visions* CD-ROM.

learning about the culture of the Beothuk. Shanawdithit tried to answer their questions, drawing pictures to describe the life her people once led. When Shanawdithit died of tuberculosis in 1829, the Beothuk went extinct. In 200 years, an entire culture had been wiped out by violence and disease.

Respond

1. In your own words, explain the main cause of the conflict between the British fishers and the Beothuk in Newfoundland.

2. If British colonists in Newfoundland had been more interested in the fur trade than the fishery, how might the relationship between them and the Beothuk have been different?

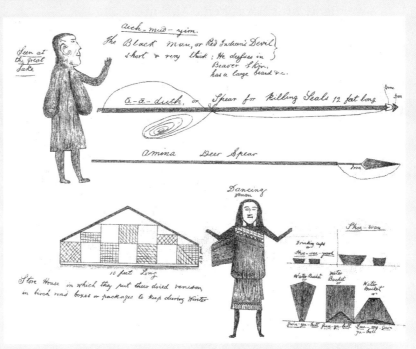

Figure 3.6 Drawings by Shanawdithit. Explain what type of source these drawings represent—are they primary or secondary? What can you tell about the Beothuk from these illustrations?

Events in Europe Affect the Colonies

Britain and France fought many wars against each other in Europe. Sometimes,

Reading
STRATEGY

The most important new vocabulary words in each chapter appear in boldface. These words are defined in the glossary at the back of this book. However, you should keep a dictionary close by in case there are other words in the text that are unfamiliar to you.

these conflicts affected their colonies in North America. In 1713, the two imperial powers signed the Treaty of Utrecht to create peace in Europe. The agreement allowed the French to keep control of the Fortress of Louisbourg on Île Royale (present-day Cape Breton), while the French colony of Acadia was given to the British. The British renamed the colony Nova Scotia. Otherwise, they let the habitants live their lives they way they always had—at least for a time. (You'll learn about the fate of the Acadians in Chapter 5.)

The Creation of Halifax

Eventually, Britain became more concerned about the strong French presence in Nova Scotia and at the Fortress of Louisbourg. So, in 1749 Britain decided to show its **sovereignty** over Nova Scotia. This means it would tighten its control over the former French colony.

The British planned to build a town and a fort in Nova Scotia at a place the Mi'kmaq [MIG-mah] called Chebucto, meaning "the biggest harbour." It was to become a base for British troops and naval ships. Sixteen ships sailed into the harbour with 2600 soldiers and colonists on board, ready to begin building the town. They called the settlement Halifax, after the British official in London who oversaw the project. The houses and buildings spread out along the waterfront at the base of a hill. At the top of the hill, the British built a military fort.

Active Citizenship in Halifax

The government at Halifax included a governor, a council of advisors, and an elected assembly. For many years, though, the governors of the colony put off elections. They worked with their advisors to govern on their own. Then, in 1758, Britain insisted that an election be held. The **citizens** of the colony could now participate actively in their government by voting. It was the first elected assembly in British North America.

As you know, citizenship involves much more than voting in elections. Halifax residents who contributed to their society by working, paying taxes, volunteering, or abiding by the law, for example, were also active citizens.

Figure 3.7 This is a modern reconstruction of the military fort overlooking Halifax harbour. Why do you think the British chose a hilltop for the fort and shaped it like a star? Check on the Internet or in the library to find the answer.

The Mi'kmaq Perspective

The Mi'kmaq people who lived in Nova Scotia were concerned about the British newcomers. The site where they had built Halifax was one of the Mi'kmaq people's preferred coastal campsites. Their French allies urged the Mi'kmaq to make life difficult for the British. In response, the governor of the British colony, Lord Cornwallis, issued orders to "annoy, distress, take, or destroy Mi'kmaq people wherever they are found."

With the hostile relations between the British colonists and the Mi'kmaq, the newcomers decided it was not a good time to build farms outside Halifax. Besides, there was little good farmland available in the colony. The Acadians already occupied most of the fertile land. This situation increased tensions between the French and British colonists in Nova Scotia. It did not seem that peace would last much longer.

VOICES ■

In 1749, the Mi'kmaq enlisted the help of some French missionaries to write a declaration of war against the British. It read in part:

66 The place where you stand, where you build houses, where you build a fort, where you wish, as it were, to enthrone yourself, this land of which you now wish to make yourselves absolute masters, this same land belongs to me. I have grown up on it like the grass, and it is the very place of my birth and my residence. ...

Show me where I, a Native, will lodge? You chase me away, and where do you want me to take refuge? You have seized nearly all of this land in all its vastness.... At the present time, you force me to speak out because of the considerable theft you inflict upon me. 99

Source: Cornelius Jaenen and Cecilia Morgan, "A Mi'kmaq Declaration of War, 1749," in *Material Memory: Documents in Pre-Confederation History* (Toronto: Pearson Education Canada, 1999).

Think It Through

1. **Citizenship and Identity.** How did the establishment of the first elected assembly in Canada increase the responsibilities of the colonists?

2. Britain gained control of Nova Scotia. What do you predict will be the long-term consequences of this for the Acadians? Give reasons to support your predictions.

3. What do you predict will be the long-term consequences for the Mi'kmaq of British expansion in Nova Scotia? Give reasons to support your predictions.

The Company by the Bay

VOICES AND VISIONS

Beaver furs were in demand throughout Europe. As a result, the imperial powers competed for furs in North America. In this section, you'll discover how the British entered the fur trade. You'll also look at the issues that affected the competition for furs among the British, the French, and the First Nations.

Focus

What was the importance of the creation of the Hudson's Bay Company?

The Europeans Explore Hudson Bay

In Chapter 2, you discovered that the Canadien *coureurs de bois* travelled with the First Nations into the interior. As they did, they heard stories about a vast sea that lay far to the north. This "sea" was Hudson Bay. You read about the adventures of two coureurs de bois, Pierre Radisson and the Sieur des Groseilliers. They thought that if they found this sea, they would find an abundant new supply of furs, too.

Radisson and des Groseilliers took their idea to the governor of New France. But he was not interested in searching for this mysterious body of water. So instead, they took their plan to Britain. They found a group of British merchants who were willing to pay for their expedition.

In 1668, two ships sailed from London. A storm forced Radisson's ship to turn back. But the second ship, carrying

Figure 3.8 Henry Hudson's last voyage, as imagined by an unknown nineteenth-century artist. Henry Hudson was the British explorer and sea captain after whom Hudson Bay was named. He was known as an avid adventurer, but not a great leader. In 1610, he was looking for a passage through the Arctic when he happened upon the huge bay. He failed to keep control of his crew, and they mutinied. The sailors set Hudson and a few of his loyal followers adrift in a small rowboat in the middle of the bay.

des Groseilliers and his crew, reached the vast body of water spoken of by the First Nations. They dropped anchor at the mouth of the Rupert River and built a small fort. During the winter, they traded with the local Cree (Nehiyawak [nay-HI-uh-wuk]) and Innu [IN-noo]. When summer came, they returned to England with a shipload of furs.

Radisson and des Groseilliers had been right. Hudson Bay provided an ocean route into the heart of the continent—and an abundant new supply of furs.

The Hudson's Bay Company

In 1670, King Charles II of England granted a monopoly to the Hudson's Bay Company. The monopoly covered all the lands drained by the rivers that flowed into Hudson Bay. It was a vast territory consisting of most of what is now Western and Northern Canada.

The British called the area **Rupert's Land**, after Prince Rupert, the first head of the company. The Hudson's Bay Company was not interested in building a colony. They were merchants, interested only in trade. They built trading posts at the mouths of important rivers. First Nations and Inuit [IN-yoo-it] hunters brought the furs to these posts.

Conflict on the Bay

Meanwhile, the French fur traders decided they could not stand by while the English grabbed up all the furs in Rupert's Land. In 1686, a French soldier named Pierre de Troyes led a bold attack on the British forts along the bay. The French surprised the

The English (Hudson's Bay Company) called their trading posts **factories**. The trader in charge of a post was called the **factor**.

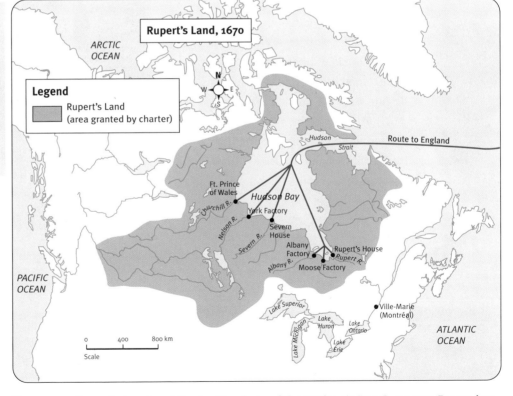

Figure 3.9 Rupert's Land and the trading forts of the Hudson's Bay Company. Fur traders were eager to gain control over Hudson Bay and the surrounding land. Look at this map. Why do you think control of this area was important to the British? How do you think the First Nations who lived there felt about newcomers taking control of the land?

British by travelling from the interior by canoe, instead of arriving in the bay by ship. De Troyes and his troops easily captured Rupert House, Moose Factory, and Albany Factory on James Bay. The British were caught off-guard. They didn't even have time to load their cannons!

The French victory was not complete, though. The British remained in control of York Factory at the mouth of the Nelson River. The most famous soldier in New France, Pierre Le Moyne d'Iberville, led French troops in several attempts to capture York Factory. In 1697, he finally succeeded. In a daring naval battle on the waters of the bay, d'Iberville's ship sank or drove away three British warships.

The French victories in Rupert's Land did not last. The Treaty of Utrecht brought peace between Britain and France both in North America and in Europe. It returned the Hudson Bay lands, Acadia, and Newfoundland to the British in 1713.

The battles over the fur-trading posts were part of a larger conflict between Britain and France for control of North America and the fur trade. The war between these two empires would last another 50 years. You'll find out how the competition ended in Chapter 5.

Canada Today

The Hudson's Bay Company is Canada's oldest company. In fact, it is one of the oldest companies in the world! Today, though, the Bay does not do business at trading posts. It operates more than 100 department stores and sells billions of dollars worth of goods every year.

When the Hudson's Bay Company first started, it had a **monopoly** on the fur trade. That meant no other British company could trade in Rupert's Land. Today, of course, the Bay no longer has a monopoly. It competes with many other companies to attract your business.

Figure 3.10 A modern Bay store in Calgary, Alberta. If the Hudson's Bay Company still had a monopoly, what effect do you think it would have on prices? How is competition good for consumers like you?

Think It Through

1. Predict how the French, English, and First Nations reacted to the Treaty of Utrecht.
2. Britain now controlled Nova Scotia, Newfoundland, and Rupert's Land.
   a) What parts of North America did the French control?

b) Predict the consequences of this situation for the future of the French fur trade. Then draw a mind map to illustrate your ideas.

The British Continue to Explore

Focus

What did the British explorers who ventured into the North and West achieve?

At first, the traders at the Hudson's Bay Company posts stayed at their forts. They waited there for First Nations peoples to bring the furs to them. Then, the French began interfering in the British fur trade. They met First Nations trappers before the trappers reached the British forts. They bought the furs the British were expecting. Now the British traders would have to travel into the interior themselves to compete with the French. In this section, you'll learn about some of their expeditions and you'll discover what the British traders and explorers accomplished.

Into the Interior

Henry Kelsey worked for the Hudson's Bay Company. In 1690, he left his trading post and set off on a journey with a group of Cree. His goal was to meet Aboriginal peoples and convince them to become trading partners with the British. He took a brass pot, a blanket, some guns, tobacco, and a hatchet with him to show any First Nations people he met.

Kelsey travelled on foot and by canoe south and west away from Hudson Bay. The Cree led him out of the forest and into the grasslands of the prairies. He was the first European to see the vast herds of buffalo that once roamed the Plains. As he crossed the prairies, the First Nations peoples he met welcomed him to their territories. The Cree already had alliances with the Siksika [sik-SIK-uh] First Nation, who lived in the West. Through this relationship, the Cree helped Kelsey gain greater access to furs.

Kelsey remained on the prairies for two years, travelling as far west as present-day Saskatchewan. Through his contact with First Nations, he increased the flow of furs from the interior to the Hudson Bay posts.

Figure 3.11 *Kelsey on the Plains,* painted by Rex Woods about 1967. It is a romanticized repainting of a work by Charles W. Jefferys in 1927. Kelsey is taking part in a buffalo hunt with the Assiniboine [uh-SIH-nih-boyn] Nation in August 1691. Like the coureurs de bois, Kelsey lived among the First Nations. He learned their languages and customs. How do you think this helped his relations with First Nations people? What impact do you think this had on the fur trade? For help in analyzing this image, see the Skill Check on page 6.

West into Alberta

Another British explorer, named Anthony Henday, ventured even farther west. Henday worked for the Hudson's Bay Company, too. In 1745, he set off from York Factory, travelling on foot to what is today Red Deer, Alberta. He also wanted to make contact with the Siksika people who lived there. He hoped to convince them to bring their furs to Hudson Bay.

Led by his Cree guides, Henday arrived at a large Siksika camp of about 200 tipis. Their leader was sitting on a white buffalo robe surrounded by 20 Elders. They smoked a pipe of tobacco with Henday, which was a symbolic act to show good faith. Then everyone feasted on pieces of boiled buffalo meat served in baskets of woven grass. Hospitality such as this was an important part of the Siksika culture. It ensured the well-being of the giver and the receiver.

The Siksika society was based on equality among its members. Its economy was based on meeting the needs of the community. Henday invited the Siksika to bring furs to the trading posts at Hudson Bay. He was suggesting they adopt an economy driven by profit. The Siksika refused his offer. The idea of trading for profit was new to them. The effect of this trade on their hunting and gathering activities would have to be carefully considered before it could be accepted.

To the Northern Lands

Beyond the tree line, in the Far North, lies a vast marshland. It's too cold for trees any larger than shrubs to grow there. The Dene [DEN-ay] people who lived there told the British stories about gold and copper along the shores of a distant northern river.

In 1770, a young sailor named Samuel Hearne set out from Hudson Bay to find the river and its rich resources. He joined a party of Dene and their leader, Matonabbee. They travelled on snowshoes, hauling their supplies on toboggans. When the snow melted in spring, they made bark canoes to carry them across the rivers and lakes.

Hearne did not find any gold or copper. However, he was the first European to reach the shores of the Arctic Ocean, and he learned from the Dene how to travel and live off the land.

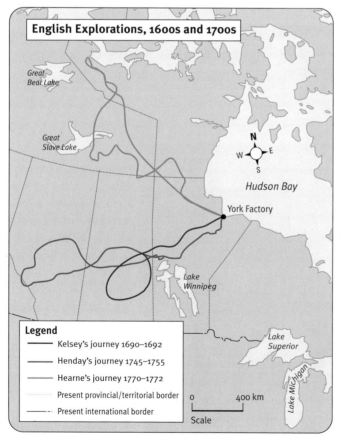

English Explorations, 1600s and 1700s

Great Bear Lake

Great Slave Lake

Hudson Bay

York Factory

Lake Winnipeg

Lake Superior

Lake Michigan

Legend
— Kelsey's journey 1690–1692
— Henday's journey 1745–1755
— Hearne's journey 1770–1772
····· Present provincial/territorial border
—··— Present international border

0   400 km
Scale

Figure 3.12 The routes into the interior taken by the three English explorers. What does this map tell you about the extent of British exploration?

Tech Link

The Hudson's Bay Company depended on maps made by the people who knew the land. You can see the map that Ac ko mok ki, a leader of the Blackfeet in Montana, made for an HBC surveyor. Just open Chapter 3 on your *Voices and Visions* CD-ROM.

VOICES ■

Tech Link

Look in the Documents section of Chapter 3 on your *Voices and Visions* CD-ROM to read more from Hearne's journal of his explorations.

Samuel Hearne's journey lasted for 19 months. Led by Matonabbee, he travelled all the way to the shores of the Arctic Ocean and back again. In his journal, he wrote about the hardship he suffered during the trip.

66 My feet and legs had swelled considerably. The nails of my toes were bruised to such a degree that several of them fell off. The skin was entirely chafed off from the tops of both my feet, and between every toe. For a whole day I left the print of my feet in blood almost at every step I took. 99

Biography

Matonabbee (about 1737–1782)

As a young boy, Matonabbee was raised at a fur-trading post, so he knew both the European and Dene ways of life. He was a skilled diplomat who spoke at least three languages. On one occasion, the Hudson's Bay Company sent him to Lake Athabasca to settle a dispute between the Dene and the Cree.

Matonabbee's leadership made Samuel Hearne's expedition a success. He knew the route to the Arctic Ocean. He showed Hearne how to travel light and live off the resources of the land.

Matonabbee was a successful fur trader. He and his people collected furs from groups as far north as the Mackenzie River and brought them to Hudson Bay trading posts. It was said that no other Dene brought as many furs to the forts.

Matonabbee was a close ally of the British at the HBC trading posts. In 1782, the French attacked and destroyed Fort Prince of Wales. Around the same time a smallpox outbreak killed most of his people. With the HBC fort and his people gone, Matonabbee killed himself in despair.

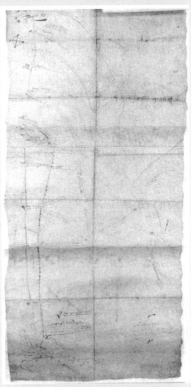

Figure 3.13 The map that Matonabbee drew. When they returned to Hudson Bay, Matonabbee presented Hearne with a map of their travels. Most accounts of Samuel Hearne's expedition describe Hearne as an explorer and Matonabbee as his guide. Do you think these are fair and accurate descriptions? Give reasons for your answer.

VOICES AND VISIONS

CASE STUDY

The Search for the Northwest Passage

Ever since the Europeans first arrived in North America, they heard rumours about a Northwest Passage through the Arctic. They were convinced this route would give them a shortcut to Asia. In the Arctic, the ice melted briefly each summer. When it did, the British sent expeditions there to search for a route to the Pacific.

One of the most famous Arctic explorers was a British sea captain named Sir John Franklin. In 1845, he and his two ships disappeared while searching for the passage. Several search parties tried to find them. With the help of the Inuit, the British finally found the missing ships frozen and crushed in a sea of ice. Franklin and all the crew were dead.

Passage Finally Found

In 1906, a Norwegian sailor named Roald Amundsen sailed his small boat, the *Gjoa*, into the waters north of Baffin Island. Three years later, he emerged on the other side in the Pacific Ocean. Amundsen had finally found the Northwest Passage. But the ice made travel extremely dangerous. Though some ships have crossed it, the Northwest Passage remains largely an unusable route to Asia.

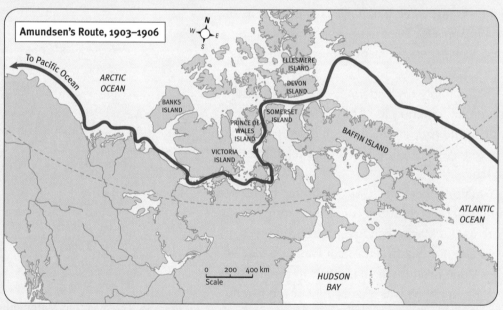

Figure 3.14 A map of Roald Amundsen's route through the Northwest Passage. Why do you think it took him three years to make this journey?

Respond

In a small group, discuss the following issues.
a) Even though it turned out to be unusable, do you think it is still important that Amundsen found the Northwest Passage?
b) **Citizenship and Identity:** Is it important for Canada to keep control of the Far North? Why?

The Issue of Ownership

Since the 1880s, Canada has claimed **sovereignty** over the Arctic. This means that the Northwest Passage and the islands there are under the control of the Canadian government. In 1969, an American ship challenged Canada's ownership. It travelled through the passage without permission. The United States argued that the Northwest Passage belonged to all countries. In the end, the US backed down. For a time, the issue was forgotten.

In 1985, however, it happened again. The Americans sent another ship through the passage without permission. Canada was angry. It feared that if it lost control over the passage, it might lose ownership of the northern islands, too. Canada was also concerned that it might not be able to protect the delicate northern ecosystem from pollution from oil tankers and other cargo ships. Canada warned that refusing to recognize its sovereignty in the Arctic would be an "unfriendly act." The Americans wanted to avoid a major conflict. They agreed and promised to ask for permission before entering the northern waters again.

Exploring the Pacific Coast

Most efforts to find the Northwest Passage began at the Atlantic coast. However, British explorers looked for a passage from the Pacific coast, too.

In 1778, the English explorer James Cook sailed his ship the *Resolution* into a harbour on Vancouver Island. Cook was sent by Britain to look for a Pacific entrance to the Northwest Passage. He was welcomed by the Nuu-chah-nulth [noo-CHAH-noolth] who lived on the island.

Cook failed to find the route he was seeking, so he left the coast and set sail across the Pacific for Asia. When his ship reached China, he and his crew discovered that the sea otter skins they had traded with the Nuu-chah-nulth were worth a lot of money. Their pelts were so valuable that the traders called the sea otter "soft gold." When word spread, fur traders rushed to the Pacific coast to grab up these precious furs.

Another British sea captain, named George Vancouver, followed in the wake of Captain Cook. He, too, came to explore the coast in search of an entrance to the Northwest Passage. From 1791 to 1794, he and his crew spent three summers exploring up and down the Pacific coast. They drew the first accurate map of the shoreline of present-day British Columbia. It proved that there was no entrance to the Northwest Passage along the coast. Today, Canada's third-largest city, Vancouver, bears his name.

Figure 3.15 Sea otters have thick fur to keep them buoyant and warm in the cold water. In the past, when the Europeans found valuable resources such as the sea otter, they hunted them until they were all gone. Why do you think the Europeans did not practise conservation in those days?

VOICES ■

The Nuu-chah-nulth have their own story about their meeting with James Cook. They talk about being eager to trade with the newcomers:

❝ We were anxious to secure trade with these new vessels. To this end, we sent out some of our best canoes and mariners to welcome and assist our visitors. This we were able to do, directing Cook's ships through the fog to an anchorage well within our territory. We were able to bind Cook to us through a ceremonial welcome and gift exchange, and to establish and maintain good relations with the captain and his crews in the hope that we could attract more visitors. ❞

Source: Alan Hoover, ed., *Nuu-chah-nulth Voices: Histories, Objects and Journeys* (Royal BC Museum, 2000), p. 19.

The British: Forging the Foundations of Canada

The British played a key role in the exploration and colonization of North America. They built colonies and benefited from the rich natural resources here. They travelled through the interior and up and down the coasts of North America. As they did, they made contact with many First Nations. In time, this contact would alter these nations forever. On the Atlantic coast, the British built the first English-speaking communities in the land that would become Canada.

Think It Through

1. Mercantilism played an important part in Britain's expansion in North America. Explain the economic factors behind each of these explorations, including the role played by the British government:
   - the Hudson's Bay Company
   - Hearne's exploration
   - Kelsey's exploration
   - the search for a Northwest Passage
   - Henday's exploration
   - Cook's exploration

   Record your information in a chart like the one below. As an alternative, you may want to record your information in a mind map.

2. The Think Ahead question at the beginning of this chapter asked you what you thought the effects of mercantilism would be on the colonies, the home country, and the First Nations. Now that you have completed this chapter, as a class review your original answer. Revise it according to what you have learned.

Exploration	Economic Factors	Role of the British Government
The Hudson's Bay Company	Wanted to make money from the fur trade	Gave a monopoly for English trade on Hudson Bay to one company
Hearne's exploration	Searching for gold and silver	None
Kelsey's exploration		
The search for a Northwest Passage		
Henday's exploration		
Cook's exploration		

Chapter 3 PROJECT   Compare and Contrast

Cultural Diversity

In Chapters 1, 2, and 3, you learned about the cultures of three First Nations (the Mi'kmaq, Anishinabe [a-nih-shih-NAH-bee], and Haudenosaunee), the French colonists, and the British colonists. You saw how they governed themselves, chose their leaders, and set up their societies and economies. They each played an equal role in forging the foundations of Canada.

   In the chapters to come, you'll learn more about the relationships among these diverse groups of people. In this chapter project, though, you'll look for the similarities and differences among their ways of life.

1. Work in small groups. Create a list of categories to use in your comparison. To prepare your list, you'll need to review the information in Chapters 1, 2, and 3.

2. Once you have your categories, brainstorm a list of questions to guide you in making your comparisons. For example, "What was the role of religion in each of these societies?"

3. As a group, review Chapters 1, 2, and 3. Take turns having each student read sections of the chapter aloud. As one student reads, another student should record point-form notes.

4. Once you have the answers to your questions, create a poster to display the information. Your poster may be a comparison chart similar to the one shown below. Or you may choose to do a visual presentation using images and drawings.

5. When your chart is complete, display it in your classroom.

Analyzing the Results

Once you have completed your poster, hold a class discussion on the following questions:
- What are the similarities in each category? What are the differences?
- What does this information tell you about the relationships among these people?
- How does this information help you understand the *equal but different* role each group played in forging the foundations of Canada?

Reflecting

As a group, critique your comparison poster and the process you used to create it. Is there any part of the project that you feel could be improved the next time?

Different but Equal			
	First Nations Peoples	French Colonists	British Colonists
Government			
Economy			

Chapter 4 Competition for Trade

Chapter INQUIRY

How did the various peoples in North America both work together in the fur trade and compete to control it?

Key CONCEPT ▶ Cultures in Contact

Vikings were the first Europeans to visit North America, in the year 1000. The next Europeans to arrive did so 500 years later. The first contacts took place with peoples who lived on or near the coast. They included the Mi'kmaq [MIG-mah], the Haudenosaunee [hah-duh-nuh-SAH-nee], and the Montagnais [MON-tun-yay]. Both First Nations peoples and Europeans were surprised to meet people who seemed so different from themselves.

We all find it hard to understand people who are different from us. We are used to our own way of doing things. Sometimes we think our way is the best way. This was probably how the Europeans and First Nations peoples felt when they first met. This is called being **ethnocentric**. Each thought that their own ethnic group was superior. After contact, both groups began a long process of learning to understand one another. They gradually found ways to get along.

Perspectives on First Contacts

Read the two accounts below. They both describe a first meeting between First Nations and Europeans on the west coast of North America.

There came to us a canoe with nine men in it. This canoe drew near to the vessel, the people in it singing. But they would not come near enough for us to communicate by means of signs. Having followed us for some time, they returned to the land. About five o'clock this canoe, and another in which there were six people, caught up with us, both drawing up to our stern. The captain made them a present of some strings of beads and they gave us some dried fish. But they would not come on board the ship. These people were well-built, with long hair, and they were clothed in pelts and skins; some of them were bearded.

—A Spaniard's account of his first meeting with a First Nation along the west coast of North America (see text credits page for source)

The Indians didn't know what in earth it was when his ship came into the harbour.... So the Chief, Chief Maquinna, he sent out his warriors... in a couple of canoes to see what it was. So they went out to the ship and they thought it was a fish come alive into people.

They were taking a good look at those white people on deck there. One white man had a real hooked nose, you know. And one of the men was saying to this other guy, "See, see ... he must have been a dog salmon, that guy, there, he's got a hooked nose."

The other guy was looking at him and a man came out of the galley and he was a hunchback, and the other one said, "Yes! We're right, we're right. Those people, they must have been fish. They've come back alive into people. Look at that one, he's a humpback [salmon]. He's a humpback!"

—A First Nation oral account of the first meeting of the Nuu-chah-nulth [noo-CHAH-noolth] and Captain Cook's ship in Nootka Sound (see text credits page for source)

SKILLS

Honing Your Skills

Do you sometimes wonder why events happen, and why they have particular results? The Skill Check feature in this chapter shows you how to **Analyze Causes and Effects.** This skill is important to your studies because it will help you analyze historical events. The project at the end of the chapter will ask you to analyze effects from a variety of perspectives.

Changing First Impressions

First Nations peoples and Europeans learned to get along because they wanted to trade. They began a long process of learning to respect one another's differences. This chapter invites you to learn how this process began. You will see how the fur trade laid the foundations of the Canadian economy. You'll look at the different partnerships among the various First Nations, the Métis [may-TEE], the Canadiens, and the British. You'll also learn how the fur trade affected First Nations and Métis societies.

Think ► AHEAD

1. Discuss with your classmates what challenges First Nations peoples and Europeans must have overcome to build a good relationship. Which do you think was the greatest challenge? Why?

2. The First Nations and Europeans began working together in the fur trade. Do your views of people change when you start working with them, for example, on a sports team? If so, in what ways do they change? Predict how a European fur trader's and a First Nations trapper's view of each other may have changed as they began to work together.

SKILL CHECK: Analyze Causes and Effects

The North American fur trade brought many peoples together. Some peoples worked together. Others competed. Many effects resulted from these forms of contact, as you'll see in this chapter.

A **cause** is something that makes an event happen. An **effect** is the result of this event. Effects are sometimes called consequences. An event may have several effects.

Cause and Effect in History

Together, a series of causes and effects may lead to a major change or event. When studying the past, study the causes and effects of an event together. This helps you see why major events happen.

Reading
STRATEGY

To identify causes and effects, use connecting words and phrases like these to connect ideas.

- As a result of ...
- Nevertheless ...
- If ... then ...
- This led to ...
- Because ...
- Therefore ...

Identifying Causes and Effects

1. Think about your favourite hobby or sport.
   a) What caused you to take up this form of recreation? Think about your early impressions of it. Think about whether someone influenced you.
   b) What are your hobby's effects? Think about how it changed you. Think about how it affects your day-to-day life.

Try It!

Analyze the causes and effects of your favourite hobby or sport. Use a cause-and-effect chart like the one here to help you.

Cause → Event → Effect
Cause → Event → Effect

Unexpected Effects

Many effects can come out of one event. Sometimes the effects, in turn, cause even more effects. When this happens, there is a chain of causes and effects over time.

Sometimes the effects that come out of an event are unexpected. For example, if you join the volleyball team, you might miss a half-day of school to go to the finals.

2. Expand your cause-and-effect chart. Add effects of effects. Add effects you didn't expect.

The Fur Trade: The Foundation of an Economy

Focus

How did the First Nations peoples work with the French and the British in the fur trade?

Generations of First Nations, Inuit [IN-yoo-it], and Métis as well as French and English adventurers took part in the fur trade. In this section, you will learn how these groups of people found ways to work together.

Partners in Trade

Initially, the fur trade was a partnership between European traders and First Nations hunters and trappers. As in all partnerships, each had something the other wanted.

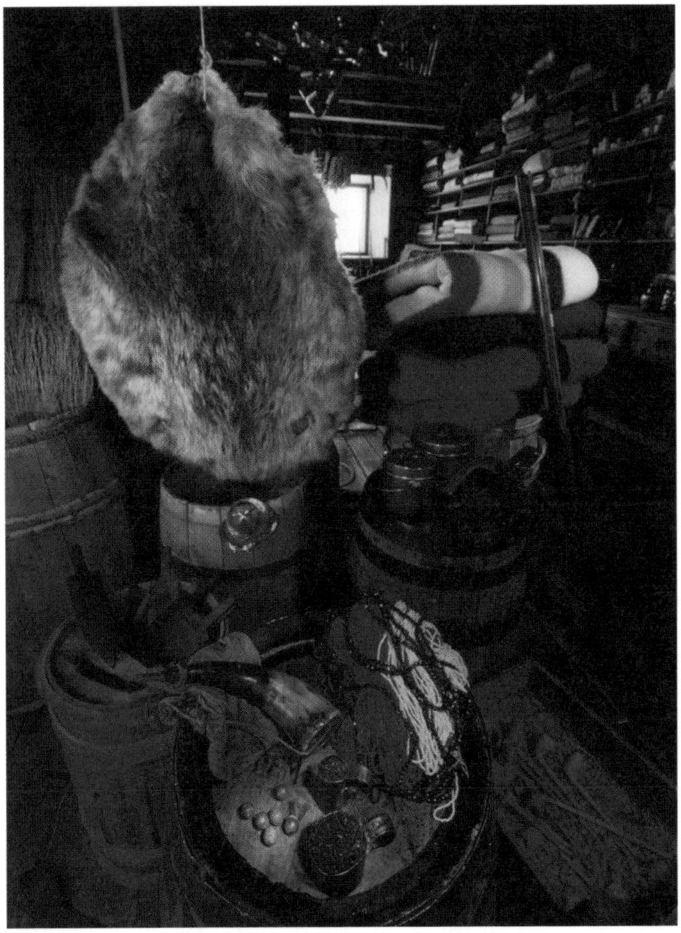

Figure 4.1 Some of the items the First Nations trappers took in trade. How do you think each of these items changed day-to-day life for First Nations peoples? SKILLS

The First Nations peoples valued the metal goods that came from Europe. These included pots, knives, axes, copper wire, and guns. These goods were stronger and lasted longer than the tools and utensils they made for themselves out of stone or wood. The First Nations traded for other goods as well, such as blankets, cloth, and thread.

What did the First Nations peoples have that the Europeans wanted? Just one thing: fur, and lots of it! Fox, marten, otter, bear, lynx, muskrat, wolf, beaver—the traders snapped up the furs of all these animals. In Europe, they used them for fashionable trims on coats and jackets. The most popular European fashion trend, however, was the beaver felt hat.

The Barter System

When you go to the store to buy something, you pay for it with money. In the time of the fur trade, Europeans used metal coins for money, but they also traded goods. The exchange of goods is called **barter**.

The First Nations had been trading among themselves for hundreds of years. They used the barter system. Trading parties carried corn, tobacco, furs, copper, pottery, and many other goods long distances to trade with their neighbours. People traded to get what they needed.

Before trade began, those who had travelled a long way would rest for a bit. They would establish feelings of respect and trust with their hosts by exchanging gifts and sharing the peace pipe. Throughout Eastern North America, wampum (strings of shells) would be offered to honour new friends and create harmony.

When the French arrived, they adopted this way of doing business.

CASE STUDY

Dedicated Followers of Fashion

Can you imagine an economy being kick-started by a fashion trend? That's what happened in Canada! Beaver pelts make fine hats. It was the huge demand for hats that fuelled the fur trade.

Respond

In the beginning, the economy of New France was based solely on the fur trade. What might have happened to the colony if beaver hats had suddenly gone out of fashion? SKILLS

At first, only wealthy Europeans could afford a beaver hat. With the many furs coming in from North America, though, prices came down. By 1700, many people could afford this trendy fashion item.

How do you make a fur hat? The fur of the beaver grows in two layers. The surface layer consists of guard hairs, which are long and thick. Beneath the guard hairs is an inner layer of fine, smooth hair. After the guard hairs are removed, the under-fur can be scraped off and crushed together to form a thick mat, or felt. The felt can then be dried and shaped into hats.

Figure 4.2 A modern-day hatter showing off his hat-making techniques. The production methods of the past are still used to make hats today. Resistol and Stetson, for example, still make good-quality cowboy hats this way.

VOICES

The Trading Ceremony

There were many ceremonies involved in the fur trade, such as gift giving. For what reasons do you exchange gifts with pe[...]

Charles Lalemant was a F[...]missionary. In this excerpt, he describes a trading session in 1626. (Europeans commonly used the term *Indian* at that time. Today, First Nations prefer to be known by the name of their nation.)

66 The day of their arrival, the French merchants erect their huts and the Indians arrive in their canoes. The second day the Indians hold a council and present their gifts. Gifts are always given when people visit each other. The French give presents then to the Indians.

The third and fourth day the Indians trade and barter their furs for blankets, hatchets, kettles, capes, little glass beads, and many similar things. It is a pleasure to watch them during this trading.

When it is over they take one more day for the feast which is made for them, and the dance. Early the next morning the Indians disappear like a flock of birds. 99

Source: Sharon Sterling, *Outlooks 4: Our Beginnings* (Toronto: Oxford University Press, 2000), p. 166.

The fur trade was a partnership in the sense that European traders and First Nations trappers engaged in it together. The question is, did they benefit equally from trade? It cost a lot of money to run trading posts and ship furs across the ocean. Even so, the European fur traders were paid about 10 times more for the pelts than they paid for goods to trade. This mark-up ensured healthy profits.

Tech Link

Look on the *Voices and Visions* CD-ROM to watch a re-enactment of a bargaining session at a fur-trading post.

1 gun	= 14 beaver
5 pounds [2.2 kg] gunpowder	= 1 beaver
1 ice chisel	= 1 beaver
1 hatchet	= 1 beaver
3 feet [1 m] cloth	= 3 beaver
1 pound [0.5 kg] tobacco	= 2 beaver
4 knives	= 1 beaver
1 kettle	= 1½ beaver

Figure 4.3 A list from the 1720 records for the Hudson's Bay Company post at York Factory. (You may want to refer back to page 65 to remind yourself of this use of the term *factory*.) Each trade item was worth a certain number of beaver pelts. Why do you think a gun was worth 14 beaver pelts while a hatchet was worth only 1?

Hudson's Bay blankets still have several narrow black lines running along one edge. These indicate the number of beaver pelts a blanket of that size was worth.

Three Key Players

Three major groups took part in the fur trade: the First Nations, the merchants, and the *coureurs de bois*.

- **First Nations.** During the winter, First Nations men hunted and trapped animals. The women skinned the animals and prepared the pelts. In the spring, when the ice on the rivers and lakes melted, the men and women loaded their bark canoes with furs. They travelled to the trading posts to trade these furs for goods. Sometimes they transported furs for other hunting groups, too.

- **Merchants.** In both the French and English fur trade, merchants financed and organized the trade. They purchased trading goods in Europe and shipped them to Canada. Then they shipped the furs back to Europe to sell to the hat makers.

- **Coureurs de bois and voyageurs.** The phrase coureur de bois means "runner of the woods." You will recall reading about these adventurers in Chapter 2. They were the French traders who paddled on long journeys into the wilderness to trade for furs with the First Nations. Later, these hardy men paddled the trade canoes from Montréal to the trading forts. They became known by another French word, *voyageurs*.

Relying on First Nations

Europeans could not have been involved in the fur trade without a great deal of help. As you have seen in earlier chapters, Europeans did not know how to cope in the North American wilderness. The First Nations helped them by

p. 79 list – if a first Nations person – what kind of goods could they trade

- showing them how to find food
- teaching them how to make medicine to cure diseases such as scurvy
  - providing advice on how to dress for the cold weather
  - providing transportation in the form of canoes, snowshoes, and toboggans
  - sharing their knowledge of the region
  - translating trade deals with various groups
- helping them negotiate
- providing a workforce to cook food, sew moccasins, prepare pemmican, snare animals, lace snowshoes, and so on

Tech Link

Look in Chapter 1 on the *Voices and Visions* CD-ROM to see the process of tanning hides first-hand.

Many First Nations women made pemmican. **Pemmican** is dried buffalo or moose meat mixed with berries and fat and then pounded flat. It keeps for years. Why do you think pemmican was so important to the fur trade and to First Nations peoples?

First Nations Women: Another Perspective

When you think of the people who took part in the fur trade, do you think of the First Nations women? They did not hunt for furs. However, First Nations and Métis women played a different but equally important role for their communities.

- **Preparing furs.** Women prepared most pelts that crossed the ocean. First, they scraped off the flesh. They rubbed the pelt with the brains of the animal, smoked it over an open fire, and soaked it in warm water. Then they worked the pelt until it was soft.
- **Working in the forts.** Women also helped in the forts. They performed many essential tasks, such as making moccasins and clothing. They collected birchbark and spruce gum for making canoes. They wove fishing nets and snowshoes and gathered firewood. They contributed to the food supply by snaring small animals and collecting nuts, roots, berries, and bulbs as well as leaves to make tea.
- **Working "on the road."** Women paddled the canoes and worked in camps, too. Matonabbee was the Dene [DEN-ay] explorer who led Samuel Hearne on his trips. (The Dene lived in the boreal forest and on the tundra of the Northwest Territories.) Matonabbee refused to travel without women to help. In Dene society, then as now, all clan members shared the duties and responsibilities of survival. These members included women and children.
- **Sharing language and geography skills.** Many First Nations and Métis women knew more than one language. This made them valuable as interpreters and negotiators. They also worked as guides.

Think It Through

1. Has your impression of First Nations women in the fur trade changed? If so, explain.
2. The fur trade was a partnership between First Nations peoples and Europeans.
   a) With a partner, discuss what each group contributed to the partnership. How did each group benefit? Show your information in a visual organizer. You might use a chart like this one.

	First Nations	Europeans
Contributions to the fur trade		
Benefits from the fur trade		

   b) In your opinion, did one group benefit more than the other did? Explain.

The French Fur Trade

In this section, you will read about how the French government influenced the fur trade and the economy of New France. You'll also see how transportation was key to making that economy work.

Focus

How did the government of France affect the fur trade and the economy of New France over time?

The Foundation of an Economy

The coureurs de bois spent their wages in the shops. The shop owners used their profits to buy food from the farmers. The farmers used that money to buy services from the cooper (a barrel maker) or other businesses. And so the trading, buying, and selling spread from one person or business to the next. In the early days of New France, the fur trade was the foundation of the economy. That situation changed as new industries developed. Eventually, the economy grew to become the economy of the country in which you live today. We owe a great deal to the First Nations trappers and European traders who paved the way for the future.

The King and the Economy

The French king controlled the fur trade and used the profits to benefit the colony. He appointed officials to carry out his plans. As you read the following section, think about how these plans changed as new officials were placed in charge.

Jean-Baptiste Colbert

In 1663, the king put Jean-Baptiste Colbert in charge of planning. Colbert wanted the colony to be part of the mercantile system. The colonists in New France would receive goods made in France. In return, New France would send the home country fish, timber, and, of course, furs. Colbert would not allow the traders to build trading posts in the interior of North America. He believed this would lead to conflict with the First Nations. Instead, the French relied on the extensive economic network of the Wendat [WAH-n-dot], who brought furs from many First Nations to Montréal.

Jean Talon

As you learned in Chapter 2, Jean Talon was in charge of the economy after 1665. He used government money to attract more colonists. He supported local industries. Under Talon, the number of French colonists doubled.

Figure 4.4 The Montréal fur fair, painted by A. Reid in 1916. It shows a summer trading fair, where First Nations people brought their furs to trade. This fair was an annual event until Frontenac approved the expansion of trade in 1672. Does the picture show trade from a European or First Nations perspective? What makes you think so?

Governor Frontenac

A French noble, the Marquis de Frontenac, became governor in 1672. He faced a problem. Many Wendat had been killed by smallpox. The Haudenosaunee had killed many more. The whole Wendat society fell apart. They could no longer bring furs to Montréal. The less powerful Odawa [oh-DAH-wuh] tried to do this. Their enemies, the Haudenosaunee, made this dangerous.

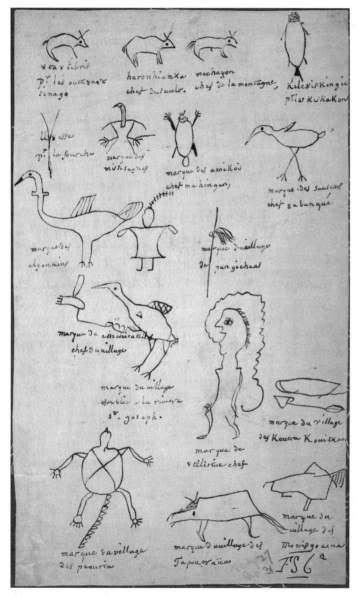

Figure 4.5 Part of *La Grande Paix*, or the Great Peace of Montréal, 1701. The governor of New France signed it. Leaders of the Haudenosaunee, Odawa, and other First Nations signed it. They drew the animal of their clan, or family grouping. How might peace affect the economy of New France?

Frontenac went ahead with a plan to send coureurs de bois into the interior. He wanted to expand the system of trading posts deep into the interior. If he didn't, he knew the English would.

The Great Peace of Montréal

Three nations banded together to fight the Haudenosaunee. The Council of Three Fires consisted of the Potawatomi [pot-uh-WAH-tuh-mee] south of Lake Erie, the Odawa on Manitoulin Island, and the Ojibwa [oh-JIB-way] on the north shores of Lakes Huron and Superior. They had many successes. Their efforts made the Haudenosaunee more and more weary of war.

After six decades, the First Nations and New France were ready to discuss peace. In the summer of 1701, 1300 delegates from 40 First Nations communities arrived in Montréal. They came in hundreds of canoes from Acadia in the east, the Great Lakes region in the west, James Bay in the north, and all points between.

All parties showed the quality of good citizenship by working hard to find a way to end the fighting. At the end of the peace talks, the French, their First Nations allies, and the Haudenosaunee signed a treaty. The First Nations would no longer battle each other or the French. New France would not attack any more Haudenosaunee villages. The trappers and traders would be able to travel safely.

"The hatchet is stopped," said Michipichy, a Wendat leader. "We have buried it during these days here in the deepest place in the earth, so that it will not be taken up again by one side or the other." (Source: Quoted in Gilles Havard, *The Great Peace of Montréal of 1701* [Montréal, Kingston: McGill–Queen's University Press, 2001], p. 145.)

Economic Development

Coureurs de bois could now travel in peace. They got furs from the Montagnais and the Odawa, who traded with distant First Nations for furs. Local beaver populations had begun to dwindle. As a result, the French expanded farther north and west in search of more beaver. This quest led Europeans to explore the entire continent.

The growing profits in the fur trade helped other parts of the economy grow. Mills, shipbuilding yards, and iron foundries sprang up. New textile industries were encouraged. The shipyards built ships for the fishing industry, trade, and the French navy. The peace lasted until the 1750s.

Global Connections

Three hundred years ago, business people shipped furs across the ocean from North America to France. This global trade was a sign of things to come. Check the tags on your clothes. Where were your clothes made? Many things Canadians buy are imported from other countries. Many things we make in Canada are exported to other countries. Now, as in the days of the fur trade, our economy depends on global trade.

Canada Today

In the days of the fur trade, the water routes of North America were a system of communication and transportation. They linked people, producers, and markets. Look at thematic maps of Canada in an atlas. What systems do we use today?

Transportation: Crucial to Any Economy

For trade to succeed, the traders needed transportation. During the fur trade, there were no trucks, trains, or airplanes. Traders relied on boats to transport their goods. As the First Nations knew, water routes were fast and convenient.

France controlled trade along the St. Lawrence River and on the Great Lakes. This gave the French fur traders a great advantage. In the Eastern United States, the Adirondack Mountains blocked English fur traders from expanding into the West. The French, on the other hand, could paddle through rivers and lakes to transport goods as far west as the Rocky Mountains.

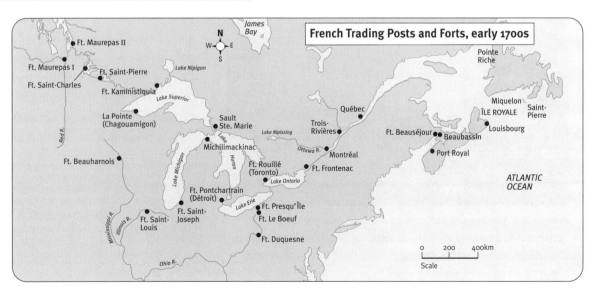

Figure 4.6 French forts in the early 1700s. Compare the pattern of forts on this map with the pattern on a current population map of Canada. What similarities can you identify?

Identity

The Canoe–A Canadian Institution

How can a little boat be part of a country's identity? For many Canadians, a summer vacation wouldn't be the same without a canoe. On the more serious side, did you know that the canoe played an important role in the fur trade?

WEB LINK

In their canoes the Indians can go without restraint, and quickly, everywhere, in the small as well as the large rivers. So that by using canoes as the Indians do, it will be possible to see all there is.

—Samuel de Champlain

Source: Library and Archives Canada, "The Exploration of Canada: Transportation," http://www.collectionscanada.ca/ explorers/h24-1403-e.html.

The word *canoe* came from Arawak, an indigenous language spoken in the Caribbean. It is just one of many Aboriginal words that have become part of the English language. What others can you think of?

Respond

In a group, talk about the ways in which the canoe is part of the Canadian identity. What other things can you think of that symbolize our country?

Travelling into the interior of North America would have been impossible without the canoe. The birchbark canoes built by the Eastern First Nations were well suited for travelling on lakes and rivers. They were lightweight. This meant they moved through the water quickly. They were easy to carry over a **portage** (overland route between two waterways). Yet they were sturdy, so they could last on long journeys.

Making a canoe was a highly skilled craft. John Kawapit, a member of the Cree (Nehiyawak [nay-HI-uh-wuk]) Nation, makes canoes. He shows his strong sense of citizenship as he describes the importance of being a canoe maker:

Figure 4.7 Voyageurs camped at the end of a portage. A Toronto artist named William Armstrong painted this image in the 1860s. What factors do you think would have influenced the way he showed what he saw?

Even long ago there were some men who could not make all the things that were needed. In each camp there were only a few who could make everything. The hardest thing to build was the canoe. The man who could make a canoe was very happy because the people depended on it so much.

—John Kawapit, Great Whale River, Québec

Source: Canadian Museum of Civilization, "Wave Eaters: Native Watercraft in Canada," http://www.civilization.ca/aborig/ watercraft/wainteng.html.

Expanding Trade

The French made good use of the First Nations' knowledge of transportation routes. They also heard stories from many First Nations peoples about a great "Western Sea" that lay beyond Lake Superior. If they could reach it, the French thought, it would take them all the way to China. Can you guess what we call this great sea today?

Biography

Pierre Gaultier de Varennes, Sieur de La Vérendrye (1685–1749)

In 1715, Pierre La Vérendrye took charge of a French trading post near Lake Superior. During his years there, he made several trips through the forests of what is now Northern Ontario. He claimed these lands for France.

In 1732, La Vérendrye, three of his sons, and a nephew travelled west to the lands the French called *le pays d'en haut*—the upper country. A group of First Nations peoples led the way. Eventually, they reached Lake Winnipeg.

As they explored the West, La Vérendrye and his group came upon the Saskatchewan River. First Nations used the Saskatchewan River as their main east-west route. It soon became the most important river for the French fur traders, too.

La Vérendrye made many alliances with the First Nations. He also started several trading posts in the West. In 1743, two of his sons travelled as far as the Rockies. La Vérendrye died in 1749. He thought he was a failure because he had not found the "Western Sea." Today, most historians feel differently about his contributions. Ask yourself: Would Canada be the same today without the efforts of this citizen of New France?

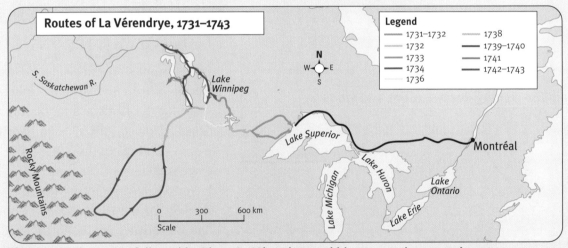

Figure 4.8 The routes followed by Pierre La Vérendrye and his sons as they moved west.

Think It Through

1. Make a cause-and-effect chart. Use it to show how the French king and his officials changed New France over time. SKILLS

2. Think about the Great Peace of Montréal in 1701. What caused this event to happen? What were its effects on various groups? SKILLS

3. Get an outline map of North America's river systems from your teacher. Trace possible water routes through lakes and rivers between Montréal and the Rocky Mountains. If possible, use GIS software for this task.

The English Fur Trade

Unlike the French, the English were not interested in creating a colony in what is now Canada. In 1670, the English king granted a charter for control of the fur trade to the privately owned Hudson's Bay Company (HBC). It had one goal: to make money. This affected the relationship between the English fur traders and the First Nations trappers. In this section, you'll learn how the English fur trade worked. You'll see how the French and English ways of trading were different.

Focus

In what ways was the English fur trade different from the French fur trade?

Reading
STRATEGY

When you read maps with routes, use the linear scale to estimate the distance of the routes.

Why Hudson Bay?

The English built their forts along the icy shores of Hudson Bay. There were some advantages to this location.

- It was close to the abundant fur supply of the northern forests. Northern furs are better because animals grow the thickest fur in the coldest climates.
- Many rivers flow into Hudson Bay. They provided good transportation routes for the First Nations trappers.
- Large supply ships could deliver heavy supplies directly to the English forts. The French route involved both a sea voyage by ship to Montréal, and a lengthy journey by canoe to reach the furs. The HBC could get furs to England in one year, while the French took two.

Biography

Isabel Gunn (1781–1861)

Isabel Gunn's boyfriend, John Scarth, travelled from Scotland to Canada to work for the Hudson's Bay Company. Gunn followed him in 1806. Women were not allowed, though, so she disguised herself as a man!

For two years, "John Fubbister" worked for the Hudson's Bay Company. She performed all the duties expected of the men at the fort. No one guessed that "John" was really a woman, until she gave birth to a baby. Her baby was the first non-Aboriginal child born in the Northwest. After the birth, Gunn was reunited with Scarth in Grandes Fourches.

Later, Gunn took her baby to a post on Hudson Bay. She worked there for another year, taking in laundry. Then she returned home to Scotland.

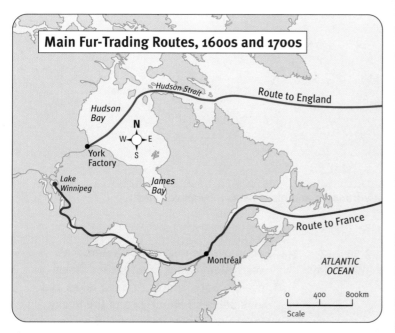

Main Fur-Trading Routes, 1600s and 1700s

Hudson Strait
Route to England
Hudson Bay
N
W — E
S
York Factory
Lake Winnipeg
James Bay
Route to France
Montréal
ATLANTIC OCEAN
0   400   800km
Scale

Figure 4.9 The two main fur-trading routes into the interior. Compare the two routes. In what ways was the rivalry for control of the fur trade a rivalry between these two transportation routes?

CASE STUDY

Life at a Hudson's Bay Company Trading Post

The English liked to trade for furs at their posts. Most posts were forts. The buildings were surrounded by a **stockade**—a wooden barrier of upright posts. Entry was controlled. The First Nations didn't like the change. They liked it better when the traders travelled to them. Would this be a problem?

The Hudson's Bay Company built many trading posts. The posts served as warehouses for trade goods, supplies, and ammunition. Employees came from Britain to live and work in the posts for years at a time.

The traders soon learned how helpful the nearby First Nations people could be in running the posts. The First Nations people learned that they could earn a good living working at the posts. The First Nations men cut wood, hunted big game, and loaded and unloaded goods. The women also played key roles, especially in making snowshoes, moccasins, canoes, and pemmican. With everyone working together, the posts became bustling hives of activity.

Nonetheless, the English still found that life at fur-trading posts was harsh. One trader at York Factory described it as "nine months of winter varied by three of rain and mosquitoes."

Respond

Sometimes it is hard to get used to new ways of doing things. How did the English and First Nations people find ways to get along?

Figure 4.10 A painting of Albany Factory (about 1804–1811). This was an HBC fort on the shores of Hudson Bay. How do you think a young HBC employee from England would have reacted on seeing the fort for the first time? How might a young Cree trapper have reacted?

Whitefish	17 346
Ptarmigan	4 663
Ducks	4 298
Geese	4 274
Deer	3 530
Plovers	3 359
Other fish	2 715
Rabbits	816
Trout	420
Freshwater cod	38
Caribou tongue	35
Caribou heads	15

Source: M. Payne, *The Most Respectable Place in the Territory* (Ottawa: Canadian Parks Service, 1989), p. 146.

Figure 4.11 The wild animals eaten at York Factory during one winter there. About 40 people lived at the fort. Which of these foods have you eaten?

Think It Through

Make a Venn diagram or comparison organizer. Use it to compare the similarities and differences in the English and French fur trades. Which trading style did the First Nations prefer? Do you think one method was superior to the other? Give reasons for your answer.

Converging in the West

The competition between French and English fur traders came to an abrupt halt in 1760, when New France came under British control. (You'll learn more about this in Chapter 5.) The French trade ended. Some of the French traders settled in the Great Lakes Lowlands with their First Nations wives. These couples created a new people—the Métis. In this section, you will learn other ways that the fur trade in the West brought various peoples together.

Focus

How did the fur trade in the West bring various peoples together?

The Nor'Westers

Within a few years, fur traders from Montréal were returning to the woods. These new traders blended the English and French ways of doing things. The traders were Scottish or English business people, mainly from Montréal. Many married Francophone women.

In 1779, a group of the new traders from Montréal formed the North West Company. Known as the Nor'Westers, they extended the fur trade farther than it had been in the days of New France. Now the goal of the company was to make money rather than to build a colony. These traders ran an efficient business while embracing the traditional methods of the French fur traders. They worked hard to improve ties made by the French with the First Nations peoples.

The hard-working men who paddled the canoes and hauled supplies across the portages were the fabled voyageurs. These were the men who used to be known as the coureurs de bois. Most were *Canadiens*— Francophone citizens of North America. They were joined by Mohawk and Anishinabe paddlers. The rest of the voyageurs were Métis.

The Métis were the children of European fathers and First Nations mothers. They played a substantial role in the fur trade. Many of them knew two languages, so they acted as interpreters. They were comfortable in more than one culture. Métis became the chief suppliers of buffalo meat to the Western trading posts.

For years, the Métis worked both as voyageurs and as employees in the forts. The 1804 list of North West Company employees, for example, includes mostly French and Métis names. Strong young men such as Jean-Baptiste Lemay, François Boucher, and Pierre Laliberté made the fur trade possible.

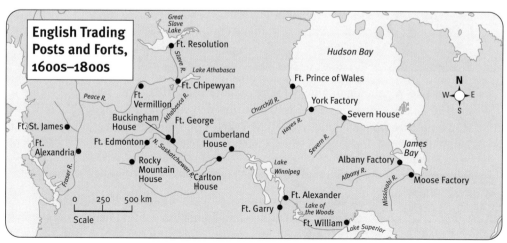

English Trading Posts and Forts, 1600s–1800s

Figure 4.12 Fur-trading posts in Western Canada. This map shows the most important posts. Describe the location of the forts in relation to bodies of water.

Tech Link

To hear two voyageur songs, open Chapter 2 on your *Voices and Visions* CD-ROM.

The Annual Cycle

The trading posts of the Western interior were very far from Montréal. The voyageurs could not make the trip there and back in one summer. Instead, canoes came from both directions and met in the middle at Fort William, on Lake Superior. Those who lived year-round at the posts were known as inlanders, or winterers. They brought the furs they had traded with the First Nations. The large canoes from Montréal brought supplies and trade items. After the goods were exchanged, the partners held a banquet and a dance to celebrate. Then each group headed back.

Life of the Voyageur

The voyageurs combined a spirit of adventure with a willingness to work hard for the good of the group. Most of them spoke both French and a First Nations language. They enjoyed good relations with First Nations communities. They worked for the Nor'Westers until 1821, when the HBC bought the North West Company.

Because of the voyageurs, French was the language of the Western fur trade. Many First Nations learned to speak French. Later, many voyageurs settled permanently in the West. They were the first Europeans to set down roots on the Prairies. They helped spread the French language and way of life across the country.

Figure 4.13 A voyageurs' camp outside the rebuilt Fort William. Parks Canada workers play the roles of people at the fort. What would Canadians get out of historical "performances" like this?

VOICES

In 1822, a former trader, Alexander Ross, gave a ride to a 70-year-old man on his way to Red River. As Ross talked with him, he discovered that the man had been a voyageur. This is part of what the man told Ross. As you read, think about this man's strong sense of pride and citizenship.

" I have now been 42 years in this country. For 24 I was a light canoeman. I required but little sleep, but sometimes got less than I required. No portage was too long for me; all portages were alike. My end of the canoe never touched the ground till I saw the end of it. Fifty songs a day were nothing to me. I could carry, paddle, walk, and sing with any man I ever saw. During that period I saved the lives of ten bourgeois [merchants], and was always the favourite because when others stopped to carry at a bad step and lost time, I pushed on—over rapids, over cascades, over chutes; all were the same to me. No water, no weather ever stopped the paddle or the song. ... Yet, were I young I should glory in commencing the same career. "

Source: CanText, "1700: The Coureurs de Bois," http://207.61.100.164/cantext/newfranc/1700ross.html.

VOICES ■

VOICES AND VISIONS

The voyageurs sang many songs to keep the time as they paddled through the day. This favourite came from France, but the Canadien tune is different. Although it began as a ballad about a young man recalling a lost love, it became a way for the Canadiens to vow to remember New France before the rule of the British. Here are the last three verses.

À la claire fontaine

You have no cares to grieve you,
While I could weep today,
For I have lost my loved one
In such a senseless way.

Refrain:
Many long years have I loved you,
Ever in my heart you'll stay.

She wanted some red roses
But I did rudely say
She could not have the roses
That I had picked that day.

Now I wish those red roses
Were on their bush today,
While I and my beloved
Still went our old sweet way.

Source: Edith Fulton Fowke, *Chansons de Québec (Folk Songs of Québec)* (Waterloo, ON: Waterloo Music Company Limited, 1957), p. 63.

The Nor'Westers in Alberta

Some Americans travelled into the Northwest to take part in the fur trade. Peter Pond was an American from Connecticut. In 1778, First Nations people persuaded him to build a small trading post on the Athabasca River.

Figure 4.14 A painting of voyageurs paddling their canoe in rapids. Frances Hopkins painted it in 1879. She was the wife of a fur-trade official. How do you think this influenced the way she portrayed what she experienced? Do you see her in the painting?

They wanted the post so they wouldn't have to go all the way to York Factory. It was the first fur-trading post in what is now Alberta.

This post was soon replaced by Fort Chipewyan [chip-uh-WY-un], a North West Company site on Lake Athabasca. It was named for the Dene people who lived east of the lake. They also supplied furs to the fort. Fort Chipewyan quickly became a major trading centre and the first European community in Alberta. It was so big that the voyageurs jokingly called it the "Emporium of the North." Today, it sits just east of Wood Buffalo National Park.

First Nations who took part in the fur trade in Alberta were the Siksika [sik-SIK-uh], the Piikani [bee-GUN-ee], the Kainai [KY-ny], the Tsuu T'ina [tsoo-TIN-uh], the Cree, and the Nakoda [na-KOH-dah]. Farther north, the Chipewyan, the Dene, the Dunne-Za [duh-nuh-ZAH], and the Dene Tha' [DEN-ay-dah] also traded with the Nor'Westers.

Fierce Competition

From Fort Chipewyan, the Nor'Westers carried the fur trade westward up the Peace and Mackenzie Rivers, building trading posts as they went. Not to be outdone, the HBC did the same. Each company wanted to be closer to the trappers. They both offered higher prices for furs.

On the down side, some rival traders also got into fist fights as they competed to get the most furs. Some traders bullied the trappers to get their furs. Some began to trade alcohol for furs, too. The relationship between the First Nations trappers and the rival traders became increasingly difficult.

Tech Link

To see a historical painting of two competing forts side by side, open Chapter 4 on your *Voices and Visions* CD-ROM.

Figure 4.15 Fort Edmonton, painted by Paul Kane in 1845. It was rebuilt at this location after flooding ruined the old fort. Kane spent three years in the West. He canoed with the voyageurs, witnessed a buffalo hunt, and crossed the Rocky Mountains. Do you think historians value Kane's paintings? Why or why not?

VOICES

Alexander Henry the Younger was the factor at Rocky Mountain House from 1810 to 1811. He kept a journal of the daily activities at the trading post. Desjarlais and Pichette, the two workers Henry mentions in his journal, were Métis.

66 Nov. 20th, 1810. B. Desjarlais hunting; seven men out to raise dog trains [cutting wood to make dog sleds]; four laying up canoes and cleaning the fort; one making a wood sled; one off for meat, one cutting wood, one carting, one making kegs. Our canoes are much split by the frost and four of our large axes broke today, being nearly as brittle as glass. Desjarlais killed nothing, as the animals about the fort have all

been roused by men going for wood for sleds; searching for horses, etc.

Nov. 23rd. Two Sarcees [Tsuu T'ina] arrived from near Wolf River, where buffalo are numerous; they brought a few beavers.

Dec. 1st. Pichette finished the fort gates, and the bastions were put in order, but they are wretched buildings for defence.

Dec. 4th. Nine young Indians arrived, each with a dog travois and a few bad wolfskins, for which they wanted tobacco. 99

Source: Elliot Coues, ed., *New Light on the Early History of the Greater Northwest: The Manuscript Journals of Alexander Henry and of David Thompson, 1799–1814* (Minneapolis: Ross & Haines, 1965).

Biography

Marie-Anne Gaboury (1780–1875)

Marie-Anne Gaboury was the first non-Aboriginal woman to live in Western Canada. She was born near Trois-Rivières in Québec. She married Jean-Baptiste Lagimodière. He was a voyageur with the HBC. Soon, he yearned to go west again. Gaboury would not allow it—unless she could go, too!

The two went to live in the fur country in Manitoba, and then to Fort Edmonton in the Northwest. In the summer, Gaboury went on buffalo hunts. She was an important leader in the community. She became godmother for many people there. Today, when people stroll down rue Marie-Anne-Gaboury in Edmonton (named in 1988), they think of this important person in Alberta's history.

One of Gaboury's daughters, Julie, became the mother of the Métis leader Louis Riel. Gaboury was a noteworthy pioneer who helped establish the French presence in Western Canada.

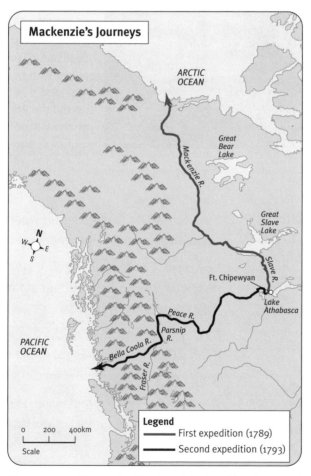

Mackenzie's Journeys

ARCTIC OCEAN

Great Bear Lake

Mackenzie R.

Great Slave Lake

Slave R.

Ft. Chipewyan

Lake Athabasca

Peace R.

Parsnip R.

PACIFIC OCEAN

Bella Coola R.

Fraser R.

0 200 400km
Scale

Legend
First expedition (1789)
Second expedition (1793)

Figure 4.16 Alexander Mackenzie's two trips in search of the Pacific Ocean. It has been said that the fur trade was the most important factor in exploring the West. Do Mackenzie's expeditions support this theory?

Crossing the Rockies

For years, the Rocky Mountains created a barrier that kept the voyageurs from pushing westward. Explorers could not find a way through the mountains. An explorer named Alexander Mackenzie wanted to solve the riddle. He was a veteran Nor'Wester who had come to Canada from Scotland to work in the fur trade when he was just 15 years old.

In 1789, Mackenzie tried a long river heading out of Great Slave Lake. It took him to the Arctic Ocean, so he called it the "River of Disappointment." What is it called now? (Hint: Look at the map at left.) A few years later he tried again. This time he travelled up the Peace River and down the Bella Coola River. A Métis named François Beaulieu accompanied him. With Beaulieu's help, Mackenzie's expedition became the first group of Europeans to cross the continent by land from east to west.

Canada Today

Historic sites are all over Canada. How can historic sites tighten our bonds with the early citizens of our country? How can they strengthen our sense of identity? When Alexander Mackenzie reached the Pacific Ocean, he wrote a message on a rock, as you can see at left. He used a mixture of animal grease and dye. Today, you can only reach this spot by water. Would you like to see this?

The Métis guide François Beaulieu was only 22 when he went with Alexander Mackenzie to search for the Pacific Ocean. He later became a leader of the Yellowknife Montagnais. He traded for the Hudson's Bay Company. What skills does a person need to be a wilderness guide?

Think It ▶ Through

1. What caused the fierce competition in the Alberta fur trade? What resulted from it? Use a cause-and-effect chart to organize your thoughts. SKILLS

2. Scan this section to make a list of individuals involved in the fur trade.

a) What did they each accomplish? With whom did each of them work?

b) Choose one person. Draw a picture or write a poem to show a scene from his or her life in the fur trade.

The Impact of Contact

In this chapter, you have seen how the fur trade was a process of contact and economic development. As with any activity that brings cultures together, the fur trade resulted in changes. In this section, you will learn about a few of those long-term changes.

Focus

What was the impact of the fur trade on First Nations' societies, economies, and sense of identity?

The Best Form of Flattery

The First Nations and Europeans got to know each other. They found things to admire in each other's culture. They began to copy the other's way of doing things. They also borrowed each other's technologies. The identities of Canada's peoples have evolved over time, as we have adapted to one another's ways of doing things.

Figure 4.17 An engraving of a soldier in New France. I.B. Scotin made it in 1722. What First Nations customs and technologies has the soldier adopted?

VOICES ■

In 1749, Pehr Kalm visited Canada from Sweden. He saw how the French newcomers copied the First Nations peoples.

66 The French in Canada in many respects follow the customs of the Indians, with whom they have constant relations. They use the tobacco pipes, shoes, garters, and belts of the Indians. They follow the Indian way of waging war exactly; they mix the same things with tobacco; they make use of the Indian bark boats and row them in the Indian way; they wrap a square piece of cloth round their feet, instead of stockings, and have adopted many other Indian fashions. 99

Source: Adolph Benson, ed., *Peter Kalm's Travels in North America* (New York: Dover Publications, 1966).

Negative Impacts

Contact between cultures was not always positive. Think about who did well over time. European companies made a lot of money from the fur trade. In time, European governments claimed First Nations territories as their own.

In contrast, the First Nations suffered greatly over time. Contact with Europeans turned their traditional ways of life upside down. It eroded their societies. It led to the loss of their lands. Societies that had thrived before contact were altered forever. The ethnocentrism of the newcomers often led to misunderstandings.

Shifting Ways of Life

The fur trade changed the way of life of many First Nations individuals. It affected their sense of identity as well.

- **Working for the fur trade.** Many First Nations people adapted their old way of life to work in the fur trade. They focused their efforts on trapping furs. Others worked at the trading posts. First Nations people hunted for food for the newcomers and paddled the canoes filled with furs.
- **Following the fur.** As time went by, beaver supplies shrank. Some First Nations moved out of their traditional territories to find more. Sometimes this displaced other First Nations and led to disputes.
- **Depending on European goods.** Before the fur trade, the First Nations met their needs using the environment around them. Some traded with other nations. Those who became involved in the fur trade began to use goods that only the traders could supply.
- **Hunting the buffalo.** In the West, First Nations such as the Cree and Nakoda hunted buffalo as a way of life. They expanded their hunt to make pemmican for the voyageurs. Later, newcomers hunted and traded for buffalo hides. The buffalo herds quickly disappeared. The way of life of First Nations of the Plains changed forever.
- **Loss of language.** French and English became the dominant languages. The slow process of Aboriginal language loss began.

The Invisible Enemy

Perhaps the greatest disaster to result from the fur trade was disease. The traders and missionaries who came from Europe brought many germs. Diseases such as smallpox, measles, influenza, and whooping cough did not exist in North America before the Europeans came. The First Nations and Inuit had no immunity to them. Their bodies were unable to fight these diseases.

Hundreds of thousands of First Nations and Inuit died in epidemics that swept across the continent. One trader, William

Walker, reported from the Saskatchewan River, "the Smallpox is raging with such great Violence over the Country, not hardly sparing any that takes it." (Source: Walker's Journal at Hudson House, 1781–1782, in E.E. Rich, ed., *Cumberland House Journals and Inland Journals, 1775–82* [London: Hudson Bay Record Society, #15, 1952], p. 265.) The 1781–1782 smallpox epidemic killed three out of every five First Nations people on the Prairie. The 1837–1838 epidemic killed even more.

CASE STUDY

Fort Whoop-Up and the Whiskey Trade

Trading alcohol for fur was not common before the nineteenth century. That changed in the 1860s. The worst misuse of alcohol occurred in what is now southern Alberta. The American government had banned alcohol in Montana Territory. Many American "free traders" came north to Canada. There was no police force here. They could do what they liked. They went after the quick profits to be had by trading alcohol for buffalo hides.

Many of these traders were hardened Civil War veterans. They cared little for the First Nations people. In fact, they were extremely callous in their dealings with First Nations.

Respond

What led to the "whiskey" trade? Think of at least three impacts it had on First Nations. SKILLS

In 1869, J.J. Healy and Alfred Hamilton built Fort Whoop-Up near present-day Lethbridge. It was the largest of about 40 whiskey-trading posts along the Oldman and Belly Rivers. Fort Whoop-Up was a frightening place. It had a four-metre-high stockade, brass cannons, and iron bars over the doors and windows. Trade at Fort Whoop-Up grew from 5000 hides in 1869 to about 60 000 in 1875.

The "whiskey" the traders offered was a vile brew. It contained pure alcohol, tea leaves, rotten chewing tobacco, painkillers, red peppers, lye, ginger, soap, red ink, and molasses. The hunters who drank this stuff got so sick that they could not take care of their families. Many died from its poisons. Violence became common. In the winter of 1872–1873 alone, about 70 members of the Kainai First Nation died in violent encounters. (The Kainai are some of the oldest residents of the western prairie region.)

In Chapter 9, you'll see how the Canadian government responded to the lawlessness in the West.

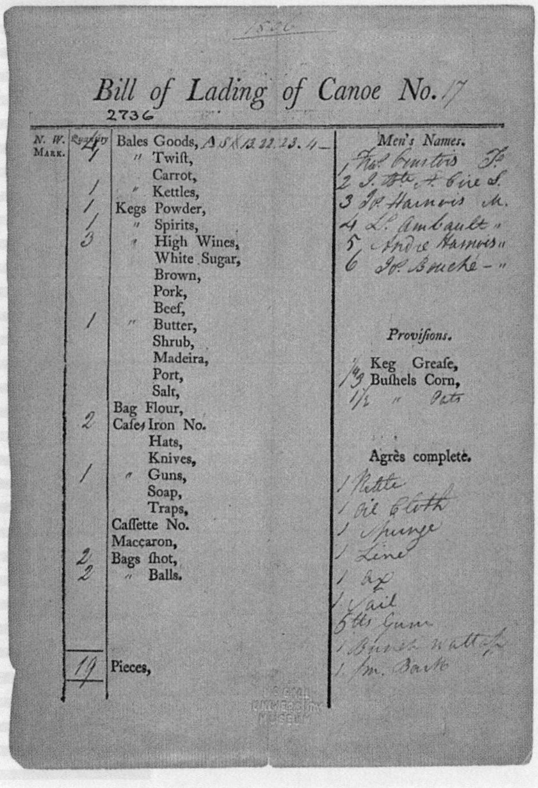

Bill of Lading of Canoe No. 17
2736

N. W. Mark. | Quantity

4 Bales Goods,
1 " Twist,
Carrot,
1 " Kettles,
1 Kegs Powder,
1 " Spirits,
3 " High Wines,
White Sugar,
Brown,
Pork,
Beef,
1 " Butter,
Shrub,
Madeira,
Port,
Salt,
Bag Flour,
2 Cases Iron No.
Hats,
Knives,
1 " Guns,
Soap,
Traps,
Cassette No.
Maccaron,
2 Bags shot,
2 " Balls.
19 Pieces,

Men's Names.

1 ...
2 ...
3 ... Harnois
4 ... Ambault
5 Andre Harnois
6 ... Bouche

Provisions.

1 Keg Grease,
1 3/4 Bushels Corn,
1/2 " Oats

Agrès complete.

1 Kettle
1 Oil Cloth
1 Sponge
1 Line
1 Axe
1 Sail
5 lbs Gum
...

Figure 4.18 The American traders were not the only ones to trade liquor. This is a list of trade goods carried by a canoe that travelled west from Fort William to Fort Lac la Pluie (later called Fort Frances) in 1806. There were kegs of "spirits" and "high wines."

Creating a New Culture

One very positive result of contact between First Nations peoples and Europeans was the creation of a new culture: the Métis. **Métis** are people of dual heritage. The first Métis were the children of First Nations women and European fur traders. Some of these children embraced the heritage of their French, English, or Scottish fathers. Others embraced the heritage of their First Nations mothers. Many others embraced both. Thus was born the unique Métis culture. You will learn more about the Métis in Chapter 8.

Canada Today

How are First Nations dealing with the results of the smallpox epidemics? Among other things, they're trying to get back the remains of their ancestors. The Haida [HY-duh] live on Haida Gwaii [HY-duh-gwy] in the Queen Charlotte Islands in British Columbia. There were once as many as 30 000. That figure dropped to 800 by 1885. The Chicago Field Museum took 160 bodies from Haida gravesites. They thought the Haida would be extinct soon. In 2003, the museum returned these remains to the Haida Nation. The Haida were then able to rebury their ancestors with respect and honour.

Figure 4.19 Andy Wilson at the Skidegate Haida Repatriation Signing Ceremony at the Chicago Field Museum in October 2003. Wilson helped make the traditional bentwood boxes that were used to bring home his 160 Haida ancestors.

Think It Through

1. Recollect the eyewitness accounts of first contact at the beginning of this chapter. SKILLS
   a) Since then, many changes took place in the lives of the First Nations. Discuss these in a small group.
   b) Create a graphic organizer to show the positive and negative impact of European contact on First Nations. You can write or draw each of the impacts in the chart.
   c) Compare your findings with those of another group. What impacts would you add if you were starting over?
   d) Are you in a good position to judge what is or is not a negative impact? Explain.
2. a) Create a three-column chart like the one below to record information about the impact of the fur trade on Canada. In the first column, list these factors:
   • There was an abundant supply of quality fur in northern North America.
   • Traders and First Nations trappers needed one another.
   • The French king used the fur trade to develop New France.
   • There was an east-west river system.
   • Pemmican was made from buffalo. Add other factors. SKILLS
   b) Choose what you think was the most influential factor. Explain your choice in writing or to a partner.
3. How did the various peoples in North America both work together in the fur trade and compete to control it?

Factor	Influence on Social Development of Canada	Influence on Economic Development of Canada

Chapter 4

(SKILLS) Chapter 4 PROJECT — Understanding Point of View and Perspective

Point of View

Our **point of view** is the way we see things as individuals. People have different points of view about things they observe.

What makes your point of view different from someone else's? Your family, your education, your culture, your personal experiences, and your personality can all affect your point of view. Think about a recent event that you and a friend saw differently. Perhaps you both saw an argument. Perhaps you disagreed on who started it.

Individuals can see historical events differently, too. Look at the engraving on this page. How would Gaboury view this event? How would a First Nations person view it? When we study history, it is important to find different people's points of view. Otherwise, we cannot truly understand the past.

Figure 4.20 First Nations people greet Marie-Anne Gaboury and her husband when they arrive in Fort William, Manitoba, in 1807. This painting was created by L'Abbé G. Dugaft the same year.

Perspective

People's perspectives are different from their individual points of view. A **perspective** is the generally shared point of view of a group. It can reflect the outlook of people from a cultural group, faith, age category, economic group, and so on. For example, the Haudenosaunee perspective on the French fur trade was quite different from the Wendat perspective on it.

Focus

Recall activity 2 on page 96. You thought about how various aspects of the fur trade affected the development of Canada. Now think about the perspectives various groups had about these impacts.

1. Think about perspectives in a small group. The east-west water system allowed the French fur trade to develop westward. It brought Europeans into the interior of the continent. What would be the perspectives of the following groups about that impact? Keep in mind that perspectives can include a variety of concerns and can change over time.
   - the First Peoples who participated in the French trade, for example, the Wendat
   - the First Peoples who did not, for example, the Haudenosaunee
   - the Canadiens
   - the English, who went west via Hudson Bay
2. With your group, choose another impact of the fur trade. Consult the final section of this chapter for ideas. Develop a cause-and-effect chart for it. Analyze the impact from a variety of perspectives. Consider it in the short term and long term. Make a graphic organizer on chart paper and present your results.

Think about It

3. Discuss with your class why students of history should try to understand a variety of perspectives.
4. Did your views of the fur trade change as a result of doing this exercise? Explain.

Chapter 5 War and Peace

Chapter INQUIRY How did military events and their consequences contribute to the foundations of Canada?

Key CONCEPT ▶ Conquest and Consequences

Canadians are proud of their ability to find peaceful solutions to problems. It is part of who we are: we work together to settle disputes without using violence. Occasionally, though, talking and negotiating fail. Sometimes, people get into fights.

Countries that cannot agree sometimes get into fights too—they go to war. War involves the use of organized force on a large scale to attain a goal.

Superpowers

You may have heard the term **superpower**. It refers to a country that is more powerful than almost all other countries. Superpowers dominate world affairs. Today, for example, the United States is the world's largest superpower.

In the 1700s, France and England were rival superpowers. Both countries had huge, well-equipped armies and strong navies. Both were wealthy. Both controlled vast empires. These empires included colonies in North America.

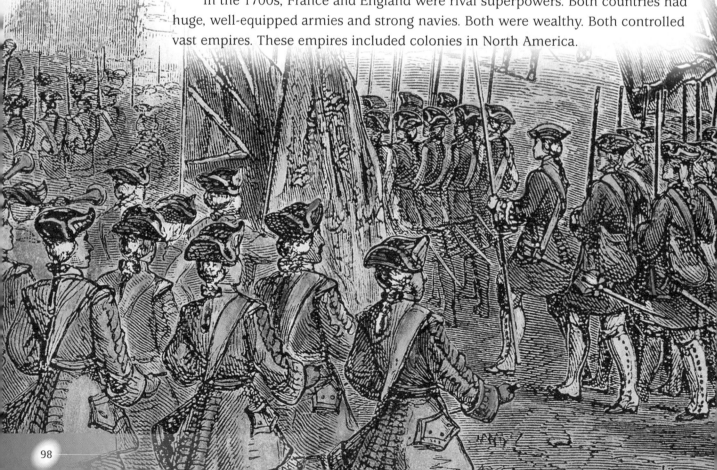

The French and English at War

France and England were often in conflict with one another. This happened because they both wanted the same thing. They wanted more territories, including those in North America. They wanted the resources in these territories. They were rivals for power in Europe and on the high seas. Between 1690 and 1763, France and England were almost always at war with each other.

In this chapter, you will learn about the Seven Years' War. France and England fought for control of New France. You will look at the causes of the war and the effect war had on different groups living in North America at the time. Finally, you will discover the long-term effects of the war, which helped to shape the country we live in today.

(SKILLS) Honing Your Skills

Do you trust everything you read? The Skill Check feature in this chapter shows you how to **Identify Facts, Opinions, and Bias**. This skill is important to your studies because it will help you think critically about your research findings. The project at the end of the chapter will ask you to use this skill as you identify a turning point in Canadian history.

Perspectives on War

As you read this chapter, think about the war through the eyes of those affected by it. Here's what some of those people might have thought about the looming war.

Halifax merchant: If our navy can defeat the French, we will have a much larger market for our goods. Should I be planning to set up business in Québec?

Acadian farmer: Why can't both sides just leave us in peace? Why do we have to choose to support one side or the other?

Canadien habitant: If the English come here, will we be forced to give up our livelihoods, homes, rights, language, and religion?

Mi'kmaq woman: We have lived peacefully with the Acadians. The British have been our enemy since they raided us to enslave us. If the British come, will they take our land?

Mohawk trapper: We have a strong alliance with the French. Will we have to defend them in this war? What is this war going to mean for the fur trade?

Think ► AHEAD

1. Have you or a relative of yours lived through war? Do you think that all people involved in an armed conflict have similar opinions about it? How and why would people's opinions be different?

2. Think about the perspectives you have read above. Then create a chart to record information about how war affected each of these people. Fill in the category "Effects of War" as you read the rest of the chapter.

Affected Group	Perspectives about War	Effects of War
Halifax merchants	need to expand business	

Skill Check: Identify Facts, Opinions, and Bias

The British won the Battle on the Plains of Abraham. This is a fact. What did the battle contribute to the foundations of Canada? That is a matter of opinion. When people give an opinion without facts to back it up, they are showing bias.

To study history, you need to know the difference between facts and opinions. You need to spot bias. Then you can judge historical accounts for yourself.

Facts

Information that is accepted as correct and true is a **fact**. It is important to get the facts right so that we can be sure of what happened and when.

Can a fact be wrong? People may believe something to be true. They think it is a fact. Then, new information comes along that proves it is *not* true. For example, long ago people believed the sun revolved around the earth. Then, new technology revealed that the earth revolves around the sun. So sometimes a "fact" can be wrong.

Opinions

When people give their point of view or judge something, they are expressing their personal **opinion**. For example, let's assume you said, "Harry Potter books are dull!" You would be expressing an opinion. Others might disagree with you.

Some people try to present opinions as facts. As a student of history, you must be on the lookout for that.

In history, if you decide that one fact is more important than another fact, you are expressing an opinion. You could be right. If you want others to respect your opinion, use facts to support your point of view.

Bias

Chances are that if you live in Calgary, you are a Flames hockey fan. If you live in Edmonton, you are likely an Oilers hockey fan. Favouring one hockey team because we live in the same city is a type of **bias**. We all have biases. They make us more accepting of some things than of others. We can be biased about something and not even be aware of it.

When studying history, you need to ask yourself if a source favours one perspective over another. Bias is harmful if it leaves out important information. This would present an inaccurate picture of the past.

When you study history, ask yourself what bias the person who created the source may have had.

Here are some questions to ask when looking for bias:

- What is the source? Who is the author? Who is the intended audience?
- When was the source created? How might this colour the point of view?
- Are strongly positive or negative words or phrases used?
- Are opinions supported by facts?
- Is important information left out? Is the information one-sided? Can I confirm the information in other sources?

Try It!

In a small group, decide which is the "best" computer game. Identify (a) facts, (b) opinions, and (c) biases.

Background to War

When the Seven Years' War broke out in 1756, it was close to being a world war. As well as in Europe, France and England fought in India, the Caribbean, and Africa. In all these places, the two countries had colonies—and resources—they were determined to protect or expand.

What were the specific causes of tensions in North America? What was each side's perspective? Were they prepared for war? In this section, you'll discover the answers to these questions.

Focus

Why were France and England drawn into conflict in North America?

The French Perspective

By 1750, the French were very well established in North America. The area France claimed was huge. French colonists lived on Île Saint-Jean (Prince Edward Island), Cape Breton, and in Louisiana in the south. Acadia belonged to the British, but it was populated by French-speaking people.

The heart of New France was the colony along the St. Lawrence River. About 50 000 French colonists lived there. By 1750, most of the population had been born in New France. These colonists were no longer Europeans. They had begun to see themselves as a new people—the Canadiens.

New France felt secure—perhaps too secure. It felt protected by the home country, which supplied soldiers, and by the mighty fortresses at Québec and Louisbourg. Surely the English armies could never get past these barriers!

The Canadiens were the Francophone citizens of Québec. A **Francophone** is a person whose first language is French. After the First World War, English-speaking Canadians no longer wished to be known as British subjects. They called themselves "Canadians". That is when the term *French-Canadian* began to be used more often in referring to Francophones.

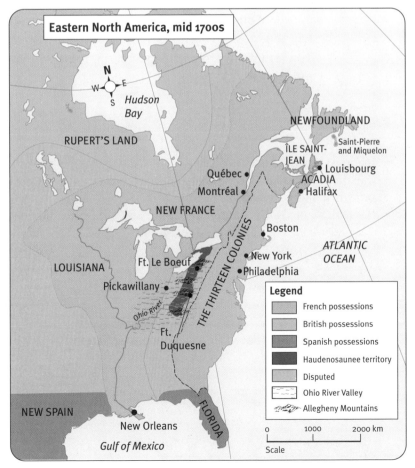

Figure 5.1 Eastern North America, about 1750. The grey areas are those territories that were in dispute. Why do you think the French and English both felt hemmed in? How would the Haudenosaunee [hah-duh-nuh-SAH-nee] feel about the tensions between the French and English?

Eastern North America, mid 1700s

Hudson Bay

RUPERT'S LAND

NEWFOUNDLAND

ÎLE SAINT-JEAN

Saint-Pierre and Miquelon

Louisbourg

Québec

ACADIA

Montréal

Halifax

NEW FRANCE

Boston

THE THIRTEEN COLONIES

New York

ATLANTIC OCEAN

LOUISIANA

Ft. Le Boeuf

Philadelphia

Pickawillany

Ohio River

Ft. Duquesne

NEW SPAIN

New Orleans

FLORIDA

Gulf of Mexico

Legend

French possessions
British possessions
Spanish possessions
Haudenosaunee territory
Disputed
Ohio River Valley
Allegheny Mountains

0   1000   2000 km

Scale

The English Perspective

English colonists from the Thirteen Colonies far outnumbered the French colonists of New France. They wanted to move into the interior of North America. They needed more farmland for their growing population. They also wanted to trade with the First Nations in the interior. Yet they could not cross the Allegheny Mountains to settle in the Ohio River Valley. France had claimed the area for itself and had built forts to protect it. The Thirteen Colonies felt blocked on the north and west.

In the Atlantic region, control of the fisheries was at stake. The Atlantic fisheries produced tonnes of cod and other fish for dinner tables back in Europe. The English wanted to control this profitable resource. England also wanted to gain control of the major gateway to the continent: the St. Lawrence River.

The English felt hemmed in. Yet they had the most powerful navy in the world. The temptation to use it against the French must have been great.

"England" versus "Britain"

In this book, you have been reading about England and Britain, or Great Britain. The terms do not mean quite the same thing. Great Britain ("Britain" for short) is an island in Western Europe. Together, England, Scotland, and Wales share the island. With Northern Ireland, they form the country called the United Kingdom of Great Britain and Northern Ireland. Historically, Great Britain is often called England because England was the largest member of the partnership.

Strengths and Weaknesses

As war approached, each side in the conflict assessed its strengths and weaknesses. Read the chart below. Which side do you think was in the stronger position? Why do you think so?

British Strengths	French Strengths
• the most powerful navy in Europe • prosperous colonies in New England, which could provide military supplies • Haudenosaunee allies (later in the war)	• the most powerful army in Europe • strong fortresses at Louisbourg and Québec • many First Nations allies, including the Mi'kmaq [MIG-mah], Maliseet [MAL-ih-seet], Canadian Mohawks, Innu [IN-noo], Algonquin [al-GONG-kwin], Wendat [WAH-n-dot], Ojibwa [oh-JIB-way], Odawa [oh-DAH-wuh], and Abenaki [a-buh-NA-kee]
British Weaknesses	**French Weaknesses**
• an army that was not used to waging forest warfare • major challenges: that is, the need to capture the well-defended French fortresses • constant bickering among the Thirteen Colonies	• dependence on France for supplies • a vast territory that was hard to defend • a single entry route to the colony: the St. Lawrence River (In time of war, an enemy could block it.) • military and government officials who could not agree on a defence policy

CASE STUDY

Fortress Québec

By 1750, Québec had grown to be the largest town in New France, with a population of about 8000. It was the centre of French power in North America.

In a way, Québec was two towns. The Upper Town was a walled **fortress** located high above the river, atop an imposing cliff. It included the governor's mansion and the homes of the wealthy. The Lower Town was the port, huddled between the river and the cliff. Stone warehouses lined the harbourfront, where ships arrived to deliver their cargoes and to take on furs and other goods bound for France. Tradespeople, labourers, and shopkeepers all lived in the narrow streets of the Lower Town.

Québec lay at a narrowing of the St. Lawrence River. It was the gateway to the colony. All ships coming up the river had to pass within range of its cannons. The French were confident that no enemy could overcome its defences.

Respond

Look at the illustration of Québec in Figure 5.2. Who or what do you think the fortress was built to protect? Who or what would not be protected by this fortress?

Locate each of the following:
A – the fort, with the governor's mansion, the Château St-Louis
B – a church
C – walls and fortifications
D – the Jesuit college
E – a cathedral
F – a seminary for the training of priests
G – the hospital
H – the home of the Catholic bishop
I – a separate fort
J – the Lower Town

Figure 5.2 Québec in 1720. Think about ways that paintings and drawings could be used as sources of information at that time.

Figure 5.3 Québec, the only fortified city in North America, as it looks today. Why do you think the United Nations named parts of the Old City a World Heritage Site?

Figure 5.4 A drummer and a soldier of New France, about 1690, drawn by historical artist Michel Pétard. At any one time, up to a third of the population of Québec were soldiers sent from France to defend the colony. Some were teenagers. How would this affect the character of the community?

War Rumblings in the West

The war for North America began in the Ohio River Valley. In 1754, a British force led by General George Washington marched into the valley. In time, Washington would become the first president of the United States. On this occasion, however, he suffered defeat. The next year, the British tried again with a much bigger force. The result was the same. The French had successfully adopted the battle tactics of their First Nations allies.

For the moment, New France was secure. Even so, the British were determined to drive the French out of North America. The British prime minister, William Pitt, promised to send more soldiers, more ships, and more money.

Figure 5.5 Louisbourg viewed from the harbour, as it would have looked about 1744. It was painted by historical artist Lewis Parker in the 1980s. The painting shows the King's Bastion barracks in the background. The governor lived in the left wing while the soldiers lived in the right wing. Louisbourg was an important port on the North Atlantic trade routes. It was also a fishing port. Why do you think it was so important to the French to defend Louisbourg?

Canada Today

Louisbourg was the French naval base on the eastern coast of Canada. After the war, all that was left of Louisbourg was a pile of rocky rubble. For nearly 150 years, the site lay deserted. Then, about 1890, amateur historians John S. McLennan and his daughter, Katharine, took an interest in the site. They researched extensively for two decades. They campaigned to restore the town. The government of Canada finally declared the area a National Historic Site in 1928. In the 1960s, work began in earnest to rebuild the fortress as it would have looked in the 1750s.

Today the Fortress of Louisbourg stands again. Visitors stroll through the streets down to the waterfront. They admire the furnishings in the governor's mansion. Costumed actors make it seem as if you've stepped back in time 250 years. Projects like this help Canadians feel a strong connection with our history. It helps us know who we are.

Figure 5.6 Activities at the reconstructed Fortress of Louisbourg. How would a local hotel operator, a Canadian historian, and a taxpayer each view the process of reconstruction? **SKILLS**

Think It Through

a) Make a two-column chart. Record the key factors leading to war from the French and English perspectives. Don't forget to think about international factors.

b) Decide which factor you think was the most important for each side. Explain your reasoning. **SKILLS**

Key Factors	
French Perspective	English Perspective

Prelude to War: Acadia

The Acadians were the descendants of the French colonists who had first farmed the shores of the Bay of Fundy in the 1600s. Acadia had changed hands many times in the seventeenth century. First the English captured it. Then the French did. Back and forth it went.

By 1710, most of Acadia was firmly under British control. Acadians had developed a unique identity because they had been cut off from the rest of New France for so long. Britain changed the colony's name to Nova Scotia. It allowed the Acadians to live their lives in peace. It seemed that the Acadians' troubles were over. As you will see in this section, however, the Acadians became victims of a war they did not want.

> An **Acadian** is a Francophone citizen of Acadia.

The Acadian Way of Life

By 1750, more than 10 000 Acadians lived on small farms and in villages nestled along the shores of the Bay of Fundy. Many had intermarried with their Mi'kmaq trading partners. They were mainly French-speaking Catholics. Over the years, they created their own way of life. It was based on fishing and their unique methods of farming.

Caught in the Middle

Britain had always wanted to populate Nova Scotia with people who spoke English. As tensions between England and France grew, the governor of Nova Scotia, Charles Lawrence, began to wonder if the Acadians might side with the French. The Mi'kmaq and Maliseet had trade and family ties with the Acadians. Over the years, they had captured hundreds of English ships. The Acadians had always refused to swear loyalty to the British Crown.

In 1755, Lawrence gave the Acadians an ultimatum (a threat of serious penalties): swear your loyalty or lose your land. The Acadians did not want to fight. They wanted to remain **neutral**. They promised not to take up arms against the English, but they refused to take the oath. That set the stage for *le Grand Dérangement*—the Great Upheaval.

Focus

Why did the English expel the Acadians from their land in Nova Scotia?

Tech Link

To see a re-enactment of Acadians preserving fish, open Chapter 5 on your *Voices and Visions* CD-ROM.

Reading STRATEGY

To better remember what you're reading, try identifying the main idea in every paragraph as you read.

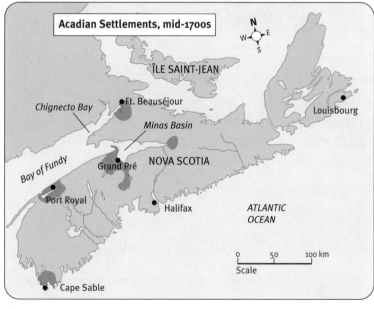

Figure 5.7 The main Acadian settlements around 1750. Think about Acadia's location. Why did both Britain and France want to control the colony?

CASE STUDY

The Expulsion of the Acadians: Was There Any Other Way?

In modern Canada, we believe that people have certain human rights. For example, Canadian citizens have a right to live in Canada. We have the right not to be torn from our families and shipped off to foreign lands. Our government has the responsibility to protect those rights.

It has not always been this way. Just consider what happened to the Acadians in 1755.

The Great Deportation—Le Grand Dérangement

Governor Lawrence was convinced that the British newcomers in Nova Scotia would not be safe with the Acadians living among them. He thought he found proof of this when British troops captured Fort Beauséjour from the French in 1755. Inside, they found 300 armed Acadians defending the fort. To Lawrence, this meant that all Acadians were disloyal.

The governor gave the order: "The French inhabitants of the province shall be removed out of the country as soon as possible." British soldiers fell upon the Acadian villages. They rounded up the people at gunpoint. They broke up families and forced them to board ships bound for distant lands. They burned homes and churches. They destroyed farms and drove off animals.

How It Ended

Most of the Acadians were deported by ship to the New England colonies. Some were sent to the Caribbean, France, or England. A few escaped and went into hiding in the woods. Others made their way to New Orleans, Louisiana, still part of New France. Their descendants formed the Cajun community, which still thrives.

Many Acadians didn't survive the deportation, though. They died of disease, drowning, or starvation. In all, about 10 000 Acadians were driven from their homes. Seeing what happened to the Acadians, the Mi'kmaq and Maliseet abided by the wishes of the British.

Figure 5.8 British soldiers forcing Acadians from their homes. The exiles could take only what they could carry. How has Lewis Parker, who created this painting, used facts and emotions to re-create the scene?

CASE STUDY *continued*

John Winslow was a British army officer who took part in the removal of the Acadians from Grand Pré. Here he tells about what he did:

Respond

Think about this question: Did Governor Lawrence have to abuse people's human rights? [SKILLS]

a) With two partners, analyze the facts about the Great Upheaval.

b) Here are three roles:

- Col. Greenhouse, a British army officer
- M. Arsenault, an Acadian who refused to take the oath
- Mme LeBlanc, an Acadian who took the oath and stayed

Think about how these characters would have viewed the facts.

c) What evidence supports your position? Record the evidence supporting each point of view in a graphic organizer.

d) Now develop an argument to support or oppose your response to the question from your own point of view.

> The whole of the French people were drawn together in a group. I then ordered Captain Adams to lead away the young men to the ships. I ordered the prisoners to march. They all answered they would not go without their fathers. I told them that "no" was a word I did not understand.
>
> The King's command had to be obeyed. I told them that I did not want to use harsh means, but there was no time for talking and delay. I ordered the troops to fix their bayonets and march towards the French. The men started off, praying, singing, and crying. Along the way they were met by the women and children who were on their knees crying and praying.

Source: Colonel John Winslow,
The Journal of Colonel John Winslow
(Nova Scotia Historical Society Collections, Vol. III).

Figure 5.9 Acadian singer Jeanne (Doucet) Currie, dressed in traditional clothing. She is attending the World Acadian Congress at Grand Pré, Nova Scotia. She and other Acadians remember their ancestors. People take part in this type of cultural event for a feeling of connection. Explain what this means using an example from your own experience.

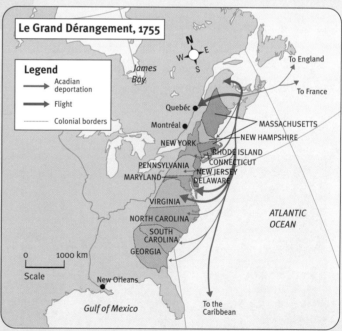

Figure 5.10 Destinations of the Acadian deportees in 1755. *Le Grand Dérangement* can also be translated as "the Great Bother." What comment do you think the Acadians were making when they labelled such a tragedy with that phrase?

Identity

A Lasting Identity

Can the Acadians' identity survive in Canada? First consider what the Acadians have done over the past 250 years.

In 1763, the war between France and England was over. The Acadians were free to come home. Some returned to the shores of the Bay of Fundy. Most chose to settle in what would become New Brunswick and Prince Edward Island, because their original farms in Nova Scotia had been taken.

The memories of their exile stayed with the Acadians. They were determined to preserve their culture and way of life. Today, about 300 000 French-speaking Acadians live in Atlantic Canada. In New Brunswick, about a third of the people speak French as their first language. The province is the only one in Canada that is officially bilingual. Acadians have their own schools, music, plays, and novels. They even have their own flag. It is modelled on the French flag to show the Acadians' bond to their French heritage.

 Respond

What factors do you think boost a people's sense of cultural identity? What could you do to help the Acadians protect their identity?

The Acadians keep their cultural identity alive in many ways. In New Brunswick, *Le Pays de La Sagouine* is a re-creation of an Acadian village. At Grand Pré, Nova Scotia, an annual festival draws 5000 Acadians. They enjoy a weekend of picnics, songs, dancing, and games. Every few years, Acadians hold a big family reunion.

In 2004, Nova Scotia hosted the World Acadian Congress. It marked the 400th anniversary of the first French settlement in North America at St. Croix Island. The event drew more than 250 000 Acadians. They came from as far away as Spain, Louisiana, and Hong Kong. Governor General Adrienne Clarkson offered apologies for the expulsion of the Acadians on behalf of the British.

Figure 5.11 Viola Léger portrays La Sagouine, an Acadian washerwoman who tells her stories of life in Acadia. Léger played this role more than 2000 times. Antonine Maillet created La Sagouine. Maillet is famous for her many plays and novels about Acadia. How has she helped keep the Acadian identity vibrant and alive?

Think It Through

Do you want to be able to identify bias? Put yourself in the time of a historical event. **SKILLS**

a) Imagine you are Édouard Arsenault, a young Acadian in 1755. Write a letter to Governor Lawrence explaining why you wish to remain neutral in the conflict between Britain and France.

b) Imagine you are Governor Lawrence. Write a letter back explaining why you have to expel the Acadians.

Alternatively, write a brief skit in which the two discuss this issue. The scene: Arsenault is assisting the governor with a broken coach wheel.

The Struggle for Canada

For a few years, the French, Canadian Mohawks, Ojibwa, and other First Nations successfully fought the English. They kept the enemy at bay in the Ohio River Valley and the Great Lakes region.

There was only one way to win New France. England would have to gain control of France's two centres of power in North America: Louisbourg and Québec. In this section, you will see how they accomplished this daunting task.

Focus

How was the Battle on the Plains of Abraham a turning point in Canadian history?

Capturing Louisbourg

Louisbourg had to be captured first. It guarded the St. Lawrence River, which led to the Québec colony.

In the spring of 1758, the British collected a huge force of warships and troops at Halifax. Arriving off Louisbourg that June, the British fleet blockaded the harbour. The British soldiers scrambled onshore with their cannons. They cut off the town from the landward side and settled in for a long **siege** (a blockade of a city).

Inside the fortress, the people were cut off from supplies and reinforcements. Their food supplies ran low. They watched as the British sank their ships, one by one. The people weakened as the British launched a steady rain of cannonballs onto the fort. After seven weeks of bombardment, the French at Louisbourg surrendered.

Onward to Canada

With the route to Canada now open, the British lost little time. The next spring, in 1759, Major-General James Wolfe led a fleet up the St. Lawrence River. He had about 200 ships carrying 9000 soldiers and 18 000 sailors. The line of ships stretched for 150 kilometres.

The battle for Québec unfolded over three months. Victory for the British was never a sure thing. The French commander was the Marquis de Montcalm. He had 16 000 troops and a stone fortress that would not be captured easily. If Montcalm could hold out until winter, Wolfe and his ships would have to retreat before the river froze.

Figure 5.12 Louisbourg as the siege began, 1758. Captain Charles Ince, a British soldier who took part in the attack, painted this scene. It shows the British moving their cannons into place. To the right, French ships are anchored in the harbour. In the distance, the British fleet waits offshore. In what ways might the soldier's bias have affected his interpretation of the scene? SKILLS

VOICES ■

The short-term effects of war in New France were dreadful. Mother Marie-Marguerite d'Youville ran a charitable home in Montréal during the war. Here she expresses her despair:

66 **We had flattered ourselves that France would not abandon us. This country is more and more forsaken. My tears are blinding me.** 99

Source: *L'Hôpital Général des Soeurs Grises de la Charité*. Montréal (nd), Vol. 1, pp. 238–240 (Trans.). Quoted in K.A. MacKirdy et al., *Changing Perspectives in Canadian History* (Don Mills, ON: J.M. Dent, 1967), p. 65.

Points of View before the Battle

Wolfe and Montcalm faced different challenges. Wolfe was on the attack. He and his troops faced a well-defended fortress perched atop a high cliff. It appeared impossible to climb. Unlike Louisbourg, Québec could not be surrounded from the countryside behind the fort. Therefore, Wolfe could not cut off supplies. Time was short. There would be only a few weeks until the cold weather set in. Wolfe's only hope was to draw the enemy out onto the open battlefield.

Montcalm, on the other hand, was on the defence. He and his French forces faced a huge fleet of British ships and a well-trained army. He believed they were safe inside the stone fortress. They could fire their cannons at will on the enemy below. They believed help was on the way. The best thing to do was to wait.

A Standoff

The French and the British bombarded each other for almost nine weeks. The fortress of Québec was in ruins, but it still had not been captured. "We do not doubt that you will destroy the town [with

cannon fire]," declared one French officer, "but we are determined that you shall never set foot within its walls." Despite major damage to the city, Montcalm would not release his army to fight.

General Wolfe wrote to his mother: "My antagonist [Montcalm] has wisely shut himself up so that I can't get at him." Wolfe unleashed a savage attack on the countryside. Troops destroyed villages and set fire to hundreds of farmhouses and barns. Frightened *habitant* families fled to the protection of the walled fortress. It was a terrifying tactic, but it did no good. The French forces would not leave the fortress.

Winter was setting in. It was time for the British to leave. For Wolfe, this was the time for one last gamble.

The Battle on the Plains of Abraham

Wolfe came up with a plan. On the high clifftop behind the fortress was a farmer's field known as the Plains of Abraham. If British soldiers could secretly make their way there, they could attack the French where their defences were weak.

Just before midnight on 12 September 1759, the first British soldiers stepped ashore. Throughout the night, they crept up a steep path leading to the field. In a few hours, the British army was in place on the

Tech Link

To see a re-enactment of the life of a French soldier at Québec before the siege, open Chapter 5 on your *Voices and Visions* CD-ROM.

Figure 5.13 The events of the Battle on the Plains of Abraham, shown as if they were all happening at the same time. It is based on a sketch by Hervey Smyth. He was a British soldier who was wounded during the battle. Locate the following: the British fleet, the landing boats, the Plains of Abraham, and the town of Québec. What distortions in the painting might be a result of Smyth's bias? SKILLS

Plains of Abraham. When dawn broke, the French were astonished to see thousands of red-coated soldiers in battle position just outside the city gates.

At the fort, Montcalm had 6000 soldiers, including 300 upper Great Lakes Odawa allies. About 4400 professional British soldiers waited on the Plains. Reinforcements had not arrived. What should Montcalm do? Should he march out and fight the British head-on? Should he stay safely behind the fortress walls? Montcalm decided he couldn't wait. It was a fateful decision.

Montcalm emerged from the city leading 4000 troops. The British launched a massive volley of musket fire. The French fired back. A fierce battle raged, and both Wolfe and Montcalm were killed. After 15 minutes of slaughter, the French turned and fled. In all, 1300 soldiers died on the Plains of Abraham. It was the bloodiest battle ever fought on Canadian soil.

The English are bringing their cannons up the cliff. The longer I wait, the stronger they become. I have more soldiers than they do on the field. I could wait for reinforcements, but if I attack now perhaps I will catch them before they are ready.

Figure 5.14 A portrait of the Marquis de Montcalm. Most historians blame Montcalm for the loss of Québec. They argue that if he had waited for reinforcements to arrive, he might have won the battle and the French may have won the war. What do you think? Did Montcalm make the best decision he could?

allies were no longer willing to fight. On 8 September 1760, the French surrendered at Montréal. New France passed into British hands.

The Legacy of the Colony

With their First Nations friends and allies, the Canadiens accomplished a great deal during the over 150 years that they controlled the St. Lawrence River Valley. They were the first newcomers in the territory that would one day be Canada. French traders pioneered the fur trade. They travelled all the way to the Western Plains. In spite of the harsh climate, the Canadiens created successful farms. They cleared the land, dug wells, and built roads. They started up shops and businesses. Through the Catholic Church, they began a tradition of public responsibility for education, health, and the disadvantaged. These are roots of values central to the contemporary Canadian identity.

The Canadiens proved that a colony could survive in this difficult land. By the time the English arrived in the St. Lawrence, the Canadiens had already laid the foundations of a successful country.

Figure 5.15 The Plains of Abraham as it looks today. In the nineteenth century, the British built the Citadel, which you can see in the foreground. In 1908, the National Battlefields Commission was created to preserve the site. Why would we want to preserve a battle site?

Following the battle, the English troops entered the city. "Québec is nothing but a shapeless mass of ruins," reported one eyewitness. "Confusion, disorder, pillage reign even among the inhabitants." French colonists and British soldiers alike scrambled to find food during the winter. More British soldiers died from disease than had died in the battle.

The remaining French soldiers fell back to Montréal. Here they held out for a few months. Many of their First Nations

---

Think It Through

1. Review the section titled "The Struggle for Canada."
   a) Make a list of the key events that took place, with their locations and dates.
   b) Put them in order and create a timeline. Alternatively, create an illustrated map showing these events. Label each event, including the date.

2. Do an Internet or library search for information about the Battle on the Plains of Abraham. Find what looks like a useful source. Then answer the following questions:

   - What are the facts? What are opinions?
   - Are the opinions supported by facts, reasoned arguments, or respected sources?
   - What is the bias? How do you know? SKILLS

3. What might have happened if French ships had arrived in Québec before the British ships did in 1759? Write a front-page newspaper story or narrative poem. In it, describe how events might have unfolded.

4. How did the citizens of New France lay the foundations of the Canada you know today?

The First Nations and the War

As you will discover in this section, the First Nations were deeply involved in the wars between the French and the English. Most First Nations supported the French, with whom they had a long history of trading. Some Haudenosaunee sided with the English.

The First Nations fought independently against the enemy. They also fought and died alongside their allies on the battlefield. At Québec, for example, 300 Odawa sharpshooters helped defend the city. They could not have known that the winner of this war would take control of all the lands, including the First Nations territories.

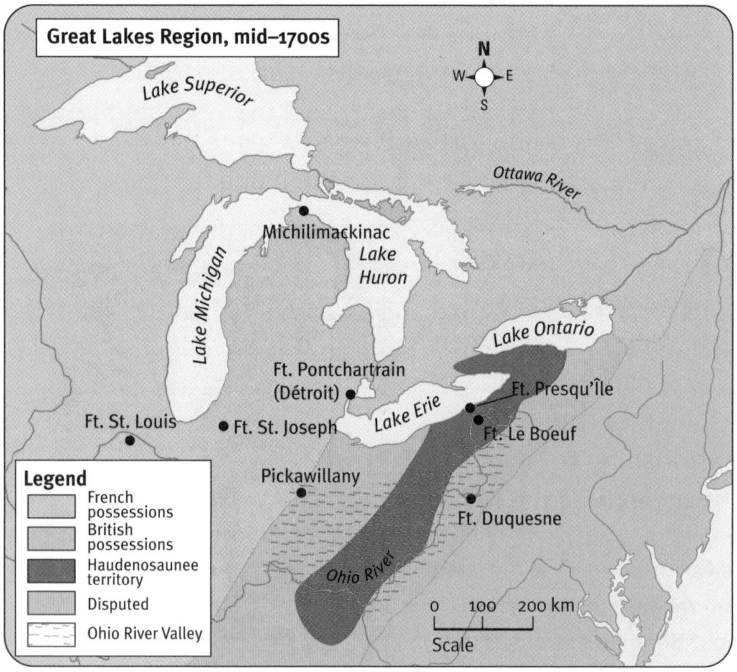

Focus

What role did the First Nations play in the war between France and England?

The First Nations did not stop fighting after the French surrendered. The First Nations and the English first had to negotiate neutrality. Only then could the English declare victory.

Reasons for Anxiety

Following the war, France and England made peace. They signed a **treaty** in 1763. It gave England possession of most of North America. The treaty disappointed the First Nations. The future of their land was at stake, yet no one had invited them to take part in the peace process. The French governor made the English promise not to take revenge against the First Nations peoples who had sided with the French.

As you learned in Chapter 4, British traders took over the French fur trade. They did not follow the same trading practices as the French. They were not as generous in giving gifts such as tobacco, ammunition, and wampum. The British did not understand that exchanging gifts was how First Nations people built trust.

The First Nations were worried about the newcomers. English farmers began to move into the Ohio River Valley. Gradually, the First Nations were losing their lands. They began to consider war.

Great Lakes Region, mid–1700s

Lake Superior
Lake Michigan
Michilimackinac
Lake Huron
Ottawa River
Lake Ontario
Ft. Pontchartrain (Détroit)
Ft. Presqu'Île
Ft. St. Louis
Ft. St. Joseph
Lake Erie
Ft. Le Boeuf
Pickawillany
Ft. Duquesne
Ohio River

N W E S

0 100 200 km
Scale

Legend
French possessions
British possessions
Haudenosaunee territory
Disputed
Ohio River Valley

Figure 5.16 The Great Lakes area, about 1750. How would the Haudenosaunee territory act like a buffer between the French and English?

VOICES

Minweweh was a chief of the Ojibwa people. He told the British,

> **Although you have conquered the French, you have not conquered us. We are not your slaves. These lakes, these woods and mountains, were left to us by our ancestors. They are our inheritance, and we will part with them to none.**

Source: Kevin Reed, *Aboriginal Peoples: Building for the Future* (Canadian Challenge Series) (Toronto: Oxford University Press, 1999), p. 36.

Pontiac's War against the British

The person who inspired a war against the English was a man named Pontiac. This leader of the Odawa convinced several First Nations to join together to drive the British out of the Ohio River Valley. In May 1763, Pontiac and the Odawa laid siege to the British fort at Detroit. Around the same time, Pontiac's allies captured forts along the trading frontier south and west of Lake Erie. They were remarkably successful, capturing seven of ten English forts.

Pontiac hoped that the French would come to help him. After all, he and his allies had aided the French in *their* war with the English. The French, however, had already surrendered at Montréal. The British sent in troops to fight the First Nations. The alliance that Pontiac had formed fell apart.

CASE STUDY

Tactics versus Physical Strength

When you play hockey or soccer, good tactics can help you beat a stronger opponent. The same is true in war.

Fort Michilimackinac [mish-il-ih-MAK-ih-nak] was held by the British. It was located where Lake Huron and Lake Michigan meet. The Chippewa [CHIP-uh-wah] who lived in the area joined Pontiac's fighting force. Their first target was the fort, but the fort was too strong to attack outright. Instead, they devised a clever plan.

The men gathered outside the walls of the fort and began a game of lacrosse. British soldiers idly watched as the players chased the ball back and forth. Suddenly, one of the players tossed the ball

Respond

Have you ever won a physical sport because of your strong tactics? With your classmates, discuss what is more important in playing team sports: tactics or physical strength.

through the fort's open gate. It seemed to be an accident. As the other players chased it into the fort, though, the women who had been watching handed the men weapons they had hidden under their clothing. Taking the British by complete surprise, the Chippewa captured the fort in just a few minutes.

Figure 5.17 Gates of the reconstructed Fort Michilimackinac. Without the element of surprise, do you think the Chippewa would have had much hope of taking over the fort?

Think It Through

1. The First Nations felt betrayed after the Seven Years' War. Were they betrayed? How did the English and French view the situation? Explain your reasoning. What might be your bias in this question? SKILLS

2. As Britain expanded its control in North America, the First Nations were concerned that their interests would not be respected. Why did First Nations have good reason to be concerned about their future?

After the War

After the war, the Canadiens, English newcomers, and First Nations and Métis peoples were faced with a new challenge. How could these new citizens of a single colony live together in peace? In this section, you will see how they struggled to find ways to meet this challenge.

Focus

How did the British treatment of their new colonies and the people who lived there influence the future of Canada?

New Challenges

Each group had its own concerns as it looked to the future. The First Nations were tired of war. They just wanted a return to normal life, but they feared that land-hungry newcomers would flood into their territories.

The Canadiens feared the worst. Those who stayed in Canada faced the challenge of rebuilding the colony. They wondered if they would be allowed to speak French and worship in the Catholic faith. After all, the British had forced the Acadians to abandon their homes. Would the same thing happen to the Canadiens?

The new British rulers faced challenges, too. They now had a colony of 70 000 people who spoke a different language and practised a different religion. The Canadiens had a different form of government, followed different laws, and had different ways of doing things. The English were worried about the First Nations, too. Many of them had been allies of the French during the war. How were the English going to make the Canadiens and First Nations peoples loyal subjects of the British Crown?

Figure 5.18 A painting of Québec in ruins by Richard Short, who was a member of the invading British forces. What aspects of the painting create mood? The war brought devastation to both the city and the countryside, where many farms were destroyed. What effect does war have on civilians?

The Treaty of Paris, 1763

The surrender of Montréal in 1760 ended the fighting over New France. As you learned earlier, though, the conflict between England and France was fought elsewhere, too. It continued for three more years in Europe and other parts of the world.

Finally, in 1763, France and Britain signed the Treaty of Paris, ending the conflict. Under the treaty, France gave up any claim to Québec or any other part of North America. In return, France received Guadeloupe, a sugar-producing island in the Caribbean. The only parts of New France still in the hands of the French were the tiny islands of Saint-Pierre and Miquelon near the coast of Newfoundland. (Find them on the map on page 118.)

Choices for the Future

The British had gained control over what had been New France. Now they had to decide how to govern the colony. What options did they have?

- **Eviction.** Should they evict the Canadiens from their homes and deport them from British North America?
- **Assimilation.** Should they pressure the Canadiens to give up their language and religion and become loyal British subjects?
- **Accommodation.** Should they leave the Canadiens alone to live as they always had, with their own religion, language, and customs?

At the same time, the British had to decide two more things. Should they make land agreements with First Nations peoples? And how could they reward the American colonists of New England? Many of these colonists had fought for Britain in the war. New England farmers wanted land in the Ohio River Valley. British traders hoped to be able to set up businesses in Canada.

Region of New France	Before 1763	After 1763
Québec	• most heavily settled part of New France	• became a British colony
Nova Scotia (or Acadia)	• all but Cape Breton became British in 1713 • Acadians expelled in 1755	• Cape Breton was added
Cape Breton	• controlled by France • called Île Royale	• controlled by the British as part of Nova Scotia
Prince Edward Island (Île Saint-Jean)	• controlled by France	• came under British control
Newfoundland	• the British won possession of the island in 1713 • the French kept a small portion of the shoreline for fishing	• the island came under total British control except the offshore islands of Saint-Pierre and Miquelon

Figure 5.19 The fate of the five regions of New France. Which country controls the islands of Saint-Pierre and Miquelon today?

The Royal Proclamation of 1763

The British did not want to evict the Canadiens from their homes. However, they did want to **assimilate** them. This means the Canadiens would become more like the British and would lose their language and culture. The British chose the second of the three options listed on page 117.

In October 1763, King George III of England signed the Royal Proclamation of 1763, which laid out the British government's plans for the colony. To attract Anglophones to Québec, the Proclamation brought in British institutions and laws.

Tech Link

To see a descriptive map related to the Royal Proclamation, open Chapter 5 on your *Voices and Visions* CD-ROM.

It also prevented settlement west of the Appalachians. This forced American colonists who wanted land to move to Québec.

Recognition for First Nations

Pontiac's acts of war were not in vain. They made the British realize that they had to pay attention to the demands of the First Nations. In the Royal Proclamation of 1763, Britain set aside a huge area of land for the First Nations. It included all lands west of the Appalachian Mountains and east of the Mississippi River. Europeans could not live there. It seemed that some First Nations had achieved what they wanted—to continue their way of life without interference.

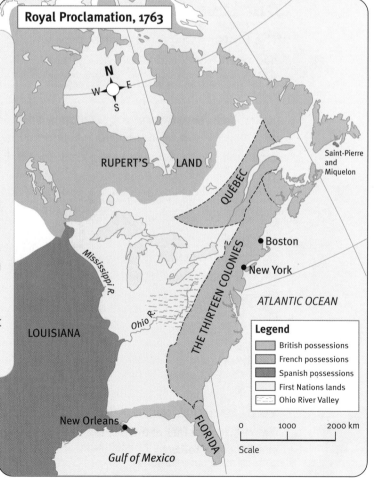

Terms of the Royal Proclamation

- *La Nouvelle-France* (New France) became the Province of Québec.

- Québec became much smaller.

- The interior was set aside for First Nations peoples.

- A system of British laws and courts replaced the French system.

- Civil government replaced the military government.

- The government would consist of a governor, appointed by Britain, and an appointed council of advisors.

- The Catholic Church lost its ability to tithe. Catholics were not allowed to sit on the council of advisors or to hold senior jobs in government.

Figure 5.20 The Proclamation reduced the size of the colony to a small area along the St. Lawrence and Ottawa Rivers. Overall, do you think the British were fair? Explain.

Royal Proclamation, 1763

RUPERT'S LAND

QUÉBEC

Saint-Pierre and Miquelon

Boston

New York

ATLANTIC OCEAN

THE THIRTEEN COLONIES

Mississippi R.

Ohio R.

LOUISIANA

New Orleans

FLORIDA

Gulf of Mexico

Legend
- British possessions
- French possessions
- Spanish possessions
- First Nations lands
- Ohio River Valley

0   1000   2000 km

Scale

Royal Proclamation of 1763

And whereas great Frauds and Abuses have been committed in purchasing Lands of the Indians, to the great Prejudice of our Interests, and to the great Dissatisfaction of the said Indians: In order, therefore, to prevent such Irregularities for the future, and to the end that the Indians may be convinced of our Justice and determined Resolution to remove all reasonable Cause of Discontent, We do, with the Advice of our Privy Council strictly enjoin and require, that no private Person do presume to make any purchase from the said Indians of any Lands reserved to the said Indians.

Source: Royal Proclamation of 1763, available at http://www.bloorstreet.com/200block/rp1763.htm#7.

Figure 5.21 An excerpt from the Royal Proclamation of 1763, signed by King George III. The duties of citizenship include recognizing the rights of others. How is the king engaged in active citizenship? What reasons does the king give for protecting First Nations lands?

Reading
STRATEGY

Formal documents like this can be hard to understand. Try "translating" each phrase into everyday, modern English.

The Québec Act of 1774

The attempt to turn Québec into a colony with a British identity failed. The Canadiens had developed such a strong sense of

Canada Today

Are modern Aboriginal land claims legitimate? According to the Proclamation of 1763, the answer is yes. In it, the British king promises to protect First Nations lands. This document laid the legal grounds for all the land treaties that followed. Today, treaties between First Nations and Canada still rely on the Proclamation as the basic guarantee of Aboriginal rights. For this reason, it is sometimes called the Aboriginal Bill of Rights. These rights are now guaranteed in the Constitution under the Charter of Rights and Freedoms.

Figure 5.22 Almira Augustine, a Mi'kmaq from the Burnt Church Reserve in New Brunswick. Augustine is taking part in a protest about the fishery in August 2000. First Nations across Canada have a legal right to a share of the fishery. Why are documents such as the Proclamation of 1763 so important to First Nations?

identity that they could not be "made" British. They were determined to survive as a people. Only a few hundred English-speaking newcomers were attracted to Québec.

Meanwhile, in the Thirteen Colonies, the colonists were becoming restless under British rule. The British did not want trouble in Québec as well. They needed to keep the colony loyal. They decided the best way to do that was to recognize the Canadiens' rights that had been taken away by the Proclamation. Therefore, in 1774, Britain passed a law with new plans for the colony.

> The Québec Act resulted in the survival of the French language in North America. Consequently, it is known by some as the Magna Carta of Francophones.

The Beginnings of a Bilingual Canada

Bilingualism recognizes two of the peoples that forged the foundations of Canada. Bilingualism means that Canada has two official languages: French and English. It means that Canadian citizens have the right to government services in either language. It means they have the right to do business in either language. Bilingualism is central to the Canadian identity.

You will learn more about bilingualism later in this book. For now, it is important to understand that the origin of bilingualism was the Québec Act. The British recognized the Canadiens' right to maintain their language and traditions. This was a foundation for peace. Québec, and later Canada, became a partnership between French- and English-speaking citizens.

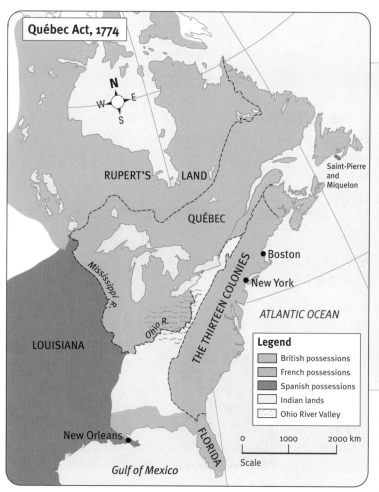

Québec Act, 1774

RUPERT'S LAND

QUÉBEC

Saint-Pierre and Miquelon

Boston

New York

THE THIRTEEN COLONIES

ATLANTIC OCEAN

Mississippi R.

Ohio R.

LOUISIANA

New Orleans

FLORIDA

Gulf of Mexico

Legend
- British possessions
- French possessions
- Spanish possessions
- Indian lands
- Ohio River Valley

0   1000   2000 km

Scale

Terms of the Québec Act

- Québec was expanded to the size it had been when it was a colony of France.
- Much of the land that had been set aside for First Nations became part of Québec. Remaining Aboriginal lands were still protected.
- French language rights were recognized.
- The French seigneurial system remained in place.
- Catholics were given freedom of religion. They were allowed to hold government jobs.
- French civil law would be used in matters of property, inheritance, and to settle disputes.
- The Roman Catholic Church got back the power to hold property and to tithe.

Figure 5.23 The Québec Act expanded the size of the colony to include the Great Lakes and the Ohio River Valley territory. This was prime fur-trading country. What might the colonists in the Thirteen Colonies think about this?

Think It Through

1. What was the impact of Britain's takeover of New France? Did the Canadiens get a bad deal or a good deal? **SKILLS**
   a) Think about the facts.
   b) Present arguments for both sides.
   c) Did your opinion change after considering the facts? Explain.

2. Working with a partner or in a small group, create any type of multimedia display on the concept of "conquest and consequences." Help your viewers understand the following:
   • the causes of the Seven Years' War
   • the effect of the war on the Acadians, the First Nations, and the Canadiens
   • the long- and short-term consequences
   Assess your findings for bias. **SKILLS**

3. How did military events and their consequences contribute to the foundations of Canada?

SKILLS Chapter 5 PROJECT Turning Points

Some events seem to change everything. After the event, life is different. A **turning point** can take place without people being aware of it. The creation of the Internet was a turning point, yet few people knew about it.

Turning Points in Your Life

Your life has taken certain twists and turns that have affected who you are.

1. Make a list of the turning points in your life.
2. Use these to create a timeline titled "The Timeline of My Life."
3. Choose one event that had major consequences for you. How did it affect who you are today?

Turning Points in Canadian History

Ask yourself what happened in North America between 1740 and 1774. Was there a turning point that changed everything?

Make a list of events that took place during this time. For ideas, review this chapter. Remember that even small events can have big consequences. For each event, note what you know about its short- and long-term effects.

Gather Evidence

For the events on your list, find out whether or not they had important long-term consequences. Conduct research on the Internet, in books, or on databases. Ask the questions listed in the Skill Check feature on page 100 to help you judge the bias in the information you gather.

Back Up Your Choice

What event is the most important turning point? What biases do you have that might affect your choice? What facts and arguments can you use to support your choice?

Present Your Turning Point

With a partner, create a visual display, write a news article, videotape a news feature, or write lyrics for a ballad. Your presentation should show how the event you chose is a turning point that affected the foundations of Canada.

Looking Back

After giving your presentation and viewing other presentations, think about how you might do things differently. How could you improve how you screened for bias? How could you back up your opinions more effectively?

Chapter 6 Becoming Canada

How did the War of 1812 and its political consequences affect the developing Canadian identity?

Key CONCEPT

A Complex Identity

When people meet you, what do they first note about you? Perhaps you are female. You might have dark hair and brown eyes. Perhaps people you meet learn that you're polite.

When people get to know you, however, they learn a lot more about you. They might really enjoy your sense of humour. They might admire your deeply held convictions. They get to know your complex **personal identity**. By getting to know one another, we understand each other better.

Like people, countries have **superficial characteristics**. When people around the world picture Canada, they think of hockey, the Mounties, the maple leaf, and snow. Maybe they recall that Canada is the second-largest country in the world.

Really, though, do these superficial characteristics say much about Canada? Do other people in the world know about Canada's 600 First Nations? Do they realize that Canada is officially bilingual? Do they know that poppies bloom on the Arctic tundra?

These are just a very few of Canada's characteristics. Canada's identity is very complex. In fact, it varies depending on where you are in Canada, and which Canadian you're talking to. Canada is many things to many different Canadians.

An Emerging Identity

A country's complex identity develops over time. It is based on its history. It changes as people build their societies. In an earlier chapter, you learned about the history and identity of the First Peoples. Later, you learned how the Francophones in New France established their unique identities as Acadians and *Canadiens*.

In this chapter, you will see that the complex Canadian identity continued to develop between 1763 and 1850. Hundreds of thousands of British immigrants came here during that time. They brought British values and traditions. You will see that the new colonists soon gained a sense of citizenship in this land.

Honing Your Skills

Do you find it hard to find meaning in numbers? The Skill Check feature in this chapter shows you how to **Use Statistics to Create Graphs.** This skill is important to your studies because it will help you analyze statistics. The project at the end of the chapter will ask you to use this skill as you examine one group's contribution to Canada's emerging identity.

Think ▶ AHEAD

Brainstorm some ideas about the characteristics that make up the complex Canadian identity. Include aspects of culture, such as language, religion, sports, music, literature, games, government, inventions, symbols, and fashion. Think of examples from your own life. Think of other perspectives. Then, working with a partner, illustrate your ideas in a web diagram. Use words or drawings to show each characteristic.

SKILL CHECK: Use Statistics to Create Graphs

In this chapter, you are investigating the developing character of Canada. Population statistics help us understand the people of a country. You can "see" statistics better by using them to make graphs. Here are three common types.

Line Graphs

Line graphs are useful for showing trends over time.

- Mark the horizontal line in regular intervals, usually in units of time.
- Mark the vertical line at regular intervals to show changes.
- Label both lines.
- Plot the information on a grid.
- Connect the points with a line.

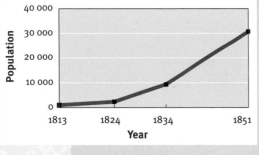

Figure 6.1 The population of York, Upper Canada, 1813–1851. What do these statistics tell you about population growth in York?

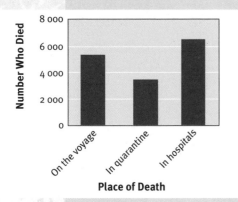

Figure 6.2 Deaths of British immigrants to Canada, 1847. What information can you learn from these statistics? What can you conclude?

Bar Graphs

Bar graphs are useful for comparing two or more sets of data.

- Mark the vertical scale in regular intervals of units.
- Place the bars along the bottom of the horizontal scale.
- To identify the bars, use labels or a colour code.
- If using a colour code, add a legend.

Circle Graphs

Circle, or pie, graphs are useful for comparing the size of parts to a whole.

- Calculate the percentages. Be sure that the total adds up to 100 per cent.
- Divide the percentages proportionately as parts of a circle.
- Add a legend and labels.

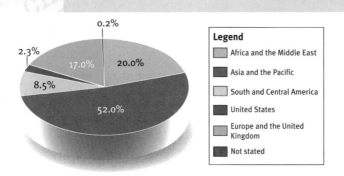

Figure 6.3 Canadian immigration by region, 2002. This graph tells us where immigrants to Canada came from. What can you conclude?

Try It!

Over the last eight months of the War of 1812, the number of British troops in North America increased from 19 477 to 48 163 soldiers. Graph these data. How would this change have affected the outcome of the war?

Rebellion in the Thirteen Colonies

In 1775, a rebellion exploded in Britain's Thirteen Colonies. As you will find out in this section, a huge migration of refugees came north. They flooded Canada with English-speaking newcomers. They changed the face of British North America forever.

Focus

How did revolution in the Thirteen Colonies and the resulting Loyalist migration affect Britain's North American colonies?

Growing Restless

Britain's Thirteen Colonies south of the St. Lawrence River were prosperous. By 1765, however, they were growing restless under British rule. They could trade only with the home country. They had to pay high taxes on British imports. Also, they wanted more control over their own affairs. Matters grew worse in 1774 after Britain passed the Québec Act. The act gave the Ohio Valley to Québec, not the Thirteen Colonies.

In April 1775, the first shots of the War of Independence were fired. The American rebels hoped the Canadiens would join their revolt. With that thought in mind, they marched into Québec. First, they captured Montréal. Then, they moved on to Québec City.

CASE STUDY

Invaders or Liberators?

American rebel soldiers invaded Québec in 1775. They thought the Canadiens would see them as **liberators**. After all, weren't the Canadiens oppressed under British rule, too? What did the Canadiens really think?

- The Québec Act kept New York traders out of the fur trade around the Great Lakes. Whom would the Canadien fur traders and merchants support?
- The *seigneurs* had influence in the government. Whom would they support?
- Most Americans were Protestant. Whom would the Catholic Church support?
- The *habitants* had regained their language and religion rights under the Québec Act. Whom would they support?

The Americans faced fierce resistance. On the last day of 1775, they attacked Québec City. It was a disaster! There was a blinding snowstorm. The rebels got lost in Québec City's maze of narrow streets. They were easy targets for the British and Canadien defenders, who fired on them from the walls. The Americans called off their attack.

Respond

What could the Americans have done to get the people of Québec on their side?

Figure 6.4 Fighting in the streets of Québec City on New Year's Eve, 1775. Local militia (wearing red toques) and British soldiers fire on the Americans, who attempt to scale a wall. Alan Daniels painted this scene 200 years after the battle. What resources can an artist use to find out how events happened?

The invasion of Québec failed. The War of Independence, however, did not. It took many years of fighting. Then Britain recognized the United States of America in 1783.

Historians sometimes like to think about "what if" questions. What do you think: What if the Province of Québec had joined the rebellion? How would our national identity have been different?

> What does the term *British North America* mean? It refers to all British colonies in North America except the Thirteen Colonies.

Citizens Loyal to the King

In 1776, people from many cultures lived in the Thirteen Colonies. Not all of them supported the rebellion. In fact, as many as a third of the people remained loyal to Britain. The **United Empire Loyalists** came from every walk of life. They had many reasons for opposing the war.

- Some did not believe in using violence to settle disputes.
- Some had business ties with the British.
- Some were in military regiments that had fought on the British side.
- Some were enslaved African Americans seeking freedom or a more welcoming society.
- Some were First Nations peoples who had lost their land to Americans.

The American rebels treated the Loyalists as **traitors**. They took away their property and possessions. They beat and jailed them. Sometimes, they painted them with hot tar, covered them with feathers, and paraded them around town.

Many Loyalists fled north, seeking shelter and safety. These **refugees** flooded Canada. They changed the Canadian identity forever.

Loyalists Head to Nova Scotia

During and after the war, almost 40 000 Loyalists migrated to the British colonies. Many travelled by ship to Nova Scotia. They doubled the population of the colony and created many new communities. Britain promised to help the Loyalists with free land and supplies. Some received land, especially those who had fought for Britain. Others did not receive the promised land. Life was difficult for all.

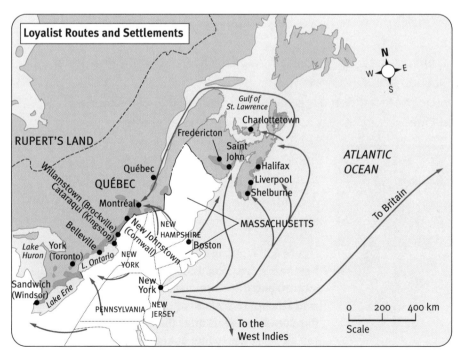

Figure 6.5 The main routes the Loyalists took to British North America, 1783–1791. The shaded areas show where the Loyalists settled. What pattern of settlement can you see? What do you think made these places attractive?

For Black Loyalists, things were even worse. They received less land than the other Loyalists did, and their land was not good for farming. Many worked as tenant farmers. They farmed a plot of land, then they gave half the money from the sale of their crops to the landowners. They faced racism and **discrimination**, too. Despite these hardships, many Black Loyalists stayed. They overcame the challenges in the colony to build a rich heritage in Nova Scotia.

New Colonies

Many Loyalists were unhappy in Nova Scotia. They had endured cruelty and hardship during the war. Some resented that the colonists in Nova Scotia had not suffered. The Loyalists wanted their own colony.

Britain agreed. In 1784, it divided Nova Scotia into two parts. The western portion became New Brunswick. Cape Breton Island became a separate colony, too. Île Saint-Jean was renamed Prince Edward Island.

VOICES ■

Hannah Ingraham (1772–1869)

Hannah Ingraham came to what is now New Brunswick with her family in 1783. She was just 11 years old. Rebel forces had taken her family's farm after her father joined a Loyalist regiment.

66 It was a sad, sick time after we landed in Saint John. We had to live in tents. The government gave them to us, and food too. It was just at the first snow then. The melting snow and rain would soak up into our beds as we lay. ...

We lived in a tent at St. Annes [Ste. Anne's Point, which became Fredericton] until father got a house ready. He went up through our lot till he found a nice fresh spring of water. He stooped down and pulled away the fallen leaves and tasted it. It was very good so there he built his house. 99

Source: Hannah Ingraham, "Reminiscences," in The Women's Canadian Historical Society of Toronto, *Transactions*, No. 11 (1911–1912).

Biography

Rose Fortune (1773–1864)

Rose Fortune was born into slavery in the southern United States. She came to Nova Scotia as an enslaved person with a Loyalist family. She was just 10 years old. The family settled in Annapolis Royal. Here Fortune gained her freedom. In 1825, she started her own business, the Lewis Transfer Company. She carted luggage between the ferry docks and nearby homes and hotels. Later, Fortune became the town's police officer, patrolling the town and wharf. She also joined the **Underground Railroad** to help African Americans escape slavery.

Figure 6.6 Rose Fortune, painted by an unknown artist in the 1820s. In what ways was Fortune an active citizen?

Canada Today

Part of active citizenship is acting to solve world problems, not just local problems. Refugees are people who can no longer live in safety in their own country. They come from countries where people are threatened by war, torture, famine, or persecution. The Loyalists were the first refugees to come to Canada. Canada now accepts thousands of refugees each year. We offer a safe place to build new lives. In return, refugees become active citizens, contributing to the growth and well-being of Canada.

Figure 6.7 Lulzim Azizi (left) and his friend Fehmi Islami, two Kosovar refugees who fled to Canada in 1999. What problems do refugees in Canada face today? How do these problems compare with those the Loyalists faced?

Figure 6.8 *Loyalists Camping on their Way up the St. Lawrence, 1784*, by Charles W. Jeffreys. What does this drawing tell you about the Loyalist experience?

The Loyalists Come to Québec

Loyalists also streamed north into Québec. They crowded into temporary camps. There, they waited for Britain to help them.

Most of the Loyalists did not want to settle in Québec. Its French language and Roman Catholic traditions were unfamiliar to them. All the good land was already taken. The governor of Québec, Sir Frederick Haldimand, agreed to give the newcomers land farther west. He chose land along the upper St. Lawrence River and the north shore of Lake Ontario. In 1784, the first group of Loyalists headed west.

CASE STUDY

Land, Identity, and the First Nations

Having land gives a people a place to live and belong. The First Nations lost much of their traditional land. How did this affect their sense of identity?

Respond

Why was it important for the Mohawk to have land of their own? What effect do you think this would have on their sense of identity? How would it affect their sense of citizenship in Canada?

Tech Link

To learn more about Thayendanegea, open Chapter 6 on your *Voices and Visions* CD-ROM.

About 2000 Loyalists were from the Mohawk Nation, one of the Six Nations of the Iroquois Confederacy. As a reward for helping them in the war, the British had promised the Mohawk land. After the war, though, Britain gave all the land west of the Mississippi River to the Americans. It gave away the land promised to the Mohawk. The Mohawk had been betrayed.

The Mohawk leader was Thayendanegea. (His English name was Joseph Brant.) He demanded that Britain give his people land. In 1776, he expressed the frustration of his people:

The Mohawks have on all occasions shown their zeal and loyalty to the Great King; yet they have been very badly treated by his people. Indeed, it is very hard, when we have let the King's subjects have so much of our lands for so little value. We are tired out in making complaints and getting no redress.

Source: History Television (Canada) website, http://www.historytelevision.ca/chiefs/htmlen/mohawk/ev_haldimand.asp.

Thayendanegea convinced the British to give the Mohawk land along the Grand River, north of Lake Erie. This became the largest Six Nations Reserve. It still exists today.

Figure 6.9 A portrait of Thayendanegea, painted by William Berczy in 1805. Berczy made a sketch of the Six Nations leader when he met him in person. He later turned it into this oil painting. What do you think the artist was trying to show? Would a Mohawk artist try to show the same thing?

A Fair Trade?

The land Haldimand chose for the Loyalists belonged to the Anishinabe [a-nih-shih-NAH-bee] Nation. The governor had bought the land in 1781 and 1783. He paid with some guns and other trade goods. Why did the Anishinabe give up so much land in return for so little?

Like all First Nations, the Anishinabe did not believe that land was something people bought and sold. They believed that everyone should share the land. They may have thought they were simply giving the newcomers permission to use the land. By the time they realized what was happening, though, it was too late.

There may be another explanation. The Anishinabe may have been afraid to say no to the governor. In the United States, First Nations that refused to give up their land had it taken from them by force. Would the British use force, too? It is possible that fear was the reason why First Nations bargained away their land for so little.

In the last chapter, you read about the Royal Proclamation of 1763. It was written to protect First Nations peoples and their lands. How did Haldimand's land deal go against the spirit of the Proclamation?

Figure 6.10 Volunteers handing out bread and blocks of cheese in the arena on the Six Nations Reserve in Ohsweken, Ontario. These are symbolic gifts. They show Britain's gratitude for the Six Nations' loyalty during the American rebellion. Queen Victoria began the annual event in 1863. How might this tradition help nurture a sense of citizenship?

Building a Bilingual Country

Most Loyalists who came to Québec spoke English. They came from colonies with British traditions and customs. In Québec, though, the Canadiens formed the majority. The Loyalists wanted to keep their British heritage. To do so, they needed their own colony and their own institutions.

Britain agreed. In 1791, the Constitutional Act divided Québec in two. The land west of the Ottawa River became Upper Canada (now southern Ontario). East of the river, the old colony of Québec became Lower Canada. Each colony had an elected assembly. The citizens of Québec kept all the rights they had gained from the Québec Act in 1774, including French civil law. This strategy allowed the French and English cultures and languages to co-exist. It was an important step in building a bilingual country.

Upper and Lower Canada

What do the terms *upper* and *lower* mean in the names of the two new colonies? They refer to a position on the St. Lawrence River. Upper Canada is *up*stream, while Lower Canada is *down*stream.

Think It Through

1. In a small group, brainstorm a list of the physical and emotional challenges each of the following would have faced in the British colonies:
   • military Loyalists
   • African American Loyalists
   • First Nations Loyalists
   How might these different challenges affect their perspectives about their new country?

2. Working with your group, create a concept poster or a web diagram that identifies the challenges one group of Loyalists faced. How did your group demonstrate a sense of citizenship? Present your work to the class.

3. What characteristics do you think the Loyalists had? How might these qualities have affected the identity of Canada?

Conflict Renewed: The War of 1812

By 1812, tensions between Britain and the United States had heated up again. War soon broke out. British North America was the battleground. In this section, you will learn how the War of 1812 affected the colonists and the Canadiens.

Why couldn't Britain and the United States get along?

- Britain was at war with France. It stopped Americans from trading with the French.
- The British were kidnapping American sailors to serve in the British navy.
- The British were supporting the First Nations in the struggle for land.
- Some Americans wanted to take over Britain's colonies.

The war began in 1812. The British wondered if they could count on loyalty in British North America. First, many of the English colonists were Americans who had arrived after the Loyalists. They had come for cheap land, not because they were loyal to Britain. They outnumbered the Loyalists four to one. Second, the Atlantic colonies depended on trade with the Americans living along the Atlantic coast. Finally, it had been only about 50 years since the French had lost New France. Would the Canadiens rise up against Britain now?

Focus

What effect did the War of 1812 have on Canada?

VOICES

How did the Americans, the Loyalists, and the First Nations view the War of 1812?

General William Hull led American troops into Upper Canada in July 1812. He said this to Canadians:

> Separated by an immense ocean and an extensive wilderness from Great Britain, you have no participation in her councils, no interest in her conduct. You have felt her tyranny, you have seen her injustice. ... The United States are sufficiently powerful to afford you every security.

Source: D.B. Read, *The Life and Times of Major-General Sir Isaac Brock, K B* (Toronto, 1894), pp. 125–127. Quoted in K.A. MacKirdy et al., *Changing Perspectives in Canadian History*, revised edition (Don Mills, ON: J.M. Dent, 1971), pp. 117–118.

Respond

Do you think the Americans were right to assume that Upper and Lower Canada could be won easily? Consider the quotations on this page and the caption for Figure 6.14 on page 133. Explain your thinking.

John Strachan was a church leader in York (Toronto). He expressed the Loyalists' perspective:

> They can never be victorious while we are united, on the contrary they shall continue daily to receive bloody proofs that a country is never more secure than when defended by its faithful, loyal, and industrious inhabitants.

Source: George W. Spragge, ed., *The John Strachan Letter Book: 1812–1834* (Toronto, 1946), pp. 11–12. Quoted in K.A. MacKirdy et al., *Changing Perspectives in Canadian History*, revised edition (Don Mills, ON: J.M. Dent, 1971), p. 120.

Shawnee [shah-NEE] leader Tecumseh (see the Biography on the next page) called on First Nations peoples to fight on the British side:

> Shall we, without a struggle, give up our homes, our lands, bequeathed to us by the Great Spirit? The graves of our dead and everything that is dear and sacred to us? ... I know you will say with me, Never! Never!

Source: Quoted on the Digital History website, "Native American Voices," http://www.digitalhistory.uh.edu/native_voices/voices_display.cfm?id=36. From H.B. Cushman, *History of the Choctaw, Chickasaw and Natchez Indians* (Greenville, TX: 1899), p. 310.

Reading
STRATEGY

When reading about people who take action, picture yourself in the same situation. Could you be as brave?

Figure 6.11 The Battle of Queenston Heights, painted by a British soldier who was there. General Isaac Brock leads British forces on a charge up the heights. Brock was killed in the battle. His death rallied Canadian citizens to fight against the Americans. Why does the death of a hero inspire people?

Biography

Tecumseh (1768–1813)

Why do the trials of war create strong bonds between allies?

In the War of 1812, Britain needed the help of its First Nations allies to defend its colonies. One of its greatest allies was Tecumseh. He was leader of the Shawnee.

Before the War of 1812, the Americans were taking First Nations land in Ohio. Tecumseh united various First Nations to oppose the Americans. When war broke out, Tecumseh went north to join the British. He led an army of 2000 to 3000 soldiers. It was the largest First Nations army the Great Lakes region had ever seen.

Together, Tecumseh and his friend General Brock won the Battle of Detroit. It was a crucial victory. Tecumseh and his army fought and won many battles. Even so, victory eluded him at Moraviantown in October 1813. In a battle against 3000 American soldiers, the British troops panicked and fled. Tecumseh and 500 First Nations soldiers fought on, but they were hopelessly outnumbered. Tecumseh and many of his soldiers died on the battlefield. Can you think of another example of such active citizenship in Canadian society today?

Brock wrote about his friend after he died. Brock said that "a more … gallant Warrior does not I believe exist." Tecumseh's death was a great blow to the British side.

Respond

What important role did Tecumseh play in the War of 1812? Think in terms of his personal relationships. Consider his abilities as a leader and his successes on the battlefield.

Figure 6.12 A portrait of Tecumseh, painted by Benson John Lossing in 1886. General Brock gave Tecumseh the red sash from his uniform. In turn, Tecumseh gave Brock his beaded belt, which Brock was wearing when he was killed in battle. Why do you think they exchanged these items?

The War Unfolds

 British soldiers, local militia, and First Nations allies fought hard against the invaders. They won many key battles. In April 1813, though, a fleet of American ships in Lake Ontario shot cannon fire at the town of York (now Toronto). American soldiers looted York's shops and houses. They burned down the colony's government building. Britain hit back in August 1814. It invaded Washington, DC, and burned down the US government buildings.

The Impact of the War

The War of 1812 ended in a **deadlock**. The Treaty of Ghent ended the war in December 1814. It required both sides to return any territory they had gained. The two sides agreed to make the 49th parallel of latitude the political boundary from west of the Great Lakes to the Rocky Mountains.

The Americans viewed the war as a triumph over Britain. People of Upper and Lower Canada had the opposite view. For a second time, they had stopped an American attack.

The First Nations could claim no victory. About 15 000 First Nations allies died in the war. This was more than the British and American casualties combined. Further, the Americans refused to create a First Nations state, as Britain had proposed.

Figure 6.13 The stamp created to commemorate Laura Secord. In 1813, Secord overheard that the Americans were planning an attack. Leaving in the middle of the night, she hiked 32 kilometres through swamp and forest to warn an outpost. Countries often make stamps featuring important citizens. In what other ways do we honour key people in our history?

Tech Link

View a re-enactment of a battle from the War of 1812 by opening Chapter 6 on your *Voices and Visions* CD-ROM.

Figure 6.14 *The Battle of Châteauguay, 1813,* by Henri Julien before 1884. In October 1813, 4000 American troops advanced on Montréal. The Canadien force, called the Voltigeurs, met them at Châteauguay. The Canadiens were outnumbered, with only 800 soldiers. Even so, they valiantly fought off the Americans. What effect do you think the war had on how Canadiens felt about the United States?

Think It Through

1. In a small group, brainstorm acts of citizenship that people demonstrate during times of war.

2. The Volunteer Battalion of the Incorporated Militia took part in the Battle of Lundy's Lane on 6 July 1814. Look at the statistics in the table below. SKILLS
   a) Select an appropriate form of graph to present these data.
   b) Produce your graph or graphs.
   c) What conclusions can you make about the battle? Which is the safest rank? Which is the most dangerous? Explain?

3. Wars give us stories and myths that become a part of Canada's identity. Myths are things that people believe and that give them pride. Even so, they are not always true. One American myth is that the United States won the War of 1812. Discuss each of the following myths. Decide whether each is reality. List facts that could be used to prove the history.
   a) The Americans won the War of 1812.
   b) The Canadians won the War of 1812.
   c) The First Nations won the War of 1812.
   d) The War of 1812 bound Canadians together in a common cause.

Rank	Numbers in the Field of Battle	Numbers Killed in the Battle
Officers	33	1
Sergeants	27	3
Drummers	10	0
Rank-and-file soldiers	309	13

Source: The War of 1812 Website, www.warof1812.ca/imuc.htm.

The Great Migration

Focus

How did the flow of immigration after 1815 reinforce the British character of Canada?

After the war, Britain was eager to open up the backwoods to farming. It planned to fill its colonies with people from England, Scotland, Wales, and Ireland. Between 1815 and 1850, more than 800 000 **immigrants** came to the ports of Halifax, Saint John, and Québec City. This influx is called the Great Migration. In this section, you will find out why the Great Migration took place. You will think about how it made the Canadian identity more British.

Why did so many people want to leave Britain to live in the colonies? There were many reasons.

- In Britain, the population was growing rapidly, but jobs were scarce.
- Farmers were being forced off the land.
- Poverty and hunger were common. Ireland suffered a terrible famine, forcing many rural people to flee.
- With peace, ocean travel was now safer.
- The colonies offered free land, new opportunities, and a chance for a better life.

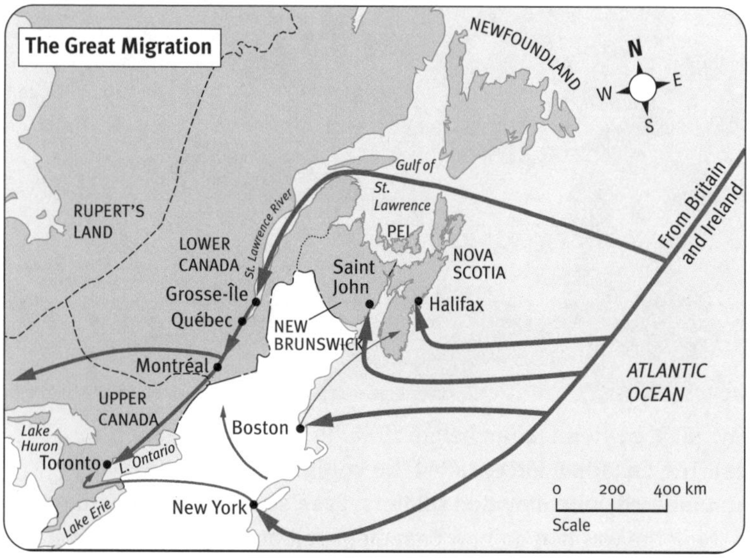

Figure 6.15 The routes taken by immigrants during the Great Migration, 1815–1850. What geographical feature influenced where people made their new homes?

The Great Migration

Canada Today

Does immigration still influence the Canadian identity, as it did during the Great Migration?

Since the Great Migration, there have been many waves of immigration. At first, most immigrants came from Britain. Later waves came from Eastern Europe. Over the past 50 years, the majority of immigrants have come from Asia. Today, Canada is home to people from all over the world. Why do you think people choose to come to Canada?

Figure 6.16 A group of young Canadians. Many of today's young Canadians were born in Asia. Others have parents or grandparents from there. In what ways do you think the immigrant experience today is similar to the immigrant experience during the Great Migration? In what ways is it different?

Coming to the Colonies

Immigrants travelled from Britain to Canada by ship. It was a long journey that lasted for many weeks. For those with money, there were comfortable cabins. Most of the immigrants, though, were poor. They were crowded into the dark and filthy holds below deck, where diseases ran rampant. So many people died on these voyages that they called the boats "coffin ships."

Some of the immigrants stopped in the Maritime colonies. Most, however, continued up the St. Lawrence River to Québec City and Montréal. From there, most newcomers travelled by land to Upper Canada.

VOICES ■

Scottish newlyweds James Rintoul and Annie Smith sailed for Québec City in Upper Canada in 1850. They travelled on the ship *Three Bells*. Rintoul described his first impressions of the city in his diary. What things struck him as different?

66 I saw a beautiful sight. The steeples and towers were glistening in the sun and the roofs of the houses which are all covered with tin. Then the Castle frowning over the town, bristling with cannon. ... We went ashore to see the town and rambled through its streets. It was easy to see that we were in a foreign land. ... The houses were very high and the streets narrow. Many of them were steep in some places. There were long wooden stairs up. We wondered at the immense number of queer looking gigs and carts. ... 99

Source: Rintoul family website, www3.sympatico.ca/david.rintoul/Voyage.htm.

The Terrible Year

At first, about 30 000 immigrants arrived from Britain each year. Two-thirds were from Ireland. Then, in 1847, immigration from Ireland leapt to 100 000. The potato crop had failed. The Irish had nothing to eat. Thousands set out for North America.

A typhus epidemic broke out aboard the ships. Thousands of people died on the voyage to Canada. Thousands more died as the ships waited on the St. Lawrence River at Grosse-Île. It was a **quarantine station**. The newcomers stayed there until doctors were sure they were not bringing diseases into the country. In 1847 alone, 5424 people were buried on Grosse-Île.

Figure 6.17 *The Famished,* by John Falter, 1847. It shows Irish immigrants coming ashore at Grosse-Île. Describe some of the mixed feelings these people might be having as they come ashore.

Pioneer Life

Once they left their ships, the newcomers made their way inland by boat and wagon. When they reached their plot of land, each family faced the same challenge: clearing the dense forest. The rugged environment and harsh climate made it difficult.

VOICES ■

Catherine Parr Trail came to live on a backwoods farm in Upper Canada in 1832. Do you think life here would be harder for women than for men?

66 The women are discontented and unhappy. Few enter with their whole heart into a settler's life. They miss the little domestic comforts they had been used to enjoy; they regret the friends and relations they left in the old country; and they cannot endure the loneliness of the backwoods. 99

Source: Catherine Parr Trail, *Backwoods of Canada*
(London: C. Knight, 1836), p. 105.

Figure 6.18 An early bush farm in Upper Canada, painted by Philip Bainbrigge in 1838. Farmhouses were far from one another. What effect do you think this isolation would have on a pioneer family?

Figure 6.19 A well-established Nova Scotia farm, painted by J.E. Woolford between 1810 and 1820. This farm shows many years of hard work. How does this farm compare with the bush farm in Upper Canada?

VOICES ■

Women worked hard with their husbands, brothers, and fathers in the home and on the farm. William Hutton, a farmer in Upper Canada, described the work his wife and five daughters did. Make a list of the chores the girls carried out. In each case, consider what you do to obtain the same things.

66 Mary milks the cow admirably and drives the horses for me in the barn when I am threshing, and they tread out the grain. She also attends to the young lambs and is most useful in a hundred ways. Frances makes our candles and does the cleaning.

The girls finish their spinning today. ... What they do not require for the house, they will "trade away" for winter dresses, boots, shoes, and a thousand little things which a large family of girls are always requiring. ... Their exertions have been wonderful, from before 5 in the morning till after 7 at night. 99

Source: Beth Light and Alison Prentice, eds. *Pioneer and Gentlewomen of British North America, 1713–1867* (Toronto: New Hogtown Press, 1980), pp. 27–28.

A Very British Colony

The arrival of so many people from Britain changed the identity of the British colonies. The newcomers opened up vast areas for farming. New industries such as logging and mining began to emerge. Towns sprang up to serve the needs of the local community.

People worked as labourers and servants, doctors and teachers, loggers and miners.

The newcomers brought another important change. They brought a British flavour to their new communities. They followed British customs and traditions, played British games, and spoke English.

	1806	1831	1851
Upper Canada	71 000	237 000	952 000
Lower Canada	250 000	553 000	890 000
Nova Scotia	68 000	168 000	277 000
New Brunswick	35 000	94 000	194 000
Prince Edward Island	10 000	30 000	70 000
Newfoundland	27 000	76 000	102 000

Source: Daniel Francis and Sonia Riddoch, *Our Canada: A Social and Political History,* 2nd edition (Toronto: Pippin Publishing, 1995).

Figure 6.20 The population of British North America, 1806–1851. What trends can you identify in this table? Note that these figures do not include the First Nations populations. In 1824, the estimated First Nations population of Upper and Lower Canada was 18 000. This dropped to 12 000 within 20 years.

VOICES AND VISIONS

CASE STUDY

The Underground Railroad

Slavery had been present in New France for many years. Some Loyalists brought enslaved African Americans with them. Then how did British North America become a haven for people escaping slavery?

In 1792, the governor of Upper Canada passed a bill to phase out slavery. In 1833, Britain banned slavery in all its colonies. The British colonies soon became known as a safe **haven**. Word passed among slaves in the southern United States: Canada was the "land of promise."

When my feet first touched the Canada shore I threw myself on the ground, rolled around in the sand, seized handfuls of it and kissed it and danced around, till, in the eyes of several who were present, I passed for a madman.

—Josiah Henson, former slave, 1830

Source: Canada's Digital Collections, "The Underground Railroad: The Hidden Road to Freedom," http://collections.ic.gc.ca/heirloom_series/volume4/264–267.htm.

Respond

Canada became a haven for many former enslaved people. Do you think this role helped form the Canadian identity we know today? Give reasons for your answer.

Many runaway enslaved people fled north via the Underground Railroad. This secret network hid the fugitives by day. "Conductors," or guides, then moved them under cover of darkness to the next "station" on the "railroad." It was dangerous work. Anyone who helped enslaved people escape risked going to jail.

The Underground Railroad helped more than 30 000 former enslaved people reach the British colonies. In 1865, the United States ended slavery. About half of the former enslaved people went back. Thousands stayed, though. They built farms, schools, and churches. They created their own strong communities and their own unique identity.

Figure 6.21 A group of African Americans escaping slavery by coming to Canada on the Underground Railroad. It was painted by Charles T. Webber in 1892. Conductors put into action their belief that all people should be free. They showed a strong sense of citizenship.

Chapter

**Think It ▶
Through**

1. Compare the Loyalist migration with the Great Migration. Use a Venn diagram or a graphic organizer of your own design.

2. Refer to the statistics on population growth in British North America in Figure 6.20 on page 137. [SKILLS]
   a) Select an appropriate form of graph to present these data. Produce your graph.
   b) What conclusions can you make about the growth in population?

c) Do you think the attempt to give Canada a British character succeeded? Why or why not?

3. What effect did the Great Migration have on the developing Canadian identity? Consider how various groups were affected. Create a mind map or write a paragraph to show your answer.

Divided Society

The population grew rapidly in British North America. Tensions grew. In time, these tensions boiled over into armed rebellion. In this section, you will explore the many factors that led people to take that drastic step.

Focus

What factors led to the rebellions in Upper and Lower Canada in 1837?

Government in the Colonies

The Constitutional Act of 1791 gave the British colonies a new form of government. Each colony had its own governor and an elected assembly.

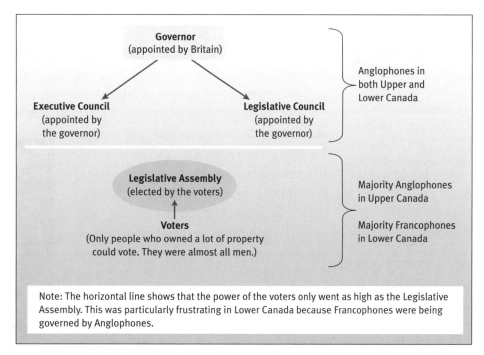

Figure 6.22 The system of government in all the North American colonies. Political leaders in Britain appointed the governors. Whose instructions do you think a governor would be more likely to follow—those of Britain or those of the colonists?

The **Legislative Assembly** was elected, but it had little power. The real power was in the hands of the governor and the two councils. The council members were Anglophone friends and relatives of the governor. In Lower Canada, they were known as the **Château Clique**. In Upper Canada, they were known as the **Family Compact**. They passed laws that favoured their own interests.

Many colonists thought this was unfair. Why was a governor appointed by Britain controlling affairs in Canada? These people called themselves **Reformers**. They demanded change. But year after year, these changes were denied.

Rebellion in Lower Canada

By the 1830s, people were unhappy with their governments in both Upper and Lower Canada. Different groups were angry for different reasons. What were these perspectives? First let's look at the situation in Lower Canada.

Democracy and the Secret Ballot

Today, Canadians have the **secret ballot**. No one knows how individual citizens vote in elections. Why is the secret ballot one of the most important rights in a democracy?

In British North America, voting to elect members of the Assembly took place in public. At the **polling stations**, voters had to announce the name of the person they were voting for. There was no privacy.

Some candidates tried to influence the way people voted. Sometimes, bullies tried to prevent people from voting for rival candidates. **Bribery** was another way to influence voters. Politicians made promises to people or paid people to vote for them. Since voting was public, they always knew if the people they had bribed voted the way they had promised. When people didn't vote the "right" way, thugs would throw old fruit at them or even beat them as they left the polling station. Despite these problems, voting remained public until 1874.

Respond

Imagine you are holding an election to vote for your class rep. Would you be more comfortable voting (a) by secret ballot or (b) by holding up your hand? Why? Use your answer to help explain why the secret ballot is important in a democracy.

Figure 6.23 Kari Vanderkloot, a university student, voting in 2003. If you were voting in an election, would you prefer to announce your vote in public or write it down in secret? Why?

VOTING SCREEN

Reading
STRATEGY

Appreciating historical perspectives can be hard. Look for one that seems familiar. Which Canadians would express a similar view about a current issue?

The Merchants' Perspective: We need more roads and canals to improve our businesses. We want the government to raise taxes so they can make these improvements.

The Château Clique's Perspective: Although we are English, we have earned the right to govern because we have the education and experience. It's our birthright. Besides, we don't want to lose all our privileges.

The Habitants' Perspective: The English Château Clique is overruling our elected representatives! Will the British immigrants start telling us what to do? They are taking what little good farmland is left. And the wheat crop has been doing poorly. What is the government going to do?

The Canadien Professionals' Perspective: The English elite benefit the most in the colony. They tax us so they can get rich! Could a stronger Assembly protect our interests?

The Patriotes' Perspective: The way it is, the governor's friends get the best land and the best jobs. Ordinary people should have more power!

Figure 6.24 Various perspectives of the situation in Lower Canada

Louis-Joseph Papineau led a group of radicals called the *Patriotes*. In 1834, they presented the **Ninety-Two Resolutions** to the Assembly. They called for sweeping reforms. Then they won 75 per cent of the votes in an election. Surely now the governor and Britain would listen to their demands.

The Patriotes waited. Then, in 1837, the British government rejected all of the demands. Papineau travelled throughout the colony urging the Canadiens to take up arms. Fighting broke out in November 1837 at Saint-Denis. The Patriotes were victorious. Nonetheless, British forces overwhelmed the rebels at Saint-Charles. Then they destroyed a rebel force at Saint-Eustache. Papineau fled to the United States. The Patriote uprising had been crushed.

Tech Link

"Un Canadien Errant" was a popular song that recalled the plight of the exiled Patriotes. To read the lyrics, open Chapter 6 on your *Voices and Visions* CD-ROM.

Figure 6.25 A scene from the Battle of Saint-Eustache, painted by Lord Charles Beauclerk in 1840. Outnumbered, the rebels hid in the village church. British troops set the church on fire. Many of the rebels died. Do you think it's fair to attack soldiers hiding in a church? Why or why not?

Figure 6.26 Various perspectives on the situation in Upper Canada

The Farmers' Perspective: The best farmland is given to the Family Compact and the Anglican Church. Then they wait until land values go up so they can sell their land at a profit.

The Merchants' Perspective: The government wants us to trade with Britain. We want to trade with the United States.

The Loyalists' Perspective: We have proven our loyalty to Britain in the War of 1812. We have earned the right to govern ourselves.

The Reformers' Perspective: We want more power for the elected Assembly. The colonies should manage their own affairs.

Rebellion in Upper Canada

Unrest was brewing in Upper Canada, too.

A Scottish immigrant named William Lyon Mackenzie led the Reformers. In 1834, he and a group of Reformers issued the **Seventh Report on Grievances**. It listed their demands. Some of the Reformers decided to take up arms. They would overthrow the government! On 5 December 1837, Mackenzie led about 700 rebels on a march toward Toronto. A few had rifles, but most carried only pikes and pitchforks. At the first clash with government supporters, the rebels turned and fled.

Other violent clashes broke out around the colony. They were quickly put down by British troops. After a few days, the rebellion was over. Like Papineau, Mackenzie fled to the United States.

The Impact of the Rebellions

From a distance, the rebellions in Upper and Lower Canada may seem to be minor events. Only a few hundred people took part.

In reality, though, the rebellions of 1837 had a lasting impact. In Lower Canada, the Francophone colonists felt dreadfully wronged. This feeling would last a long time. In both colonies, it was clear that many people agreed with the goals of the Reformers. Britain had to face the fact that reform was necessary.

Figure 6.27 A historical drawing of the hanging of Reformers Samuel Lount and Peter Matthews in 1838. Lount had blown up a bridge. Matthews had led a small force. Not even an 8000-signature petition could save their lives. What effect do you think these hangings had on the colonists?

Think It Through

Nearly every country in the world goes through a period when people rebel against their government. Most rebels have a strong vision about what their country should be.

a) Were the Reformers and Patriotes responsible citizens? Explain your thinking.

b) What do the rebellions in Upper and Lower Canada tell us about the Canadian character?

c) How has your opinion about Canada changed after learning about the rebellions? Explain.

The Road to Responsible Government

Focus

How did Britain respond to the issues raised by the rebellions?

The Reformers in all of Britain's North American colonies shared one common complaint. The governor and councils did not have to follow the will of the people. In this section, you will see how the British government responded. You will learn how Canada finally achieved **responsible government**.

Lord Durham's Report

The British government decided to find out more about the causes of the rebellions. In 1838, they sent Lord Durham to Canada. He was a wealthy British noble and politician. His job was to find some answers.

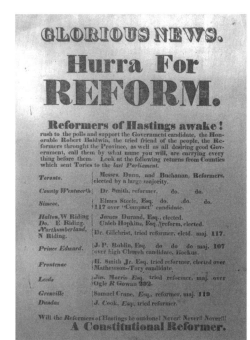

Figure 6.28 An election poster supporting the Reformer Robert Baldwin in the 1841 election. What techniques does the poster use to convince voters to elect Baldwin?

Durham spent five months in Canada. During this time, he tried to understand the issues. When he returned to England, he produced the famous Durham Report. In it, he made two main recommendations for change:

- Unite Upper and Lower Canada into a single colony.
- Grant the colonies responsible government.

The Union of the Canadas

Durham blamed the troubles in Lower Canada on one thing: the conflict between the Canadiens and the English colonists. It was, he said, "two nations warring in the bosom of a single state."

Durham was prejudiced. In his report, he called the Canadiens "a people with no history and no literature." He failed to understand that the Canadiens had a distinct national identity tied to their language and heritage. He failed to credit the Canadiens for their many contributions to Canada.

Durham wanted to get rid of the French language in Québec. He would do this by uniting the two colonies. A British society would gradually absorb the Canadiens. Britain agreed to the plan. In 1841, the Act of Union created a single colony with two provinces. Lower Canada became Canada East; Upper Canada became Canada West. English became the only official language of government. The Canadiens were very unhappy with this arrangement.

Canada Today

If Lord Durham had had his way, the use of French would have petered out. The Canadiens would have gradually become more like their English-speaking neighbours. In the 1840s, the British even tried to send enough Irish immigrants to Canada East to swamp the Canadiens. Instead, the Irish became like their Canadien neighbours. This explains the many unilingual Francophone O'Reillys and Fitzpatricks in Québec today.

How did the Canadien culture survive such blatant attacks? The people fought for their rights, which bound them together in common cause. The phenomenon of "the revenge of the cradle" helped too—after the 1840s, Canada East had one of the highest birth rates in the world. As the population grew, so did a strong sense of nationhood. You can see both in the many vibrant Francophone communities across the country today.

Figure 6.29 École La Vérendrye in Lethbridge, Alberta. Francophone schools like this one are for French-first language students. These schools exist because Franco-Albertans fought for them. How do you think it has affected the Franco-Albertan community to fight together to help their language survive?

Achieving Responsible Government

In responsible government, elected representatives in the Assembly would express the wishes of the citizens. In turn, the governor would follow the wishes of the Assembly. Responsible government would keep the governor's power in check.

At first, British rulers opposed the idea.

Despite this, in 1848 the Reformers won a huge election victory. The people wanted change. The governor, Lord Elgin, chose two Reformers to lead a new government. They were Robert Baldwin and Louis-Hippolyte LaFontaine. Elgin agreed to accept their advice. In 1849, he did just that when he passed the Rebellion Losses Bill even though he did not like the bill. At last, responsible government was a reality.

Think It Through

1. The British government responded to the rebellions with two major policy changes.
   a) Describe them in two paragraphs, or make jot notes about each.
   b) How was each of these changes an honest attempt to resolve the issues?
   c) Do you agree with the strategy in each case? Why or why not?

2. Research Canada's journey to responsible government in the 1840s. Then make a timeline showing Canada's progress.

3. Design an election campaign poster, or write a brief campaign speech. Show the perspective of the Reformers or the Patriotes.

4. How did the War of 1812 and its long-term political aftermath affect the developing Canadian identity? Has your opinion of Canada's identity changed? Explain.

SKILLS Chapter 6 PROJECT

A Visual Presentation on Canadian Identity

In this chapter project, you will create a visual presentation. It will show one group's contribution to Canada's emerging identity. You may want to work on your own, with a partner, or in a small group to complete this project.

Focus

Below are three aspects of Canada's complex identity. Explore one, as it was developing before 1850.

- our First Nations identity
- our Francophone identity
- our British identity

Gather your information by reviewing Chapters 1 to 6. Use the index in this book to find specific information. Extend your research in books or on the Internet. Find some statistics related to your chosen group. In point form, record information that shows how this group contributed to the shaping of the Canadian identity. Decide what subtopics you will use.

Possible Subtopics

- key events (for example, the Battle of Queenston Heights)
- important places (for example, Québec City)
- turning points (for example, suppression of rebel forces at Saint-Eustache)
- leaders and heroes (for example, Tecumseh, LaFontaine)
- ideas (for example, responsible government)
- facts and figures (for example, population data of British colonists)

Your Presentation

After gathering your information, prepare a display that shows what your chosen group contributed to the Canadian identity before 1850.

1. Determine how much text and how many visuals you can use in your display. Plan to include at least one graph.
2. Plan the content of your text boxes and visuals. If you are working in a group, assign specific subtopics to each person. Set deadlines for everyone.
3. Do not copy information. The text should be written in your own words.
4. Use techniques that encourage your viewers to think about the information in your display. You may want to ask questions or pose problems to encourage critical thinking.
5. Give your text boxes titles. Write titles and captions for your visuals.
6. Select the colours and type styles you want to use. Make your work easy to read.
7. Create a title for your project that will attract your viewers' attention.
8. Present your project to the class.
9. After seeing the other presentations, ask yourself how you might have done things differently to create a better presentation.

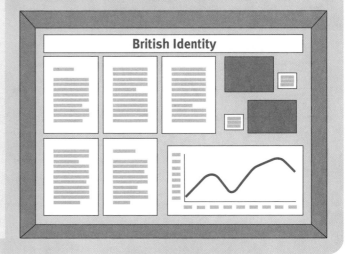

Chapter 7 Creating a New Country

Key CONCEPT ▶ People and Government

Government is the way societies organize themselves to make decisions and get things done. Suppose that someday you share a house with three or four other students. How would you make decisions? Most people would talk to one another and then decide what to do.

How do we make decisions in a community where thousands of people live? Or in a country where millions of people live? Some kind of organization is needed. That organization is called government.

Canada's Government

Today, Canada is a **democracy**. That means that the people hold the power. It is also a **representative democracy**. That means that citizens elect people to make decisions for them. These representatives must make laws in the best interest of the people.

In Canada, the prime minister chooses a small group of these representatives to work with him or her. This group is the Cabinet. It runs the government. Canada has **responsible government** because the Cabinet must answer to the elected representatives.

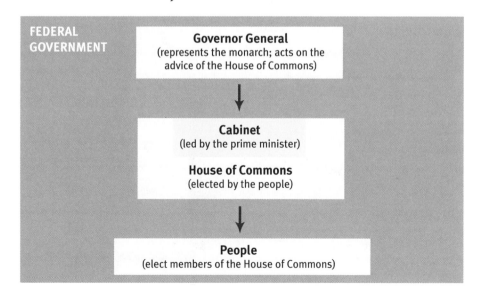

FEDERAL GOVERNMENT

Governor General
(represents the monarch; acts on the advice of the House of Commons)

↓

Cabinet
(led by the prime minister)

House of Commons
(elected by the people)

↓

People
(elect members of the House of Commons)

Chapter 7

Honing Your Skills

Did you ever find out that research information you used was wrong? The Skill Check feature in this chapter shows you how to **Identify Reliable Sources of Information**. This skill is important to your studies because it will help you research effectively. The project at the end of the chapter will ask you to use this skill to research Confederation.

How did we get the system of government that we have? It all began over 150 years ago. As you saw in Chapter 6, the colonies of British North America had achieved responsible government. In the mid-nineteenth century, they began to think about joining together. The new government would have to give a say to all the different regions. It would have to meet the needs of many people. What form of government would work in the new country?

This chapter invites you to discover how and why the colonies created a new country in 1867. This process was called Confederation. You will see the form of government the founders of Confederation chose for Canada.

Think AHEAD

The diagram on the previous page shows the structure of government created in 1867. We still use it today. In Canada, you hear and read about government every day. It's mentioned in school, in the newspapers, on television, and on the Internet. Government affects your daily life, too. As a class, brainstorm what you know about government in Canada. Use the RAIN formula to help you bring out as many ideas as you can.

R Recognize all ideas.
A Aim for understanding.
I Innovate by building on the ideas of others.
N Numerous ideas are best.

Source: Sharon Sterling, *Global Citizens 6 Teacher's Resource* (Toronto: Oxford University Press, 2001).

Skill Check: Identify Reliable Sources of Information

As you investigate which problems Confederation might solve, you will research the topic. How do you find reliable information? The following tips can help guide you. If you're still not sure, ask a librarian or your teacher.

1. **Use books and other print sources with good reputations.**
   - Check the facts in encyclopedias and atlases. These sources give accurate and reliable information.
   - The facts in news stories are usually accurate. The publishers employ people called fact checkers. They check the facts in articles.

2. **Be careful using the Internet.**
   - Look for websites posted by universities, governments, and museums.
   - Avoid websites without an author, a date, or contact information.
   - Be careful with sites hosted by interest groups. Their purpose is to present one point of view.
   - Never trust what you read in chat rooms or blogs (online journals).

3. **Use current sources.**
   - Unless you're using primary sources, use current information.
   - In books, check the copyright date.
   - In newspapers and magazines, check the date of publication.
   - On websites, check when the page was last updated.

4. **Use sources that tell you where they got their information.**
   - Check to see if a source has a bibliography. If so, the author is trying to be accountable.
   - Use sources that provide footnotes for quotes and other information taken from other sources.

5. **Conduct first-hand interviews.**
   - Do you want information about a specific topic? Then talk to someone who has knowledge of that topic.

6. **Assess the information.**
   - Think about whether the source is presenting facts or opinions. Watch out for opinions that pretend to be facts. (See Skill Check: Identify Facts, Opinions, and Bias on page 100.)
   - Look for bias.
   - Avoid sources that present stereotypes or use bad language.
   - Avoid sources with sexist or racist ideas.
   - Avoid sources that contain errors in spelling and grammar.

7. **Have an inquiring mind!**
   - Ask questions as you read. If something doesn't make sense, double-check it.

Try It!

Which of the following would be reliable sources? Why?
- a government document
- a documentary film
- an advertisement
- a televised session of the House of Commons

Conditions for Confederation

By 1858, there were seven colonies in British North America. (See the map below.) Each colony had its own history. Each had a unique identity. The colonies still had many things in common. They were all part of the British Empire. They had parliaments like the one in Britain. First Nations peoples lived in every colony. Except in Canada East, the people were largely of British origin.

Focus

What factors in British North America led to Confederation?

In the 1850s, many colonists began to think about what they had in common. They began to wonder if they could be stronger by uniting as a single country.

In this section, you'll investigate the three main factors that led these colonies to think about union:

- political deadlock in the Province of Canada
- shifting trade relations
- defending British North America

"French Canadian" versus "Québécois"

After Confederation, the term *French Canadian* was used to identify Francophone citizens of Canada. Since the 1960s, however, most Francophone Québeckers prefer *Québécois*. Today, *Québécois* refers to Francophones of Québec origin or residents of Québec. Canada also has Franco-Albertans, Franco-Manitobans, and so on.

Colony	Population
Province of Canada	
Canada West	1 396 000
Canada East	1 112 000
Nova Scotia	331 000
New Brunswick	252 000
Newfoundland	122 000
Prince Edward Island	80 000
British Columbia	
Vancouver Island	51 524

Figure 7.2 The population of the British colonies, 1861. Think about how many people were in each colony. What big concern do you think people in the four eastern colonies had about union?

City	Population
Montréal	107 225
Québec	59 700
Toronto	56 000
St. John's	30 475
Saint John	28 805
Hamilton	26 700

Figure 7.3 The largest cities in the colonies by population, 1861. Do an Internet search or check your atlas to find the current population of each of these cities. How have the rankings changed? What factors might explain these changes?

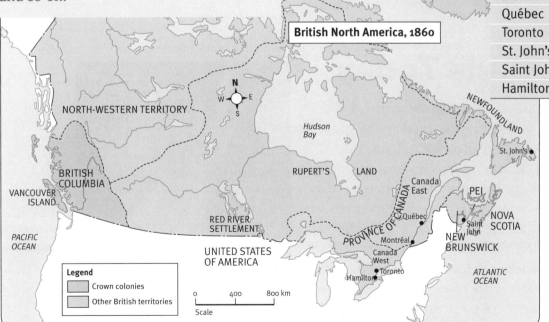

British North America, 1860

Legend
- Crown colonies
- Other British territories

0   400   800 km
Scale

Figure 7.1 The colonies of British North America in 1860. Rupert's Land was not a colony. The Hudson's Bay Company controlled it. Early on, talk of unity focused on the five colonies in the East. Speculate on the reason.

Political Deadlock in the Province of Canada

By the 1850s, people were unhappy with the political system. You learned in Chapter 6 that Upper and Lower Canada were united as a single colony in 1841. It was called the Province of Canada. The English members in Canada West and the Canadien members in Canada East had just one Assembly between them. The English made up a majority. The Canadiens were often outvoted on matters that were very important to them.

Some Canadiens then began to talk about dividing the province of Canada. A moderate Reformer, Louis-Hippolyte La Fontaine, disagreed. He thought he could make the system work for the Canadiens. La Fontaine was a big supporter of French language rights. He often spoke French in the Assembly. He did this even though he was supposed to speak English.

La Fontaine knew that the English were not as united as they seemed. In fact, they were divided into two groups, the Reformers

Who were the parties in the Assembly, and what did they want?

- The **Clear Grit Party** was a group of radical Reformers. They wanted a more democratic government. They were impatient with the demands of the Canadiens. Their leader was George Brown.
- *Les Rouges* (the **Reds**) were a group of Canadien radicals. They wanted independence for Québec. Their leader was Antoine-Aimé Dorion.
- *Les Bleus* (the **Blues**) were a group of conservative, business-oriented Canadiens. They were in favour of co-operating with the English. Their leader was George-Étienne Cartier.
- The **Liberal-Conservatives** were conservative, business-oriented English Canadians. They were in favour of co-operating with the Canadiens. Their leader was John A. Macdonald.
- The **Independents** were individuals who had not joined any party. They voted as they wished.

Figure 7.4 Parties in the Canadian Assembly during the 1850s. The Assembly was ineffective because rival parties could not agree. Which of the parties might have formed alliances? Why?

Canada Today

Baldwin and La Fontaine were partners in a Great Ministry from 1848 to 1851. They made many changes that benefit us today. They began Canada's first public school system. They fought for responsible government. They even made French one of Canada's two official languages. These leaders also started the first **municipal government**. Municipal, or local, governments provide many services that we use every day. For example, they provide the fresh water that pours out of our taps. What are some of the services that your local government provides?

and the Tories (also called the Conservatives). He joined forces with his good friend, the English Reform leader Robert Baldwin. Together, they formed a "Great Ministry" and developed laws to improve life in Canada.

Responsible government gave more power to the elected assemblies. It did not mean that the government ran smoothly, though. Things got worse after the Great Ministry ended. During the 1850s, the Assembly was deadlocked by rivalries between groups. It seemed that no one could agree on anything.

One of the issues that divided the Assembly was **representation by population**—or "rep by pop." Under this system, elected members all represent the same number of people. The larger the population, the more representatives. This was not the system in Canada. People were frustrated.

The Act of Union had given Canada East and Canada West the same number of seats in the Assembly. Earlier, in the 1840s, Canada West had had a smaller population than its neighbour to the east. As a result, people in Canada West were happy to have the same number of seats. Then, in the 1850s, the population of Canada West began to outgrow that of Canada East. Politicians in

Figure 7.5 Calico printing in a British cotton mill, 1834. In the nineteenth century, Britain began to make many products in vast quantities. Why do you think it needed more places to sell goods?

Canada West began to demand more seats. They wanted rep by pop. The Canadien politicians in Canada East objected. The Canadiens would be outnumbered if Canada West got more seats. The fight over rep by pop led to deadlocks in the Assembly. It was time for a change.

Shifting Trade Partners

Political deadlock was not the only reason for change. There were economic reasons, too. Under the mercantile system, the British colonies had helped make Britain rich. For a long time, the furs, timber, wheat, and fish from the colonies boosted Britain's economy. The system helped the colonies do well, too. Britain taxed imports from all countries except its colonies. This made the colonial goods inexpensive and popular in Britain. The colonies could depend on the British to buy their goods.

Then the situation changed.

Britain Lets Go

By 1846, the mercantile system was no longer working. Britain's new **manufacturing** industries were getting bigger. Britain needed to find more places to sell its goods. It decided to reduce or remove taxes on goods imported from all countries. In turn, Britain could sell its goods to more countries. In other words, Britain began **free trade**, or tax-free trade, with all countries. The colonies no longer had an assured market for their goods.

At the same time, the British began to wonder why they were keeping the colonies. Britain no longer needed them for trade. It wanted the colonies to pay for their own governments and defence. In return, Britain would give the colonies greater control over their own affairs.

Global Connections

Global Trade

Today, many businesses in Canada rely on global trade. We **export** goods and services to people in many other countries. This brings money into Canada. It creates jobs. This graph shows Canada's most important export markets in 2003.

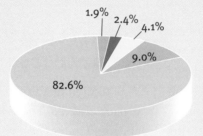

1.9% 2.4% 4.1% 9.0% 82.6%

Legend
- Britain
- Japan
- Other European countries
- Other countries
- United States

Source: Statistics Canada, CANSIM table 228-0003.

Trade with the United States

Britain urged its colonies to look for other markets. The colonies in British North America turned to the United States. In 1854, they signed a trade agreement. It created **reciprocity** between the colonies and the United States. Fish, timber, and grain could flow both ways across the border free of any import taxes.

Reciprocity was good for the colonies. Their businesses did well. However, the Americans decided they weren't getting enough out of the trade deal. After just 10 years, the United States cancelled the deal.

The colonies faced an economic crisis. Now they had lost their special trade relationships with both Britain *and* the United States. What were they to do? For many people, the answer was union. If the colonies were united, they would trade more among themselves.

Good Business Sense

Business leaders had their own reasons for wanting a union of the colonies. They thought it made good business sense. It would give businesses in Canada East and Canada West access to the Maritime ports. They could use these ports to transport their goods overseas. In turn, the Maritime ports would gain more customers. In a united market, the colonies could exchange goods without paying taxes. Building a stronger market at home was one way to make up for the reduction of trade with Britain and the United States.

Figure 7.6 The Great Western Railway station in London, Canada West, in 1858. The large building in the background is the Tecumseh House Hotel. Imagine a small London button manufacturer. Would the workers in the factory welcome the coming of the railway? Would the hotel owner? Why or why not?

CASE STUDY

The Railway Revolution

Better transportation systems make good business sense. Could a desire for better transport also help create a country?

Respond

Other forms of travel at the time were the canoe, steamboat, stagecoach, wagon and team, saddle horse, and sleigh. What are the benefits and drawbacks of the railway compared with those of these forms of transportation?

In the mid-nineteenth century, a railway boom was taking place in British North America. "The days of stagecoaches have come to an end," boasted one newspaper, "and everywhere is to be heard the snorting of the iron horse, and the shrill blast of the steam whistle." By 1861, more than 3000 kilometres of railway track stretched across the colonies.

Before railways, geography had kept the colonies isolated. Then the railway came. Farmers could get their crops to market. Tracks connected towns and cities from east to west. Businesses could move their goods quickly and easily.

Businesses wanted even more railway track. People began to talk about building a railway linking Canada West with Halifax. The project would cost a lot of money. It could only go ahead if the colonies were united. Then all the colonies could share the cost.

Defending British North America

The end of the reciprocity trade deal brought change. It soured relations between the colonies and their southern neighbour. Colonists worried that the United States might send its mighty armies north.

In 1861, civil war broke out in the United States. It was the northern states versus the southern states. The two main issues were slavery and the power of the states to make their own laws. Most of the colonists in British North America opposed slavery. They supported the North. Britain's textile industry, however, depended on cotton from the southern plantations that enslaved African Americans. It seemed that Britain was supporting the South. As a result, the North looked on Britain *and* its colonies with suspicion. This concerned the colonists in Canada. If the North won the war, would the United States turn its mighty

army north? When the North did win the war in 1865, some Americans wanted to do just that. They wanted to punish Britain for supporting the South. Other Americans wanted to take over the colonies for another reason. They believed in **Manifest Destiny**. They thought it was the natural right of the United States to control all of North America.

The colonists feared the United States. In union, though, perhaps the colonies could protect themselves better. It was one more good reason to think about union.

The colonists had to think about another defence issue, too. The Fenians were a group of Irish Americans. They wanted Ireland to be freed from British rule. In 1866, Fenians attacked some border towns in the British colonies. They thought this would force Britain to free Ireland. It didn't work. However, these events made the colonists even more nervous about the security of their borders.

Figure 7.7 A grand review of the armies after the Civil War, Washington, DC, 1865. When the war ended, the United States suddenly had a large and powerful army with nothing to do. Did the colonists have good reason to worry about an American invasion? Why or why not?

CASE STUDY

Choosing a Capital

Have you ever wondered why Canada's capital isn't one of our big cities?

Every country has a capital city. It is the centre of government. In the 1850s, no one could agree where the capital should be. They even thought of switching the capital! It would be Toronto for two years, and then Québec City for the next two.

In 1857, the Assembly asked Queen Victoria to choose the capital. To everyone's surprise, she chose a small logging town called Bytown. (It was later renamed Ottawa.) Bytown was on the border between Canada East and Canada West.

Why would the queen choose such an out-of-the-way place? Location! Ottawa was located where three rivers met. This meant people could get there easily by water. It was right between Canada East and Canada West, too. This made it a good choice for both French and English Canadians. Most important, though, was Ottawa's location relative to the US border. This location made it less vulnerable to attack. On 31 December 1857, Ottawa became the capital of Canada.

Respond

Look at an atlas map of Canada. Why was Ottawa more secure than Québec City, Montréal, or Toronto? If you could choose today, where would you put the capital city of Canada? Give reasons for your choice.

Figure 7.8 The Parliament Buildings under construction in Ottawa, 1863. Most of these were destroyed by fire in 1916. The Parliament Buildings you see in Ottawa replaced the originals. What are the advantages of being the capital city of a country?

Chapter 7

Think It ▶ Through

1. Choose any two facts from this section and find reliable sources to confirm that they are true. List the two sources you used. **SKILLS**

2. a) Make a chart to record information about the factors that led colonists to think about union. Here is one way you could organize your ideas. Was any one factor more important than the others?

b) Imagine you are a colonist in favour of union. Write a letter to the editor of the *Novascotian* newspaper. Explain your reasons for supporting union.

Alternatively, imagine you are a colonial artist in favour of union. Create a series of colour sketches. They should show your reasons for supporting union.

Factor	How It Encouraged Confederation

Confederation and the Maritime Colonies

The Maritime colonies had little in common with the Province of Canada. Geography kept them far from the large, inland population. The Maritime colonists made a living from the sea. Many fished for a living. Others traded with other countries. The goods leaving Maritime ports were bound for Britain, the United States, and the Caribbean.

In this section, you'll learn about the Golden Age of the Maritimes. You'll also learn some Maritime colonists' opinions about union.

Focus

To what extent was Confederation an attempt to strengthen the Maritime colonies?

The Golden Age of the Maritimes

The years between 1840 and 1870 were a "Golden Age" for the Maritime colonies. It was the age of wind, wood, and sail. Maritime shipbuilders were respected for the wooden sailing ships they made. British North America had the fourth-largest shipping fleet in the world. Only Britain, the United States, and Norway had bigger fleets. Of these ships, 70 per cent were built in the Maritimes. It's no wonder that shipbuilding came to symbolize the Maritimes.

Facts about the Maritime Colonies

New Brunswick	Prince Edward Island
• economy: forestry and fishing • most important city: Saint John • famous for its wooden sailing ships • Acadians in the north • largest group of colonists: the Irish	• economy: fishing and farming (fertile soil) • most important city: Charlottetown • no bridges to the mainland • the smallest colony in both area and population
Nova Scotia	**Newfoundland**
• economy: fishing • most important city: Halifax (naval centre) • land good for farming: 10 per cent • trade with colonies in the Caribbean • largest group of colonists: the Scots • about 1500 Mi'kmaq [MIG-mah]	• economy: fishing (exported to Britain) and seal hunting • most important city: St. John's • land good for farming: none • isolated from the other colonies • very close ties to Britain

Fish, lumber, and grain were major exports. Coal mining was about to make Nova Scotia one of the largest coal producers in the world. The economy of the Maritimes was growing.

Benefits Not for All

The eastern colonies were growing. There were the first peoples, the Mi'kmaq and the Maliseet [MAL-ih-seet] who lived throughout the region. There were Scottish immigrants in Cape Breton. There were the Acadians, Loyalists, and Irish immigrants in New Brunswick. There were Black Loyalists and German immigrants in Nova Scotia.

The mid-nineteenth century was not a golden age for all these people. The Mi'kmaq and Maliseet peoples did not share in the economic benefits. Many First Nations signed treaties and were assigned limited reserve lands. Much of this land was not good for farming. The natural resources on which the First Nations made a living were disappearing. It was not a good time for Black Loyalists, either. They experienced racism and discrimination. And while exports in timber were strong, the workers on the lumber gangs endured many hardships in the backwoods. How would those not enjoying the prosperity feel about the "Golden Age"?

Most people in the Maritimes, though, did well. For them, the mid-nineteenth century was truly a Golden Age. Would union make the Maritimes stronger—or weaker?

Would Union Help or Hinder?

Many people opposed union because they thought it would end the good times. They wanted to expand their trade with Britain and the United States, not Canada.

People who supported union saw that the world was changing. New technologies based on coal, iron, and steel threatened to end the age of wood, wind, and sail. Union would give them access to the bigger economies of the Canadian provinces. In time, supporters thought, trade within the union would grow.

The proposed railway was very attractive. It would be good for business. Further, if there were an American invasion, the proposed railway could move in troops to help fight the Americans off.

Reading
STRATEGY

To remember a list of important names, try this. Make a "word" out of the first letter of each name. For example, you could use PNNN to help you remember the names of the Maritime colonies.

Figure 7.9 The tall ship *Marco Polo*, built by Smith Shipbuilding of Saint John and launched in 1851. (John Lars Johnson painted this image about 1930.) The *Marco Polo* was described as the fastest ship in the world. Who would benefit from a strong shipbuilding industry in the Maritimes?

Biography

Joseph Howe (1804–1873)

Joseph Howe was the leading politician in Nova Scotia in the Confederation period. When he was just 23 years old, Howe bought a Halifax newspaper called the *Novascotian*. Once, he published a letter that said the government was stealing from the people. He was arrested and put on trial. Howe argued that a newspaper had to be free to criticize the government. The judge agreed. Howe went free. He became a popular hero in the colony.

In 1836, Howe was elected to the Assembly. He was the leader of the Reform party. He and the Reformers helped bring responsible government to Nova Scotia. They did so with fewer struggles than the Canadians did.

Howe was fiercely loyal to Nova Scotia. He spoke out against union with Canada. He believed Confederation favoured Canada at the expense of the Maritime colonies. With his newspaper, Howe made his views well known. Howe became a hero for his defence of the colony.

Respond

A Nova Scotian would probably say that Howe showed the qualities of a great citizen. Would a colonist in Canada West agree? Explain your opinion.

Figure 7.10 A photograph of Joseph Howe, taken about 1871. Howe called Confederation the "Botheration Scheme." In other words, he thought it would be a lot of trouble, with little benefit to Maritimers. Howe was ahead of his time. Think of a modern advertisement that uses humour to get a message across. Is it effective?

Think It Through

1. a) What were the reasons that people in the Maritime colonies began to consider union with Canada? Make a chart to record this information. Here is one way you could organize your ideas.

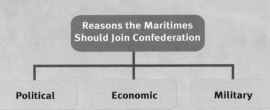

   b) Make a similar chart titled "Reasons the Maritimes should *not* join Confederation."

   c) Decide whether Confederation would be the best choice or not.

2. Write a speech or create a poster about the Maritime colonies joining Confederation. To promote union, show how it would strengthen the colonies. To oppose union, show how it would weaken the colonies.

Confederation Discussions

Not everyone in British North America liked the idea of Confederation. Politicians had a lot of work to do. They had to work out a deal that everyone could accept. In this section, you'll see how deadlock was finally broken. You'll hear different points of view about Confederation. You'll discover what each colony decided and why.

Focus

How was Confederation finally achieved?

Breaking the Deadlock

As you saw earlier in this chapter, political deadlock was making it hard to govern in Canada. Then, in 1864, there was a breakthrough. George Brown, leader of the Clear Grits, convinced his party to join a coalition. They would vote with the Liberal-Conservatives and Les Bleus (the conservative party of the Canadiens).

In return, Brown wanted these two parties to support a plan that he had—a plan to unite all the colonies. Brown proposed **federalism**. Each colony would keep its own government to run its own affairs. A central government would look after matters that affected the whole union. This arrangement would reduce concern in the Maritimes that central Canada would control their affairs. It was a good plan for Canada East and Canada West, too. If they each had their own government, it would break the long-running political deadlock.

Federalism was well suited to British North America, with its scattered colonies. The Liberal-Conservatives and Les Bleus agreed to Brown's idea.

The Talks Heat Up

In 1864, delegates from New Brunswick, Nova Scotia, and Prince Edward Island were going to meet in Charlottetown. They wanted to talk about a union of *their* three colonies. The politicians in Canada asked to be invited. The Maritime leaders listened to their plan to unite all four colonies. They agreed to meet again.

1. John A. Macdonald, leader of the Liberal-Conservative Party in Canada West
2. George-Étienne Cartier, leader of Les Bleus in Canada East
3. George Brown, leader of the Clear Grits in Canada West
4. Charles Tupper, premier of Nova Scotia
5. Leonard Tilley, premier of New Brunswick
6. J.H. Gray, premier of Prince Edward Island

Figure 7.11 A charcoal sketch of the founders of Confederation. These political leaders attended the conferences in 1864. In 1883, the government asked Robert Harris to portray the group as they had looked in 1864. Some had died. The rest were older. Harris worked from photographs and interviews with those who had been there. How do you think the process affected the accuracy of his work?

A month later, the founders all gathered at Québec City. For two weeks, they argued. They all tried to persuade the others to see things their way. Then they found ways to **compromise**—everyone gave up a little to get an agreement they could all live with. They finally reached **consensus**. The delegates had drafted the Seventy-Two Resolutions. These were the foundations for a new country and a new government. First, though, the colonial assemblies had to agree.

The Great Debate

Now the great debate began. Politicians and ordinary citizens alike talked about union. Families talked about it at the kitchen table. Neighbours debated it across the farm fence. People stopped to express a point of view at the general store. In the end, though, the decision was in the hands of the politicians.

Tech Link

To see a photo of the provincial delegates to the Québec Conference, open Chapter 7 on your *Voices and Visions* CD-ROM.

VOICES ■

Some politicians supported the idea of union. Others did not. Here are opinions from five leading politicians of the day.

❝It is said that the Canadians have outgrown their Constitution. Well, if they have, what of that? If they are in trouble, let them get out of it; but don't let them involve us in distractions with which we have nothing to do. Are not the Canadians always in trouble?❞

—Joseph Howe, Nova Scotia

Source: *Halifax Morning Chronicle*, 11 January 1865.

❝If union were attained, we would form a political nationality with which neither the national origin, nor the religion of any individual, would interfere.❞

—George-Étienne Cartier, Canada East

Source: Parliamentary Debates on the Subject of the Confederation of the British North American Provinces (Québec, 1865) pp. 59–61. Quoted in K.A. MacKirdy et al., *Changing Perspectives in Canadian History*, revised edition (Don Mills, ON: J.M. Dent, 1971), p. 214.

❝We would be such a small portion of the Confederacy, our voice would not be heard in it. We would be the next thing to nothing. Are we then going to surrender our rights and liberties?❞

—Cornelius Howatt, Prince Edward Island

Source: *The Charlottetown Examiner*, 27 August 1866. Quoted in Paul W. Bennett and Cornelius J. Jaenen, *Emerging Identities*, (Scarborough: Prentice Hall, 1986), p. 252.

❝The dangers that have arisen from this [American] system we will avoid if we can agree upon forming a strong central government. If we can only obtain that object—a vigorous general government—we shall not be New Brunswickers, nor Nova Scotians, nor Canadians, but British Americans, under the sway of the British Sovereign.❞

—John A. Macdonald, Canada West

Source: Edward Whelan, comp., *The Union of the British Provinces* (Toronto, 1927), pp. 29–30. Quoted in K.A. MacKirdy et al., *Changing Perspectives in Canadian History*, revised edition (Don Mills, ON: J.M. Dent, 1971), p. 212.

❝I oppose Confederation because I foresee innumerable difficulties with the joint powers given to the local and general governments in several areas. These conflicts will always be resolved in favour of the general government.❞

—Jean-Baptiste-Éric Dorion, Canada East

Source: Philippe Sylvain, "Jean-Baptiste-Éric Dorion," *Dictionnaire biographique du Canada*, Vol. IX. (Québec, Presses de l'Université Laval, 1977), p.235. Quoted on http://www.collectionscanada.ca/confederation/h18-2322-e.html.

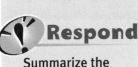

Respond

Summarize the arguments listed here for and against Confederation. Which is most convincing? Why? Do some research to find another opinion about the issue. Don't forget to judge your sources carefully. SKILLS

What the Colonies Decided

The Province of Canada

Most of the people in Canada West were in favour of union. This was not the case in Canada East. Many Canadiens worried that English Canadians would control the new country. George-Étienne Cartier disagreed. He believed that federalism would give the Canadiens control over matters that affected them directly. Francophones received promises that their language and other rights would be respected. Section 93 of the BNA Act gave the provinces control over education. The vote passed 91 in favour, 33 against.

Reading
STRATEGY

Try taking turns reading paragraphs out loud with a partner. After each partner reads, the other partner describes what he or she heard.

New Brunswick

Many people in New Brunswick worried that the larger Canadian colonies would dominate the union. At first, the Assembly voted against the idea. Then Britain put pressure on New Brunswick to accept the deal. The promise of a railway appealed to many colonists, too. New Brunswick politicians changed their minds. They voted to support union.

Nova Scotia

Joseph Howe worried that Nova Scotia would have little influence in the new country. He argued that the people of Nova Scotia would have to pay higher taxes, but that the money would be spent elsewhere. On the other hand, union meant Nova Scotia would get a railway. In the end, Nova Scotia voted to join union, too.

Prince Edward Island

This island colony was isolated from the other colonies. People thought that Prince Edward Island was too small. It would be swamped by the other colonies. Prince Edward Island did not join Confederation until 1873.

Newfoundland

Newfoundland had little in common with the other colonies. The people did not think they would have much influence in such a distant government. They were more interested in their ties to Britain. Newfoundland and Labrador stayed out of Confederation until 1949.

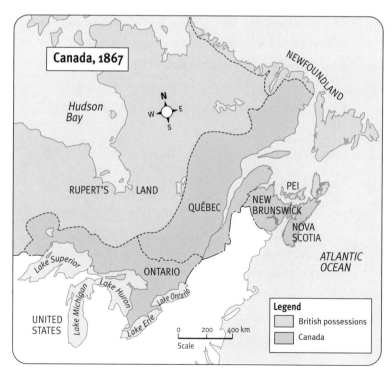

Figure 7.12 Canada and its first four provinces, 1867. In that year, Nova Scotia, New Brunswick, Canada East, and Canada West formed a union. Look at a modern political map of Canada. Compare Canada's original size and shape with its size and shape today.

Working Together

The man who argued, cajoled, and finally convinced politicians across the colonies to join in Confederation was John A. Macdonald. He believed that Canada had to be a partnership between Canadiens and English Canadians. To make this happen, he formed an alliance with George-Étienne Cartier from Canada East.

Union was George Brown's idea. Macdonald, however, was the one who led the campaign at every step.

He was the unofficial "architect" of Confederation at the early discussions in Charlottetown and Québec. At the London Conference in 1866, he headed the meeting that drew up the British North America Act (also called the BNA Act). In fact, Macdonald wrote much of the BNA Act himself.

Tech Link

To see a painting of the young John A. Macdonald, open Chapter 7 on your *Voices and Visions* CD-ROM.

The new country's name, Canada, came from the Haudenosaunee [hah-duh-nuh-SAH-nee] word for village: *kanata*. Many people are proud that our country's name has roots in the language of one of the First Peoples. Why might they hold that opinion?

Biography

George-Étienne Cartier (1814–1873)

George-Étienne Cartier was the leading Québec politician of the Confederation era. He and John A. Macdonald worked tirelessly to achieve their shared vision. After Cartier's death, Macdonald said, "Cartier was bold as a lion. He was just the man I wanted. Without him, Confederation would not have been carried."

The Cartier family had been in Lower Canada for more than 200 years. As a young and fiery lawyer, Cartier had fought with the Patriotes during the rebellion of 1837–1838. After exile in the United States, he returned to Montréal. There he began a career as a lawyer and railway promoter. Cartier won election to the Assembly in 1848. He worked many long hours to adapt the French civil code to Canada East. The civil code is still used in Québec today.

Cartier spoke passionately in the great Confederation debates in 1865. "We must either have a confederation of British North America or be absorbed by the American union." He knew, however, that union might be disastrous for the Canadiens. He and another moderate, Étienne-Pascal Taché, fought to achieve the right compromises. Cartier and Taché worked tirelessly. They convinced the Canadiens to give the new scheme a chance.

Cartier's career reminds us that citizens of different languages and cultures can work together to make great things happen.

Respond

What qualities of citizenship did Cartier have? Do Canadians still value these qualities today?

Dawn of a Dominion

July 1, 1867, saw the creation of a new country: the Dominion of Canada. Citizens

celebrated together in many communities across the country. At midnight, church bells began ringing. Bonfires lit up the night skies. Cannons boomed. Soldiers fired rifle salutes. British naval ships in Halifax Harbour discharged their guns. When daylight broke, people took to the streets. People waved flags. Crowds cheered. Then, at 11 o'clock in the morning, mayors and officials in towns and villages across the country read a proclamation from Queen Victoria. Canada was now a country.

Figure 7.13 Young Canadians in Vancouver celebrate their country on Canada Day. How do citizens in your community celebrate Canada Day?

Think It Through

1. Imagine it is 1 July 1867. Design a poster to celebrate the birth of Canada. Your poster should include symbols that reflect the new country's identity. Consider what various groups would find important about the new country. Alternatively, write lyrics for a rap song that tells the story of the birth of the country.

2. John A. Macdonald was one of the top 10 nominees for the 2004 CBC contest *The Greatest Canadian*. Do some research about Canada's first prime minister. Why do many Canadians admire him? Did he have faults? Discuss this statement: Politicians should be perfect. SKILLS

The Structure of Canadian Government

The founders of Confederation made many compromises. What decisions did they make? In this section, we'll look at how those decisions laid the foundation for Canada today.

Focus

What did Confederation achieve for the Canadian system of government?

Making It Official

In 1867, the British Parliament passed the BNA Act. It was official: the Dominion of Canada was a country. Britain still controlled defence and foreign affairs. Canada remained part of the British Empire. The British monarch was Canada's head of state. A Governor General would represent the monarch in Canada. Since 1935, he or she has been chosen by the prime minister.

Parliament was divided into two parts. There was an elected House of Commons and an appointed Senate. The number of seats a province had in the House of Commons was based on rep by pop. Therefore, Ontario and Québec had more representation. Senate seats were based on region. The senate would give the less populated provinces a larger voice in government. It would also protect the rights of minorities. It was the House of Commons, however, that held the real power.

A Federal System

The BNA Act called for a **federal system** of government. This created two levels of government. The central government had power over matters affecting the whole country. The provincial governments had power over local and regional matters.

Identity

Peace, Order, and Good Government

Why did the founders of Confederation divide the powers the way they did? The provinces wanted to retain their unique identities. The founders, however, had just witnessed the Civil War in the United States. In part, this war had been a fight about who should have more power: the states or the central government.

The founders of Confederation did not want a civil war in Canada. They chose to have a strong central government. The BNA Act states that the federal government has the power to make laws for the "peace, order, and good government" of Canada. This phrase has become part of the Canadian identity.

Look in the chart below to see what the Founders of Confederation did about **residual powers**. These are the powers over things that no one knew about in 1867. They include things such as telephones, airplanes, and the Internet.

Respond

Brainstorm a list of things that exist today that did not exist in 1867. Then, working in a small group, decide which level of government you think should control each one. Give reasons to support your decisions.

Federal Powers	Provincial Powers
• defence • the post office • trade and commerce • weights and measures • currency and coinage • taxation • navigation • fisheries • copyright • banking • First Nations • criminal law • naturalization • marriage and divorce • residual powers • the power to cancel any provincial laws that went beyond the bounds of provincial power	• property and civil rights • education • local works • highways • hospitals • municipalities • courts • provincial and local police

Shared Powers
• agriculture • immigration

Figure 7.14 The powers the federal and provincial governments were granted by the BNA Act. In what ways could the provincial powers help provinces maintain their unique identities? If you were to reassign any powers, which would you change? Why?

A Limited Democracy

In 1867, Canada was a democracy—to a degree. Who had the vote in 1867? Only citizens over the age of 21 who owned property or rented large amounts of property had the vote. Married women could not vote, and very few single women owned property. Neither did various visible minorities, farm labourers, or unskilled workers. Neither did First Nations, Métis, or Inuit. In all, only 11 per cent of the population had the vote.

Today, all Canadian citizens aged 18 and older can vote.

Canada Today

The decisions that went into the BNA Act have strongly influenced what Canada has become. For example, the BNA Act made education a provincial responsibility. Besides Québec, the provinces used this power to deny the right to instruction in French. As a result, many Francophones did not receive their schooling in French until recently. How would this affect the number of Francophones across Canada today?

Not Included

The Canadiens and English Canadians far outnumbered the First Nations peoples. Should the politicians have consulted the First Nations about Confederation? The idea probably didn't even cross their minds. Even so, the results very seriously affected First Nations. Section 91(24) of the BNA Act gives the federal government responsibility over "Indians, and Lands reserved for the Indians." How had the relationship between the new Canadians and the First Nations changed since first contact?

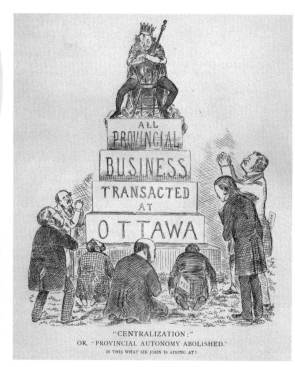

Figure 7.15 A political cartoon about the relationship between the federal and provincial governments, published in a collection in 1886. John A. Macdonald is shown as a king surrounded by the provinces. What is the cartoonist saying about federal-provincial relations? Do you think this message holds true in Canada today? Explain.

Think It Through

1. Choose one decision that the Founders of Confederation made. In a paragraph or brief speech, describe how it affects your Canada.

2. Recall the Iroquois Confederacy, which you read about on page 20. In your opinion, was this nation more or less democratic than Canada in 1867? Give reasons for your answer as jot notes or a paragraph.

3. Voting is the responsibility of all adult citizens. What do you think the voting age should be? Working with a small group, list the reasons for your choice. Give evidence to support your answer. Then, as a class, try to reach a consensus.

4. To what extent was Confederation an attempt to solve existing problems and lay a foundation for a new country?

Chapter 7 PROJECT   Researching Confederation

Confederation was a defining moment in Canadian history. Therefore, there is a lot of information about this subject. This chapter project challenges you to use your research skills. Your task is to find reliable sources of information about the problems that Confederation was meant to solve.

Focus

Look for information on Confederation in the library or on the Internet. Use Skill Check: Identify Reliable Sources of Information on page 148 to guide you. Find as many of the following types of sources as you can.

- **Primary sources.** Speeches, letters, newspapers, the BNA Act, photographs, and artwork.
- **Secondary sources.** Canadian history books, textbooks, and political biographies.
- **Canadian Encyclopedias.**
- **Atlases.** Check for Confederation-era maps. Try the *National Atlas of Canada* website.

Recording Your Sources

After you find your information, record your sources so you can back up your research.

Use a record sheet like the ones shown at the bottom of the page. You can use the given examples to guide you.

Sharing Your Sources

After you have recorded your sources, display your record sheets on a class bulletin board. Look over the other record sheets. Record the details of two sources of information you missed. Find them in the library or on the Internet.

Drawing Conclusions

How much information on Confederation is available? What problems does this create?

Making Recommendations

Choose two sources of information on Confederation that you would recommend to the class. For each one, explain why you believe it is a reliable source. Explain your recommendations to a small group or in written form. How could you find more reliable sources next time?

Figure 7.16 A chart to help you keep track of books.

Author	Title	City	Publisher	Year	Page Nos.
Alfred Duclos De Celles	La Fontaine et son temps	Montréal	Librairie Beuchemin, limitée	1912	24–26

Figure 7.17 A chart to help you keep track of magazines.

Author	Article Title	Magazine Title	Volume or Issue Nos.	Date	Page Nos.
Dan Palmer	His Legacy Lives On	Edmonton Sun	–	12 Nov. 2004	A1

Figure 7.18 A chart to help you keep track of websites.

Web Address	Organization	Article Title	Date Updated or Copyright Date
http://www.cbc.ca/greatest/top_ten/nominee/macdonald-john.html	CBC	Sir John A. Macdonald	2004

Part 2

At the time of Confederation, conditions in Canada were not very good for many Canadians. How did things improve? People like Nellie McClung took action. Nellie McClung was an active citizen.

As a journalist, McClung saw many problems in early twentieth-century Canadian society. She started telling people about them. Women could not vote. They earned lower pay than men did, and many worked in dreadful conditions. They had few property rights, and women were not allowed to hold high office because, by law, they were not considered "persons." Would McClung stand for this? No. She and four other Alberta women formed the "Famous Five" to fight for a woman's right to be recognized as an equal citizen.

In this unit, you will learn about the history of our country after Confederation. You will meet many people who worked hard to change Canada for the better. You'll meet the Métis, who fought to have their rights recognized. You'll meet the many immigrants who travelled by sea, by rail, and by ox cart to start a new life on the Prairies. You'll meet the North West Mounted Police, Chinese railway workers, First Nations leaders, politicians, soldiers, and many more. Canadians from all walks of life have—in their own way—helped make the Canada you know today. What do you see as your role as an active citizen in your Canada?

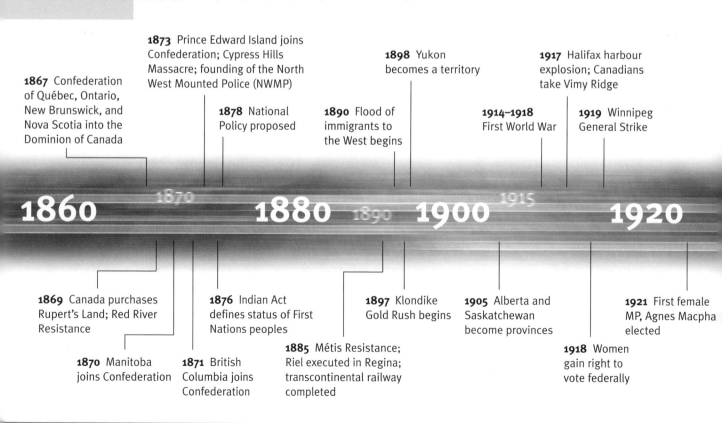

1867 Confederation of Québec, Ontario, New Brunswick, and Nova Scotia into the Dominion of Canada

1873 Prince Edward Island joins Confederation; Cypress Hills Massacre; founding of the North West Mounted Police (NWMP)

1878 National Policy proposed

1890 Flood of immigrants to the West begins

1898 Yukon becomes a territory

1914–1918 First World War

1917 Halifax harbour explosion; Canadians take Vimy Ridge

1919 Winnipeg General Strike

1860   1880   1900   1920

1869 Canada purchases Rupert's Land; Red River Resistance

1870 Manitoba joins Confederation

1871 British Columbia joins Confederation

1876 Indian Act defines status of First Nations peoples

1885 Métis Resistance; Riel executed in Regina; transcontinental railway completed

1897 Klondike Gold Rush begins

1905 Alberta and Saskatchewan become provinces

1918 Women gain right to vote federally

1921 First female MP, Agnes Macpha elected

Active Citizenship Project Two

Do active citizens work alone? Sometimes. In other instances, people work together, as did Nellie McClung and the Famous Five.

Consider what you might do as a class to improve your small corner of Canada. With your classmates, come up with an idea for a community improvement project. Here are a few possibilities:

- cleaning up a local park or stream bed
- conducting a petition and campaign to put in a crosswalk or speed bump to improve road safety
- creating an educational video or audio tape about an event in local history
- advocate for the rights of others

With your class, work together to plan a community project. Your plan should

- describe the purpose of your project
- list all required tools, equipment, or materials
- state any permission you would need to get for anything involving private or public property
- list experts you might need to consult for advice
- list media you would like to inform of your project

Later in your course of study, you will have a chance to put this plan, or a similar one, into action.

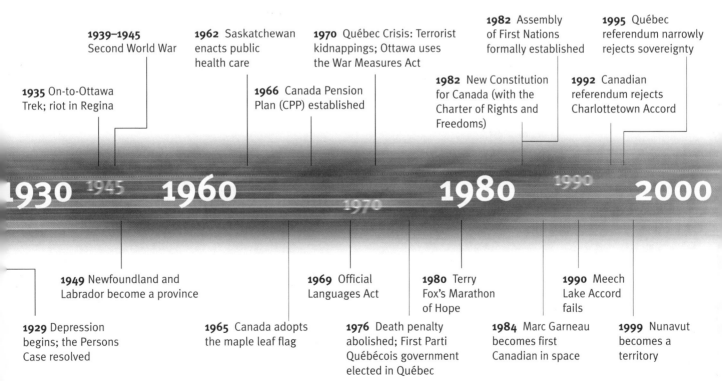

1935 On-to-Ottawa Trek; riot in Regina

1939–1945 Second World War

1962 Saskatchewan enacts public health care

1966 Canada Pension Plan (CPP) established

1970 Québec Crisis: Terrorist kidnappings; Ottawa uses the War Measures Act

1982 Assembly of First Nations formally established

1982 New Constitution for Canada (with the Charter of Rights and Freedoms)

1995 Québec referendum narrowly rejects sovereignty

1992 Canadian referendum rejects Charlottetown Accord

1930 **1945** **1960** **1970** **1980** **1990** **2000**

1929 Depression begins; the Persons Case resolved

1949 Newfoundland and Labrador become a province

1965 Canada adopts the maple leaf flag

1969 Official Languages Act

1976 Death penalty abolished; First Parti Québécois government elected in Québec

1980 Terry Fox's Marathon of Hope

1984 Marc Garneau becomes first Canadian in space

1990 Meech Lake Accord fails

1999 Nunavut becomes a territory

Chapter 8 The Métis

In what ways did the Métis have an impact on the development of Western Canada?

Key CONCEPT

Emerging Identities

In earlier chapters, you read about the concept of **identity**. Your identity is the set of characteristics and values you use to express who you are. Different groups within a country can have their own identities, as can individuals. We recognize that some people may dress differently or follow different religions, speak different languages, and hold different perspectives or points of view. These are all ways of expressing an identity.

Citizenship and Identity

One important result of contact between First Nations and Europeans was the emergence of the **Métis** [may-TEE]. The Métis population grew quickly, spreading across the land. By the mid-1800s, it was in Red River, Manitoba, however, that the largest number of Métis lived. The different groups of Métis who lived in Red River came together as a solid community with a shared identity. They considered themselves citizens of a Métis Nation, distinct from the Europeans, Canadiens, and First Nations.

This chapter explores the unique identity of the Red River Métis. You will learn about the role they played in the development of the West. You will also examine the Métis struggle to protect their identity and way of life.

Chapter 8

Honing Your Skills

Whether we are in class, at home, or out with friends, we are often asked to share our thoughts on different topics. The Skill Check feature in this chapter, **Develop an Opinion**, shows you how to do this. This skill is important to your studies because it will help you become a critical thinker. The project at the end of the chapter will ask you to form and state your opinion on Métis leader Louis Riel.

Points of View and Perspectives on Métis Identity

Different people described the Métis in different ways. As you read the following comments, think about how each one describes the identity of the Métis people.

> *They one and all look upon themselves as members of an independent tribe of natives, entitled to a property in the soil, to a flag of their own, and to protection from the British government.*
>
> —William McGillivray, fur trader, 1818

Source: Entry on "Métis" in *The Canadian Encyclopedia* (Toronto: McClelland & Stewart, 1988), p. 1345.

> *They are the ambassadors between East and West.*
>
> —Lord Dufferin, Governor General of Canada, 1872

Source: Alexander Morris, *The Treaties of Canada with the Indians* (Toronto: Belfords & Clarke, 1880), pp. 293–295.

> *We may be a small community ... but we are men, free and spirited men, and we will not allow even the Dominion of Canada to trample on our rights.*
>
> —Louis Riel, Métis leader, 1869

Source: Jennifer Brown, *Strangers in Blood* (Vancouver: University of British Columbia Press, 1980).

> *We are Indian, we are white We are rejected by them both Although we are so lost between We continue in our growth As a Métis*
>
> —Joel Anderson, 10-year-old Métis from Manitoba, 1982

Source: Hope MacLean, *Indians, Inuit, and Métis* (Toronto: Gage Publishing Ltd., 1982), p. 101.

> *Identity is multi-layered. While I paint flowers to express and celebrate my Métis-ness ... I also have other reasons that don't necessarily have anything to do with me being Métis. They have more to do with a broader sense of myself as a member of the human race desiring to contribute something positive to the world.*
>
> —Christi Belcourt, Métis artist from Lac Sainte-Anne, Alberta, 2002

Source: "Purpose in Art and Moving Beyond the Self," http://www.blackrobin.co.nz/ARCHIVE/MAR2004/BELCOURT/belcourt.html.

Think ▶ AHEAD

Brainstorm reasons why you think it is important to respect another person's or community's identity. What could happen if we do not?

SKILL CHECK: Develop an Opinion

When we see and experience the world around us, we form opinions about the people, places, and events in it. An **opinion** is a person's thoughts or beliefs on something. We are all individuals, and our identity, values, and knowledge influence our opinions. This Skill Check feature will show you how to put careful thought into forming and stating your opinion.

Explain the Issue

An issue is a question to which there are many answers, but none of the answers is right or wrong. Here is one issue:

• Should school cafeterias stop selling junk foods to students?

State Your Position

Take time to consider what you already know about the issue. Ask yourself: Do I have enough information about this issue to know how I truly feel about it? If your answer is no, then you should do more research. After you have gained a better understanding of the issue, you are ready to state your point of view.

Write your opinion as a position statement; for example: school cafeterias should stop selling junk foods to students and instead offer healthy choices such as fruit and salads.

Research for Evidence

The goal of an opinion piece is to get the reader to agree with your point of view. This is a lot easier if you include good reasons for your opinion.

Research to find

• *facts* (Junk foods can be harmful.)
• *examples* (Chocolate bars and pop, for example, can cause tooth decay.)
• *figures and data* (A survey of students in my school found that 70 per cent would prefer healthy foods at lunch.)
• *observations* (When I eat unhealthy foods, I don't have the energy to do the things I like, such as playing basketball.)

Write the Closing

Restate your opinion using different wording than you did at the beginning. You may also want to summarize the main reasons you hold your opinion.

You could end your piece with a thought-provoking statement or question to get the reader thinking.

Review Your Piece

• Is your position statement clear? Will readers easily understand where you stand on the issue?
• Is your opinion supported by facts and examples? Are these organized in a logical way?
• Are your spelling and grammar correct? (Proofread your piece or ask a classmate to check it to make sure.)

Try It!

Read the opinion or editorial page of a local or provincial newspaper. Identify one letter to the editor that you feel is especially good. Bring it to class and explain why you feel it is an effective opinion piece.

An Emerging Identity in the West

Focus
What are the origins of the Métis culture in Red River?

As you learned in earlier chapters, the first Métis were the children of First Nations women and the European men who came to North America to explore and trade for furs. Métis lived all over North America, wherever these peoples came into contact.

It was in present-day Manitoba, however, that the largest Métis community grew. The Francophone Métis of Red River (where Winnipeg is located today) had a unique culture and identity. In this section, you will discover how the Métis came to identify themselves as a nation.

The Demographics of Red River

Although the French-speaking Métis were the largest group living at Red River, they weren't the only people there. When we speak about the characteristics of the people of a particular place, we are referring to the **demographics** of the place. Demographics include information such as the number of people who live in a town. The ratio of male to female residents is another example.

By 1840, there were about 4000 Francophone Métis in the region. They were mainly Catholic, like their Canadien ancestors. However, they also kept some of their First Nations spiritual beliefs. About 1000 other people also lived near Red River:

- **Country Born Métis.** The Country Born were the children of First Nations women and British traders from the Hudson's Bay Company. Like their fathers, the Country

Figure 8.1 Red River was located where the Assiniboine [uh-SIH-nih-boyn] and Red Rivers meet. How might this location be important to the Métis economy? Using GIS software (or another mapping software) choose two themes of information to add to a map of this area. For example, you could include climate and vegetation layers. Then, explain how these geographical features might have contributed to the Métis sense of community and identity.

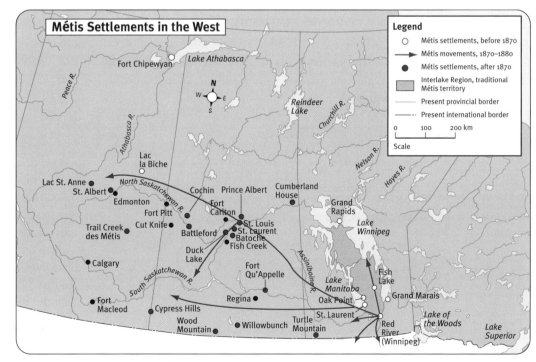

Métis Settlements in the West

Legend
○ Métis settlements, before 1870
→ Métis movements, 1870–1880
● Métis settlements, after 1870
▨ Interlake Region, traditional Métis territory
.... Present provincial border
—--— Present international border

0   100   200 km
Scale

Born were usually Protestant. They also held some First Nations beliefs.

- **Cree and Anishinabe** [a-nih-shih-NAH-bee] **First Nations.**
- **Roman Catholic missionaries.** They began arriving in the West in 1818. The missionaries built churches and schools. These became the centres of Francophone Métis communities.
- **Canadiens.** They lived in St. Boniface.
- **British employees of the Hudson's Bay Company.**

Shared Culture of the Red River Métis

In Chapter 1, you examined the various aspects of culture (see page 4). You saw how the First Nations, the Canadiens, and the English colonists each had their own distinct ways of life. The Red River Métis shared a unique culture in the 1800s that helped shape their identity. They developed their own language, artistic style, poetry, music, dance, economy, and values.

Language

The Métis were raised by parents of both First Nations and European descent. This gave them the opportunity to learn several languages, including French, English, and one or more First Nations languages.

Many Métis at Red River also spoke their own language, called *Michif* [mee-SHEEF]. It linked their First Nations and Canadien or English identities by mixing French, English, Cree, and Anishinabe words. Fewer than a thousand people still speak Michif in Canada today.

Figure 8.2 Many Métis women, such as Mrs. La Vallée from Waskesiu, Saskatchewan, were skilled leather workers. They decorated leather items and clothing with colourful thread, beads, tin, and other materials. Some First Nations called the Métis the "flower beadwork people." The date of this photograph is unknown. Analyze the photo for clues that might lead you to an approximate date.

VOICES ■

Some Michif Phrases

Michif	English
Tánishi kiya?	How are you?
Dishinikáshon Alice.	My name is Alice.
Tánde wékéyan?	Where do you live?
Marsé eki pe'itoteyek.	Thank you for coming.

Respond

1. Some people are trying to make sure that the Michif language never disappears. Think of some ways a community can help keep a language alive.
2. Some Canadians learned another language before they learned English. Should these people make an effort to maintain their first languages? Write a short opinion piece on this issue. **SKILLS**

Identity

Pierre Falcon (1793–1876), "The Bard of the Prairies"

Pierre Falcon was one of the best-known Métis poets and songwriters. He was a Francophone-Cree fur trader who later farmed at Red River. His songs tell the stories of important events in Métis history. For example, he wrote a song about the armed clash at Seven Oaks (a battle you will read about in the next section).

…We took three foreigners prisoners when
We came to the place called Frog, Frog Plain.
They were men who'd come from Orkney,
Who'd come, you see,
To rob our country.

Well, we were just about to unhorse
When we heard two of us give, give voice.
Two of our men cried, "Hey! Look back, look back
The Anglo-Sack coming for to attack" …

Source: Margaret Arnett MacLeod, comp. and ed.,
Songs of Old Manitoba (Toronto: Ryerson Press, 1959),
pp. 5–9, translated by James Reaney.

Figure 8.3 Pierre Falcon. Are song lyrics primary or secondary sources of information? Refer to the Skill Check feature on page 6 to remind yourself of the differences between these types of sources.

Falcon also wrote ballads about life in the fur trade and on the buffalo hunt. Métis sang his songs as they sat around campfires or paddled canoes. Falcon Lake in Manitoba was named after him.

Tech Link

Open the *Voices and Visions* CD-ROM to hear one of Falcon's songs sung by Métis people of present-day Manitoba.

Figure 8.4 Members of the Turtle Mountain Dancers, a Métis troupe, performing at the Manitoba Indigenous Summer Games, 2003, in Brandon, Manitoba. What kind of music do you like? Explain the roles music and dancing play in your life.

Canada Today

There are different views on the question "Who is a Métis?" About 300 000 people identified themselves as Métis in the 2001 Canadian census.

Like their ancestors, present-day Métis face many challenges. They still struggle for land rights and hunting and fishing rights. The Métis have formed associations that promote their identity. These groups also help the Métis in their struggle to gain rights and opportunities equal to those of the First Nations.

Figure 8.5 The Métis flag dates back to the early nineteenth century. It is about 150 years older than the Canadian flag! The infinity symbol represents the coming together of European and First Nations peoples to form a new people, the Métis. It also suggests that the Métis people will exist forever. **Citizenship and Identity:** Why do you think it was important to the Métis people to have their own flag?

Shared Economy

Over the years, the Métis developed a unique **economy**. They made a living based on the climate of their territory and on the resources found in it. They took jobs in the fur trade and hunted the buffalo that grazed in the western grasslands. When they weren't hunting, they grew crops on narrow river lots, similar to the seigneurial system used in Québec. The Métis expressed both their First Nations and European or Canadien identities through this mix of fur trading, hunting, and farming.

The Métis in the Fur Trade

The Métis were very important to the success of the fur trade. They were employed at every trading post and supplied buffalo meat to the people who lived there. Many Métis knew two or more languages, so they often acted as interpreters. They worked in all aspects of

Figure 8.6 A York boat. Reaching 12 metres in length, the boat required six to eight rowers. If a breeze was blowing, the boat flew along under sail. It was too heavy to carry, so it was dragged across the portages on wooden rollers. List some advantages that the York boat had over the canoe. Can you think of any disadvantages?

the trade, as trappers, traders, and freighters. To deliver the furs, the Métis rowed large **York boats**. These boats replaced canoes as the main means of transportation on western rivers and lakes.

An Independent People

The Cree called the Métis the *Otipemisiwak* [oh-tee-puh-MIH-soo-ak], a word that means "the people who govern themselves," or "the people who are their own bosses." This term refers to the fact that the Métis often worked for themselves as independent traders, hunters, and farmers.

Tech Link

Open the *Voices and Visions* CD-ROM to see a video called "The Country Wife." This will give you an idea of the lives of women in nineteenth-century Métis society.

The Buffalo Hunt

The Métis from Red River were expert buffalo hunters. The hunt became the focus of their way of life. Before setting out, they chose a council to organize the hunt. They also chose a set of captains to lead the hunt.

After the hunt, the women cut up the meat. Back at camp, they spread it out to dry and then pounded it into shreds. They mixed the shredded meat with fat and berries to create a food called **pemmican**. The Métis took the pemmican to the trading posts, where they sold it to the fur traders. Pemmican was a very important food for people in the West. It could keep for years. No explorer or fur trader would venture onto the plains without a bag of it to eat.

Figure 8.7 The Métis invented a unique form of transportation called the **Red River cart** to haul buffalo meat. These carts had large wooden wheels that were wrapped in buffalo hide. The cart was also used as a boat. The wheels were removed and hooked to the bottom. Why do you think it became the most dependable form of transportation in the Canadian West?

Figure 8.8 *Métis Hunting Buffalo on Horseback*, painted by Paul Kane, 1848–1852. There were strict rules to guide the buffalo hunt. The rules were enforced by the captain and his "soldiers." Here are a few examples:

1. No hunting buffalo on Sunday
2. No lagging behind or going forward without permission
3. No running buffalo before the general order

The punishment for disobeying was having your saddle and bridle cut up. Why do you think it was so important to the Métis to have rules and follow them?

Canada Today

Many Métis wore a long colourful sash around their waist. When necessary, a sash could become a dog harness, a strap for carrying baggage, a washcloth, or a bridle, for example. Over the years the sash became an important symbol of the Métis identity. Today, Métis who make an important contribution to their community receive the Order of the Sash.

 WEB LINK

Figure 8.9 L'Assomption sash was named after the town in Québec where many were made. Think of three things that symbolize *your* identity. Find pictures of them or draw them, and then explain your choices to the class.

Think It Through

1. As you have learned, the Métis are descendants of European or Canadien and First Nations peoples. However, they have an identity that is distinct from all of these groups. Collect evidence from this section and from other resources to make a poster that supports this statement. **SKILLS**

2. **Citizenship and Identity:** What different groups are there in your community? Choose one of these groups and investigate how the people express their identity and keep it strong. Consider the three factors we have discussed: shared language, arts, and economy.

Conflict at Red River

In the early 1800s, a Scottish nobleman named Lord Selkirk bought a huge piece of land from the Hudson's Bay Company. It was located where the Red and Assiniboine Rivers meet in present-day Manitoba. He brought dozens of families to the land from the Highlands of Scotland, where they were being forced off their farms to make room for sheep pastures. Selkirk hoped that the Highland Scots would be able to turn the land at Red River into a great farming colony.

However, as you have just learned, this land was not empty. A large Métis community was already living there. In this section you will examine the conflict that developed between the new colonists and the Red River Métis. You will also assess the impact of these events on development in the West.

Focus

How did the arrival of colonists threaten the identity of the Red River Métis?

Métis Reaction to the Colonists

The Métis had no legal papers to say they owned the land they had been farming for more than 100 years. They feared the colonists would try to push them off their farms. The Métis were also concerned that their way of life could be overrun by the British culture of the colonists.

The North West Company employees (called **Nor'Westers**), who were allied with the Métis, also opposed the colony. The North West Company was competing against the Hudson's Bay Company for control of the fur trade. The employees believed that the Hudson's Bay Company had sent Selkirk and the colonists to disrupt their trade.

Conflict over Resources

While the colonists prepared the land to grow their first crops, they relied on the buffalo as food. The governor of the colony worried that his colonists would starve if too much buffalo meat left the colony. So, in 1814, he banned the Métis from exporting any meat, fish, or vegetables from Red River. This order was known as the **Pemmican Proclamation**.

The Nor'Westers and the Red River Métis were outraged! The buffalo meat trade was a very important part of the Métis identity and economy. Yet, the newcomers had put a stop to this trade without discussing it with the Métis.

Together the Nor'Westers and the Métis set about driving the Selkirk colonists from

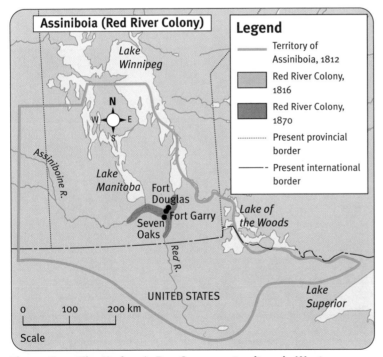

Figure 8.10 The Hudson's Bay Company territory in Western Canada was known as Rupert's Land. This map shows the boundaries of the Selkirk colony. Officially, it was called Assiniboia [uh-sih-nih-BOY-uh], but it was commonly called the Red River Colony. Why might the location and size of this new colony be a concern for the Métis?

the area. They stole farm equipment and horses, and they shot off their guns to frighten the settlers. A series of natural disasters, including a locust infestation, made matters worse for the Scottish colonists. In the summer of 1815 many of them loaded their belongings into canoes and left.

Battle of Seven Oaks

The tensions between the remaining Scottish colonists and the Métis remained high. In June 1816, a group of Métis led by Cuthbert Grant was passing by Fort Douglas. The fort was the headquarters of the colony. The governor, Robert Semple, led an armed group out of the fort to challenge Grant.

The two sides faced each other near a grove of oak trees beside the Red River. Angry words were exchanged. Suddenly, a shot rang out! Fierce fighting followed, and within a few minutes a Métis and 21 colonists lay dead.

Eventually, many of the key people involved in these incidents were arrested and put on trial. An investigation showed that one of the settlers was the first to open fire at Seven Oaks. The issues dividing the colonists, the Métis, and the fur-trading companies remained.

The Battle of Seven Oaks was the first time the Métis stood up as a united group against the Canadian government. Country Born Métis joined with the Francophone Métis to defend their common interests. This event marked the beginning of the Métis nation.

Migration Further West

In 1821, the Hudson's Bay Company took over its rival, the North West Company. This meant that the Red River Colony and all the

Figure 8.11 *Battle of Seven Oaks*, 1816, by Charles W. Jefferys. Analyze this painting using Skill Check: Interpret Images (page 6). Determine what biases, if any, are present in this scene.

land surrounding it now belonged to the British. There would be no further violent clashes between the two fur-trading companies. Red River recovered from its troubled beginnings. It grew into a stable community. Not all the Métis were content to stay, however.

One important business for the Red River Métis was the buffalo robe trade. As you know, the Métis had long hunted the buffalo. During the 1840s, there was increased demand for the furry hide of the animals. The hides were made into blankets and coats. Buffalo fur was thickest during the coldest months. Therefore, Métis hunters and their families spent the winter on the plains close to the herds.

As the buffalo began to die out, hunters had to travel very far from the Red River Colony to find a herd. As a result, many Métis were away from their homes and farms in Red River for most of the year. Some gave up farming in favour of hunting buffalo out on the plains. They **migrated**, or moved, west and set up communities such as Batoche (near Duck Lake, Saskatchewan) and St. Albert (in Alberta). They also settled in the Cypress Hills in southern Saskatchewan. Catholic missionaries who ran churches and schools joined the Métis in these new communities. These were some of the earliest Francophone communities in Western Canada.

Figure 8.12 A caravan of Red River Métis on the way to hunt buffalo. It was painted by the Toronto artist Paul Kane, who took part in a hunt during a visit to Red River in 1846. Create a cause-and-effect flow diagram to explain the development of Métis settlements in present-day Saskatchewan and Alberta.

Think It Through

a) How did the Selkirk colonists and the Hudson's Bay Company show a lack of respect for the Métis identity and way of life?

b) How did the Métis respond to this threat to their identity?

c) Can you think of any other ways the Métis and the colonists could have tried to resolve the conflict?

d) How do Canadians resolve conflicts like this today?

Red River Resistance, 1869

VOICES AND VISIONS

The Red River Métis felt that Rupert's Land belonged to them. They had been living there with their families for over 100 years. Their livelihood depended on being able to farm, trap animals, and hunt buffalo in this vast territory. However, the government of Canada was beginning to see it as a good place to send more European colonists. This section investigates these differing perspectives on Rupert's Land.

Focus

How did the conflicting points of view between the Métis and the government affect the identity of the Métis and the future of Rupert's Land?

Canada Takes an Interest in the West

For many years, outsiders believed that the prairies were barren lands that could not be farmed. This vast territory, known as **Rupert's Land**, was left to the Aboriginal people who lived there.

Things began to change during the 1850s. In 1857, the Canadian government sent scientific teams to the West. They wanted to learn about the climate and resources of the area. The scientists reported that parts of Rupert's Land were well suited to farming. They also said the land had a wealth of natural resources. Suddenly, outsiders started to take notice of the West.

At the same time, good farmland was becoming scarce in Ontario. People began to look outside central Canada for new areas to colonize. Rupert's Land looked like just such a place. Many Ontarians felt it was time for Rupert's Land to join Canada.

Figure 8.13 The scientific expeditions collected all sorts of information about the West, including photographs. This photo, by H.L. Hime, shows members of the Canadian Exploring Expedition at a camp on the Red River in June 1858. What other forms of information do you think the explorers brought back with them? Why was this information so important to the Canadian government?

Points of View on the West

Different people in Canada had different ideas about the future of the West.

Let the merchants of Toronto consider that if their city is ever to be made really great—if it is ever to rise above the rank of a fifth-rate American town—it must be by the development of the great British territory lying to the north and west.

—George Brown

Source: *The Globe* newspaper, 26 December 1856.

Figure 8.14 George Brown was owner and publisher of Canada's first national newspaper, *The Globe*. He was also a politician in Ontario and a supporter of western expansion.

I am perfectly willing to leave Rupert's Land a wilderness for the next half century, but I fear that if the Canadians do not go in, the Yankees will, and with that fear I would gladly see a crown colony established there.

—John A. Macdonald, 1865

Source: J. Bradley Cruxton and W. Douglas Wilson, *Flashback Canada* (Toronto: Oxford University Press, 2000), p. 82.

Figure 8.15 Sir John A. Macdonald was the first Prime Minister of Canada. He served from 1867 to 1873 and from 1878 to 1891.

This is our land! It isn't a piece of pemmican to be cut off and given in little pieces to us. It is ours and we will take what we want.

—Pitikwahanapiwiyin (Poundmaker), 1874

Source: Peter Erasmus, *Buffalo Days and Nights* (Calgary: Fitzhenry & Whiteside, 1974), p. 244.

Figure 8.16 Pitikwahanapiwiyin, known in English as Poundmaker, was a well-respected Cree leader at the time Rupert's Land was being sold to Canada. He voiced the concerns of many First Nations people living in the region.

Rupert's Land Joins Canada

By the 1860s, the Red River Colony was connected by a steamboat route to Minnesota in the United States. A trickle of American newcomers was arriving. Trade with the US was growing steadily. Some people in Ontario who favoured western expansion and some British colonists in Red River began to worry that if Canada did not quickly claim Rupert's Land, the United States would.

Following Confederation in 1867, the government of Canada began talks with the Hudson's Bay Company. In 1869, they

struck a deal. Canada purchased the territory from the HBC for $1.5 million.

Fears of Assimilation

Now Canada claimed to own Rupert's Land. The First Nations and Métis living there felt uncertain about their future. They had not been consulted about the sale of the land. The West belonged to them, they said. It could not be bought and sold by outsiders.

The First Nations and Métis were also worried about assimilation. **Assimilation** is a process by which a culture or individual is absorbed into another culture. Sometimes whole cultures or individual members may assimilate by choice. In this case, members of the culture freely adopt another group's culture and language. But sometimes assimilation is forced on people. The Aboriginal peoples worried that they would be forced to give up their way of life. They feared they would become like the English-speaking newcomers who were moving into the West. They had many questions:

- Would there be a role for Métis and First Nations in the new government?
- Would the Red River Métis be able to keep their French language and Catholic religion?
- Would they be able to keep their farms and way of life?
- Would English-speaking Protestants from the East overwhelm them?

At that time, there were few answers.

The Red River Resistance, 1869

Canada was ready to take control of Rupert's Land on 1 December 1869. Just before this, the federal government sent surveyors to Red River. Their job was to

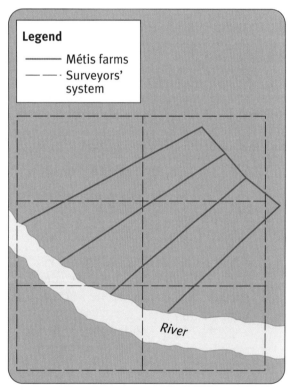

Figure 8.17 The Métis divided up their farmland in river lots, similar to the seigneurial system used in Québec. This method allowed the families to live closer together. It also gave each farm access to the water, which was used for travel. The government surveyors wanted to re-divide the land into square lots. How would this plan have affected the Métis community?

prepare the land for the expected rush of farming colonists. The government did not warn the local First Nations and Métis that the surveyors would be coming in October of 1869. So, when the Métis saw these strangers measuring lots along the river, they confronted them and asked them to explain what they were doing. However, the surveyors spoke only English and the French-speaking Métis could not understand them. So, they sent for one of their fellow villagers, a Métis named Louis Riel, who spoke French, English, and Cree fluently. Riel stopped the surveyors in their tracks and told them to leave Red River immediately.

Although they had bought themselves some time, the Métis knew the surveyors would be back. In the meantime, they had to decide how they would protect their land from what they saw as a foreign government. The Métis were used to governing themselves. They set up a National Committee to protect their right to the land. Louis Riel became an important member of the committee. He was a member of a well-known Métis family in the Francophone community of St. Boniface. Riel was a devout Roman Catholic who had been studying to be a priest in Montréal.

In December the Métis took control of Fort Garry, a major fur-trade centre in Manitoba. There they established a **Métis Provisional Government** (*provisional* is another word for temporary). They chose Louis Riel, a 25-year-old Métis who was passionate about his people's rights, to be president.

Métis Bill of Rights

If they had no choice about joining Canada, the Métis at least wanted to negotiate terms. The provisional government drew up a **Bill of Rights** to present to the government of Canada. It was a clear attempt to protect the varied interests of the peoples already living in the territory. It was also a clear demand for certain provincial powers, such as the right to elect a legislature.

Figure 8.18 This image shows the Métis National Committee in 1869. Louis Riel is seated in the centre of the middle row. He became the leader of the Métis resistance to the government's takeover. What qualities made Riel an effective leader for the Métis?

- Either French or English would be used in the Legislature. Government documents would be printed in both languages.

- Laws for the new province would be decided by the residents.

- The Métis would keep the rights to their land.

- Local officials (sheriffs, magistrates, school commissioners, and so on) would be elected by the local people.

- The federal government would negotiate treaties with the First Nations living there.

French and English Canada Take Sides

Not everyone in Red River supported the Métis resistance. Members of the "Canada Party," for example, were looking forward to the Canadian takeover. This group was made up of English-speakers originally from Ontario or Britain, and they were furious at the actions of the Francophone Métis. Some of them took up arms against the provisional government. The Métis put them in jail. One of these prisoners was Thomas Scott, a 28-year-old labourer from Ontario. Scott threatened to kill Riel and insulted his Métis guards until they lost patience with him. He was put on trial, found guilty, and placed in front of a firing squad. It is still unclear today whether the guards were ordered only to scare Scott or to fire at him. Nevertheless, he was shot and killed.

Tech Link

To see images of Louis Riel at different stages of his life, open Chapter 8 on your *Voices and Visions* CD-ROM.

The Anglophone Perspective

Scott was an English-speaking Protestant. His death set the huge British population of Ontario against the Métis Provisional Government. Newspapers in Ontario called for revenge against the Métis leaders who were responsible.

The Francophone Perspective

The Canadiens in Québec reacted differently. The Red River Métis were mainly Francophone Roman Catholics. (Remember, for example, that Louis Riel was a Francophone who had been educated to be a priest.) Because of this, many Canadiens saw the Métis as defenders of the Francophone Catholic way of life in the West. The Canadiens took up the cause of the Métis as their own and demanded that they be given their rights.

The conflict between the Francophone Métis and English-speaking colonists in the West revived the old anger between the English-speaking Protestants in Ontario and the French-speaking Roman Catholics in Québec. The situation at Red River threatened to become a national crisis.

Think It Through

1. At the time and since, some people have called the creation of the provisional government in Red River a "rebellion." This text uses the term *resistance*. Consult your dictionary and discuss as a class the differences between these two terms. Then, write your own answers to the following: **SKILLS**

   a) Why did the Métis feel they needed the provisional government?

   b) Were the Métis trying to overthrow the government of Canada?

   c) Were the Métis attempting to set up an independent nation of their own?

   d) Why do you think the Métis people today refer to this event as a "resistance?"

2. a) Why do you think people might fear assimilation? Create a web diagram to show your thinking, or write a short opinion piece following the guidelines in the Skill Check feature on page 170. **SKILLS**

   b) Do some research at the library or on the Internet to find out about some Métis organizations that promote Métis identity today. Give a short description of one of them, and explain its importance to the Métis community it serves.

The Creation of Manitoba

Prime Minister John A. Macdonald wanted to find a solution that would seem to please all sides in the Red River crisis. The Métis Provisional Government sent representatives to Ottawa with its Bill of Rights. The prime minister recognized the provisional government as legal. He met with them and agreed to almost all the items on the list. In July 1870 the government passed the **Manitoba Act**, which created the province of Manitoba.

But this solution was not as easy as it sounds. This section investigates the compromises that were necessary to bring Manitoba into Canada.

Focus

What impact did the Red River Métis have on the creation of the province of Manitoba?

WEB LINK

The Manitoba Act

The Manitoba Act created Canada's fifth province. Some of the important terms of the Act were the following:

- Manitoba would have its own provincial government.
- Both French and English would be used in the government and courts.
- The province would be able to send four elected members to the House of Commons in Ottawa and two members to the Senate.
- There would be two publicly funded school systems, one for Protestants and one for Catholics. (It would be similar to the school system in Québec, which was meant to meet the needs of both the French-speaking Catholic majority and the English-speaking Protestant minority.)
- An area of land (560 000 hectares) would be set aside for the Métis to use.
- The natural resources of the new province would remain under the control of the federal government. (This meant that unclaimed land, for example, belonged to Ottawa.)

The Canadian government promised to grant a pardon to any Métis who had been involved in the resistance at Red River. However, in the end, a pardon was not included in the Manitoba Act.

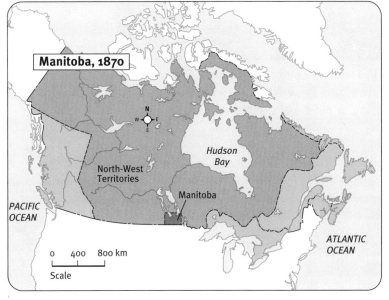

Manitoba, 1870

North-West Territories

Hudson Bay

Manitoba

PACIFIC OCEAN

ATLANTIC OCEAN

0   400   800 km
Scale

Figure 8.19 Manitoba occupied only a small portion of what had been Rupert's Land. The rest passed into the hands of the Canadian government. This larger area was called the North-West Territories, and it was ruled by officials appointed by the government of Canada. Compare this map to a modern map of Manitoba. How has it changed?

Soldiers on the March

At the same time as he discussed Métis terms, the prime minister sent 1200 soldiers to Red River. The government said that the soldiers were meant to keep the peace in the new province. Their job was also to defend the territory in case the United States tried to claim it. But many of the soldiers were Ontario volunteers who thought their job was to punish the Métis and capture Louis Riel. "I should like to hang him from the highest tree," said the commander of the troops.

Knowing that he was in danger, Riel escaped across the border into the United States. Later, the federal government agreed not to put him on trial for the death of Thomas Scott. However, it did banish him from Canada for five years. (While Riel was away the people of Manitoba showed their continued support for him by electing him to Parliament in Ottawa even though he could not serve there.)

Meanwhile, some of the soldiers took out their anger on the Métis when they arrived at Red River. Several Métis were killed. Others were jailed and beaten. It was a sour beginning for the new province.

Tech Link

To see a series of 10 images about the Red River Expedition from Ontario to Red River, open Chapter 8 on your *Voices and Visions* CD-ROM.

Figure 8.20 This painting from 1877 by Frances Hopkins, the wife of a fur trader, shows the military force making its way from Ontario. It took them 13 weeks to reach Manitoba. Do you think sending the military to Red River was a good decision, or did it make things worse? Explain your thinking.

Think It Through

1. The Manitoba Act was a compromise between the different parties involved in the dispute at Red River. Make an organizational chart to show what each of the following groups achieved from the compromise: First Nations, Métis, English-speaking residents, and Francophones.

2. Compare and contrast the federal government's Manitoba Act and the Métis Bill of Rights. (You may want to refer to Skill Check: Compare and Contrast on page 54 before beginning.)
   a) Create a chart that compares the two under different headings: language rights, education, political representation, and so on.
   b) Assess the success of the Métis in gaining their rights.

Second Métis Uprising, 1885

The creation of the province of Manitoba did not solve all the concerns of the Métis and First Nations. There were still disagreements over land ownership. Also, the Métis' fears of assimilation grew as more and more newcomers flooded into the area.

This section explores what happened after the government ignored the Aboriginal peoples' complaints. You will also investigate how the government managed to gain even greater control over the West.

Focus

What was Louis Riel's role in preserving the Métis identity?

Reading
STRATEGY

Read this section of the chapter with a partner. One of you will be the reader and the other will be the coach. First, the reader reads a paragraph out loud. Then, the coach summarizes the main idea of the paragraph in his or her own words. Continue through the section, switching roles for each paragraph.

Problems Persist

When Manitoba was created, land was set aside for the Métis. Each family was supposed to receive a scrip giving them ownership to about 240 acres (97 hectares). (A scrip is like a coupon.) But the system did not work well, and many Métis did not receive their land.

Newcomers from the East did not show respect for the Métis identity and way of life. They wanted to build a society in Manitoba that was similar to Ontario's. They dreamed of bringing in so many Anglophones that Manitoba would become a place of English-speaking, Protestant farmers. Feeling cheated and frustrated, many Métis left Manitoba to move farther west and north where they could live as hunters, trappers, and farmers. As the buffalo began to disappear from the plains, the Métis turned to other ways of making a living, such as ranching, logging, and running small businesses.

In some of these new Western settlements, the Métis set up their own governments with their own laws. The village of St. Laurent, on the South Saskatchewan River, was one example. Gabriel Dumont became president, and an elected council collected taxes and governed the community. The laws in the community were based on the traditional rules of the buffalo hunt (see Figure 8.8), with additional laws for keeping the peace. In other words, the Métis were looking after their own affairs as they had always done. But to outsiders, it seemed as if they were opposing the Canadian government.

Métis and First Nations Grievances

By the 1880s the Métis faced a number of challenges to their way of life, such as starvation and poverty that resulted from the drastically reduced buffalo population. The First Nations people were facing similar threats. In response, many First Nations people had no other option but to make treaties with the Canadian government. You will read more about those treaties in Chapter 12. The Métis were sometimes allowed to join a First Nation's treaty, but they did not qualify for their own treaties.

Métis Concerns	First Nations Concerns
• Some Métis felt that they had been cheated out of their land in Manitoba. • Outside of Manitoba, land ownership was unclear. Some of the Métis were living on property that had also been claimed by the Hudson's Bay Company or the railway company. • Newcomers were moving into the West, and the Métis feared losing their land and jobs. They also feared being assimilated into the new society that was emerging. • The buffalo were disappearing due to over-hunting. The livelihoods of many Métis were disappearing along with them. • The federal government was ignoring their problems. The Métis sent 15 petitions to Ottawa that were not answered.	• The government had not kept some of the promises it had made to provide food rations and farming equipment. • The buffalo were disappearing due to over-hunting by outsiders. • Some First Nations people were starving, in part because the government restricted their movements. This made it difficult for them to hunt and find food. The government owed them food rations as repayment, but none were given. • With the arrival of so many newcomers, they worried that they would not be able to hold on to what little land was left to them. • Some First Nations leaders wanted a large territory where their people could live together. The government, however, forced the people to live on small **reserves** separate from each other.

Figure 8.21 After hunters killed the buffalo, bone-pickers collected the skeletons. They shipped them to the East where they were ground up and used to make a variety of products. Recall what you have learned about the importance of the buffalo to the way of life of Western First Nations and Métis. In small groups, discuss the impact of the disappearance of the buffalo on these peoples. Compare ideas with the other groups.

The Government Ignores Warnings

Government officials working in the area that would one day become Saskatchewan were aware of the growing tension in Manitoba. They offered advice to Ottawa about how to avoid another Métis uprising. However, the federal politicians would not listen. They were focused on what they considered a more important issue—the westward expansion of the Canadian Pacific Railway (CPR). The building of this railway through the prairies was a priority for Ottawa because it would encourage more colonists to move onto the prairies and develop the land.

Riel Returns

The Métis and First Nations sent at least 15 petitions to Ottawa to address their concerns (outlined in the chart above). The government ignored all of them. In the summer of 1884, a group of Métis, led by Gabriel Dumont, travelled to the United

States and invited Louis Riel back to Canada. The Métis were angry and impatient that the government was not doing anything about their complaints. They wanted Riel to be their voice.

Led by Riel, the Métis set up their own government at the community of Batoche. From there, they sent a Bill of Rights to Ottawa. Among other things, they wanted the land issue solved and two new provinces created west of Manitoba. They also demanded more food rations for the First Nations. When nothing happened, Riel suggested they take up arms. Many Métis didn't want to go to battle because they knew they would be outnumbered. However, Dumont was a strong supporter of Riel. Many Métis respected Dumont, and so they decided to join the uprising. Dumont was named general of the Métis forces.

Rising in Arms

The Northwest Resistance of 1885 was violent, but brief. On 26 March, the Métis defeated a group of North West Mounted Police at a place called Duck Lake, forcing the police to retreat. A few days later, a group of Cree joined the resistance. At Frog Lake they killed nine people and captured a police post. The police and neighbourhood farm families were allowed to leave unharmed.

Reading
STRATEGY

When reading sections of text, it is sometimes helpful to try to picture in your head the people and events being described. If you prefer, you could draw sketches on paper to illustrate what you have read. This could be done in a storyboard format, which is similar to the series of boxed drawings in newspaper cartoons.

The Government Reacts

The federal government rushed thousands of soldiers west aboard the newly built railway. This army advanced on the Métis village of Batoche. Many Métis women remained in the village during the battle to help in whatever way they could. They carried food, messages, and supplies to the men. They melted down lead plates to make bullets. It wasn't long before the Métis ran out of bullets and were firing stones and nails.

After three days of fighting, the 200 to 300 Métis and their Cree and Dakota allies surrendered. The resistance was over. A total of 53 soldiers from Ontario died in the fighting, and 118 were injured. Thirty-five First Nations and Métis people were killed.

Figure 8.22 Gabriel Dumont (1838–1906) was the military general for the Métis. He was a famous buffalo hunter who could speak French, English, and six First Nations languages. "Louis Riel was the heart of the Métis people, and Dumont was their sword" is a historical saying of unknown origin. Explain this saying in your own words.

Biography

Mistahimaskwa, Leader of the Cree (1825–1887)

Cree Leader Mistahimaskwa, known in English as Big Bear, headed the largest group of Cree on the Plains (in the area around Frog Lake). He was very suspicious of the outsiders who were coming into the West. In 1883, Mistahimaskwa spoke to a council of Cree elders and a visiting government agent.

Long before the advent of the Palefaces this vast land was the hunting ground of my people, this land was then the hunting ground of the Plains and the Wood Crees, my fathers. It was then teeming with buffalo and we were happy. This fair Land … is now the land of the white man—the land of the stranger. Our Big Game is no more. You now own our millions of acres—according to treaty papers—as long as grass grows on the prairies or water runs in our big Rivers. We have no food. We live not like the white man, nor are we like the Indians who live on fowl and fish. True, we are promised great things, but they seem far off and we cannot live and wait.

Source: Robert S. Allen, "The Breaking of Big Bear," *Horizon Canada*, vol. 5 (1987), p. 1191.

He hoped to form an alliance of all the First Nations so that they would be stronger in their dealings with the government. He feared that his people would lose their freedom, and their land, if they made a treaty. The government promised food rations as part of the treaty agreement. In the end, the starvation of his people forced Mistahimaskwa to sign.

Even as conditions for his people got worse, Mistahimaskwa opposed the use of violence. He hoped to solve the issues through peaceful talks with the government. This did not work. Instead, fearing trouble, the federal government made it illegal for First Nations people to leave their home reserves without permission. Such permission could only be granted by the government agent on each reserve.

When the Métis took up arms, a few Cree people joined them against Mistahimaskwa's wishes. After the resistance was over, the soldiers tracked down the Cree group and arrested its members. Mistahimaskwa was sent to jail for treason. He was released in 1887 but died soon after.

Respond

1. Write a letter from the government of Canada responding to Mistahimaskwa's speech.
2. Refer to the Skill Check feature on page 170 to learn how to write an opinion piece. Then, write a few paragraphs stating your opinion on the government's treatment of Mistahimaskwa. If you find you do not have enough information to write your piece, you should do some more research on Mistahimaskwa (Big Bear) on the Internet or at the library. [SKILLS]

Figure 8.23 This painting shows Canadian troops surrounding the Métis at Batoche. The Métis held the soldiers off by firing at them from the shelter of their trenches. In the end, the government troops overran the town. Imagine you are a reporter covering the battle for your newspaper. Write a story describing the scene, the colours, the sounds, and the smells. Explain the background to the fighting.

The Fate of Louis Riel

Following the resistance, more than a dozen Métis ended up in prison. Louis Riel surrendered and stood trial for **treason**—the betrayal of one's country. A jury found him guilty and Riel was sentenced to hang. Prime Minister Macdonald could have stepped in and saved Riel's life. Twice Macdonald delayed the execution while he debated what to do.

Macdonald's government was heading into a federal election after the trial. Whatever decision he made, it would cost his party votes. However, the number of voters in Ontario was larger than the

Macdonald's Dilemma	
Many Ontarians thought the Métis leader Louis Riel was a traitor and a murderer. They wanted him hanged.	Canadiens considered Riel a hero. They thought of him as a defender of French language rights and the Catholic religion in the West.

number in Québec. Macdonald knew that if he sided with Ontario, his party would likely win the election.

Finally, the prime minister made up his mind. "Riel shall hang though every dog in Québec shall bark," he was heard to say. On 16 November 1885, Riel was taken from his Regina jail cell and hanged. When news reached Québec, flags were dropped to half-mast. Macdonald was burned in effigy in the streets. The Canadiens blamed English Canadians in Ontario for Riel's death. The Riel execution confirmed the suspicions of the Canadiens that their Confederation "partnership" with English Canada was unequal.

The Government Tightens Its Grip

Once the uprising of 1885 was over, the government finally responded to some of

A RIEL UGLY POSITION.

Figure 8.24 Analyze this cartoon using the Skill Check feature on page 218. Explain the cartoon. Is it effective, in your opinion? Support your opinion with reasons. SKILLS

Tech Link

To learn more about Mistahimaskwa (Big Bear) and Pitikwahanapiwiyin (Poundmaker) and their efforts on behalf of their people, open Chapter 8 on your *Voices and Visions* CD-ROM.

the complaints that had led to it. The North-West Territories did not become two new provinces as the Métis had demanded in their Bill of Rights. The government began issuing scrip (certificates for land) again to Métis people at Red River. However, the Métis remembered how difficult it was to actually obtain their land the last time scrip was issued. So, this time they sold their scrip, often for much less than it was worth.

Figure 8.25 This photograph shows Louis Riel (standing, centre) at his trial. Riel was found guilty of treason. What did Prime Minister Macdonald mean when he said, "Riel shall hang though every dog in Québec shall bark"?

Aboriginal people in the West were punished for their role in the resistance. Along with the Métis, 44 First Nations men were found guilty of crimes. Eight of them were hanged; the rest were sent to prison. Only a few First Nations had joined the resistance, but whole communities were punished severely by having their government food rations stopped even though, in all of Canada, there were only 100 buffalo left. First Nations people were told to stay on their reserves unless they had permission from a government agent to travel. These restrictions on the First Nations opened up the land to more European farmers. It also allowed the government to continue expanding the CPR without fear of another resistance.

As an independent nation, the Métis had tried to deal peacefully with Canada. They wanted rights equal to those enjoyed by people in other provinces, but the government ignored their requests. The outcome of the resistance set back the Métis and their struggle to be recognized as a distinct people. The government of Canada, backed by the army, gained firm control of the West. Many of the issues that led to the violence of 1885 would remain unsettled in the years to come.

Think It Through

1. Make a chart to compare the Red River Resistance (1869) to the Second Métis Uprising (1885). You may want to refer to Skill Check: Compare and Contrast on page 54 before beginning.
   a) Compare the issues and concerns that led to each resistance. Compare the government responses in both cases. Also compare the outcomes of each resistance.
   b) Were some of the factors the same? What do you think is the most important difference between the two events? Explain your answer.

2. a) What compromises were made by the Métis, First Nations, and Francophone and English peoples in order to create the province of Manitoba?
   b) How would each group have felt about the final outcome?

Chapter 8

Chapter 8 PROJECT — Writing an Opinion Piece on Louis Riel

From his own day to the present, Louis Riel has been a person of controversy.

To us, you are … the valiant leader of this population that is strongly confident that, God willing, you will one day bring to victory our just claims.

—Residents of the Métis community of St-Louis de Langevin, 1885

Source: Letter in the Riel Papers, Manitoba Archives, cited in Maggie Siggins, *Riel: A Life of Revolution,* (Toronto: HarperCollins, 1995), p. 364.

Had I been born on the banks of the Saskatchewan, I would myself have shouldered a musket to fight against the neglect of the government and the shameless greed of speculators.

—Sir Wilfrid Laurier, future prime minister, after Riel's hanging in 1885

Source: Peter Russell, "Laurier and the Prairie West." www.collectionscanada.ca/04/042423_e.html.

Louis Riel, Métis leader, executed November 16, 1885, political martyr! Guilty of having loved his oppressed compatriots! Victim of fanaticism, to which politicians without soul and without heart have sacrificed him.

—A poster handed out in Québec, 1885

Source: R. Douglas Francis, et al., *Destinies: Canadian History Since Confederation* (Toronto: Harcourt Brace Canada, 2000), p. 96.

Grievances did not give anyone the right to organize and lead a rebellion in which more than a hundred died.

—Desmond Morton, historian, 1998

Source: *Ottawa Citizen,* 22 January 1998.

And the province of Manitoba? Without our provisional government it would still be nothing more than a colony tied to the apron strings of Canada. I deserve to be called the Father of Manitoba.

—Louis Riel, August 1885

Source: Quoted in the Montréal newspaper the *Weekly Star,* August 1885.

This chapter project challenges you to analyze this historical issue in order to form and support an opinion.

State Your Position

Using Skill Check: Develop an Opinion (page 170) as your guide, write a one-page opinion piece on the issue: *Was Louis Riel a hero, a traitor, or neither?*

Research for Evidence

Review the details in Chapter 8 that provide facts, figures, and quotations to support your opinion. Take notes in your own words. Identify direct quotes with quotation marks, and include the page numbers where they are found.

You may also need to review information found on the Internet or at your local library.

Organize Your Opinion Piece

Before you begin writing, organize your ideas using an outline or graphic organizer.

Write Your Opinion Piece

Write a strong opening paragraph. Follow it with facts to support your opinion. Conclude with a thought-provoking summary. Create a title that sums up your opinion in a few words.

Polish and Present

In a small group, share your writing. Use informal debate to discuss the differing viewpoints regarding the issue. Take note of comments, concerns, and questions raised by other students. Decide if your piece needs more work, and then revise accordingly. Do a final proofread. Present your opinion piece in writing or as a speech.

Chapter 9 Growth in the West

Chapter INQUIRY How did Canada secure the West and prepare for a massive influx of immigrants?

Key CONCEPT ▶ Natural Resources and History

Natural resources are the parts of nature that people can use. They include fish, land, trees, furs, water, oil, and minerals. Earlier in this book, you read about the ways that various First Nations used natural resources. After first contact, First Nations and newcomers used these resources to meet their needs.

Canada is rich in natural resources. Canadians cut down trees to make lumber. We drill for oil and gas to heat our homes and fuel our cars. We grow wheat to make bread. Our use of natural resources can harm the environment. However, our natural resources have created many jobs.

Natural Resources in Canada's Story

Natural resources have played a big role in Canada's story. They affected where people chose to live. For example, the First Nations on Canada's northwest coast chose to live where they could fish for salmon.

Why did Europeans first come to Canada? They were searching for China. Why did they stay? Natural resources. First these visitors harvested fish off the Atlantic coast. Then they travelled inland for fur. These were important stages in Canada's history. In part, the history of the Canadian people is the history of our natural resources.

The Importance of Land

The land itself is an important natural resource. It has value because it is the place where we live. It also has value because of what it provides. First Nations peoples made use of the water, plants, and animals on the land. Later, people used it to produce other resources, such as cattle and grain. After Confederation, thousands of newcomers began arriving in the West. The vast majority wanted one thing: land.

In this chapter, you will learn how the government of Canada tried to gain control of this land for newcomers. You'll learn how the government built a railway so immigrants could travel into the West and farm the land.

Honing Your Skills

Do you like stories? The Skill Check feature in this chapter shows you how to **Read and Write Historical Fiction**. This skill is important to your studies because it will give you an enjoyable way to learn about history. The project at the end of the chapter will ask you to write a story set in Canada shortly after Confederation.

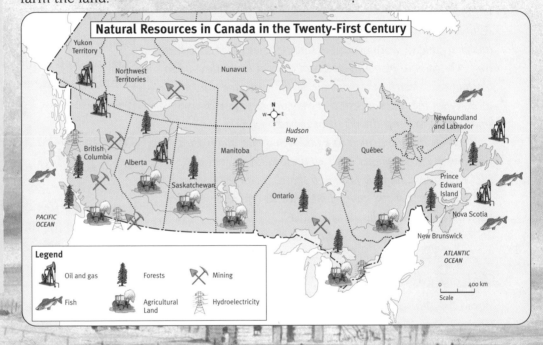

Natural Resources in Canada in the Twenty-First Century

Yukon Territory

Northwest Territories

Nunavut

Hudson Bay

British Columbia

Alberta

Saskatchewan

Manitoba

Ontario

Québec

Newfoundland and Labrador

Prince Edward Island

Nova Scotia

New Brunswick

PACIFIC OCEAN

ATLANTIC OCEAN

Legend

Oil and gas

Forests

Mining

Fish

Agricultural Land

Hydroelectricity

0   400 km
Scale

Think AHEAD

1. a) Using the map above, list one important natural resource for each province.
    b) Extend your list by brainstorming ways each resource is used today.
    c) Which of the resources on the map would have drawn newcomers in the late 1800s?

2. Which Inuit or First Nations peoples lived in or near your community at the time of first contact? You can check on the map on page 7. Speculate on what natural resources they used.

3. Imagine that an out-of-town visitor asks what your community is like. How you answer will depend partly on the ways that people use local resources. Name natural resources people develop in or near your community. Together, create an answer for your visitor.

SKILL CHECK: Read and Write Historical Fiction

How can we get a feel for the exciting times in the West after 1867? Historical fiction can help us "experience" what it was like. In historical fiction, authors write about real places and real events, but they make up the details of the story. They often make up characters as well.

Read the following excerpt. It comes from the historical fiction story *White Jade Tiger*. In it, author Julie Lawson shows us what conditions were like building a railway through the Rockies in the 1880s.

A tunnel was being dug into the mountain. Near the roof of the tunnel, a gang [a work group] of Chinese [men] was already at work. On galleried platforms at several different levels, they drilled blasting holes, inserted the dynamite, lit the fuses, and ran for cover. When the explosion settled, a gang armed with pick-axes smashed the rock into chunks and removed the debris.

Outside the tunnel, more rock had been drilled and blasted, then broken into fragments to fill up the roadbed. "That's our job," Keung said, handing Jasmine a shovel. "Load the loose rock into a wheelbarrow and dump it into the cuts and hollows. Once the roadbed's finished, the tracks are laid."

Pile after pile of shattered rock had to be moved. Soon every muscle in [Jasmine's] body was screaming. And she'd thought digging the garden was back-breaking work. Bend, lift, bend, lift. Her body was one long, deep groan ...

Source: Julie Lawson, *White Jade Tiger* (Victoria: Beach Holme Publishing, 1993), pp. 124–125.

Try It!

Read the *White Jade Tiger* excerpt. What do you learn from it about opening the West?

Reading Historical Fiction

1. First, read historical fiction to enjoy it.
2. What facts did you learn?
3. How did the characters feel about their experiences?
4. What is the author trying to tell you?

Feeling inspired? Writing your own historical fiction is another way to have fun with history. This is how you do it.

Choose a Topic

Identify a period of history that you find exciting. You could choose an event from Canadian history, your community history, or your family history.

Research

Now become an expert on the historical period you're going to write about. What happened? How did people dress? What did they do for fun? Interview people for facts and details. Explore archives and museums online or in your community. Use your local library. Read historical fiction. Take accurate notes.

Planning

- Decide on your story's characters.
- Create a plot to organize the events.
- Consider the point of view. Will you tell it in first person or third person?
- What tense will you write in?

Writing and Editing

- Tell about the events of the period from your character's point of view.
- Describe the setting accurately.
- Tell about historical events accurately.
- Include occasional facts and details.
- Use historically appropriate dialogue.
- Check your grammar and spelling.

Securing the Land

A country is not a country without land. Canada wanted to secure its claim to the land in the West before the Americans could occupy it. You have read that the government of Canada bought Rupert's Land from the Hudson's Bay Company in 1869. This vast region came to be known as the North-West Territories. Many Canadians looked forward to the day when the North-West Territories would be home to thousands of successful farm families.

Focus

What role did the North West Mounted Police play in the development of Western Canada?

First, though, the government had to gain control of the land. That is why it signed treaties with the First Nations. These agreements will be discussed in Chapter 12.

As you will learn in this section, the government also began to mark the Canada–US border. Then it sent in a new police force, the North West Mounted Police (NWMP). In the American West, homesteaders arrived before the law did.

Violence was common. Canada would do things differently. The police were intended to make the land safe for all the expected newcomers.

Marking the Border

The government could not give land to settlers until it knew exactly what land it had. The 49th parallel was the border west of the Great Lakes. In the early 1870s, with the help of Métis guides, American and British surveyors marked this boundary.

Surveyors carefully measured the land and marked the border. Every 1.6 kilometres (1 mile), they planted an iron post in the ground. About every 5 kilometres (3 miles), they built a low mound of earth. The markings showed the exact limit of Canadian territory.

In the nineteenth century, Canadians measured distance in miles. One mile equals about 1.6 kilometres.

Trouble in Whoop-Up Country

The Cypress Hills rise up from the flat prairie in southern Saskatchewan and Alberta. For centuries, the Cree, Nakoda [na-KOH-dah], and Siksika [sik-SIK-uh] came here in winter. They hunted the game animals. They cut pine trees to make poles for their lodges and tipis. Later, Métis hunters and traders also lived in the hills.

During the 1860s, the Cypress Hills became known as Whoop-Up Country. The area got this name because of whiskey traders, mainly from the United States.

Figure 9.1 A party of surveyors building a boundary mound on the prairie. It is the summer of 1873. What benefits come from marking boundaries between countries?

These outlaws crossed into Canada to trade liquor for furs and buffalo robes. Selling liquor was illegal, but no one was around to enforce the law.

Americans also came to Whoop-Up Country to hunt wolves. When buffalo died, wolves would feed on their carcasses. The wolf hunters, called wolfers, put poison in the carcasses. The wolves would eat the poisoned meat and die. The wolfers would then collect the wolf pelts.

Wolves weren't the only animals to eat the poisoned meat. Dogs belonging to the local First Nations people also died this way. Some First Nations people got back at the wolfers by taking their horses. The wolfers and First Nations people did not get along.

Creating a Police Force

The government was worried about the violent way of life in Whoop-Up Country. Prime Minister Macdonald decided that a new police force was needed. The North

West Mounted Police would

- show the United States that Canada controlled the territory
- shield the Aboriginal peoples from American outlaws
- help newcomers adjust to the frontier
- keep the peace between First Nations and the newcomers

A Massacre Spurs on a Prime Minister

In the United States, the army had killed thousands of First Nations people to get their land. They had forced the rest off the best land. Prime Minister Macdonald wanted to avoid such violence in the Canadian West. He hoped the NWMP would enforce the law and keep the peace. Without it, Canadian occupation of the land would be difficult.

On 1 June 1873, an event took place that showed how much the West needed law and order. Nakoda people were camped near Farwell's and Solomon's Trading Posts in the Cypress Hills. A group of American wolfers thought that the Nakoda had stolen their horses. They hadn't, but that didn't matter to the wolfers. They ambushed the Nakoda camp. They murdered as many as 36 men, women, and children before the rest could escape. The event became known as the Cypress Hills Massacre.

Macdonald soon heard news of the massacre. He was outraged. He made it a priority to get the North West Mounted Police to the area as soon as possible.

The Great March West

Police recruits rushed to Manitoba for training. The next July, in 1874, 300 mounted police headed west in a caravan. There were ox carts, horses, and wagons.

Figure 9.2 Four mounted police officers at Fort Walsh in the 1870s. Red was the colour of the British Empire. American Cavalry wore blue. In your experience with team sports, how does the colour of a uniform help the team?

This so-called Great March soon turned into a fiasco. Food supplies ran low. Horses died for lack of water. The expedition even got lost. Local Métis guides had to rescue them.

Finally, the police arrived safely. Part of the force went south. Here, they established Fort Macleod, west of present-day Lethbridge, and Fort Walsh, in the Cypress Hills. Another group went north to Fort Edmonton, where they built another outpost.

Calgary also began as a police fort, briefly known as Fort Brisebois.

The Role of the Mounted Police

The North West Mounted Police had one major task: to make life in the territory peaceful. The officers made sure that people obeyed the law.

The mounted police were few, but they performed many tasks.

- They cleared out the whiskey traders.
- They arrested lawbreakers of all types and put them on trial.
- They delivered the mail.
- They fought grass fires and assisted the new farmers.
- They fought in the second Métis Uprising of 1885.

Tech Link

To hear the "Mounted Police Waltzes" composed by an NWMP officer in the West, open Chapter 9 on your *Voices and Visions* CD-ROM.

Figure 9.3 Fort Walsh, the NWMP post built in the Cypress Hills in 1875. Over the next few years, the NWMP erected a string of posts between Manitoba and the Rocky Mountains. Why would a string of posts be required? How would First Nations feel on seeing the forts going up?

WEB LINK

Canada Today

In 1919, there was a very big strike in Winnipeg. Canada needed a national force, so the NWMP absorbed the Dominion Police from Eastern Canada. It became the Royal Canadian Mounted Police (RCMP). Today, the RCMP deals with problems such as illegal drugs, counterfeit money, and organized crime. It provides policing services for towns, rural areas, and Aboriginal communities.

Figure 9.4 A charge in the Musical Ride. This RCMP spectacle dates back to the days of the NWMP. Officers practised riding in regular drills. Why would the RCMP perform for the public?

CASE STUDY

Tagging Along on the Great March

Can journalists avoid being biased when the government pays their way?

Colonel G.A. French of the NWMP wanted people to know about the Great March West. So, he invited Henri Julien to come along. Julien was a Montréal artist with the newspaper *Canada Illustrated News*. (He painted *The Battle of Châteauguay* on page 133.) The government would pay for all expenses.

Julien accepted, although he didn't really know what he was getting into. You can see this in the following excerpt from his diary:

Respond

The government paid all of Julien's expenses. How might this have affected how Julien viewed and interpreted what he saw?

July 10th It was in the neighbourhood of the Grande Coulee that we first [met] the hostility of the mosquitoes.

As soon as twilight deepens, they make their appearance on the horizon, in the shape of a cloud, which goes on increasing in density as it approaches to the encounter. At first, a faint hum is heard in the distance, then it swells into a roar as it comes nearer. The attack is simply dreadful. Your eyes, your nose, your ears are invaded.

*If you open your mouth to curse at them, they troop into it ....
And not one or a dozen, but millions at a time ....*

Source: Henri Julien's diary, http://www.ourheritage.net/julien_pages/Julien2.html.

Julien made many illustrations about what he saw. These were printed in his newspaper and made him famous. Look at the drawing on this page. Julien is presenting his opinion. What facts or arguments does Julien present to back up his opinion? What stereotypes does he use?

Develop Your Skill SKILLS

Draw on your own experience to better understand what the NWMP went through on the Great March. You have probably had a day when the mosquitoes wouldn't leave you alone. Jot down the facts of your experience: who, what, where, when, and why. Now write a short piece of historical fiction. Just make up a character who might have been with you on that day. Then write a funny scene as he or she fights off the mosquitoes.

Figure 9.5 An 1876 drawing by Henri Julien. He is comparing the American West (top) with the Canadian West. How does he view each approach? How might these drawings be different if an American had drawn them?

Biography

Jerry Potts (1840–1896)

The NWMP could not do their job alone. They needed the help of local guides and interpreters. One of these was Jerry Potts.

Potts's mother, Naamopia, was a Kainai [KY-ny] woman. His father was a Scottish trader who died when Potts was just a baby. Potts's Kainai name was Ky-yo-kosi, meaning "Bear Child." He grew up partly with his mother's people and partly at a trading post in Montana. He worked as a guide and interpreter. He helped the Kainai as a protector of the people. He was also a skilled hunter and trapper.

Potts was invaluable to the NWMP. He seemed to know every trail and coulee (deep, dry ravine) in the territory. He also gave excellent advice about the Plains First Nations. He took part in talks that led to the signing of treaties. Many scouts whom he trained went on to have long careers with the force. Potts worked for the NWMP all his life.

VOICES ■

People did not always agree about the North West Mounted Police.

❝ The NWMP came out to keep the Indians under control so they wouldn't bother the White people ... so they had a whole bunch of soldiers present when they signed the treaty—some people were scared. ❞

—Helen Meguinis, a Tsuu T'ina [tsoo-TIN-uh] elder

Source: Treaty 7 Elders et al., *The True Spirit and Original Intent of Treaty 7* (Montréal: McGill–Queen's University Press, 1996), p. 135.

❝ If the police had not come to the country, where would we all be now? Bad men and whiskey were killing us so fast that very few, indeed, would have been left today. The police have protected us as the feathers of the bird protect it from the frosts of winter. ❞

—Isapo-Muxika (Crowfoot), Siksika chief

Source: Alexander Morris, *The Treaties of Canada with the Indians* (Toronto, 1880; reprinted Toronto: Coles Publishing Co., 1971), p. 272.

❝ The Indians welcomed our residence among them, and looked upon us as their friends and deliverers from the many evils they had suffered at the hands of unprincipled white men. ❞

—Cecil Denny, one of the first police officers in the West

Source: Cecil Denny, *The Law Marches West* (Toronto: JM Dent, 1939), p. 72.

Think It Through

1. Imagine you work for the NWMP in 1874. Create a poster calling for recruits for the force. What qualities make a good recruit? What languages should a recruit speak? In your poster, describe the work the force is doing in the West. Show how it is helping to develop Western Canada. Alternatively, write a speech for a recruitment officer.

2. Find out more about Canada's mounted police by finding and reading a piece of historical fiction featuring a NWMP officer. Share it with a classmate. SKILLS

Building the Iron Road

Prime Minister Macdonald wanted a new policy for Canada. It was called the National Policy.

Focus

How did building the Canadian Pacific Railway affect the growth of Canada?

A Three-Pronged Policy

By 1878, the government had secured the land in the West. To use the land resource effectively, though, Canada needed three things:

- a transportation system to reach the resource
- a population to harvest the resource
- an **economy** to nurture the new resource industry

The National Policy was made to achieve these three things. It was like three policies in one:

The National Policy had such a big influence on Canada that we cover its three parts in the next three sections.

- a *transportation policy*—to build a railway across the continent
- an *immigration policy*—to encourage farmers to populate Western Canada
- an *economic policy*—to build a strong national economy for Canadians

In this section, you will learn more about the first part of the National Policy: building the railway.

Finding a Route

In the 1870s, work began on the **transcontinental railway**. By building it, Canada hoped to bring British Columbia into Confederation and keep the Americans out. Building the railway was a monumental task. Canada is a huge country, the second largest in the world (by land area). The railway had to cross thousands of kilometres of forested wilderness and prairie grassland. Swamps had to be filled. Rock had to be blasted out of the way. Bridges had to be built across raging rivers.

Before a railway could be built, surveyors had to find the best route. Surveyors first looked at a northerly route. It would go northwest from Winnipeg to Edmonton. Then it would cross the Rockies through the Yellowhead Pass. In the end, the route ran farther south. It crossed the prairie to Calgary. Then it crossed the Rockies through the Kicking Horse Pass. The southern route had several advantages.

- The land was flatter and had fewer trees. This made it easier to build the railroad.
- Coal deposits near Lethbridge, Alberta, could provide fuel for the steam engines.
- The route was close to the border, so most people would take the Canadian railway, not the American one.

VOICES

On 7 March 1878, Prime Minister Macdonald proposed his National Policy in the House of Commons. How did he think it would benefit Canada?

66 The welfare of Canada requires the adoption of a National Policy, which ... will benefit and foster the agricultural, the mining, the manufacturing and other interests in the Dominion; that such a policy will retain in Canada thousands of our fellow countrymen now forced to leave in search of jobs denied them at home, will restore prosperity to our struggling industries ... [and] will encourage and develop trade between provinces. 99

Source: House of Commons debates, 7 March 1878, pp. 858–859.

- In the south, the railway company controlled most of the land and would keep the profits from its sale.
- Scientists reported that the southern prairies were well suited for farming. (They were wrong, but no one knew that.)

You can see both routes on the map below.

Building the Line

A private company built the railway in stages. It raised money from investors. The government provided grants. The work crews faced different challenges in each section of the country. On average, one kilometre of track cost half a million dollars. (That's in nineteenth-century dollars!)

During the heat of summer, mosquitoes and flies buzzed around the workers' heads. In the winter, bitter cold sliced through their clothes. Work crews lived together in dark, smoky bunkhouses. They slept in piles of hay infested with fleas and rats. Their meals were salt pork, corned beef, molasses, beans, and tea.

Impact of the Railway

The railway had a huge impact on the development of Canada. Over time it brought many newcomers. They changed the face of the prairies forever.

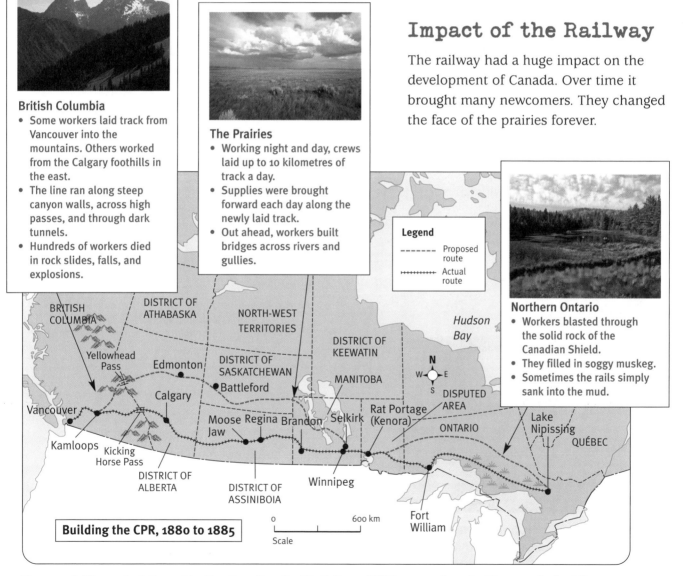

British Columbia
- Some workers laid track from Vancouver into the mountains. Others worked from the Calgary foothills in the east.
- The line ran along steep canyon walls, across high passes, and through dark tunnels.
- Hundreds of workers died in rock slides, falls, and explosions.

The Prairies
- Working night and day, crews laid up to 10 kilometres of track a day.
- Supplies were brought forward each day along the newly laid track.
- Out ahead, workers built bridges across rivers and gullies.

Legend
- – – – – Proposed route
- ++++++++ Actual route

Northern Ontario
- Workers blasted through the solid rock of the Canadian Shield.
- They filled in soggy muskeg.
- Sometimes the rails simply sank into the mud.

Building the CPR, 1880 to 1885

0   600 km
Scale

Figure 9.6 The route followed by the Canadian Pacific Railway (CPR) across Canada. The grey dashed line shows the rejected northerly route. Towns tended to spring up where the railway passed. Towns located far from the track faded away. Speculate on why communities thrived close to the railway.

Identity

Canada's First Chinese Immigrants

Did Canada mistreat some of its first citizens? Faced with a shortage of workers, the CPR employed about 17 000 Chinese workers to help build the railway in the mountains between 1881 and 1885. The work here was so hard and so dangerous that no one else would do it.

The Conditions

Chinese labourers were paid about $1.50 per day. This was about half of what other workers received. They had to pay $4 per week for room and board. Even so, the tents were flimsy and the food was poor. Most Chinese were not prepared for the bitterly cold conditions.

The work assigned to the Chinese was brutal. They were the earth movers. Hanging from ropes, they chipped away at the rock faces with chisels and hammers. They laid the dynamite to blast a path through the rock. At least 700 of these workers died. They were crushed in landslides, blown up by explosives, and lost in river torrents when bridges collapsed. Many simply died of scurvy or other diseases in the work camps.

Mary Chan's grandfather came to Canada in 1879 on a sailing ship. She recalls his work on the railway:

Many people died during the construction of that railroad. They lived in tents along the track, and it was cold. Some people got arthritis. They were attacked by mosquitoes and blackflies, and some people eventually went blind. And then, after it was finished, there was no other work.

Source: *Sound Heritage* (Victoria: Provincial Archives of British Columbia), vol. VIII, nos. 1–2, http://collections.ic.gc.ca/time/galler05/frames/chinese.htm.

The Accomplishment

As John A. Macdonald said, "Without the Chinese, there would be no railway." Without them, the railway would have been too expensive. Without the railway, Canada could not have been connected from west to east. Rock by rock, the Chinese workers shouldered their way through the Rocky Mountains. They earned an honourable place in Canada's history. Many Chinese railway workers stayed and made Canada their home.

Tech Link

To find out more about the experiences of the Chinese workers, open Chapter 9 on your *Voices and Visions* CD-ROM.

Respond

How did the Chinese railway workers contribute to Canada? How was what they did an act of citizenship? How were they treated? Why do you think they were treated this way?

Figure 9.7 James Pon in front of the Chinese Railway Workers Monument, which he lobbied to erect. It was made in 1989. Why would Pon want to immortalize the actions of people who lived so long ago? What would it have to do with citizenship?

Biography

Father Albert Lacombe (1827–1916)

Father Albert Lacombe is the most famous Catholic missionary in Alberta's history. A Canadien, whose great-great-grandfather was Anishinabe, [a-nih-shih-NAH-bee] he devoted himself to helping the Métis, the Canadiens, and the First Nations in the west. The Cree gave Lacombe the name Kamiyoatchakwêt, "the noble soul." The Siksika called him Aahsosskitsipahpiwa, "the good heart."

CPR employees began surveying the route of the CPR through the Siksika reserve. The Siksika got angry. Lacombe convinced Chief Isapo-Muxika (Crowfoot) to stop a dangerous confrontation and allow the track on the reserve. To thank him, the CPR made Lacombe president of the company for an hour and gave him a lifetime pass on the railway.

Figure 9.8 Crowfoot, Father Albert Lacombe, and Three Bulls, 1886.

Figure 9.9 A party of officials watching Donald Smith, head of the CPR. Smith hammers in the last spike at Craigellachie, BC. Think about how these officials must have felt about getting the railway finished.

Tech Link

To see the first locomotive to travel across the continent in one trip, open Chapter 9 on your *Voices and Visions* CD-ROM.

Figure 9.10 A group of workers staging their own ceremony in Craigellachie. Why aren't there any Chinese labourers in this photo? Speculate on what these workers thought about getting the railway finished.

VOICES ■

What does each of these opinions say about the purpose or impact of the railway?

❝ Like a vision, I could see it driving my poor Indians before it, and spreading out behind it the farms, the towns, and cities …. No one who has not lived in the West since the Old-Times can realize what is due to that road—that CPR. It was magic. ❞

—Albert Lacombe, missionary

Source: Katharine Hughes, *Father Lacombe: The Black-Robe Voyageur* (Toronto: William Briggs, 1914), p. 273.

❝ The Canadian Pacific was built for the purpose of making money for the shareholders and for no other purpose under the sun. ❞

—William Cornelius Van Horne

Source: W. Kaye Lamb, *History of the Canadian Pacific Railway* (Toronto: Macmillan, 1977), p. 1.

❝ Next summer, or at the latest next fall, the railway will be close to us, the whites will fill the country and they will dictate to us as they please. It is useless to dream that we can frighten them; that time has passed. ❞

—Pitikwahanapiwiyin (Poundmaker), Cree chief, speaking to his people in 1882

Source: Pierre Berton, *The Great Railway: Illustrated* (Toronto: McClelland and Stewart, 1972), pp. 224, 226.

❝ If [Macdonald] had not found ways and means of constructing the railway when he did, Canada would almost certainly not extend today from sea to sea. ❞

—W. Kaye Lamb, historian

Source: W. Kaye Lamb, *History of the Canadian Pacific Railway* (Toronto: Macmillan, 1977), p. 436.

Opinions about the Railway

• **A British Columbian:** The railway brought us into Confederation!	• **A Resident of the Prairies:** It's not fair: the railway company received so much land for free while we have to struggle.
• **A CPR Shareholder:** Finally we can make some money from the land we got for making the railway.	• **A Prairie Farmer:** The CPR charges us far too much to ship our crops. And the government won't let any other railway build lines into Western Canada. Without competition, the CPR can charge whatever it likes!
• **An Ontario Farmer:** Now we can move west. We will grow crops and move them by rail to market.	
• **A Manager for a Manufacturer in the East:** Now we'll have a way to bring our products west.	
• **A BC Logger:** We'll sell more lumber. They need lumber to build houses in the new prairie towns.	• **A Cree:** It is the railway that is bringing the flood of newcomers into our territories. If only it had never been built!
• **A Prairie Miner:** Trains need coal. We'll have jobs!	

Figure 9.11 Opinions about the railway. Use each opinion to identify a way the railway affected the person's life.

Think It ▶ Through

1. Divide your class into three groups. Imagine that each group is a survey party hired to find a route through one of three sections of the railway: Northern Ontario, the prairies, or BC.
   a) Find out any problems that the railway will face building along your route. Check the text as well as an atlas.
   b) In point form, draw up a report.
   c) Present your findings to the class.
   d) As a class, vote to decide which survey team faces the greatest challenge.

2. Imagine you are Sandford Fleming, Chief Engineer of the Intercolonial Railway. You need to convince the prime minister to give you more money for construction. Write a letter to him, or give a speech to Cabinet. Make a list of arguments and facts you will use. Why are costs so high? What benefits will the railway bring?

Farming the Frontier

Y ou will recall that the second part of the National Policy called for immigration. The government needed to convince people to come and farm the land.

Focus

What role did agriculture play in the growth of Western Canada?

As you will learn in this section, it succeeded to a certain degree. New farming communities appeared. They became the backbone of a new Canadian West. You will learn about the earliest immigrant groups. These people arrived in the 1870s and 1880s.

Land Policy in the West

Before the new farmers came, the government surveyed the land.

- Surveyors divided the land up into large chunks. These were called townships.
- Each township was divided into 36 squares called sections.
- Each section was divided into four quarter sections. Each quarter section was 64 hectares (160 acres).

The surveyors drove iron stakes into the ground to mark off each quarter section. The whole of the North-West Territories was measured in this way. The surveyors did not follow any of the established farm borders, which were patterned like farms in the seigneurial system.

The government set aside two sections in each township. These were later sold to pay for schools. Other sections belonged to the Hudson's Bay Company, left over from

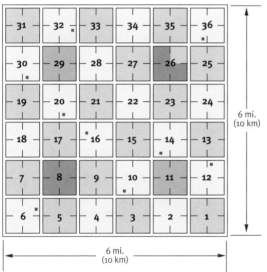

A Prairie Township

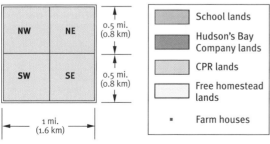

Sections

School lands

Hudson's Bay Company lands

CPR lands

Free homestead lands

▪ Farm houses

Figure 9.12 *Settler's Home*, 1900, by Edward Roper. During the 1880s, the artist visited Manitoba. That's when he painted this scene at Carberry, Assiniboia [uh-sih-nih-BOY-uh]. What in the painting makes homesteading seem pleasant? How could an artist change things to make it seem unpleasant? Can we trust paintings to "tell the truth"?

Figure 9.13 A diagram showing how the land was surveyed in the North-West Territories. Calculate the area of a township, section, and quarter section. Why was it important to survey the land before the newcomers arrived?

the sale of Rupert's Land. Still other sections went to the CPR to pay for building the railway. The rest were open for new arrivals.

Figure 9.14 The interior of a Canadian Pacific Railway car drawn by Melton Prior in 1888. Between 1867 and 1899, 1.5 million immigrants came to Canada. Virtually all of them went west on rail cars like this. What do you think the people in this illustration might be thinking?

In 1872, the government passed the Dominion Lands Act. It said that any head of a family could apply for land. So could any male at least 21 years old. They each received a quarter section of land called a homestead. It cost only $10. After 1882, women could apply, too.

Each applicant had to promise three things: to live on the land for at least six months of the year, to build a house, and to start farming. After three years, the homesteader got to keep the land if he or she had fulfilled these terms.

A Rough Life

The life of a homesteading family was difficult. Most of the new arrivals were poor. They could not buy seed, farm tools, livestock, or the materials to build houses and barns. Nature often worked against them. Crops could be ruined by grasshoppers, lack of rain, early frost, or hail. Many newcomers gave up in disgust.

VOICES ■

Alexander Kindred had a homestead. It was in the Qu'Appelle Valley, near Moffat, Saskatchewan. He describes a series of bad farming years:

❝ In 1886 we had 80 acres [32 hectares] under crop. Not a drop of rain fell from the time it went in until it was harvested. I sowed 124 bushels and threshed 54. In 1888 we began to think we could not grow wheat in this country. I had now 120 to 125 acres under cultivation. We put in 25 acres of wheat, 10 to 15 acres of oats, and let the rest go back into prairie. That year we got 35 bushels [of wheat] to the acre! So we went to work and ploughed up again. The next year wheat headed out two inches high. Not a drop of rain fell that whole season until fall. [In 1890] we had wheat standing to the chin but on the 8th July a hailstorm destroyed absolutely everything. ❞

Source: Gerald Friesen, *The Canadian Prairies: A History* (Toronto: University of Toronto Press, 1984), p. 222.

 **Respond**

Compare this account with the painting by Edward Roper on the previous page. Which image of the West do you think the government wanted to show potential immigrants? Why?

Canada Today

Farming has always been a hard life in Canada. Every season, farmers face threats to their livelihood. For example, in 2003, inspectors discovered a sick cow. It was infected with Bovine Spongiform Encephalopathy (BSE), or mad cow disease. The United States stopped all imports of older cattle from Canada. Many farmers couldn't sell their herds. They lost everything.

Figure 9.15 Farm hands at work on a modern Alberta farm. When disasters strike today, the government usually provides some help to farmers. What happened in the past?

The First Newcomers: From Ontario

The government was eager to attract newcomers to the North-West Territories, so it put on a campaign. It appointed agents to "sell" the West.

They began close to home. The earliest newcomers came from Ontario. That province had many people. Farmland was scarce there, whereas land in the West was plentiful. During the 1870s, many Ontarians moved to Manitoba. It even got the nickname "New Ontario."

Land was scarce in Québec as well. But no government agents tried to convince Canadiens to move West. Instead, the Canadiens travelled to New England for jobs.

The Arrival of the Mennonites

Mennonites do not believe in fighting wars. The czar of Russia wanted them to serve in the army. What would they do?

A Canadian immigration agent visited Russia. He invited the Mennonites to move to Canada. They would be able to practise their religion. They would be able to farm collectively (all together on a big farm).

The first group took up land southeast of Winnipeg. In all, about 7000 Mennonites came. They brought a heavy plough that was effective at breaking the prairie sod. They proved that the Canadian prairie could be farmed with the proper tools. They started about 100 communities in the West.

Figure 9.16 The steamboat *International*. This boat brought the first group of Mennonites to Manitoba in 1874. What did the Canadian West offer these new arrivals?

From Iceland to Canada

Another early group of immigrant farmers came from Iceland. Iceland is an island in the North Atlantic Ocean. In March 1875, the Askja volcano in Iceland erupted. The falling volcanic ash poisoned the land. It killed the cattle.

Many refugees from the disaster fled to Canada. The government gave them nearly 800 square kilometres of land. They would have the freedom to speak their language and keep their customs. They would be able to make their own laws.

The first party of 235 arrived in 1875. They travelled to the shores of Lake Winnipeg. They called their lands New Iceland. Their main community was Gimli, which means "paradise."

New Iceland was no paradise for the newcomers. The climate was harsh. Floods forced colonists off their land. Some people starved to death. Others died in a horrible smallpox epidemic. Many people left, but the rest held on. In 1881, Manitoba absorbed New Iceland. Some of those who left made their way to Alberta. They settled near Red Deer, in a community called Markerville.

Figure 9.17 *The Landing*, painted by Arni Sigurdsson in 1950. It shows the Icelandic immigrants landing at Willow Point, Manitoba, in 1875. They had just finished a frightening and dangerous journey over Lake Winnipeg in wooden boats called scows. What mood does the painting create? How did the artist create that mood?

Legend

	British Columbia		Prince Edward Island
	Manitoba		Northwest Territories
	Ontario		British possessions
	Québec		District of Keewatin
	New Brunswick		Disputed area
	Nova Scotia		

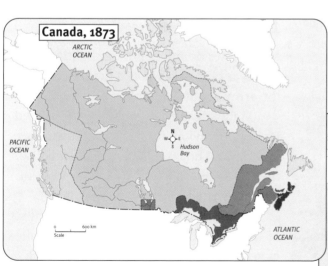

Figure 9.18 Two maps showing Canada in 1873 (left) and 1882 (right). List the changes that took place between those years. How does the 1882 map compare with a map of Canada today?

CASE STUDY
Farming and the First Nations

Some First Nations were farmers, too. Did they have a fair chance to succeed? When the buffalo began to disappear, many First Nations people wanted to farm. They were not strangers to farming. At Red River, the Anishinabe had farms. Farther west, some Nakoda and Cree farmed.

When the First Nations signed **treaties**, the government agreed to help them become farmers. The treaties guaranteed the First Nations land. The First Nations would receive farm animals, tools, and seed. In some cases, these obligations were fulfilled. First Nations welcomed machinery that would help them farm. They appreciated learning farming skills, such as making butter. However, many obligations went unfulfilled.

- Most land assigned to First Nations was not good for farming.
- Much of the equipment they were owed did not appear.
- Instructors were supposed to teach farming skills, but few instructors arrived.
- First Nations farmers were often prevented from buying farm machinery.
- Those who did farm successfully had a hard time selling their crops.

Many First Nations farmers gave up.

Respond

The government let the Mennonites farm collectively. It allowed the Icelanders to keep their own laws. It did not allow the First Nations to keep their own laws or farm collectively. Why did it not treat all citizens equally?

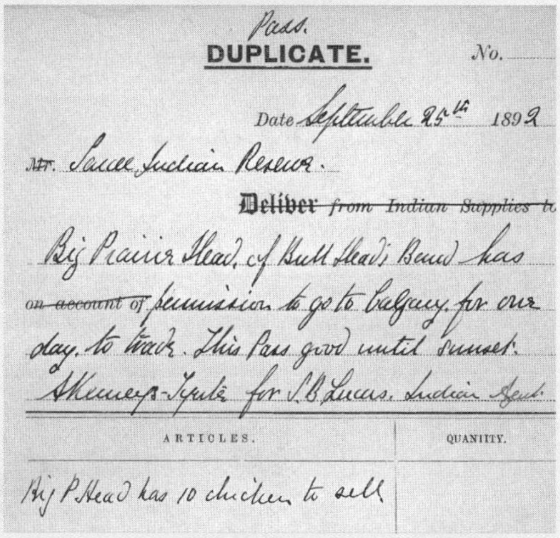
Pass.
DUPLICATE. No.

Date September 25th 1892

Mr. Sarcee Indian Reserve.

~~Deliver from Indian Supplies to~~

Big Prairie Head of Bull Head's Band has ~~on account of~~ permission to go to Calgary for one day to trade. This Pass good until sunset.

[illegible] for S.B. Lucas, Indian Agent.

ARTICLES.	QUANTITY.
Big P.Head has 10 chicken to sell	

Figure 9.19 A pass for Big Prairie Head. On it, a government representative gives him permission to leave the Sarcee (Tsuu T'ina) Indian Reserve. What did Big Prairie Head get permission to do? First Nations people on some reserves needed signed passes like this to leave their reserve lands. How would this system make it easier or harder to sell produce?

Think It Through

1. Pretend you're going to write a piece of historical fiction about an early immigrant group. In this activity, you will do just three preparation steps. SKILLS
   a) First, gather reasons why the three groups of newcomers described in this section moved to the West. Use a graphic organizer to collect your information. Alternatively, for each group, draw a picture to illustrate one reason for moving. Now choose one group.
   b) Using the text and pictures in this section, make notes about this group.
   c) Speculate on what these people were thinking about when they arrived.
2. a) The population grew in Western Canada in the late nineteenth century. By how much did it grow? (Hint: See page 208.)
   b) Did plentiful, inexpensive land help populate Western Canada? Was it a key factor? Support your opinion with facts and arguments.

Helping Industry

The third part of the National Policy was to build a strong economy. Farming in the West was going to be crucial to the Canadian economy. So was manufacturing in the East. The government wanted to build farming and other industries. This would create jobs for Canadians.

In this section, you will learn how the government tried to boost the economy. It used tariffs with some success. You will see that Canadians had mixed opinions about tariffs.

Focus

How did the National Policy strengthen the Canadian economy?

Reading
STRATEGY

When you see a complicated diagram, first look it over. Then read the separate parts. You might find it helpful to draw your own version of the diagram.

The Scenario:
- The Massey Company is a Canadian company. It makes a plough that it sells for $110.
- John Deere is an American company. It sells a plough for $100.
- The Canadian government puts a tariff of $20 on the imported plough.

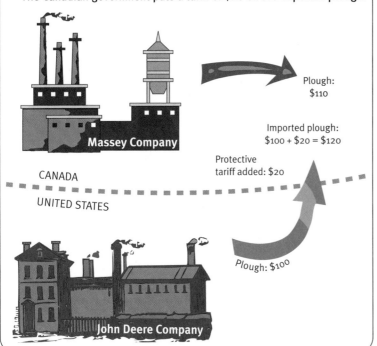

Plough: $110

Imported plough: $100 + $20 = $120

Protective tariff added: $20

CANADA

UNITED STATES

Massey Company

Plough: $100

John Deere Company

The Problem of Competition

As you have learned, the colonies joined Confederation for many reasons. One of the reasons was to increase trade with one another. Creating the railway was one way of making this trade possible.

Canadian manufacturers in the East faced a huge problem, though. American businesses could produce goods in vast quantities. This kept their unit costs low. So, American goods sold at a lower price than Canadian goods. Canadian producers worried that Canadians would buy the less expensive US goods. They were right.

The Solution: Protective Tariffs

For the third part of his National Policy, Macdonald put a tariff on goods coming into Canada. A **protective tariff** is a tax placed on a product crossing the border. This tax adds to the cost of the product. The product becomes more expensive. Macdonald knew that the tariff would make American goods more expensive than Canadian goods. Then Canadians would buy the goods made in Canada.

Figure 9.20 A diagram showing how a protective tariff works. How much more expensive is the American plough after the tariff? How would you feel about the tariff if you worked in a Canadian factory? If you were a Canadian farmer, which plough would you buy? How would you feel about the tariff? Explain your conclusions.

In Favour of the Tariff	In Opposition to the Tariff
• New manufacturing industries created jobs. • Adding manufacturing made Canada's economy more diverse. • Canada's industries were young. They needed more help so they could grow. • The high tariff kept foreign products out. People bought Canadian products instead. • The tariff brought in a lot of money. It paid for programs that people wanted.	• Canadians paid more for many goods. The tariff made them more expensive. • Farmers paid more for their tools and equipment. Nonetheless, they could only earn what buyers were willing to pay. • Most industry was in Ontario and Québec. Westerners and Maritimers had few industries. They had to pay higher costs even though they got no benefits.

Figure 9.21 Imagine a meeting with an Ontario plough maker, a Western farmer, a worker from a Montréal clothing factory, and a Halifax fisher. What would each person think about the tariff? Which of the above arguments would each person use?

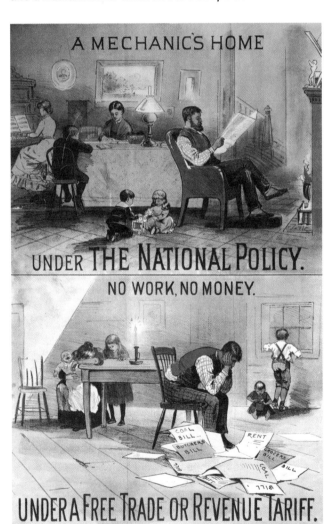

Figure 9.22 A poster dating from 1891. It gives one point of view about the impact of the National Policy. Compare the two panels of the poster. What does it say about life with and without the National Policy? What is the main message of the poster? Would a manufacturer agree with this poster? What about a Western farmer?

A **diverse economy** has many types of industry. If one industry is suffering, the others can keep the country healthy.

Slow but Steady Progress

The changes in the North-West Territories in the late nineteenth century were remarkable. New arrivals from Europe and Eastern Canada were farming the land. Grain began to replace furs as the region's chief export. Ploughed fields covered the prairies where countless buffalo used to roam. The railway replaced the canoe and the Red River cart. Trading posts changed into bustling business centres for farms.

The First Nations and Métis faced many problems. The government neglected them. Many newcomers were unfriendly. Nonetheless, they did their best to adapt to the changes in their land.

By 1891, Manitoba and the North-West Territories had a population of 281 000. This was more than double what it had been 10 years earlier. (This includes 30 000 First Nations people.) It was not quite the rapid growth that the government had hoped for. Nonetheless, it was a start.

Tech Link

To compare this 1891 poster about free trade with another from that year, open Chapter 9 on your *Voices and Visions* CD-ROM.

Canada Today

The National Policy did not help Aboriginal industries or farmers. Nonetheless, many Aboriginal businesses have done well over the years. Dolly Watts is just one of more than 27 000 Aboriginal people who ran their own businesses in Canada in 2005. She is a member of the Gitksan [git-KSAHN] First Nation from northern British Columbia. In 1995, she opened the Liliget Feast House in Vancouver, BC. It brings in more than $400 000 every year.

People travel from as far away as Germany and Japan to taste her alder-grilled salmon, buffalo smokies, venison strips, oysters, duck breast with wild-berry sauce, mussels, and steamed fiddleheads. Watts's Aboriginal staff cook these traditional foods over an alderwood grill. This makes the food taste just as Watts remembers it from her childhood.

Aboriginal women draw on their heritage to help them reach goals in the Canadian economy and in their personal lives. Read what Watts says about this important human resource.

Do Aboriginal women want to become warriors? Of course. Not for war, but as trail blazers for self and others. They're proving to be courageous, willing to take risks, empowered through improved self-esteem in the face of competitive forces all around. Armed with knowledge and skills, standing beside our helpers (resources) and our spirit helpers. I can say that many of us have become warriors, not for militancy, but for personal challenges.

Source: "Dolly Watts: Woman Warrior," http://www.first nationsdrum.com/biography/spring99_watts.htm.

Think It Through

1. The National Policy had three parts: transportation, immigration, and protective tariffs. The government hoped that each part would have certain effects. List what these were. Use the skill of distinguishing cause and effect that you practised in Chapter 4 (see page 76).

2. a) The National Policy had an impact on citizens all across Canada. It is important to think about different perspectives. Form small groups. Each member of your group should explain the impact on one of these groups:
   - Chinese railway workers
   - Icelandic immigrant farmers
   - Siksika buffalo hunters
   - factory workers in Ontario

   Think of other perspectives you could add to your group discussion.

   b) Was the National Policy good for Canada?
   - State your opinion on this question.
   - Collect facts and arguments to support your opinion.
   - Use your written list of facts and arguments in a class discussion.

3. How many Aboriginal people in Canada run their own businesses? Some of them got started with the help of band council grants or loans. How is this the same or different from the National Policy's assistance to new immigrants in the nineteenth century?

4. How did Canada secure the West and prepare for a massive influx of immigrants?

Chapter 9 PROJECT   You Be the Author

In this chapter project, you have the chance to write a historical fiction story. While studying Canadian history, you have learned about events and individuals that helped mould our country. You've seen the great dramas that built the railroad and brought law and order. You've seen the lives of people turned upside down as they travelled to the West to start a new life. These are the kinds of events and people that inspire authors to write historical fiction.

Focus

Scan through the chapter, looking at headings and pictures. What part of the chapter do you find most exciting? Does a particular event intrigue you? Choose an event that raises difficult issues. Imagine what some of the people of that time period must have been experiencing. This is your starting point.

Planning, Drafting, and Writing

As an author, you should develop an authentic but original plot. Set your story in the time and places featured in this chapter. Your story should be at least 500 words long. Use Skill Check: Read and Write Historical Fiction on page 196 to guide you through the process.

Revising

When revising your writing, ask these questions:
- Did I hook the reader with a strong opening?
- Did I make my characters believable?
- Did I choose words that made my writing interesting?
- Did I give the reader a clear picture of the setting and the historical events?
- Did I hold my reader's attention with a strong plot?

Presenting

After you finish writing your story, publish and present it. Share your story with other students in the class. Describe what you found most difficult and most interesting about writing historical fiction.

1. What historical events did the other students write about? What did you learn from their stories?

2. Discuss how historical fiction can help form a country's identity.

Figure 9.23 As you progress through your years of schooling, you will have many chances to discuss the process of writing. How is writing historical fiction different from writing other kinds of fiction? How did writing historical fiction help you understand history?

Chapter 10 Expanding Confederation

Chapter INQUIRY	What factors led British Columbia, Prince Edward Island, Alberta, Saskatchewan, and then Newfoundland to become provinces of Canada, and what were the consequences?

Key CONCEPT ▶ Historical Perspective

Imagine you woke up one day and you had no memory. You wouldn't know who you were. You wouldn't know your family and friends. You wouldn't remember your school or your favourite television program. You would find yourself in a world where nothing was familiar. How do you think you would feel if you knew nothing about your past?

History is similar to your memory. It is the record of what has happened in the past. Without history, we do not know how things came to be as they are today. All events have their roots in the past. Things happen because other things have happened. History helps us to understand why things are the way they are. We call this **historical perspective**.

Like all countries, Canada has a history. By learning about our history, we discover the traditions and values that are important to Canadians today. Knowing about the past helps us to understand the present. It also helps us think about what may happen in the future.

Honing Your Skills

Political cartoons can be a fun way to learn about history. The Skill Check feature in this chapter will show you how to **Analyze Political Cartoons** for meaning. The project at the end of the chapter will ask you to create your own political cartoon on one of the issues you have read about.

Time and Change

In Chapter 8, you learned about the events that led to Manitoba becoming the fifth province of Canada. In this chapter, you'll find out how Canada gained five more provinces. These were British Columbia, Prince Edward Island, Alberta, Saskatchewan, and Newfoundland and Labrador.

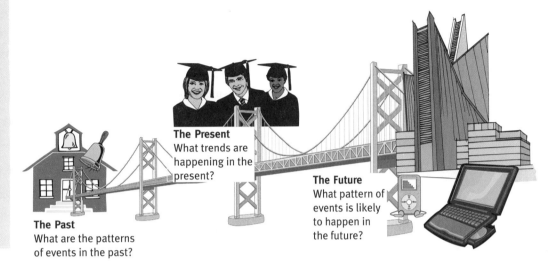

The Present
What trends are happening in the present?

The Future
What pattern of events is likely to happen in the future?

The Past
What are the patterns of events in the past?

Figure 10.1 Building a bridge between the past, the present, and the future. We can make history come alive by building bridges between events in the past and events that are happening today. Then we can study these patterns and trends. They can help us think about what may happen in the future. For example, in the previous chapter, you learned about the railway expanding in Canada. What forms of transportation are in use in Canada today? What pattern do you see? Predict how transportation will change in Canada's future.

Think AHEAD

Use a Know-Wonder-Learn chart like the one below to organize your thoughts about the expansion of Confederation.
- Think about what you already know about Confederation. Think about the reasons why some colonies joined the union in 1867. Think about why others did not. Record everything you know about the topic in the "Know" column.
- Then, in the "Wonder" column, record those things you would like to know about the expansion of Confederation after 1867.
- When you have finished this chapter, return to your chart. Check off the questions in the "Wonder" column that you have answered.
- Then, summarize what you have learned in the "Learn" column.

Expansion of Confederation		
Know	Wonder	Learn

SKILL CHECK:
Analyze Political Cartoons

Political cartoons have been around for a long time. They have been printed in Canada's newspapers since before Confederation. They are still popular today.

Political cartoons poke fun at politicians. They use humour to make statements about important events and issues. When we look at such cartoons from the past, we get an idea of what people were thinking about at that time. In this way, political cartoons help us gain historical perspective.

To understand political cartoons, we need to interpret what they are trying to say. Here are some tips to help you in your analysis.

1. **Look to see if the cartoon has a title.** If it does, what does it mean?

2. **Examine the overall scene in the cartoon.** What is the key issue or event?

3. **Describe the setting.** Where and when does the action take place?

4. **Identify the people or characters in the cartoon.** What are they saying? What does their mood appear to be?

5. **Identify any keywords or symbols.** What do they mean?

6. **At whom or what is the cartoonist poking fun?**

7. **What is the message in the cartoon?** Is it expressed effectively? Why or why not?

WEB LINK

8. **What techniques has the cartoonist used (for example, labels or exaggeration of physical features)?** How has the cartoonist created humour?

Try It!

Analyze the political cartoon on this page. Just follow the steps outlined at left.

 Tech Link

Different artists use different techniques. To compare the cartoon on this page with one drawn by an American, open Chapter 10 on your *Voices and Visions* CD-ROM.

Note: This cartoonist is using the term responsible government for representative government.

Figure 10.2 "The Bridge to Prosperity," published in the St. John's newspaper *The Independent*, 29 March 1948. This political cartoon was printed during the debate over Confederation in Newfoundland. In your opinion, is it effective?

British Columbia Joins Confederation

After 1867, many newcomers came to Canada to settle on the vast prairies of the North-West Territories. They were lured here by the promise of fertile farmland. British Columbia, though, seemed all rock and mountain. At first, farming was only possible in mountain valleys and river deltas. Why did people come to British Columbia? They came for one thing: gold! In this section, you'll find out how the gold rush and the events that followed led British Columbia to join Confederation.

Focus

What factors led to British Columbia joining Confederation?

Reading
STRATEGY

You'll notice that the text in this section is divided into "chunks." This is done using headings, subheadings and features. As you progress through the section, write each heading in your notebook. Then, summarize the main idea of each chunk in your own words.

A Gold Colony

The fur trade attracted the first Europeans to the Pacific coast. The number of explorers and traders was small, though. In those days, there were far more First Nations peoples than Europeans. They lived along the coast and in the interior. In fact, by 1849, the only European settlement was a small British colony at Fort Victoria on Vancouver Island.

In the 1850s, all that was about to change. The First Nations who lived along the Fraser River had been mining gold for hundreds of years. When the Hudson's Bay Company set up a trading post nearby, the First Nations miners brought their gold there to trade. Word that there was gold in the mountains quickly spread to the outside world. Before long, **prospectors** in search of gold stampeded into the region. The gold rush was on! In 1858, about 25 000 prospectors were scrambling along the banks of the Fraser River.

At first, Vancouver Island was a colony, and the mainland was British territory. The governor was James Douglas. He grew alarmed as thousands of miners—mostly Americans—flooded into the area. There had been lawlessness in the California gold rush a few years earlier. Douglas did not want the same thing to happen here. He began issuing licences to the miners. Then, to maintain law and order, he created a police force and appointed **magistrates** (judges) to enforce the law.

The Stó:lô [STAH-loh] and Nlaka'pamux [unth-lah-KAH-pum] Nations lived along the Fraser River. They relied on salmon for their livelihood. The miners searched for gold all along the river. This scared the fish away. In August 1858, the Stó:lô and the Nlaka'pamux blocked the river to keep the miners out. The standoff turned violent. Many First Nations people were killed. The two sides were close to war before Douglas and a band of soldiers arrived to restore

Figure 10.3 A prospector panning for gold, as painted by William Hind in 1864. The quest for gold has often spurred people on to seek adventure in foreign lands. What role did this quest play in the Europeans' early explorations?

Figure 10.4 Wagon trains on the Cariboo Road in the early 1870s. When the road was finished, it opened up the Cariboo territory. Miners and ranchers settled in the area. What impact do you think they would have had on the First Nations people who lived here?

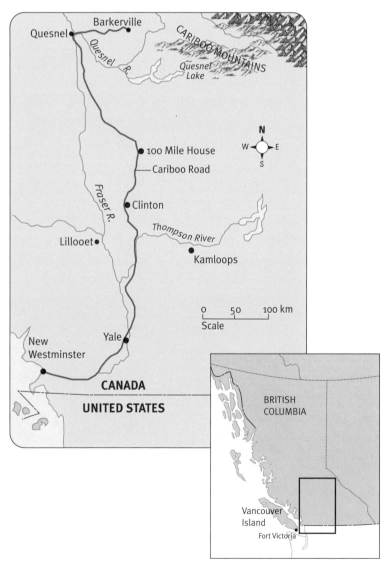

peace. They assured the Stó:lô and the Nlaka'pamux they would be protected from the miners.

Then, to bring law and order to the region, Britain created the colony of British Columbia in 1858. Fort Victoria would be the administrative centre. Douglas was appointed governor of both colonies. The two colonies had a population of about 50 000, including First Nations.

The Road to Gold

In time, the prospectors moved farther north. They were searching for the main source of the gold nuggets the river had carried downstream. They finally discovered more gold along the Quesnel River in the Cariboo Mountains. It was hard to get supplies to these remote mining camps, though. The Fraser River was too rough to travel by boat. Governor Douglas decided to build a wagon road.

In 1865, the Cariboo Road was finished. It had cost more than a million dollars to build. Now, though, horse-drawn wagons could carry supplies to the distant mining camps. Over time, 100 000 miners would start out in New Westminster on the coast. They would make their way up the Fraser River, teetering along the road that clung to the steep canyon walls. Then they would travel over land for 650 kilometres. Finally, tired out, they would reach Barkerville, a supply town for the goldfields in the central interior. For a brief time, boomtown Barkerville was the largest city north of San Francisco and west of Chicago.

Figure 10.5 British Columbia in 1865, during the gold rush. Refer to a topographical map of British Columbia in an atlas. Examine the terrain that the Cariboo Road followed. Imagine you're talking to a prospector in New Westminster. He wants to find gold. Write him a detailed set of directions.

Biography

Catherine Schubert (1835–1918)

Most prospectors travelled to British Columbia by boat. Some, however, made the trip over land from the East. Known as the Overlanders, they travelled by wagon and canoe, on horseback and on foot, led by First Nations guides. They followed the fur-trading routes across the prairies and over the mountains. It was a long and often dangerous journey.

The only woman among the Overlanders was Catherine Schubert. She and her husband, Augustus, were desperate to reach the trading post at Kamloops quickly. Schubert was pregnant with her fourth child. There was no time to spare! They were rafting down the Thompson River when Schubert's labour began. The family reached a Secwepemc [SUHK-wep-muhk] village near the Kamloops trading post. There, the Secwepemc women took care of Schubert. She quickly delivered a baby girl.

The Schuberts finally bought a farm at Lillooet. But Schubert's husband was more interested in finding gold than in farming. He made frequent trips to the goldfields. He was never very successful, though. To support her family, Catherine Schubert opened a roadhouse and rented out rooms to travellers. She ran the farm and taught school to local children in her home. Later, she sold her hotel to take a teaching job at a boarding school. In 1881, Augustus Schubert vowed to give up prospecting. The family moved to a farm in the Okanagan Valley. Once again, Schubert opened a roadhouse for travellers.

Catherine Schubert served her community until she died in 1918. She was 83 years old. A monument was built in her honour in 1926. It says, simply, "A brave and notable pioneer."

Respond

Why is Catherine Schubert described as a "notable" pioneer? Think about how she helped build the new communities in the BC interior. Do you think she should also be described as an active citizen? Explain.

A New Beginning

The gold rush lasted only until about 1868. This was the year that Barkerville burned to the ground. Yet the gold rush marked a turning point for British Columbia. During the height of the rush, the sleepy town of Victoria was transformed into a thriving centre. After the rush, many of the newcomers stayed on. They built farms and started up businesses. British officials arrived to set up a government. The Cariboo Road marked the beginning of a whole network of roads. Out of the hustle and bustle of the gold rush, a permanent settlement emerged on the Pacific coast.

Over time, other economic activities got going. Logging was one of the most important of these. How does an economic activity help get towns started? Let's look at one example. The Fraser Mills Company needed people to work in its sawmill. It invited 40 Canadien families to come to BC from Québec in 1909. They founded Maillardville, near Vancouver. It was the first BC Francophone community. Many BC towns were started for people who wanted to work in the logging industry.

Figure 10.6 Two loggers cutting down a Douglas fir tree in British Columbia. The loggers are standing on springboards that go right inside the tree trunk. Logging became the backbone of the provincial economy. What transportation networks do you think were needed to make this happen?

First Nations in British Columbia

Various First Nations lived on the mainland and islands of British Columbia. They hunted sea mammals in the ocean, gathered shellfish along the coast, and fished the mountain rivers. The Pacific Coast has a lush temperate rain forest. The First Nations relied on it as a dependable source of food. They also had a highly developed trading network.

Before the gold rush, the First Nations peoples tried to adjust to the newcomers in their territories. It wasn't easy, though. The newcomers didn't understand the First Nations' way of life. They didn't understand the importance of the land and waters to these peoples.

In 1850 and 1854, Governor Douglas bought 14 parcels of land on Vancouver Island from the First Nations. These become known as the Douglas Treaties. Douglas set up small reserves where the First Nations people could live. He recognized their right to hunt and fish on unoccupied territory. In return, the people agreed to move off their traditional lands. These were the only land deals between the British and the First Nations in British Columbia for many decades. To this day, most BC First Nations have not signed treaties. They have not received any compensation for land taken from them. For the most part, the newcomers did not ask permission to take the land.

Figure 10.7 A fishing weir in British Columbia, 1866. The Tsilhqot'in [tsil-KOH-tin] used fishing weirs like this one to trap salmon as they swam upstream. The miners panned for gold on the same rivers. How might the miners' activities disrupt the fishing weirs?

Before the gold rush, about 60 000 First Nations people lived in BC. A devastating epidemic of smallpox began in 1862. By the time it was over, about 35 000 First Nations people had died of it.

Sometimes the First Nations fought back. In 1864, this happened in Tsilhqot'in territory. A road crew was building a road through Tsilhqot'in lands without Tsilhqot'in permission. The work was scaring off the animals and fish. In addition, some of the road crew were raiding the villages. They were looting graves for valuable artifacts. In response, a group of Tsilhqot'in attacked and killed members of the road crew.

A group of British soldiers was dispatched to end the conflict. They arrested five Tsilhqot'in men and charged them with murder. During the trial, the judge agreed that the Tsilhqot'in people's land had been invaded and that the road crew had provoked them. Still, the Tsilhqot'in were found guilty and were hanged. The next year, though, a law was passed making it illegal to loot First Nations graves. A hundred years later, the government of British Columbia apologized for the way the Tsilhqot'in had been treated.

Tech Link

To learn more about Barkerville, the boomtown of the gold rush, open Chapter 10 on your *Voices and Visions* CD-ROM.

One Colony on the Pacific

You'll recall that the purpose of colonies was to provide wealth and power for the home country. On the Pacific coast, first furs, and then gold, added to Britain's wealth. Britain valued its two Pacific colonies for their location, too. They provided a base for the British fleet on the Pacific coast. In return for these benefits, Britain paid for the colonies' defence and government.

As the gold rush wound down, though, the colonies almost went bankrupt. The gold was nearly gone. The fur trade was in decline. Britain began to think it cost too much money to run two colonies. In 1866, it decided to unite Vancouver Island and British Columbia. Now there was just one colony: British Columbia.

By now, though, the colonists were unhappy with their relationship with Britain. The colony was deeply in debt. It had spent most of its money building the Cariboo Road and other roads and providing public services. There were not enough people to pay taxes or to buy land. Therefore, there wasn't enough money for the government to meet its financial needs.

VOICES

At first, the newcomers saw the First Nations peoples as partners in the fur trade. As the gold rush began, however, the newcomers took over more and more land to meet their needs. Before long, the newcomers saw First Nations peoples as obstacles to their progress. A Nuu-chah-nulth [noo-CHAH-noolth] chief expressed his people's perspective:

66 We see your ships, and hear things that make our hearts grow faint. They say that your King-George-men [Europeans] will soon be here, and will take our land, our firewood, our fishing grounds; that we shall be placed on a little spot, and shall have to do everything according to the fancies of the King-George-men. 99

Source: Gilbert Malcolm Sproat, *Scenes and Studies of Savage Life* (London: Smith, Elder & Co., 1868), p. 4.

Things were changing outside the colony, too. East of the Rockies, Canada was expanding across the prairies. To the north, the United States had bought Alaska from Russia in 1867. To the south, the state of Washington was quickly filling up with homesteaders. In British Columbia, the colonists felt the time had come to decide about their future. They had three choices:

- to remain a British colony
- to become a province of Canada
- to join the United States

Confederation Achieved

In 1870, three delegates from British Columbia travelled to Ottawa. They wanted to talk about joining Canada. They were determined to drive a hard bargain. If the colony was to join Confederation, they wanted several things in return.

VOICES ■

The future of British Columbia was the topic of a great debate. Thomas Lett Wood was a member of the colonial government. He wanted British Columbia to stay a British colony.

66 The bond of union between Canada and the other Provinces bears no resemblance to the union between England and her colonies. There is no natural love and feeling of loyalty. The feeling of loyalty towards England is a feeling blind, instinctive, strong, born with us and impossible to be shaken off; and I believe that it is impossible to transfer a feeling of loyalty at will. 99

Source: The BC Legislative Council, *Debate on the Subject of Confederation with Canada, 1870* (Victoria, 1912), p. 28.

Joseph Trutch played a leading role in the shaping of British Columbia. He was eager to see a Canada united from sea to sea.

Respond

Summarize each of these quotations in your own words. Choose one. Illustrate what the speaker is saying by drawing a picture or retelling it in your own words. SKILLS

66 I advocate Confederation because it will secure ... this Colony under the British Flag, and strengthen British interests on this Continent; ... it will benefit this community, by [reducing taxes] and ... securing the aid of the Dominion Government, who are ... able to ... develop the natural resources and to promote the prosperity of this Colony; and by affording, through a railway, the only means of acquiring a permanent population, which must come from east of the Rocky Mountains. 99

Source: The British Columbia Archives, *Debate on the Subject of Confederation with Canada, 1870.*

The following letter appeared in the *British Columbian*. The author believed that joining the United States was the best choice.

66 I am a loyal Briton, and [I] would prefer living under the institutions of my own country, were it practical. But I ... would prefer the flag and institutions of the United States, with prosperity, to remaining as we are, with no prospect of succeeding as a British colony. 99

Source: *The British Columbian*, 1870.

- They wanted Canada to pay the colony's debts.
- They wanted a road to be built across the prairies to the Pacific. It would link British Columbia with the rest of Canada.
- They wanted Canada to make payments to the new province every year.

Much to their surprise, Canada agreed.

What's more, Canada offered to build something better than a road. They offered to build a transcontinental railway—and they would do it within 10 years.

The delegates went home. They had little trouble winning approval for the deal. On 20 July 1871, British Columbia became Canada's sixth province.

CASE STUDY

The Growth of Vancouver

The city of Vancouver began as the tiny sawmill village of Granville. People also knew it as Gastown. The name came from a talkative saloon keeper known as "Gassy Jack" Deighton.

Respond

What factors affected the pattern of growth in Vancouver?

Life in Granville got busy after the village became the western end of the railway line. In April 1886, Granville became the City of Vancouver. This name was chosen to honour George Vancouver. He was the British explorer who surveyed much of the West Coast. A year later, on 23 May 1887, the first train arrived from Montréal.

The port quickly grew into the centre of activity on the West Coast. Cargo was transferred from the trains onto ships from Asia and Australia, and vice versa. Industries were set up along the railway line. At first, working families lived near these industries so they could walk to work. Wealthier families lived alongside the waters of English Bay. In the early 1900s, though, business and industry began to spread throughout the city centre. Streetcars and trams allowed working families to move to the suburbs. Wealthy families moved, too.

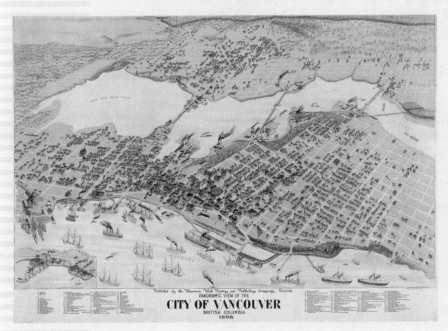

They built homes south of the city with views of the snow-capped mountains to the north. The patterns created in these early days in Vancouver can still be seen today.

Figure 10.8 An illustrated map of Vancouver, looking south, 1898. This map shows Vancouver from the air, as a bird would see it. Locate the following features: the harbour, downtown, industrial areas, residential areas, and railway tracks. In what ways do you think the railway influenced the layout of Vancouver?

Canada Today

Today, Vancouver is still a major port. More cargo passes through here than any other port in the country. Huge freighters sit anchored in the harbour. They wait to unload their cargoes and take on others. They will transport loads of grain, lumber, and minerals across the Pacific.

Vancouver is the third-largest city in Canada. Only Toronto and Montréal are bigger. Vancouver is the centre of business in British Columbia. The residents enjoy a beautiful ocean setting, with a backdrop of snow-capped mountains. These make Vancouver popular with tourists. They also attract newcomers to Canada. These new immigrants help make Vancouver unique.

Figure 10.9 An aerial photo of Vancouver, taken in 1991. What patterns can you identify in the layout of the city? How are these similar to and different from the patterns in Figure 10.8?

Think It Through

1. a) Record the arguments for and against British Columbia joining Confederation. The chart below shows a way you could organize your ideas.
   b) Which side of the debate do you think had the strongest arguments? Give reasons for your answer.

2. In Chapter 7, you learned about the factors that led to Confederation in 1867. Compare these with the arguments you listed for British Columbia.
   a) What are the similarities?
   b) What factors were unique to British Columbia?

The Issue: Should British Columbia Join Confederation?	
Arguments For	Arguments Against

Prince Edward Island Joins Confederation

Prince Edward Island was one of the colonies that took part in the talks that led to Confederation in 1867. After debating the idea, though, the Islanders decided not to join Canada. In this section, you'll learn more about why PEI stayed out of Confederation. Then you'll find out why the Islanders changed their minds.

Focus

What factors led to Prince Edward Island joining Confederation?

Reading STRATEGY

Before beginning this section, flip to its end and read the Think It Through activity. Then, as you read the section, look for possible answers.

Rejecting Confederation

As you saw in Chapter 7, PEI rejected Confederation in 1867. The people of Prince Edward Island had wanted two things. They wanted more money and more Members of Parliament. The other colonies wanted PEI to join them. However, they were unwilling to meet PEI's demands. For the time being, Prince Edward Island remained on its own.

Rethinking Confederation

What factors convinced the people of PEI to change their minds?

- The "Land Question" helped to persuade the Islanders to rethink joining Canada. Absentee British landowners owned most of the island. This meant that, instead of owning their own homes and farms, most Islanders paid rent to the landowners. Canada offered a way out of this dilemma. If PEI joined the country, Canada promised to buy the land for them.

- In 1871, the government of PEI decided to build a railway across the island. It argued that a railway would provide jobs. It could help farmers get their produce to market. A railway was expensive to build, though. What was the solution? After union with Canada, the federal government could help pay for it. Those who opposed the railway thought it was just an excuse for bringing the colony into Confederation.

Tech Link

To see an image of an early PEI farm, open Chapter 13 on your *Voices and Visions* CD-ROM.

Figure 10.10 The sailing ship *Fanny Bailey*. Shipyards in Prince Edward Island produced many wooden sailing vessels such as the *Fanny Bailey*. They traded these ships and most of the other goods they received with other countries, not the colonies. How would this affect PEI's interest in union?

- Prince Edward Island was trying to make a trade deal with the United States. It wanted goods to move tax-free across the border. This angered the British government. After all, Prince Edward Island was just a colony. It could not make trade deals with other countries. As a result, the talks went nowhere. Therefore, PEI had to look elsewhere for a market for its produce. The only option left was Canada.

Figure 10.11 The Tryon Woollen Mills on Prince Edward Island. Local sheep farms provided the mill with wool to make cloth. If you had been the owner of the mill in 1873, what political future would you have supported for PEI?

- Britain wanted to rid itself of the cost of running the colony. Canada worried that the Americans secretly planned to take over the island. As a result, both Canada and Britain put pressure on PEI to join the union.

A Better Deal

In 1873, delegates from PEI went to Ottawa. They wanted to discuss joining Canada. They were tough negotiators. As part of the deal, Canada agreed to

- pay the island's debts

VOICES

Was the railway a way to force the people of Prince Edward Island to join Confederation? Some politicians believed it was.

  66 The railway is so far beyond our means that I am convinced that the Government are fully aware that they cannot accomplish one-third of the undertaking without aid, and that aid, I have no doubt, they expect to obtain from their friends in [Canada], in exchange for delivering the Island into their hands. ... Confederation is, in my opinion, the object sought, and not the prosperity of the Island. 99

—Benjamin Davies, PEI politician
Source: *Debates of the House of Assembly of PEI*, 1871, p. 193.

The cost of building the railway was bankrupting the colony. Were the critics of the railway scheme right?

  66 Looking at the question fairly in the face, my Ministers see that there are only two courses open to them: either they must impose heavy taxes on the people, or seek admission into the Union, provided that Canada would make our railway debt her own. 99

—Lieutenant Governor W.F.C. Robinson
Source: Francis Bolger, ed., *Canada's Smallest Province: A History of PEI* (Halifax: John Deyell Company, 1991) p. 208.

- pay the province an annual sum of money
- take over the cost and building of the island's railway
- provide year-round steamboat service between the island and the mainland
- give PEI six MPs in the House of Commons (which is high in relation to the number of people represented)
- buy back land from the absentee landowners in Britain

On their return to PEI, the delegates put the deal to a vote. The Islanders voted in favour of joining Canada. On 1 July 1873, Prince Edward Island became the seventh province of Canada.

CASE STUDY

The Acadians of Île-du-Prince-Édouard

The first Europeans to live on Prince Edward Island (then called Île Saint-Jean) were about 200 people from France. They settled at Havre Saint-Pierre and Havre-aux-Sauvages in 1720. Here, they fished cod. They had a good relationship with the local Mi'kmaq [MIG-mah]. In the following decade, the first Acadians joined the first homesteaders. Over the next 35 years, the communities expanded to include about 5000 people. They made a living from farming and fishing. Jean Pierre de Roma built the first road in 1731 to connect all the settlements.

In 1758, the British deported 3000 Acadians from the island to France. A third of them died of disease or drowning during the voyage. About 2000 escaped the deportation by hiding on the island or fleeing to New Brunswick. It took many years for the Acadian population to build up again. (For more on the deportation, see page 107.)

At the time of Confederation, the Acadian population was small but politically active. In fact, the first Acadian MP in the House of Commons came from PEI. Stanislaus F. Perry (Poirier) was elected in 1874. Perry was known for his integrity. He was called "Perry the Noble."

About 12 per cent of PEI's current population has Acadian roots. The provincial government provides many services in French. To read more about the Acadians, see pages 106 to 109 in Chapter 5.

Respond

You know that most Prince Edward Island residents were concerned that a government in far-off Ottawa would not be able to represent their interests. How do you think the Acadian minority on the island would feel about it?

Figure 10.12 Ignatius and Domithilde Buote got married on 7 June 1843. They settled in Rustico, an Acadian community on PEI, and had 16 children. The 13 who survived infancy are shown here. From left to right (standing) are Hilaire, Mathias, Urban, Pierre, Amédée, André, Anaclet, and Adelaide. From left to right (seated) are Ignatius, Domithilde, Ignatius (the father), Domithilde (the mother), Isidore (who was the first Acadian doctor on PEI), and Ladislas. Domitien is in front. The photographer won a prize for this photograph in the Chicago World's Fair in 1893. What reasons might the judges have had for giving this prize?

VOICES AND VISIONS

CASE STUDY

The Island Mi'kmaq

The arrival of Europeans had greatly affected the Mi'kmaq of Prince Edward Island. In 1767, the British government had divided the island into 67 townships. It held a lottery, and gave the island away to British landowners. In this one act, the Mi'kmaq of PEI lost all their hunting and fishing grounds. As a result, the number of Mi'kmaq on the island steadily dropped. In the 1800s, only about 300 Mi'kmaq were left in PEI.

However, in its lottery, the British government had overlooked one piece of land. It was a 534-hectare (1320-acre) island off the north coast. It had been the favourite campsite of the Mi'kmaq for as long as they could recall. In 1834, David Stewart of England bought the island for the purpose of "protecting the Indians and to prevent their being annoyed and driven about." The Mi'kmaq lobbied the colonial government to buy the island from him and make it a legal reserve. But the government was not willing to pay for it. Then, in 1870, a British group called the Aborigines Protection Society bought the island (known as Lennox Island) from Stewart. This group set the island aside for the Mi'kmaq. In 1912, they gave the island to the Crown in trust for the Mi'kmaq. Finally the Mi'kmaq had some recognition that Lennox Island was theirs.

However, no treaty negotiation had taken place. The colonial government did not look after the needs of the Mi'kmaq. After 1873, neither did the Canadian government. The people lived in poverty and isolation.

Today, nearly 600 Mi'kmaq live on Lennox Island. They have joined with the people of the Abegweit [A-buh-gwit] band to create the Mi'kmaq Confederacy of PEI. Since the people never gave up title to the land, they are planning a land claims case. They hope to gain back their land rights in PEI.

Respond

In 1972, the government built a causeway to link Lennox Island with the rest of the province. How would this help the Mi'kmaq? What kinds of things make a government take action to solve a problem?

Figure 10.13 Mi'kmaq children at the Lennox Island school, 1895. At the time, several Mi'kmaq families lived on the island. They started a school and earned a living farming, fishing, and making baskets and other handicrafts.

Biography

William Henry Pope (1825–1879)

William Henry Pope was a lawyer, politician, and newspaper editor. He was a strong supporter of union with Canada. He thought it would be good for the economy. Few of the island's politicians agreed with him. Neither did the premier of the colony—Pope's younger brother, James.

When PEI decided to stay out of Confederation in 1867, William Pope quit politics. He didn't give up on the idea of union, though. He wrote editorials and gave lectures. He kept close ties with Prime Minister John A. Macdonald. He talked to politicians in London. Eventually, in 1873, he helped to persuade the Islanders, including his brother, to change their minds. In 1873, PEI joined Canada.

Canada Today

For more than 100 years, the ferry service was the only way for Islanders to travel to the mainland and back. In the 1990s, though, people began thinking about building a bridge. Islanders were asked to vote on the idea in 1993. A minority expressed concern that the island would lose its unique island character. The majority, however, voted in favour of a bridge. Construction began later that year. The Confederation Bridge was completed in 1997. It now links PEI to New Brunswick. At almost 13 kilometres, it is the longest bridge in the world that crosses water that is ice-covered for part of the year.

Figure 10.14 The Confederation Bridge, looking south toward New Brunswick. The promise of a link to the mainland was important to the people of PEI when they decided to join Confederation. What benefits do you think the bridge provides for PEI?

Think It Through

Create two posters about PEI joining Canada. One poster will support Confederation. The other will oppose it. Your posters should refer to the problems the Islanders believed Confederation would either solve or create. [SKILLS]

Two New Provinces in the West

After Prince Edward Island and British Columbia had joined Confederation, Canada stretched from sea to sea. But in the middle, between Manitoba and the Rocky Mountains, lay the North-West Territories. They were part of Canada, but they were not provinces. In this section, you'll discover what factors led to two new provinces on the prairies. You will also look at how the creation of these provinces tried to meet the needs of the people in the West.

Focus

What factors led to the creation of the provinces of Alberta and Saskatchewan?

"Province" versus "Territory"

Provinces and territories are both political regions. What is the difference? A **province** owns its lands, while a **territory** does not. Instead, Canada owns territorial lands. A territory has less power to govern itself than a province has.

Government for the Territories

Canada purchased Rupert's Land from the Hudson's Bay Company in 1869. It had carved out part of the area as the new province of Manitoba. The rest became the North-West Territories.

The North-West Territories Act made Regina the capital city. It also put a government in place. An appointed lieutenant-governor led a small, appointed council. As the population grew, elected members replaced appointed members. In 1888, the council was replaced. In its place, the people got an elected Legislative Assembly of 22 members. Within a few years, the lieutenant-governor no longer ran the Assembly. In 1897, the North-West Territories were granted full **responsible government**. In the meantime, the North-

Figure 10.15 Two homesteaders stand outside the first post office at Lake Saskatoon, Alberta, in 1909. Governments pay for the services they provide by collecting taxes. Alberta and Saskatchewan could not tax residents until they got provincial status. What services might they start providing?

West Territories had been given four seats in the federal House of Commons in 1887.

Provincial Status

Responsible government was not enough for the people of the North-West Territories. The population was growing quickly. Surely they deserved the same status that people in the provinces had. The arrival of so many newcomers was putting pressure on local services. Schools, roads, railways, and other services were badly needed. The people wanted their territory to become a province. Then they could collect taxes to pay for the things they needed.

The North-West Territories were not like British Columbia and Prince Edward

The Klondike Gold Rush brought many people to the northwest region of the North-West Territories. Local government was needed. So, in 1897, the federal government created the Yukon Territory.

Island. Those two provinces had been colonies. For them, the issue had been whether or not to join Canada. The North-West Territories were *already* a part of Canada. The issue was not whether or not to join the country. Instead, it was whether or not they should become a province. Three additional issues had to be settled first:

- the number of provinces to be created
- the division of powers and ownership of resources
- minority rights

One Province or Two

Frederick Haultain was a lawyer and the leading politician in the North-West Territories. He led the fight for provincial status. In 1905, he wrote a letter to Prime Minister Wilfrid Laurier. He laid out his arguments on the key points. Here is what he said about whether to create one province or two:

> *I am more convinced than ever that there is no need for dividing the country into two provinces .... The new Territories have for a number of years been under one government and legislature .... There does not seem to be any reason why ... they should be suddenly divided in two ... and obliged to do with two sets of machinery and institutions what they have been doing quite well with one.*
>
> Source: The Saskatoon *Phoenix*, 17 March 1905.

Laurier insisted that two provinces were better than one. He argued that a single province would be too large to manage. He was afraid that a single large province would be too powerful. By dividing it in two, Laurier hoped that one of them would support minority education rights. In 1905, the Saskatchewan Act and the

Alberta Act created two new provinces. Saskatchewan and Alberta each had a government with control over local matters.

Federal versus Provincial Power

The second question concerned land and natural resources. Haultain wanted the provinces to own the land and control the natural resources. Laurier disagreed. To populate the West, his government needed control of the land. Laurier wanted to make sure that new immigrants could obtain cheap land for settlement. Unlike the other provinces, the North-West had never been a colony, which owns its lands. This is what Laurier said:

> *When the two new provinces came into the Dominion, it cannot be said that they can retain the ownership of their lands, as they never had the ownership.*
>
> Source: Doug Owram, *The Formation of Alberta: A Documentary History* (Alberta Records Publications Board, Historical Society of Alberta, 1979), p. 279.

The federal government did keep control of public lands and resources. In return, it paid each province just over a million dollars. The two provinces did not receive title to their lands for another 25 years.

Minority Rights

The third issue that had to be settled before the deal was that of minority education rights. Tensions on this topic had been building for quite some time.

The first schools in the North-West Territories were Catholic, Francophone schools. The Roman Catholic Church ran them. This included the first school in the West, in St. Albert. Father Albert Lacombe established it for the children of Fort Edmonton. Catholic nuns such as the

Types of Schools

Public schools and separate schools are both paid for by the public through their taxes. A **public school** is for all students. A **separate school** is a public school meant for a particular group, such as Catholic students.

A **private school** is different. A private school is funded by parents through tuition fees.

A **Protestant school** is for Protestant students. A **Catholic school** is for Roman Catholic students. Most Catholics in the West were Francophone. That explains why French tended to be the language of instruction in Catholic schools.

Soeurs Grises (Grey Nuns) usually ran these early Catholic schools.

In 1875, the North-West Territories Act allowed Catholics to have their own separate schools. French could be used in the classroom. This law agreed with the BNA Act, which sets out the right to denominational schools. Citizens of Edmonton took action to make this a reality. They gathered many signatures on a petition. In 1889, the government let them create the Saint-Joachim Roman Catholic School District #7.

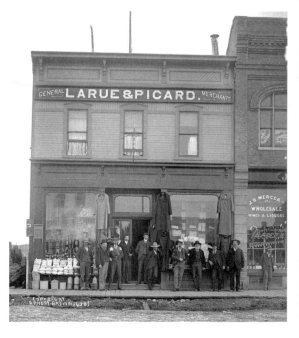

Over time, a great many newcomers arrived. They wanted their children educated in English. The Francophones had become a tiny minority. So, in 1892, the territorial government changed its mind. It now wanted just one education system for all—an English one. Ordinance #29 made English the language of instruction in all schools. (An ordinance is a type of law.) Francophones were very disappointed. Imagine a one-room schoolhouse filled with Francophone, Catholic students. They would have to take their lessons in English! Only one hour of French language instruction was allowed each day.

Francophones turned to Prime Minister Wilfrid Laurier for help. Would he enforce the minority education rights that were in the Constitution? Would he get back their Catholic, Francophone schools?

Here is what Haultain thought about the issue:

> *With regard to the question of education ... the provinces should be left to deal with the subject .... The question is one of provincial rights. It is not the question of the rights of a religious minority, which must be properly, and may be safely, left to the provincial legislatures to be dealt with ....*

Source: Doug Owram, *The Formation of Alberta: A Documentary History* (Alberta Records Publications Board, Historical Society of Alberta, 1979), p. 279.

It turned out that Laurier partly agreed with Haultain. He believed that provinces should be independent. However, he also thought that the Catholic minority should keep its right to a separate school system. This is what he said:

Figure 10.16 Larue & Picard Merchants (about 1899) on the corner of Jasper Avenue and 104th Street, in Edmonton. At this time, Francophones had a strong, visible presence in the city of Edmonton.

> *My opinion is very clear, that when the territories are admitted as a province, the [Francophone/Catholic] minority should not be placed in a worse condition than it is today; that its schools ought to receive the same degree of protection as is granted to the minority in Ontario and Québec where separate schools existed at the first establishment of Confederation.*
>
> Source: Doug Owram, *The Formation of Alberta: A Documentary History* (Alberta Records Publications Board, Historical Society of Alberta, 1979), p. 268.

Laurier made sure that the Alberta Act gave a guarantee of separate schools. In the schools, however, English would still be the language of instruction. An hour of French instruction would still be permitted.

Some Francophones in Québec and the new provinces were satisfied with the compromise. Others were very angry about it. They accused Laurier of not protecting their rights. They believed that, outside of Québec, Canada wanted to create a single Canadian identity—an identity based on the culture of an English Canada.

CASE STUDY

Choosing a Capital: Calgary or Edmonton?

When Alberta and Saskatchewan became provinces in 1905, a decision had to be made about where to have the capital cities. In Saskatchewan, Regina seemed the obvious choice. It had already been the capital of the North-West Territories. In Alberta, the choice was harder. Calgary and Edmonton were the two largest cities in the area. They both had populations of about 12 000, they were both on the railway lines, and they were both important centres of business.

Respond

In a small group, brainstorm ways to choose a capital city. Select what you think is the fairest approach. Fine-tune your idea, and share it with classmates.

The prime minister had the power to decide. Laurier chose Edmonton. In the 1904 election, voters in Edmonton had supported Laurier's Liberal party, while Calgary voters had supported his rival—Robert Borden of the Conservative Party. Laurier made Edmonton the capital as a reward.

The rivalry between the two cities has continued to the present day. Sports is a good example. Just think how excited people get when the Stampeders play football against the Eskimos, or the Flames take on the Oilers in a hockey game.

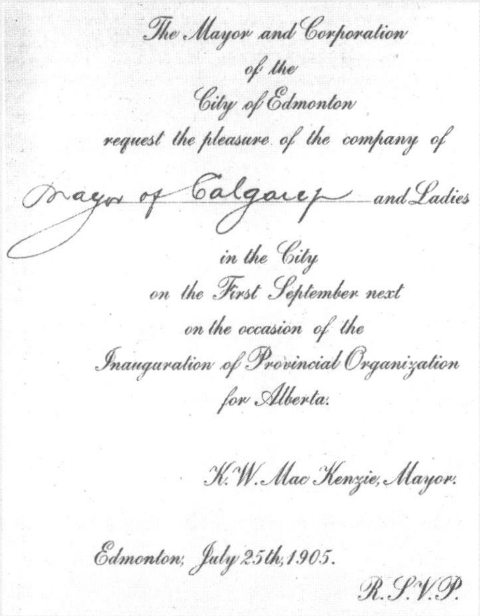

The Mayor and Corporation of the City of Edmonton request the pleasure of the company of

Mayor of Calgary and Ladies

in the City on the First September next on the occasion of the Inauguration of Provincial Organization for Alberta.

K. W. Mac Kenzie, Mayor.

Edmonton, July 25th, 1905.

R.S.V.P.

Figure 10.17 Invitation to the celebrations in Edmonton, 1905. Edmonton is getting ready to celebrate being made capital of Alberta. In your opinion, how fair was Wilfrid Laurier's method of choosing a capital?

Canada Today

The Northwest Territories still exists in a much smaller area than in 1900. It lies between Yukon to the west and Nunavut to the east.

Nunavut is Canada's newest territory. It was created on 1 April 1999, out of an eastern portion of the Northwest Territories. The name *Nunavut* means "our land." The territory is larger than any other territory or province. However, it has the smallest population. Only about 28 000 people live there.

Most of the people who live in Nunavut are Inuit. They are shaping their government to reflect their identity. One way they are doing this is by making Inuktitut one of the official languages. Their identity is also reflected in their flag (see Figure 10.18). The object in the centre is an **inukshuk**. These stone monuments were built to guide travellers, mark special places, or encourage caribou to head toward hunters. The star on the flag is the North Star. It symbolizes the leadership of the Elders in the community.

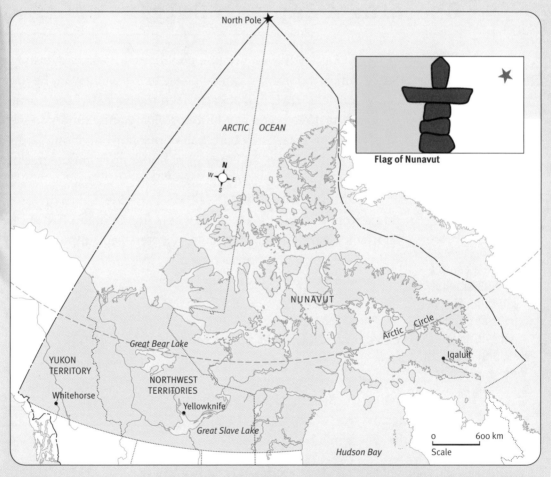

Figure 10.18 Modern map of Canada's three northern territories. None of these territories has the status of a province. Do some research to find out what a territory needs to do to become a province. Do you think Nunavut, Yukon, and the Northwest Territories should become provinces? Give reasons for your answer.

First Nations in the New Provinces

The changes that led to the creation of Alberta and Saskatchewan had a major impact on the First Nations and Métis peoples who lived there. As you will see in Chapter 12, the federal government signed many treaties with First Nations. The treaties moved the people onto **reserves**.

Further, Canada adopted a policy of **assimilation**. It wanted to absorb the First Nations and Métis into a uniform Canadian society. It demanded that First Nations parents put their children into **residential schools**. In these boarding schools, children were forced to adopt English ways. However, the First Nations and Métis resisted the efforts to assimilate them.

Figure 10.19 A one-room schoolhouse in Bruderheim, Alberta, taken in 1915. Laurier said of the education issue that it was "the most important of all that we have to deal with." Why do you think people feel that education issues are so important?

Think It Through

1. Create a timeline. Use it to show the events that led to the creation of Alberta and Saskatchewan.
2. Discuss the three issues that Haultain and Laurier argued about. How do the final decisions affect your life?
3. Organize information about British Columbia, Prince Edward Island, and Alberta and Saskatchewan becoming provinces of Canada. This chart is one way you might organize your ideas.

Arguments for Becoming a Province	Arguments against Becoming a Province	Terms of the Deal and Date of Agreement	The Impact on Canada

Newfoundland and Confederation

As you discovered in Chapter 7, Newfoundland chose not to join Confederation in 1867. Newfoundland and Labrador remained outside of Canada for more than 80 years. In the 1930s, though, the winds of change began to blow. In this section, you'll find out what led the colonists to think again about joining Canada.

Focus

Why did Newfoundland join Confederation? What were the consequences?

Economic Disaster

The economy of the colony of Newfoundland and Labrador was based on exporting natural resources such as fish, wood, and minerals. During the Great Depression of the 1930s, this became a problem. As the world economy collapsed, prices plummeted. No one had the money to buy natural resources. Thousands of Newfoundlanders lost their jobs. At the same time, the colonial government faced a crisis. It could not afford to pay the interest on money it had borrowed. The colony was about to go bankrupt.

In response, Britain threw out the colony's elected government. In 1934, it replaced it with a commission. Commission members, appointed by the British government, would run the colony's affairs until the economy returned to normal. Things did not get better, though, until the

At first, the new province was called Newfoundland. It wasn't until 2001 that the name was changed in the Constitution to Newfoundland and Labrador.

Second World War broke out in 1939. Then Canada and the United States built military bases in the colony. The economy picked up. Soon there were jobs for just about everyone.

Confederation Revisited

At the end of the war, Britain wanted Newfoundland to take over its own affairs once again. The people had three alternatives:

- to return to colonial status
- to leave the commission in place
- to become the tenth province of Canada

The Debate over Confederation

Once again, deciding the future of the colony sparked a huge debate. Those in favour of joining Canada were eager to point out all the potential benefits. These included more social services and a stable economy.

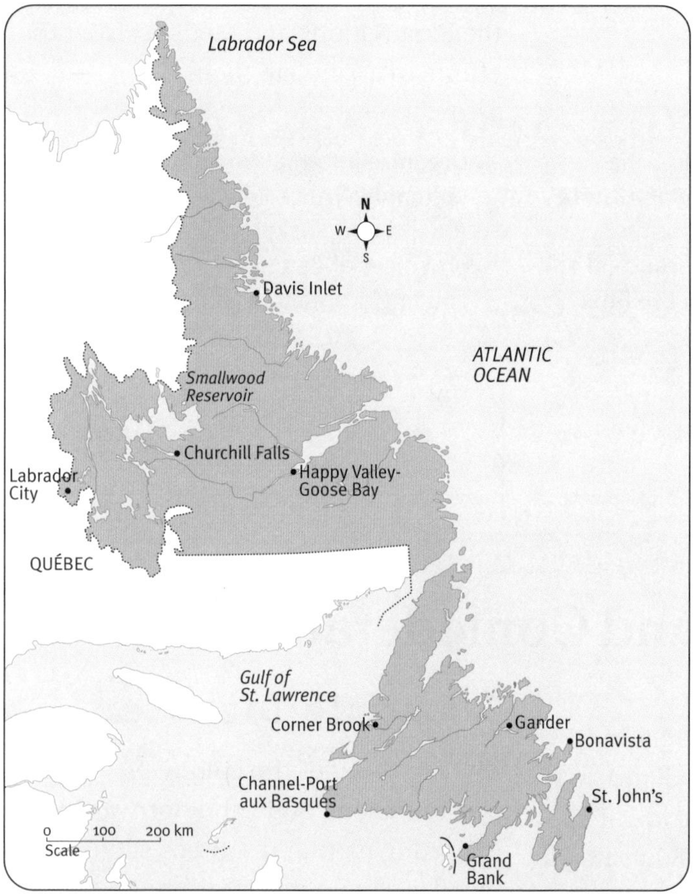

Figure 10.20 Newfoundland and Labrador, 2005. Labrador is on the mainland northwest of the island of Newfoundland. Look at an atlas to compare the distance from Newfoundland to Alberta with the distance from Newfoundland to London, England. Use this information to help explain Newfoundlanders' strong bond to Britain.

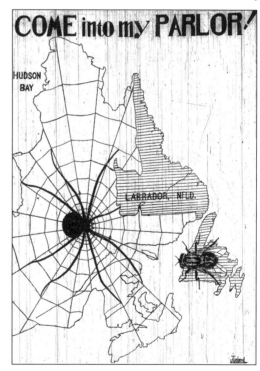

Figure 10.21 "Come into My Parlour," published in the St. John's newspaper *The Independent*, 31 May 1948. Use the Skill Check feature on page 218 to analyze this political cartoon. In your opinion, is it effective? Compare its message with the message of the cartoon in the Skill Check feature. SKILLS

Are You in This List?

To All Mothers: Confederation would mean that never again would there be a hungry child in Newfoundland. If you have children under the age of 16, you will receive every month a cash allowance for every child ....

To All War Veterans: Canada treats her veterans better than any other country in the world ....

To All Wage-Workers: All wage-workers will be protected by Unemployment Insurance. Newfoundland, under Confederation, will be opened up and developed. Your country will be prosperous. Your condition will be better.

To All Railroaders: You will become employees of the biggest railway in the world, the Canadian National Railway. You will have security and stability as CNR employees ....

To All Light Keepers: You will become employees of the Government of Canada. Your wages and working conditions will be greatly improved.

To All Fishermen: The cost of living will come down. The cost of producing fish will come down. ... The Fish Prices Support Board of Canada, backed by Canada's millions, will protect the price of your fish.

To All Newfoundlanders: The cost of living will come down. The 120 000 children in our country will live better. The 10 000 Senior Citizens of our country will be protected in their old age. Newfoundland will be linked up with a strong, rich British nation. Newfoundland will go ahead with Canada.

Figure 10.22 A re-creation of a real advertisement that appeared in the St. John's pro-Confederation newspaper *The Confederate* on 31 May 1948. It points out the many benefits of Confederation. Ads sometimes stretch the truth. Identify one or two statements that you think may do this.

VOICES ■

Those who opposed joining Canada made a strong pitch. The following editorial appeared in an anti-Confederation newspaper in 1948.

66 Newfoundland is your country. Have faith in it and your own ability to make it richer and better in every way. Strangers cannot do for you what you can do for yourselves. Canada cannot give us the only thing we need for our prosperity—markets. Britain has no dollars and cannot buy from us. America is the best customer we have and we need self-government so we can approach the Americans with proposals for improved trade between us. ... That is the only courageous course for Newfoundland to take at this critical moment in her history. 99

Source: *The Independent*, 31 May 1948, p. 7.

Deciding the Issue

On 3 June 1948, the people of Newfoundland voted in a **referendum** about their future. (A referendum is a public vote on an issue.) Few people wanted to keep the commission. Otherwise, the results were unclear. A second referendum took place on July 22. The result was close: 52.3 per cent voted to join Canada; 47.7 per cent voted to stay a British colony. The majority ruled. On 31 March 1949, Newfoundland and Labrador became the tenth province of Canada.

The Consequences of Confederation

In the short term, Confederation benefited the new province. The people gained access to Canada's social programs. These included employment insurance, health care, and old-age pensions.

In the 1950s, an economic boom swept across Canada. Premier Joey Smallwood took advantage of the good times. His government brought electric power to rural areas. It expanded the iron mines in Labrador. The fishing and forest industries did well. By 1965, the Trans-Canada Highway stretched across the province.

Over the longer term, however, things did not remain as good as in the early years. The fishing industry declined, and the cod fishery was shut down. Limitations were placed on the seal hunt. A way of life tied to the sea had become unworkable. Still, in a poll taken in 1999, 85 per cent of the people in the province said they believed Confederation had been a success.

The Impact on First Nations and Inuit

In the other provinces, the federal government was responsible for First Nations and Inuit. This was not the case in Newfoundland and Labrador. That province decided to take on the role itself. It would provide services such as schools and health care. In return, Canada agreed to pay the province money. The province had little experience providing these services, though. In the past, missionaries had filled this role. As a result, the government failed to meet the needs of First Nations and Inuit.

The people soon saw that their way of life was threatened. They began to fight to revive their cultures. The Mi'kmaq at Conne River gained recognition under the Indian Act. Their community was recognized as a reserve. In Labrador, the Inuit, Innu, and Métis formed associations to promote their cultures and reclaim their traditional lands.

Tech Link

Open Chapter 10 on your *Voices and Visions* CD-ROM to see a 1947 photograph of the delegates negotiating the entry of Newfoundland to Canada.

Figure 10.23 Joseph ("Joey") Smallwood signing the Confederation agreement, 1949. Joey Smallwood played a key role in bringing Newfoundland into Confederation. Afterwards, he was elected the first premier. He held this position for 23 years. What qualities would help a politician keep the support of voters for so long?

Cultural Background

Many Newfoundlanders still feel a strong tie with Britain. After all, more than half of the people have British ancestry. This is a higher proportion than in any other province. There are other groups, however. Starting in the eighteenth century, fishers from France settled along the west coast of the island. This area became known as the French Shore. Some Acadians joined them after their expulsion from Nova Scotia. The descendants of the two groups make up the 27 785 Francophones in the province as of 2001.

Think It Through ▶

1. Create a visual timeline. It should show the key events that led Newfoundland to join Confederation.
2. Return to the Know-Wonder-Learn chart you created in the activity on page 217.

a) Choose one of the unanswered questions in the "Wonder" column or think of a new question. Do some research to find the answer to it.
b) Present your findings in a visual, oral, or written presentation.

Chapter 10 PROJECT   Create a Political Cartoon

In Chapter 8, you wrote an opinion piece. It presented your point of view. In this chapter project, you will present a point of view *visually*. You will create your own political cartoon. Political cartoons are creative illustrations. They use humour and sarcasm (cutting irony) to make a point.

Choose a Topic or Issue

Before beginning to draw, you have to decide exactly what your cartoon is going to be about. Choose something from this chapter. What political issue, event, or behaviour would you like to present? Try to think of something controversial. What is your stand on this issue? What message do you want to send?

"Showing" Your Message

Which of these visual devices will you use?

- *Exaggerating a well-known person's physical characteristics*. This is called creating a **caricature**. For example, imagine a person has a large chin in real life. The artist might draw him with a *huge* chin.
- *Using symbols*. Symbols help the reader understand the cartoon. For example, a maple leaf can be used to symbolize Canada. A dove means peace; a hawk could mean war.
- *Including captions*. Cartoonists often add a short comment under the cartoon. They can

also add dialogue in "bubbles" above the peoples' heads. Captions and dialogue allow the artist to give the audience extra information to clarify what is happening in the cartoon. They can also add humour.

- *Adding a title*. Titles can be used to make your message immediately clear to the audience.

Draw!

Create your political cartoon in a 15 cm by 15 cm square. This will help you keep your cartoon simple. You may colour your cartoon, if you wish. Use Skill Check: Analyze Political Cartoons on page 218. It can help you make sure you have done everything necessary to make your point.

Share

Form groups of three or four students. Each person will take a turn presenting his or her cartoon while the others in the group analyze it. Listen carefully to your group members' comments, and write down anything that you feel will help you improve your cartoon.

What Did You Learn?

Did the other students "get" your message right away, or did they need help understanding your cartoon? What was the most successful part of your cartoon? What part do you need to work on?

Chapter 11 Encouraging Immigration

| Chapter INQUIRY | How did the massive immigration to Canada near the turn of the twentieth century affect the complex identity of our country? |

Immigration and Identity

As people grow older, we change. We see new places, make new friends, and meet new challenges. All these experiences influence who we are. The same thing happens to a country. Over time, the characteristics that seem to describe it change. Canada is a different country today from the Dominion of Canada of a hundred years ago. It's also different from what it will be a hundred years from now.

One of the important factors that change a country's identity is immigration. Many people come from other places to live in Canada. They change the makeup of the country. They bring their own ideas and customs. These become a part of life in Canada. In this way, the newcomers add to what it means to be Canadian.

Coming to Western Canada

At first, Canada did not attract many immigrants. The trip from other continents was very long. Most people who did come to North America went to the United States. Then, in the 1890s, things changed. Newcomers flooded the West.

Over the next 20 years, many different groups of immigrants came to Western Canada. In this chapter, you will learn more about a few of these groups. You'll learn why they left their home countries and why they chose Canada. As you read, think about how they added to the character of our country.

EARLY IMMIGRANTS
Mennonites, Icelanders, Hutterites, Mormons, Doukhobors, Chinese

THE MÉTIS

CANADIENS AND ENGLISH CANADIANS

FIRST PEOPLES
Siksika, Kainai, Piikani, Nehiyawak, Nakoda, Tsuu T'ina, Dene, Dene Tha', Dunne-Za, Anishinabe

WESTERN CANADA: A PLURALISTIC SOCIETY

Honing Your Skills

Do you like to "wow" your audience? The Skill Check feature in this chapter shows you how to **Design a Multimedia Presentation**. This skill is important to your studies because it will enable you to communicate what you know effectively. The project at the end of the chapter will ask you to design a multimedia presentation about the cultural pluralism of the West.

Think AHEAD

Examine the graphic at left. It includes the First Peoples, the Canadiens and English Canadians, the Métis, and some of the immigrant groups that lived in Western Canada in the early twentieth century.

a) Brainstorm some contributions each of these groups made to Canada.

b) Another band could be added to the rainbow to include immigrant groups that have come to Canada more recently. To find out who they are, go to the website for Statistics Canada.

c) Brainstorm some contributions these recent citizens are making today.

d) Canadians from which of these groups live in your community today?

e) Draw a different graphic to illustrate the cultural mix in your community.

SKILL CHECK: Design a Multimedia Presentation

Multimedia can turn a boring presentation into an exciting experience. By the end of this chapter, you'll have learned a lot more about the pluralistic nature of Canada. When you tell others about what you've learned, don't just read them a report. Try livening it up. Make social studies come alive with visuals, sounds, videos, and music.

Choosing the Media for Your Presentation

Any presentation can be a multimedia presentation. You just need to use more than one form of media. For example, spruce up a bulletin-board display with illustrations, graphs, and a tape recorder set up to play traditional music. Make people pay attention to your spoken presentation by showing a "slide show" of digital photographs. Look at this concept web. It shows a few of the forms of presentation you could use. Then read about what you might do with each to make it truly multimedia.

Multimedia Presentations

- Video or DVD
- Dramatization
- Website
- Computer Presentation
- Audiotape or CD

Try It!

What form of presentation would you choose to illustrate Canada's pluralistic society? Brainstorm different types of media you could incorporate, with examples (for example, drawings of immigrants' homes).

Video or DVD

Create a documentary or a commercial. Write the dialogue. Include costumes, props, scenery, and sound effects. These make the video authentic. Present your documentary or commercial on the computer or television.

Dramatization

Write an original script and present a play. Build a set and design costumes. Use music and sound effects to bring the play to life. Videotape it or present it live.

Website

Design a website on your topic. First, sketch out the web pages for your site, with one sheet of paper for each web page. The home page will need links to sub-pages. Decide what photographs, text, sound clips, cartoons, or video clips would enhance your site. Provide a list of links to useful websites on your topic, including libraries, museums, and archives. If your school has the technology, create your website.

Computer Presentation

Create a slide show with text, sound, graphics, and video clips. You could use PowerPoint, HyperStudio, AppleWorks, or another program.

Audiotape or CD

Become a radio broadcaster. Present an interview, a radio drama, a book on tape, or a newscast. Include sound effects, music, and personal interviews.

The Need for Immigrants

In 1881, 4 381 256 people lived in Canada, including 108 547 Aboriginal people. Nearly 89 per cent of Canadians were of British or French descent. The vast majority of them lived in the East.

In the West, the First Nations and Métis were struggling to adjust to a life changed by the railway. Also in the West were the Canadiens. Through the fur trade, they had explored this region. Some had established farms. Then there were the English Canadians. The English had come from Eastern Canada, Britain, and the United States.

All in all, there weren't very many people in the West. In this section, you will see who wanted more people in the West, and why. You will learn that migration within Canada was not enough to do the job.

Focus

Why did Canada need immigrants?

> In 1881, Canadiens made up 41.5 per cent of the non-Aboriginal population of the North-West Territories. English Canadians made up 41.2 per cent.

Reading
STRATEGY

Don't forget that the glossary and a dictionary are both useful sources of information. If there is a term in this section that is not familiar to you, look it up!

The Laurier Factor

Sir Wilfrid Laurier was Canada's first French Canadian prime minister. Laurier's most famous remark was "The twentieth century belongs to Canada." He meant that Canada's economy would soon get very big. He thought Canada would become a great nation.

What did Laurier need? People. Laurier could not build a thriving country without more people. In particular, he wanted newcomers to start farms in the West. As you learned in Chapter 9, a strong farm economy in the West would help the whole country.

Laurier also needed more workers for all the country's growing industries. Mines were producing three times more gold, copper, and coal in 1914 than they were in 1896. The West was producing ten times more wheat. Many factories opened.

> Note that Laurier already had people who could have taken some of these jobs: the First Nations and Métis. People didn't even think of that possibility. Why would this be so?

Figure 11.1 Wilfrid Laurier (at centre) on the campaign trail in 1908. Laurier spoke both French and English. His Francophone parents had sent him to English-language schools. Looking at the photograph, think about how knowing both English and French could help a Canadian politician. How could it enable us to be more active citizens? Are there other languages to learn that would help us be better citizens?

Year	Immigrants	Year	Immigrants	Year	Immigrants
1890	75 067	1899	44 543	1908	143 326
1891	82 165	1900	41 681	1909	173 694
1892	30 996	1901	55 747	1910	286 839
1893	29 663	1902	89 102	1911	331 288
1894	20 829	1903	138 660	1912	375 756
1895	18 790	1904	131 252	1913	400 870
1896	16 835	1905	141 465	1914	150 484
1897	21 716	1906	211 653		
1898	31 900	1907	272 409		

Source: David J. Hall, "Room to Spare," *Horizon Canada*, 1985, vol. 7, no. 76, p. 1803.

Figure 11.2 The number of immigrants entering Canada, 1890 to 1914. Most of the immigrants that came to the country from 1890 to 1914 went to the West. How many people came to Canada in Laurier's first year in office (1896)? How many came in his last year (1911)?

Laurier succeeded in bringing more people to Canada, as you can see in Figure 11.2. How did he do it? His government doubled the amount of railway track, making travel into the West easier. It advertised for immigrants in far-off countries. Government agents went overseas to find interested groups. Canada offered them special treatment. Some groups, for example, received large tracts of land.

Partners in the Effort

The government worked hard to attract people to Canada. As you'll see in this chapter, it was not the only organization eager to bring newcomers to the country. Some private companies got involved. They bought land in the West and sold it to immigrants at a profit.

Church groups took an interest. They wanted to build religious communities in a new land. They liked Canada's policy of religious freedom.

The railway companies were involved, too. The government gave them land for building the railway. For example, the Canadian Pacific Railway owned land along 109 Street and Jasper Avenue in Edmonton. It still owns land in downtown Calgary. In total, the CPR got about 100 000 square kilometres of prairie land. This is almost as big as the area of the island of Newfoundland. Other rail companies got more than 20 000 square kilometres. All the companies made big profits by selling their land.

Think It Through

1. a) Write "A Pluralistic Society" at the centre of a concept web. Put the groups who wanted immigrants to move to Canada on the second level. Put the reasons they wanted these immigrants to come to the West on the next level.
   b) Describe another way to present this information.

2. Graphs make an excellent addition to a multimedia project. Look at the statistics in Figure 11.2. **SKILLS**
   a) What type of graph would best display this data visually? Why? (See Skill Check: Use Statistics to Create Graphs on page 124.)
   b) What trends do you see?

Canada Calling

You've learned that the Canadian government wanted immigrants. It was very successful in bringing them here.

Focus

How did the Canadian government encourage immigrants to come to Canada from Europe?

In this section, you'll look at the strategies the government used to persuade newcomers to come west.

Spreading the Word

The person in charge of immigration to Canada was Clifford Sifton. Sifton was a Member of Parliament from Manitoba. He was also the Minister of the Interior from 1896 to 1905.

Sifton started a publicity campaign. The goal was to attract people to Canada. You know how products are advertised today. In the same way, Canada was advertised as a good place to live.

- Millions of posters and pamphlets were made in many languages.
- The government brought foreign journalists to Canada. They toured the country. They wrote newspaper stories about it when they returned home.
- The government sent speakers around the world. They spread the word about the great Canadian West.

Some of Canada's efforts seem a little odd. In 1907, a huge buffalo died at the Banff zoo. The government had it stuffed and sent to the Canadian office in London,

Figure 11.3 Clifford Sifton, 1907. Some people didn't like Sifton's policies. Even so, no one questioned his loyalty to the Prairies. Do you think Francophones already in the West would have agreed with his policies? Why or why not?

England. Here it stood in the front window as a symbol of the West. Later, it was displayed at fairs all over Europe. This strategy worked. It got people excited. Would it work today?

Who the Government Targeted

Sifton sent advertisements to three regions.

- **The United States.** American farmers knew how to farm on the prairies. By the 1890s, though, the United States was running out of good farmland. The ads sent there called Western Canada "the last, best West."
- **Great Britain.** Most Canadians were of British origin. Some of them wanted other Britons to move here. They thought this would strengthen the British character of the country.
- **Eastern Europe.** Sifton believed that farmers from Eastern Europe were ideal settlers for the prairies. They were experienced at growing crops. They would put up with the hardships of pioneer life. He also believed they would assimilate to English culture.

Reading
STRATEGY

Notice how lists with bullets (•) make it easy to understand several key points. Think about how you could use these kinds of lists in your own work.

CASE STUDY

Land for Sale!

False advertising is using ads to mislead people. Was the Canadian government guilty of false advertising? Examine these government ads to find out.

WANTED

14,000 men to build Railways in Canada.

100,000 men to take, cultivate and own farms in Canada.

Highest wages in Railway work.

160 acres of the best land in the world free.

The industrious poor man's chance....

Figure 11.4 A re-creation of an ad that appeared in a 1908 pamphlet. It was called *Canada: Work, Wages, Land: The Railway Route to a Free Farm*. Who would be interested in this information?

BECAUSE of the dryness of the inland climate, the cold is much less noticeable than a stranger might expect. Less snow falls on the prairies than in the East, and on account of the dryness of the air, it brushes off one's coat like dust.

Everywhere the appearance of snow is hailed as seasonable and beneficial. Sleighing parties of pleasure are arranged for the period of the full moon, and the sound of the sleigh bells is a merry one. The snow protects the autumn-sown wheat from the frost and aids ... the farmer in hauling his produce to market, and so contributes alike to business and pleasure.

Figure 11.5 A description of Canada that appeared in a 1906 pamphlet. It was called *Twentieth-Century Canada*. What feeling do you get when you read this? Which phrases are exaggerations? Which don't tell the whole story? Reword the passage to make it more accurate.

Figure 11.6 Two posters distributed around 1910. Compare the two posters. How are they alike? How are they different? Is either misleading? How?

Figure 11.7 A young woman dressed up as Canada. She appeared at a rural fair in Exeter, England, in 1907. Her bicycle is decorated with sheaves of wheat. What kind of effect might this form of publicity have had on people?

Respond

How realistic are the images of Canada on this page? Find examples of misleading information. What information was left out?

Betrayal of the Promise of Confederation

Sifton and the government most wanted new citizens who either spoke English or would learn it. The government did not try to convince Canadiens from Québec to move west. Farmland was scarce in Québec, yet the government did not advertise there. It did not offer free rail tickets.

The government had a vision of Canada as one nation with one language. Over the years, Francophones began to feel betrayed. Hadn't Confederation made Canada officially bilingual? Why wasn't the government trying to make the West a place for both Anglophones and Francophones? Within a few decades, Francophones were far outnumbered in the West. They began to feel a great pressure to learn English, especially after the use of French stopped being protected.

The Trap

For many immigrants, the move to the West was "a trap." Life here was much harder than the advertisements had led them to believe. When homesteaders arrived in the West, they needed to build shelter before winter. On much of the prairie there are few trees, so most newcomers made sod houses. These were made of slabs of soil, grass, and grass roots cut from the prairie. After a downpour, it would continue to "rain" inside for days. Only later, when they had more money and time, did homesteaders build more permanent, wood-frame houses. Few had money to pay for the trip back home.

Tech Link

Look on the *Voices and Visions* CD-ROM to learn about the long hours and tedious work involved in a task we take for granted today—making bread.

VOICES ■

It was sometimes said that Sifton had an "open-door" policy. This meant that everyone was welcome to come to Canada.

> **❝** I do not care what language a man speaks, or what religion he professes, if he is honest and law-abiding, if he will go on that land and make a living for himself and his family, he is a desirable settler. **❞**
>
> Source: Debates, House of Commons, July 1899.

Did Canada really have an "open door"? Let's look at the facts. The government advertised in the United States, Britain, and Eastern Europe. It did not advertise in Québec or Asia, and it advertised very little in France and Belgium. Also, Sifton wanted certain *types* of people to enter the country.

Respond

What kind of people did Sifton really want to attract to Canada? Who did he think would not be suitable? Do you agree with Sifton's reasoning? Explain.

> **❝** I think a stalwart peasant in a sheep-skin coat, born on the soil, whose forefathers have been farmers for ten generations, with a stout wife and a half-dozen children, is good quality. A Trades Union artisan who will not work more than eight hours a day ... is, in my judgement, ... very bad quality. **❞**
>
> Source: *Maclean's Magazine*, April 1922.

VOICES ■

Mary Louisa Cummins and her husband, Colin, came from England. They moved to Saskatchewan.

66 At the time, the CPR was plastering the country with fascinating pictures of glorious wheat fields on the great western prairies. There was a fortune for everyone in three years, not to mention glittering promises of practically free land. Hopes were high. So we, poor fools, fell into the trap. **99**

Source: Don Gillmor and Pierre Turgeon, *Canada: A People's History*, vol. 2 (Toronto: McClelland & Stewart, 2001), p. 13.

Figure 11.8 A sod house in the Camrose area of Alberta, likely about 1900. It had a dirt floor. What would be the benefits or drawbacks of raising young children in this house?

Canada Today

Perhaps potential immigrants to Canada would have been better off if they had viewed Canada's ads critically. Are you media savvy? Look at this screen capture of a 2005 Travel Alberta web page. Think about it critically. What is it trying to get you to do? Does it exaggerate? Does it leave out information? Do you believe everything it says? **WEB LINK**

YOUR ADVENTURES AWAIT

Seems you never were much of a watcher. You're definitely more of a do-er. And that's why Alberta is a holiday mecca for people just like you. So snoop around, and find your fit.

It's fascinating and beautiful and daunting and a mind-blowing blast. It's bigger than a Spielberg movie and better than the top five best things you can count on your right hand. You can see for yourself. Just head to Fort McMurray in Alberta's North...

If there's one word to describe skiers and boarders this time of year, it's eager. So powder hounds listen up! The countdown has begun to the coolest season of the year. And the time left before the opening of the ski season is narrowing from more or less infinity to mere days!

Think It ► Through

1. The government hoped to attract immigrants from three regions in the early 1900s. What were they?
   a) Make a three-circle Venn diagram to compare these regions.
   b) Write two sentences saying why these areas were targeted, and not others.
   c) What media did the government use to attract immigrants?

2. Imagine you're working on a government campaign to promote Alberta today.

   a) Prepare two posters. On one, show an Alberta that would be an ideal destination for immigrants. On the other, show an Alberta that is more realistic.
   b) Which one do you think your boss will choose? Why?

3. On paper, design a website to advertise Canada. Alternatively, write the script for a radio or television commercial. First, brainstorm possible text, pictures, sounds, and video clips you might include. **SKILLS**

Push and Pull Factors

The government promoted Canada vigorously. Was that enough? In this section, you'll find out that the people who came here had good reasons for leaving their homelands. They also had good reasons for choosing Canada.

Focus

Why did the government's immigration policy succeed?

Reasons for Emigrating

Why were Canada's new immigrants looking for a place where they could make a better life? For many, the conditions in their homelands made them want to leave. The factors that push people to leave their homelands are called **push factors**. The newcomers to the West were affected by a variety of push factors. Here are the main ones.

Tech Link

To see a wagon train of new homesteaders travelling north of Edmonton, open Chapter 11 on your *Voices and Visions* CD-ROM.

- **Population growth**. Europe was going through a dramatic increase in population. There were not enough jobs for everyone. There was not enough land to farm.
- **Religious persecution**. A **persecuted** person is one who is treated badly because of his or her beliefs. Several groups of people in Eastern Europe were persecuted for their religious beliefs.

- **Political persecution**. Several groups of people were persecuted for their political beliefs.
- **Natural disaster**. Famine, such as the Irish potato famine of 1847 (which you read about in Chapter 6), can lead people to leave their homes.
- **Affordable travel**. Steamships made voyages shorter and cheaper. After 1896, a worldwide economic depression drew to a close. With the return of better times, people could afford to move.

Figure 11.9 A family of Scottish immigrants. They arrived at Québec City in 1910. This was their first stop on a long journey to the prairies. What would it take to convince you and your family to move to a different country? What would hold you back?

Reasons for Immigrating to Canada

Near the turn of the twentieth century, millions of people were on the move. Europeans were moving to the United States, Australia, New Zealand, and South America. Why did some of them choose Canada? Canada offered plenty of reasons. Factors that influence people to choose a certain country are called **pull factors**. Here are the main pull factors that drew people to Canada.

"Emigrant" and "Immigrant"

Emigrant and *immigrant* are similar terms, but they mean different things. **Emigrants** are people who leave their homelands. They become **immigrants** when they come to live in a new land. New Ukrainian Canadians, for example, *emigrated from* Ukraine. They *immigrated to* Canada.

- **Free land.** Everyone could afford the inexpensive, plentiful land offered in Western Canada.
- **Jobs.** The developing West needed shopkeepers, coal miners, school teachers, and so on.
- **Completed railway.** Immigrants who became Western farmers would be able to sell their grain in Eastern markets.
- **Better machinery.** Farms produced more crops with better farm machinery.

- **Improved farming techniques.** Newly developed kinds of wheat were better suited to the prairie climate.
- **Growing demand for wheat.** As the demand for wheat grew, so did the price. A wheat-farming family could do well.
- **Religious and political freedom.** Canada allowed people to hold their beliefs.
- **Friends and family.** Some people chose Canada to be close to friends and family already here.

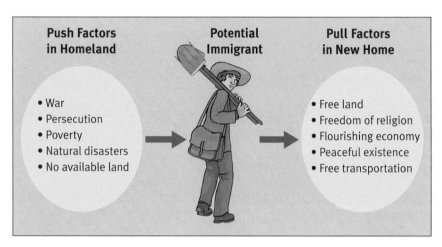

Figure 11.10 Examples of push and pull factors. Think of an instance where push and pull factors work together.

Figure 11.11 Sources for immigrants to Canada, 1901–1911. From which two places did most immigrants come before the First World War? Is a pie graph a good way to present this information? Why or why not?

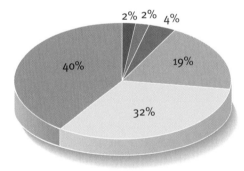

Legend

- Russia
- Asia
- Northern Europe
- Rest of Europe
- United States
- British Empire (mainly the United Kingdom)

Note: As a result of rounding, figures do not add up to 100 per cent.

Source: Daniel Francis, et al. *Canadian Issues* (Toronto: Oxford University Press, 1998), p. 23.

Think It Through

1. Imagine you are a young man who can't find work in Scotland. Write an entry in your journal in which you try to decide whether or not to immigrate to Canada. Mention the push and pull factors you might be thinking about. Alternatively, present a soliloquy (a scene in which a character talks to himself or herself). Include sound effects to make your scene realistic. **SKILLS**

2. Some push and pull factors can be controlled. Others cannot. A huge tsunami slammed into the shorelines of Southeast Asia in December 2004. It pushed many people to leave their ruined communities. Many push and pull factors influenced the people who came to Canada at the turn of the twentieth century. List them. Which were created by policies in Canada? Which could the government not control?

Churches and Immigration

Churches and religious groups took a special interest in immigration. They believed that the Canadian West offered a chance for their members to have a better life. In some cases, church members were being persecuted for their religious beliefs in their home countries. The Doukhobors, for example, were **pacifists**. Even so, the Russian government wanted to force them to fight in the army. Canada offered them a safe haven. It seemed to be a place where they could follow their faith in peace.

Focus

What strategies did missionaries and religious communities use to attract immigrants to Western Canada?

The Barr Colony

Anglican Church leaders helped many British Anglicans come to Canada. (The Anglican Church is the Church of England.) One of these leaders was a Canadian-born Anglican minister named Isaac Barr. In 1902, he placed an ad in British newspapers. It called for people who wanted to go to Canada. Barr thought that the Canadian West should be filled with English-speaking Anglicans. He thought this would strengthen its "British" character. His advertisement said, "Let us take possession of Canada. Let our cry be 'Canada for the British.' "

Barr acquired a large tract of land on the border of Saskatchewan and Alberta. In 1903 he led a party of 2684 men, women, and children from England. He did not plan the expedition well. To begin, the ship he'd arranged for, the SS *Lake Manitoba*, could carry only 900. He crammed everyone aboard anyway. After the colonists arrived in Saint John, they discovered that no rail transport had been organized. Reverend George Lloyd stepped in and made the arrangements. The immigrants ended up losing most of their luggage. They had to travel with few supplies by ox cart from Saskatoon. But the immigrants came from industrial towns. They didn't know how to drive oxen. The journey was a disaster, and many gave up.

Finally the colonists forced Barr to resign. They replaced him with Lloyd, who was experienced in the West. Lloyd helped the newcomers at every step. The colonists named their main town Lloydminster.

Figure 11.12 Barr colonist camp in Saskatoon, April 1903. The government frantically put up these tents when the Barr colonists came unprepared. It provided them with wagons for the rest of the journey. Before Barr left Canada for good, the newcomers tried to pelt him with eggs. Why would they be so angry?

The Hutterites

The Hutterites are a Protestant religious group with a unique identity. Their religious beliefs inspire them to live collectively in isolated communities and to refuse to fight as soldiers—they are pacifists. In Russia, the Hutterites had been persecuted for their beliefs, including their belief in pacifism. In 1864, they fled to South Dakota in the United States.

Things were fine until the First World War. Then Americans began to view the Hutterites with suspicion. The Hutterites spoke German, the language of the enemy. Further, the Hutterites refused to take up arms. So other Americans took the Hutterites' cattle and sheep. They made the whole community feel unwelcome.

The Hutterites decided to move to southern Manitoba and Alberta. They would be permitted to avoid military service. They would be allowed to teach their children in their own schools. A few instances of **discrimination** did not discourage them. Today, about 25 000 Hutterites live in Alberta in about 60 colonies.

CASE STUDY

A Different Settlement Pattern

Can a religious belief affect geography? Let's think about settlement patterns. **Settlement patterns** are the way human dwellings are arranged. They are part of human geography.

Most early farming families on the prairies lived on large farms. Each family lived far away from other people.

The Hutterites lived differently: they had a **communal lifestyle**. That means that there was no private property. Everyone in the colony owned everything. That included farm equipment, books, toys, and even bank accounts. A group of elders made all important decisions.

This way of life affected the settlement pattern of Hutterite colonies. About 100 to 130 people lived in each colony. A colony was known as a *bruderhofe*. Everyone lived together in a small village. All the houses and the dining hall were in the centre of the village. The farm buildings lay on the perimeter of the village. All around the village were the colony's farmlands. For the most part, Hutterite colonies function the same way today.

Respond

Draw two diagrams. Draw one to show the settlement pattern of Hutterite farming colonies. Draw another to show the pattern that was more common in the West. (See page 197 in Chapter 9.)

Tech Link

Open Chapter 11 on your *Voices and Visions* CD-ROM to see an aerial view of a Hutterite colony.

Figure 11.13 Hutterite women at work in modern times in Lethbridge, Alberta. What are they doing? How is this scene the same as it would have been had the photo been taken early in the last century? How is it different? Hutterites still live separately from the rest of Canadian society. How would this affect the lives of Hutterite teenagers?

British Home Children

Between 1867 and 1924, 100 000 British children were sent to Canada. They travelled on ships and by train, sometimes all on their own. They hoped to join Canadian families.

Two types of groups set up these ventures:

- *religious organizations*—for example, the Church of England Waifs and Strays Society
- *charitable organizations*—for example, the Society for the Suppression of Juvenile Vagrancy

CASE STUDY

Dr. Barnardo's Children

Were the home children lucky to come to Canada?

Irish-born Thomas Barnardo was a young medical student in London, England. He saw many children who were orphans or whose parents were too poor to care for them. They had to make their own way in the world by working, begging, or stealing. Many slept in the street. Some lived in workhouses, where they worked long hours for no pay.

Dr. Barnardo felt he must help these "lost" children. In 1870, he opened his first "home" where boys could live and receive some education. In time, a series of Barnardo's homes opened for boys and girls.

England did not offer much of a future for these children. On the other hand, Canada needed more young workers. Further, many Canadian families were willing to adopt these children. Barnardo believed that Canada offered these youngsters a better life. He began sending some of the children to live with families in Canada. The families were supposed to look after the orphans and make sure they went to school. Many children went to live on farms in the West. Here they worked hard to pay for their keep. It was hoped that they would grow up to become homesteaders with farms of their own.

Respond

What is the issue? What would each of these people think about the issue?

- a worker at a Barnardo home in England
- a child taken from her penniless mother
- an orphan welcomed into a Canadian family
- a farmer hoping for more help on the farm
- a teenager forced to work long hours on the farm

Figure 11.14 A group of Barnardo children, 1905. They're on the dock in Saint John, New Brunswick. About 1000 Barnardo children came to Canada every year from 1883 to 1914. Would immigration like this be allowed today? Explain.

VOICES ■

Consider the statements of these home children. Describe what you think would be the best experience for a home child. What would the worst be like?

❝In April 1907 I was called into a conference of the family. I was 15 years old, nearly six feet tall and weighed 160 pounds—pretty skookum. They asked me how I would like to go out to western Canada and help to open up the country. Well, after reading all the books of that time about the Golden West—full of Indians, cowboys and Mounties—I naturally agreed. Who wouldn't at that age? ...

I feel it has been a privilege to have had a hand in opening up the country. ❞

—Dave J. Brims

❝My first recollections of Canada are travelling on the train through Québec to Montréal. We were sitting three in a seat with the window open. I had a doll, and the little girl next to me said, "You know when you get to Canada they will take everything away from you." "Well," I said, "They won't get my doll," and I threw it out the open window. I seemed to realize then that I was really alone and I started to cry. ❞

—Girl, name withheld

❝I was sent out to Arrow River in Manitoba, where I was put on contract to this farmer for seven years. ...

Those seven years were hell. I was beat up with pieces of harness, pitchforks, anything that came in handy to hit me with I got it. I didn't get enough to eat. ...

They would buy me shoes that wouldn't fit. I used to cry with the pain. My feet are still crippled over that. ❞

—Charles W. Carver

Source: All quotations from Phyllis Harrison, ed., *The Home Children: Their Personal Stories* (Winnipeg: Watson & Dwyer Publishing Ltd., 1979), pp. 59, 84–85, 90.

Think It ▶ Through

Many groups of immigrants came to Canada because of the influence of a religious organization. Choose one such group.
a) What did the religious organization do to encourage the move?
b) Think of other push and pull factors affecting your group.
c) Create a push–pull diagram for your group by following the model in Figure 11.10 on page 252.

Francophones in the West

Focus

How did Francophones contribute to the overall development of Western Canada?

As you have learned, Francophones had lived in the West for generations. They were the first non-Aboriginal people in the West. They had been trading furs and living off the land here since 1730. In this section, you will learn ways in which Francophones put their mark on the West.

Leaving Their Mark

The Canadiens and Métis named rivers, lakes, and regions. You can see the Francophone presence in the many streets and parks with French names. Many of the communities we live in have French names, such as Batoche and Bellegarde in Saskatchewan, and Beaumont, Morinville, St. Paul, and Lac La Biche in Alberta.

You can see the mark left on the land by the early Francophone farmers. For example, the farms on the Red and Saskatchewan Rivers are quite distinct. They are long and narrow, with houses near the water. In other words, they are similar to the farms of the seigneurial system of New France.

Many Canadiens went west as missionaries. The Sisters of Charity are a good example. They are better known as the *Soeurs Grises* (Grey Nuns). They started a convent and school in St. Boniface. They started the hospital at Lac Sainte-Anne in 1859. Francophone villages and towns grew near the French Catholic missions. These included Lac Sainte-Anne, St. Albert, and St. Boniface. By the 1880s, the West had many Francophone communities.

Early Francophone businesses gave people jobs and helped get the economy rolling. For example, the West Canadian Collieries operated coal mines in the Crowsnest Pass area of Alberta. It was owned by business interests in France and run by local Francophones. Revillon Frères, the second-most important fur-trading company, had a major warehouse in Edmonton. In Albertville, Saskatchewan, a group of Francophone residents formed Saskatchewan's first credit union in 1916.

Internal Migrants

Many Canadiens and English Canadians moved westward during the period of massive settlement from about 1890 to 1914. People who move from one region to another within one country are called **internal migrants**.

At first, many Canadien migrants felt welcome. They were confident that Manitoba was meant to be bilingual. They were attracted to the educational system. It was modelled on the Québec system, which allowed for Catholic (Francophone) schools. People had the right to speak French in the courts and in government. Many Canadiens moved to Edmonton. Here 60 per cent of the non-Aboriginal population spoke French by 1880.

As time went by, Canadiens began to see that the government would rather make the West Anglophone. Fewer migrants from Québec moved West.

> The newspaper *L'Ouest canadien* began publishing in Alberta in 1898. It was founded to encourage people from Québec to move west.

Figure 11.15 Le Musée de St-Boniface, built 1845–1851. The goal of the museum is to collect and safeguard artifacts related to early Canadien and Métis life in the West. The building began as the convent of the Grey Nuns and the first hospital in the West. It also served as a boarding school. It is the oldest building in Winnipeg and the largest oak log structure in North America. How would Western Francophones have felt about having this centre in their midst?

Identity

One Very Canadien Community: St. Boniface

What makes a community a cultural centre?

St. Boniface is a very important centre for Francophone artists, authors, publishers, and festivals. It is the largest Francophone community west of Montréal. St. Boniface became part of Winnipeg 30 years ago. It began, however, more than 150 years earlier. In 1818, Bishop Provencher came here to set up a mission.

Today, St. Boniface has a population of 18 000. A majority of the people who live here are fluent in both French and English. You can see the Canadien character of the community by strolling through the town. The street signs for the many lovely, tree-lined streets are in both French and English. Many business signs are in French, and when you go into the shops, you will find a distinctive Francophone atmosphere.

Taking a Stroll through Old St. Boniface

Walking along avenue de la Cathédrale, you come upon St. Boniface Basilica. At the end of the evening Mass or liturgy (celebrated in French), you will see crowds pour out of the basilica! (Attending church is important to many Franco-Manitobans.)

Walking along boulevard Provencher, you will come upon cozy bistros, chocolatiers, and tiny clothing shops. Right on boulevard Provencher is the Centre culturel franco-manitobain. It works to make sure everyone in Manitoba has a chance to experience Francophone culture.

Respond

You have read about many signs of vitality in the Francophone community of St. Boniface. Form a small group. Share signs of the vitality of various groups within your community.

Figure 11.16 St. Boniface Basilica with the grave of Louis Riel in the foreground. The original cathedral was built around 1908. It burned down in 1968. When the cathedral was rebuilt, the community saved the original stone front. Why would they do that?

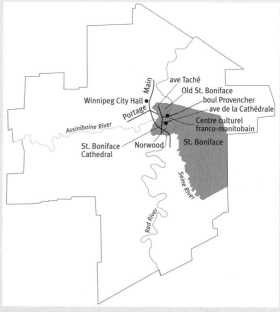

Figure 11.17 St. Boniface, which is now part of Winnipeg. Old St. Boniface was built at the turn of the twentieth century. Norwood is a lovely residential neighbourhood. Describe where St. Boniface is in relation to downtown Winnipeg.

Boosting the Francophone Population

It soon became clear that internal migration would not be enough to keep the Francophone community strong. The Canadiens saw that they might become a tiny minority.

The Catholic Church took on the job of attracting more French Catholics to the West. It gave a number of priests the task of attracting them. Father Jean-Baptiste Morin alone drew 2475 Francophone migrants to Alberta from 1891 to 1899.

Between 1860 and 1900, half a million Canadiens from Québec had moved south to New England (on the east coast of the United States). This was about a third of the Québec population. Most went because of the many jobs in factories. Francophone Westerners tried to lure these people back to Canada. For example, they made a special edition of the newspaper *Le Courrier de l'Ouest* in 1907. It was distributed in Québec, the Eastern United States, and France.

Francophone settlers came from Belgium and France, as well. One group of French army officers was led by Colonel Armand Trochu. In 1905, they started Le Ranch Sainte-Anne (St. Ann Ranch Trading Company) northeast of Calgary. The surrounding town became Trochu.

In 1886, the Francophone population of the prairies was about 16 000 people. Half of them were Métis. By 1921, that number had climbed to 137 000. Francophones made up about 7 per cent of the population of the prairies.

Biography

Gabrielle Roy (1909–1983)

Gabrielle Roy was born in St. Boniface, the youngest of 11 children. Roy grew up to be a world-famous author. Three of her books won the Governor General's Award, which is Canada's top literary prize. Her most famous book was *Bonheur d'occasion*, known in English as *The Tin Flute*. Roy's grandfather was a homesteader from Québec. Her father helped relocate migrants. Roy remembers one of the Catholic priests who convinced Québecers to go west:

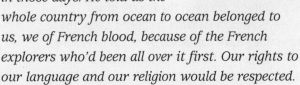

He talked about beautiful rich land and all the Canadian West where we should hurry to go and get established before the Scots and English, who were arriving in droves in those days. He told us the whole country from ocean to ocean belonged to us, we of French blood, because of the French explorers who'd been all over it first. Our rights to our language and our religion would be respected.

Source: Gabrielle Roy, *Enchantment and Sorrow: The Autobiography of Gabrielle Roy* (Toronto: Lester & Orpen Dennys, 1987), p. 16.

Think It Through

1. Identify a community with Francophone roots in Alberta. Do some research to find out about its beginnings. How did it help the West develop?

2. Imagine that the government had tried hard to attract Francophones to the West. What if a million Francophones had travelled to the West instead of 100 000?
   a) How might various peoples already in the West have reacted to such a policy?
   b) Using a paragraph or poem format, describe how the Canadian identity would be different today.

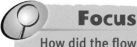

Focus

How did the flow of immigration influence the character of Western Canada?

Settling In

The newcomers in the West lived through many years of hardship. This section looks at the new prairie society that began to emerge.

A Pluralistic Society

By 1911, more than 80 per cent of the people living in the Western provinces had been born outside Canada. They had left the communities where they were born to travel thousands of kilometres to a foreign land. Here they endured years of hardship. They built their own homes. They ploughed under the prairie sod with animal-drawn ploughs. They struggled every year to bring in crops of wheat in Canada's short growing season.

What was special about all this? They did it alongside people from a wide variety of backgrounds. Many Canadians wondered how all these people would get along. Would they argue all the time? Would this be the beginning of a pluralistic society?

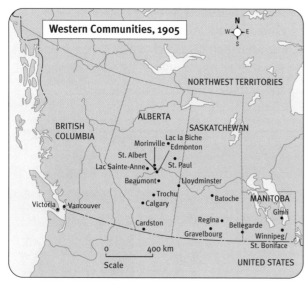

Figure 11.18 Some communities in the West by 1905. In 1871, there were only a few villages west of Ontario. By 1914, there were about 600 towns and cities. What problems might these communities have had when they first developed? Here's a hint: first think of all the goods and services you have access to in your community.

Tech Link

To see several historical photographs of the early Ukrainian community in the West, open Chapter 11 on your *Voices and Visions* CD-ROM.

Ethnic Origin	1881	1901	1911
British*	2 548 514	3 063 195	3 999 081
French	1 298 929	1 649 371	2 061 719
German	254 319	310 501	403 417
Scandinavian	5 223	31 042	112 682
Aboriginal	108 547	127 941	105 611
Jewish	667	16 131	76 199
Ukrainian	0	5 682	75 432
Dutch	30 412	33 845	55 961
Italian	1 849	10 834	45 963
Russian	1 227	19 825	44 376
Asian	4 383	23 731	43 213
Polish	0	6 285	33 625
Other European	5 760	23 811	97 101
Other**	64 980	49 121	52 263
Total	**4 324 810**	**5 371 315**	**7 206 643**

* The British and French numbers include the many Canadians whose families had been in Canada for centuries.
** "Other" refers to people having ethnic origins besides those listed here.

Source: Daniel Francis and Sonia Riddoch. *Our Canada*, second edition (Toronto: Pippin Publishing, 1995), p. 59.

Figure 11.19 Ethnic origins of Canadians. Describe the trend you see in this table. Which ethnic group grew the most from 1881 to 1901? From 1901 to 1911? What type of graph would you choose to display this data? Why?

VOICES ■

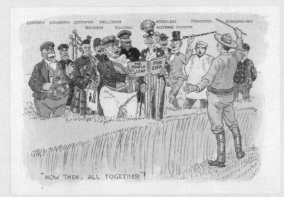

"NOW THEN, ALL TOGETHER"!

Figure 11.20 A 1903 political cartoon. Which figure is meant to be Canada? What song is the choir singing? This song was once Canada's unofficial anthem. Why is the choir standing in wheat? What is the artist trying to say about the changes taking place in Canada? What groups of people were not included in the cartoon? What does this say about Canadian society?

Points of View on Immigration

As you read, choose one quality that you think each of the speakers might use to describe a valuable Canadian citizen. What do you think makes a valuable Canadian citizen?

Ralph Connor was a church minister and author. He wrote about the changes in Western Canada.

❝In Western Canada there is to be seen today that most fascinating of all human phenomena, the making of a nation. Out of [people] diverse in traditions, in ideals, in speech, and in manner of life ... one people is being made. ❞

Source: Ralph Connor, *The Foreigner: A Tale of Saskatchewan* (Toronto: Westminster Co., Ltd., 1909).

J.S. Woodsworth was another church minister who wrote about the West. He called immigrants "strangers within our gates."

❝Foreigners in large numbers are in our midst. More are coming. How are we to make them into good Canadian citizens? ❞

Source: J.S. Woodsworth (James Shaver), *Strangers Within Our Gates* (Toronto: University of Toronto Press, 1909, 1972), p. 234.

In ethnically diverse Canada, people could be cruel to people from other groups. Ka Kita Wa Pa No Kwe, or Wise Day Woman, tells about coping with bad treatment.

❝All the difficult times I had with the white people did not make me condemn them. I just figured I had to face whatever came along and accept how we were going to be used by white man. I made no fuss about it for the longest time, I just took it all. Little did I know there were some good people in this world besides those who put me down and kept me low. ❞

Source: Madeline Katt Theriault, *Moose to Moccasins: The Story of Ka Kita Wa Pa No Kwe* (Toronto: Natural Heritage/Natural History Inc., 1992), pp. 116–117.

Lily Chang's grandfather came from China. He helped build the Canadian Pacific Railway. She remembers what he said about people learning to get along:

❝These things, the coming together of different cultures, they take time, like the flowering of a cherry tree. And, like a cherry tree, when the blossom comes it is a thing of beauty. ❞

Source: "The Building of the CPR," http://www.auraltrad.com/goldrush/s-l/chang-e.html.

Respond

What question does Woodsworth ask? Many people believed that assimilation was necessary to create "good citizens" and a strong country. What do you think the various immigrants thought about that? Would the Canadiens in the West have a different perspective? Why?

The Great Grain Growers

The homesteaders living on the prairies came from a variety of ethnic groups. Most worked from sun-up to sundown, and they knew their neighbours worked hard, too. The homesteaders had something else in common: nearly everyone was farming wheat.

The Machinery

When homesteaders first arrived at their land, they had to clear away brush. Then they "broke" the hard sod with a team of oxen and a plough. This prepared it for seeding. After planting and a long summer, the harvest was brought in by hand, too. The grain was cut, tied into bundles, and piled into stooks.

By the end of the nineteenth century, new machinery was being produced that made farming much easier. Steam-powered tractors replaced horses and oxen. Farmers used binders to harvest the wheat. A binder cut the wheat, rolled it into bundles called sheaves, and tied each sheaf with twine. Farmers then used mechanical threshers to separate the grain from the stalk. The railway was there to carry the crop to distant markets.

The Wheat

Early farmers used a type of wheat known as Red Fife. It made excellent flour, but it ripened late in the season. An early frost could wipe out an entire harvest. Early in the 1900s, Canadian government scientists William Saunders and his son Charles produced a new type of wheat. It was called Marquis, and it ripened quickly. Marquis wheat made it possible to open vast new areas of the West for farming. For this reason, Westerners called it "the discovery of the century."

The Exports

Wheat became the most important crop in Canada. It was shipped around the world to feed many people. The first shipment of wheat left Manitoba in 1876. It was a tiny cargo of 884 bushels of wheat. It travelled to Ontario. By 1921, Canada produced 156 billion bushels of wheat, most of it from the new prairie farms. Other grains, such as barley and oats, added to the harvest. In the West, though, wheat was king.

Figure 11.21 The photo on the left shows homesteaders breaking prairie sod. After a few decades, a farmer's fields looked more like the photo on the right. It was taken near Edmonton about 1910 and shows a thresher at work, harvesting "prairie gold." Compare and contrast the work required of the farmers in these two photographs.

Identity

The Prairie Way

Most prairie families lived far apart. They worked in isolation. What kind of community identity evolved from this?

Most prairie homesteaders didn't see their neighbours for days and sometimes weeks. So people learned to depend on themselves. Self-sufficiency is a proud prairie trait. Even so, the homesteaders learned together that the best way to survive was to help one another in times of need. The First Nations were probably the first to begin this tradition.

It was about 1909. Jim Grey-Eyes was a well-established farmer on the Muskeg Reserve.... One day, Grey-Eyes went riding along the Saskatchewan River and came to the Doukhobor village of Petrofka. The Doukhobors had just recently come to Canada from Russia, and they did not have any horses. What Grey-Eyes saw was twenty women, big strong Doukhobor women, hitched up to a wooden walking plow cutting furrows in the ground. Grey-Eyes watched for a while and then went home, rounded up four of his horses, and took them plus harnesses and eveners to Petrofka the next day. It was difficult to carry on a conversation because Grey-Eyes spoke only Cree and the Doukhobors spoke only Russian, but he did his best.

Grey-Eyes left the horses there and went home. About a week later he returned to see how they were making out. He was dismayed at the condition of the horses. They had been overworked and underfed. At home, these animals were used to a daily ration of oats, but here all they got was what they could forage on the prairie. The Doukhobors had been so pleased with the amount of land that could be broken with the horses that they had worked the animals far more than the horses could take. Grey-Eyes was so mad that he took his horses home.

When he got home, he decided that help was needed. So he got another team of four horses and took along his hired man, Mike Otterchild. He left Otterchild with the Doukhobors for a short while to show the Doukhobors how to look after and work the horses. A firm bond was established between the [Cree] and Doukhobor communities. Nick Popoff, one of the Doukhobor leaders, came to visit Jim Grey-Eyes every year.

Tech Link

Look on the *Voices and Visions* CD-ROM to see photographs of the Doukhobors.

Source: Shirley Bear, et al., *... And They Told Us Their Stories*, edited by Jack Funk and Gordon Lobe (Saskatoon: Saskatoon Tribal Council, 1991), p. 80.

In another form, this spirit of helpfulness showed itself in the tradition of the community bee. Bees were held for any big job that could be done quickly with a lot of workers. They included barn-raising bees and quilting bees.

In 1998, grain farmer Scott Bonnor got his foot caught in the auger at the bottom of his combine hopper. He was rushed to hospital, but his foot was mangled.

Respond

Homesteading families had hardship and hard work in common. How would these experiences encourage active citizenship? Do you think they helped forge a unique Western identity? Explain. What community traditions reflect a spirit of citizenship in your community?

Bonnor would not be able to harvest nearly 800 hectares (2000 acres) of grain on his farm. Westerner Mike O'Brien tells the story of the modern combine bee that helped Bonnor in a time of need.

The next Saturday, one week after the accident, six combines came together on Bonnor's fields. By Sunday, there were 10. Over those two days, Bonnor's neighbours took almost all of his crops off the fields. "They were still combining themselves," Bonnor said from his bed in the Regina General Hospital. "But they gave up a day to work on our farm.... That took a lot of pressure off."

The neighbours' wives brought food both days and turned the task into an old-time social event. And it was "old-time." Things like this have happened ever since farmers first planted their futures in this vast quilt of land. "It's something money can't buy," Bonnor said. "It's the people. The generosity of the people. You can't get that just anywhere. We help each other. It was my time to get help."

Source: Mike O'Brien, *Calling the Prairies Home: Origins, Attitudes, Quirks & Curiosities* (Vancouver: Raincoast Books, 1999), p. 2.

Think It Through

1. Look at the artifacts below. Immigrants brought these items to Canada in the early twentieth century.
   a) These items are an important part of Canadian heritage. Why is that so?
   b) Imagine that your family has decided to move to another country. You are told that there is room for you to bring only one possession. Think about it. Will you take something to remind you of the place you have left? Or will you choose something that will be useful in the place you are going? Describe your choice. Why did you choose this item?
   c) Take a picture of your chosen item, or make a drawing of it. Show this to the class. Explain why you would bring it with you to a new country. **SKILLS**

Figure 11.22 A Ukrainian chest. It carried family belongings to Saskatchewan in 1902.

Figure 11.23 A silk-lined bassinet. An American family brought it with them when they moved to British Columbia in 1908.

Figure 11.24 A brass samovar (a type of tea-kettle). A Russian army officer carried it across the ocean when he came to Canada in 1917.

Think It ▶ Through (continued)

2. Create a map like the one in Figure 11.18, using GIS if possible. Label each community with the major ethnic groups associated with it.

3. Various groups of immigrants came to Western Canada near the turn of the twentieth century. Investigate one group. (Refer to Figure 11.19 for ideas.) Here are six questions you might use to focus your investigation:
   - When did most of the people in this group come to Canada?
   - What were the push and pull factors affecting their decision to move?
   - Where in Canada did most of them settle?
   - What are two or three of this group's traditions or customs?
   - What contributions has this group made to Canada?
   - What impact did this group have on First Nations peoples, and vice versa?

   Collect your information. Refer to the chapter project to create a multimedia presentation of your findings. **SKILLS**

4. How did the massive immigration to Canada near the turn of the twentieth century affect the complex identity of our country?

(SKILLS) Chapter 11 PROJECT The Prairie Patchwork Quilt

The West became the destination of choice around 1890. Europeans, Americans, and Eastern Canadians joined the First Nations there. Together they become a prairie patchwork of ethnic groups, religious groups, and language groups. In this chapter project you will develop a multimedia presentation. It will explore the cultural pluralism of the West.

Focus

1. Refer to the research you completed in Think It Through activity 3 above. You will use this research to make your multimedia presentation.

2. Form a group with three other students. Each of you should have researched a different immigrant group.

3. Brainstorm with your class. How does the theme "Patchwork Quilt" reflect the Canadian identity? How could you use this theme in a multimedia presentation?

4. With your group members, decide what type of multimedia presentation you want to develop.

Find and Select

5. With your group, plan your presentation, and decide what types of media you would like to include.

6. On your own, collect multimedia segments for the immigrant group you researched. For example, you might collect or create visuals, audio clips, or video clips.

7. Work together to create your "Patchwork Quilt" presentation. A storyboard is a useful tool.

Prepare to Present

8. Organize all the tools you will need for your presentation. For example, you might need a television, computer, stereo, or DVD player.

9. Rehearse your presentation to ensure a smooth show.

Present and Reflect

Present your multimedia presentation to your class. Return to your group and discuss the finished project. How would you fix the glitches? Were your choices of media suitable to the topic? What would you do differently next time?

Chapter 12 Changing Societies in the West

Chapter INQUIRY   Was the impact of Canada's immigration policy on each of the peoples in Western Canada positive or negative?

Key CONCEPT ▶ People and Policies

There are two meanings for the word *policy*. Governments have general policies, or understandings, about the way the country should be run. For example, it is the policy of the Canadian government to maintain a healthy economy. A formal policy, on the other hand, lays out a plan of action to achieve a specific goal.

Policies have the power to affect individuals and communities in many ways—both negative and positive. This chapter describes the effects of government policies on the peoples of Western Canada in the late 1800s and early 1900s. Investigating this topic might help you understand the policies that affect you and your community today.

SKILLS Honing Your Skills

Role-playing gives us the opportunity to see historical events from a different person's point of view. The Skill Check feature in this chapter will show you how to **Research and Perform a Role Play.** The project at the end of this chapter will give you a chance to role-play a scene from the chapter.

Government Policies and the Peoples of the West

You may recall from earlier chapters that the National Policy was the main idea the government had for helping Canada grow strong as a nation. The National Policy was like three policies in one:
- an immigration policy—to encourage farmers to settle in the West
- a transportation policy—to build a railway
- an economic policy—to help the economy grow by setting tariffs on foreign goods (encouraging Canadians to buy Canadian goods)

In time, these policies achieved their goals. Along the way, they also created a new society in the West.

Many Perspectives

This chapter invites you to think about policies from the perspectives of some of the people whose lives were most affected by them: First Nations, Métis, newcomers from Eastern Europe, Chinese immigrants, Francophone Westerners, and farmers and ranchers. This organizer imagines what individuals from these groups might have said about the big changes happening in their lives at this time.

The NATIONAL POLICY

I don't think the government cares what happens to Prairie farmers. I'm going broke from the high cost of shipping wheat by rail.
Homesteader from Britain

J'ai peur que notre langue et notre culture se perdent. Il y a beaucoup de nouveaux arrivants, et la majorité d'entre eux ne parlent pas français.
Francophone Doctor

ᐁᐲᑖᒥᒥᐦᑕᐤ ᐆᒪ
ᒥᐦᒋᐟ ᐯᑐᐣ ᐊᓯᑲᓈᐊᐧᐠ
ᐁᐄᐧᐤᓀᐱᒋᑖᐧ ᑭᑕᐢᑫᓇᐦᐠ
ᑕᓂᓯ ᐳᑯ ᐃᑲᐧ
ᑳᐄᐧ ᐃᐢᐸᔨᐠ.
Nehiyaw Elder

Dawn looest tehkeh taapitow ni shipwepichinawn li terraen chi mishkamawk maka ya pawt plaas ayiiwawk chiytootehk ehkwa.
Métis Grandmother

鐵路工作很艱苦
現 在我希望我能把
我家庭的其他成員
從中國帶過來
開始經營一個小生意
Chinese Store Owner

Мені подобається
в цій новій країні, бо тато
кажуть ми матимем своє
господарство невдовзі.
Я все гадаю - яким
воно буде?
Ukrainian Girl

Think AHEAD How many of these languages can you understand? What does that tell you about one of the challenges people faced as they tried to build a new society in the West? (If you're curious about the comments you can't read, see the translations on page 284 at the end of this chapter.)

SKILL CHECK: Research and Perform a Role Play

Role-playing is one way to show your understanding of how people in history were affected by the events around them. For example, refer to the organizer on the previous page. Each quotation gives a different person's point of view on the government's National Policy and its impact on his or her life.

When you play a role, you pretend you are a real or imaginary person. You act and speak as that person would. Here are some tips for doing a good job.

1. **Start by researching the period at the library or on the Internet.** Find out everything you can about the time, place, people, and events you are studying. Look for interesting details such as clothes your character might have worn or typical expressions of the time. You might not use all this information, but it will help you understand your character. Actors call this "getting in character."

2. **If you're playing a real individual, research that person's history.** Try to find out some of his or her characteristics, such as values, religion or faith, language, ethnicity, community, livelihood, and so on. Include a copy of a photograph or painting of the person along with your written character sketch.

3. **Prepare by making notes.** Include
   - the facts of the situation or event to be role-played
   - your character's perspective
   - how your character feels
   - how your character acts (voice, gestures)

4. **Decide whether you will work from a script or make up the dialogue as you go along.** If you are working in a group, make sure everyone agrees in advance what will happen.

5. **You might want to use music, props, or appropriate clothing to make your role play more interesting.** Remember not to stereotype and to be respectful of the cultures you represent. (You may recall learning about stereotyping in previous chapters. It occurs when we make assumptions about individuals because they belong to a particular group.)

Try It!

Create a character sketch of a historical figure. You can choose someone you read about in Chapter 11, or skim ahead and choose someone from this chapter.

Figure 12.1 These students are performing a role play for their peers. What do you think the topic might be?

Treaties in the West

The First Nations and Métis were the first to feel the effects of new settlement in the West. On the plains, the buffalo had become scarce because so many newcomers were hunting them. In the north, more and more miners and trappers were moving into First Nations territories. All across the prairies, land that was good for hunting was being turned into farms.

Focus

Why did First Nations and the government of Canada sign the Numbered Treaties?

Reading
STRATEGY

Before you begin reading this section, skim through it. Read the headings and subheadings. Read the first and last sentence of each subsection. Note the titles of features and the captions under the photographs that catch your attention.

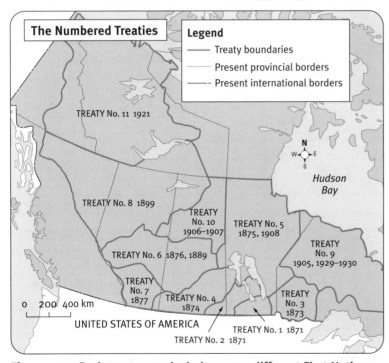

The Numbered Treaties

Legend
— Treaty boundaries
········· Present provincial borders
— Present international borders

TREATY No. 11 1921

Hudson Bay

TREATY No. 8 1899

TREATY No. 10 1906–1907

TREATY No. 5 1875, 1908

TREATY No. 6 1876, 1889

TREATY No. 9 1905, 1929–1930

TREATY No. 7 1877

TREATY No. 4 1874

TREATY No. 3 1873

0   200   400 km

UNITED STATES OF AMERICA

TREATY No. 1 1871

TREATY No. 2 1871

Figure 12.2 Each treaty area includes many different First Nations. Which treaty area do you live in? Compare this map to the map of Aboriginal Language Groups and Peoples in Canada (see Chapter 1, page 7). Identify all the First Nations covered by the treaty area in which you live.

Europeans also brought diseases, such as smallpox and tuberculosis, that were especially dangerous for Aboriginal people.

Chapter 8 explained some of the actions the Métis took during this time. This section describes how First Nations and the federal government tried to reach understanding through the treaty process. You'll see that First Nations and the Canadian government had different reasons for signing treaties. They had different understandings of what the treaties meant.

Different Reasons

From 1871 to 1921, the First Nations living between the Great Lakes and the Rocky Mountains made 11 treaties with the Canadian government. These are known as the **Numbered Treaties**.

The Canadian government's main reason for making these treaties was to gain control of the land and natural resources. Government officials knew that if First Nations did not agree to allow homesteaders onto their lands, then the government's immigration plans would fail. At the time, there were wars between First Nations and government troops in the United States. Prime Minister John A. Macdonald didn't want that to happen in Canada. He knew it would cause great suffering. He also knew that violence would slow down his efforts to expand Canada westward.

First Nations' main reason for agreeing to treaties was to protect their rights to their lands and natural resources. First Nations leaders realized that the future would bring even more newcomers. Also, the First Nations needed the food and money the government was promising. Many communities were threatened with starvation and disease

CASE STUDY

Treaty Number 7

Treaty 7 involved five First Nations: the Kainai [KY-ny], the Piikani [bee-GUN-ee], the Siksika [sik-SIK-uh], the Nakoda [na-KOH-dah], and the Tsuu T'ina [tsoo-TIN-uh]. Canadian officials and leaders from the five nations met at Blackfoot Crossing on the Bow River in September 1877. For four days they talked back and forth about what would be in the treaty. The chiefs also talked among themselves. Finally, both sides reached an agreement.

- In the written agreement, the Canadian government recorded that the First Nations had surrendered 90 600 square kilometres of land in exchange for benefits such as yearly payments, reserve lands, hunting and fishing rights on unoccupied lands, salaries for teachers, and farm equipment. The Canadian government thought it now owned the land.

- The First Nations Elders recorded in memory that they had agreed to share their land with the newcomers in exchange for the government's promises to provide for their needs. They did not think the land was sold.

Figure 12.3 This painting is A. Bruce Stapleton's interpretation of Isapo-Muxika speaking at the Treaty 7 negotiations. What questions might you ask about it? (You may want to refer to Skill Check: Interpret Images on page 6 for guidance.)

Isapo-Muxika was a Siksika chief who took part in the Treaty 7 talks. He was also known as Crowfoot. The Canadian government reports on Treaty 7 include the following record of what Isapo-Muxika said at the time.

I have to speak for my people, who are numerous, and who rely upon me to follow the course which in the future will tend to their good. The plains are large and wide. We are the children of the plains, it is our home, and the buffalo has been our food always. … The advice given me and my people has proved to be very good. If the police had not come to the country, where would we all be now? Bad men and whiskey were killing us so fast that very few, indeed, would have been left today. The police have protected us as the feathers of the bird protect it from the frosts of winter. I wish them all good, and I trust that all our hearts will increase in goodness from this time forward. I am satisfied, I will sign the treaty.

Source: Alexander Morris, *The Treaties of Canada, with the Indians of Manitoba and the North-West Territories* (Toronto: Belfords, Clarke, 1880).

 **Respond**

What do you notice about each side's understanding of the treaty? What issues might there be because it was the government that recorded Isapo-Muxika's speech?

because the buffalo were disappearing. First Nations had other reasons for signing the treaties, as well. Some saw the treaties as a better alternative than war with the newcomers and the government. Others decided to sign in return for help in setting up farms. Still others felt that, if they did not sign, the land would be taken from them anyway.

Through the treaties, the government promised to hold at least some land in trust for the First Nations. The First Nations peoples believed the treaty negotiations were a way to meet the government on a nation-to-nation basis. They hoped to ensure that their peoples and cultures would survive.

Tech Link

To learn more about the Numbered Treaties, open Chapter 12 on your *Voices and Visions* CD-ROM.

The Treaties

WEB LINK

Each treaty was slightly different, but the main agreement in all of them was that the Canadian government promised to provide First Nations with cash payments, certain goods (such as fishing gear and farm equipment), and certain services (such as education and health care). In exchange, First Nations would allow homesteaders onto their lands. Certain areas of land, called reserves, were set aside for First Nations' sole use—newcomers could not live there.

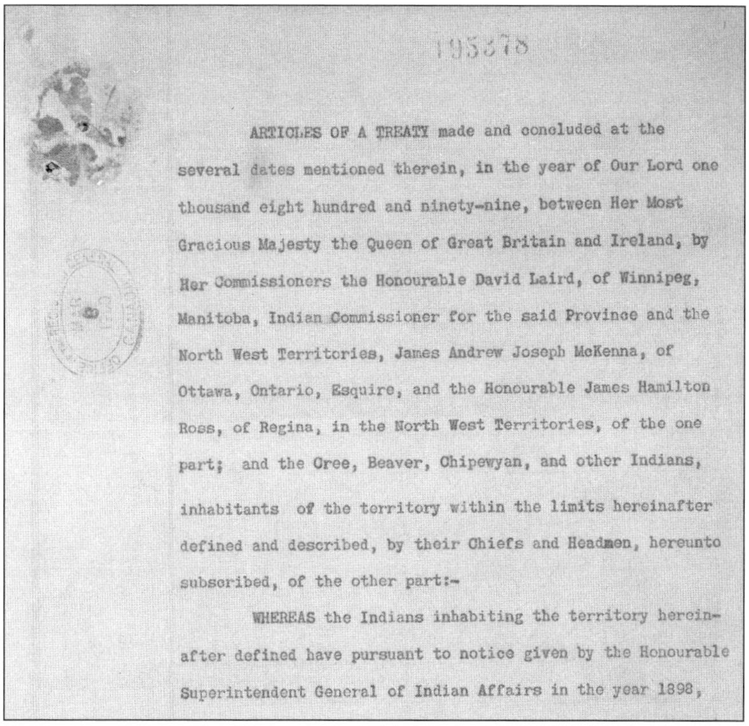

Different Understandings

In the Case Study of Treaty 7, you may have noticed that the Canadian government and First Nations ended up with different understandings of the treaty. This happened with every treaty that was signed. At the time, both sides did their best to communicate clearly. However, language and cultural differences made this difficult.

Assimilation

The Canadian government had another policy in mind that it didn't discuss at the treaty negotiations. This was a policy of **assimilation**. Assimilation means that one culture dies out because of the strong influence of a dominant group. Sometimes a language dies out that way, too. The Canadian government thought that, as time went by, First Nations would lose their cultures and languages. They would become more like the newcomers. To accomplish this, it targeted First Nations children. It separated them from their parents by making them attend **residential schools**. Here, they were forbidden from speaking their own languages or practising their own beliefs. Because these children spent much of their childhoods away from their families, they could not benefit from their parents' guidance and teachings—they were cut off from their roots.

195378

ARTICLES OF A TREATY made and concluded at the several dates mentioned therein, in the year of Our Lord one thousand eight hundred and ninety-nine, between Her Most Gracious Majesty the Queen of Great Britain and Ireland, by Her Commissioners the Honourable David Laird, of Winnipeg, Manitoba, Indian Commissioner for the said Province and the North West Territories, James Andrew Joseph McKenna, of Ottawa, Ontario, Esquire, and the Honourable James Hamilton Ross, of Regina, in the North West Territories, of the one part; and the Cree, Beaver, Chipewyan, and other Indians, inhabitants of the territory within the limits hereinafter defined and described, by their Chiefs and Headmen, hereunto subscribed, of the other part:-

WHEREAS the Indians inhabiting the territory hereinafter defined have pursuant to notice given by the Honourable Superintendent General of Indian Affairs in the year 1898,

Figure 12.4 Part of the Canadian government's record of Treaty 8. How did First Nations record treaties? How could these different recording methods lead to different understandings?

Canada Today

Aboriginal peoples and the government of Canada are still dealing with misunderstandings about the treaties. Many First Nations, for example, are involved in ongoing court cases. They argue that their ancestors never signed over ownership of the land. Therefore, they believe they still have rights to it. Hunting and fishing rights are another point of disagreement. It can be hard to know the intentions of the treaty makers as time goes by.

The treaties created 2300 reserves. Life on these reserves continues to pose many challenges for First Nations people. High unemployment, housing shortages, education issues, and lack of medical services are some examples. Use the library, news sources, or the Internet to try to learn more about one of the present-day impacts of the treaties or of assimilation policies. Prepare a written report or an oral presentation.

Think It ▶ Through

1. Refer to the Skill Check feature on page 268. In a small group, role-play a scene from the Treaty 7 negotiations. Choose actual people from history to use in your scene. You may have to do some extra research in order to develop your characters fully. SKILLS

2. In your own words, describe why each side agreed to the Numbered Treaties. Think about how the descendants of the treaty participants are doing now. How did each side benefit—or not—over time?

3. Make a chart for recording information on how Canadian government policies affected peoples and communities in the West. Here is one way you could organize your ideas. Fill in the chart as you read the rest of this chapter.

Effects of Government Policies			
Policy	Who was affected?	How were they affected?	My thoughts and questions

Peoples from Eastern Europe

Peoples from Eastern Europe were one group that benefited from Canada's immigration policies. Next to the British and Americans, Eastern Europeans formed the greatest number of newcomers to the prairies in the late 1800s and early 1900s. Poles, Ukrainians, Romanians, and Hungarians were just some of the Eastern Europeans who came. Most settled on the Canadian prairies. This section describes how they helped build a new society in the West.

The Push and Pull Factors

Life in Eastern Europe around 1900 could be very hard. The people were proud of their cultures and countries. Many families, however, lived in poverty with little chance of getting ahead. In some places, a person

Focus

How did immigrants from Eastern Europe contribute to the development of Western Canada?

could be imprisoned or killed for practising a religion different from the one most people practised. Doukhobors, Mennonites, and Jews were some of the peoples who suffered from this kind of prejudice. The Canadian government promised immigrants free land and religious freedom. These promises drew these people to Canada, even though some of them did experience discrimination after they arrived.

Making a Home

If you've ever been homesick, you have some idea of what life might have been like for the Eastern European immigrants. Most of them would never see old friends, family, and familiar places again. To help ease their feelings of homesickness, many immigrants settled close to other people from their homelands. Living near others who shared their culture helped immigrants adjust to their new lives. They could talk to neighbours in their first language and help each other with work. They could get together for common cultural celebrations.

In their new communities, people set up all the services they needed, including health care, businesses, places of worship, and schools. As these communities grew, people from different cultures began to do business together and share traditions. In this

Figure 12.6 St. Nicholas Church, built in 1908. Sometimes a whole building can be an artifact. This church was moved from Kiew, Alberta, to the Ukrainian Cultural Village. Here it was restored so people could visit it. What can we learn by preserving the past in this way?

way, people from Eastern Europe contributed to all parts of society in the West.

Contributing to the Economy

Many people from Eastern Europe were farmers who settled on the land to grow food crops. The Métis and Canadiens most often had small family farms on the prairies. The Eastern Europeans preferred large wheat farms. These farms became the base of Canada's agriculture industry. The land and climate of the prairies were very similar to what they had been used to back home. This meant they already had the skills and knowledge needed to farm in the West. Winters in Canada, however, were colder and longer than in Eastern Europe. Many European immigrants did not come prepared for the cold and snow.

Other Eastern Europeans worked in the mines and logging camps or helped to build the railways. Still others opened stores. These were just some of the ways they supported the economy that was growing in Western Canada.

Figure 12.5 The borders and names of countries in Eastern Europe have changed several times since the early 1900s. This region is home to at least 10 different countries and 15 languages.

VOICES ∎

Millie Melnyk was a young girl when she came to Alberta with her parents from Ukraine in the late 1800s. Her description of what it was like going to school is evidence of the importance of English in schools at the time.

❝ I didn't know a word of English when I went to school at five. I remember the first day, I started to cry, and Mr. Cameron [the teacher] put me in a chair in front of his desk, the chair he used to sit on. He gave me a book to read, and I remember looking at the pictures but the tears were coming down. The Italians, or Hungarians or whatever, they didn't know English either, but they taught us first to sing. We sang in the morning and before noon. I learned all the Scotch songs and all the Irish songs. And of course you had to sing "God Save the King," all for learning English. ❞

Source: Eliane Leslau Silverman, *The Last Best West: Women on the Alberta Frontier 1880–1930* (Calgary: Fifth House Publishers, 1998).

Figure 12.7 Students at Huxley School, Alberta, 1909. What similarities and differences are there with your own school population?

Education and Health

In the early years, many families were so busy with work on the farm that schools were not the first thing on their minds. As soon as they could, however, people built schools in their communities.

For new immigrants, getting sick could be a disaster. They might not have family to help them, and they probably could not afford a doctor if they needed one. Many areas didn't have medical facilities of any sort. Many groups formed benefit societies. These offered a simple form of health insurance that helped members when they were sick and could not work. One example was the Hungarian Sick-Benefit Society that started in Lethbridge, Alberta, in 1901.

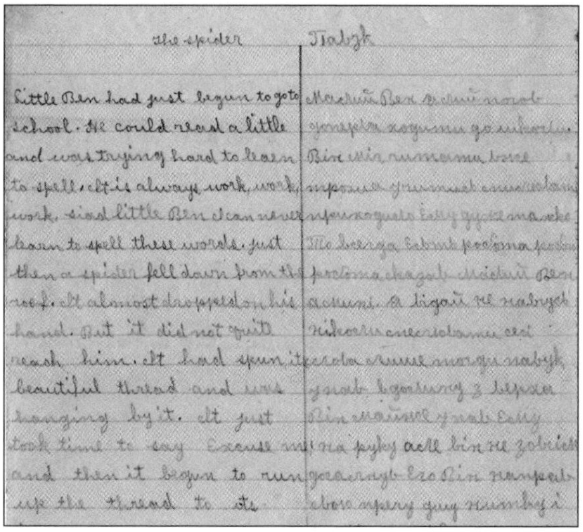

Cultural Activities

As soon as enough people had settled in an area, they built a church or synagogue where they could worship according to their faith. They also formed sports clubs, musical societies, dance groups, choirs, and other organizations that allowed them to

Figure 12.8 Child's lesson book, from about 1920. Why do you think this story is written in two languages? Dual-language lesson books like this were not common.

follow their customs and enjoy pastimes together. Many communities started newspapers in their own languages.

Culture, however, as you learned in previous chapters, involves much more than simply belonging to organizations. Culture is a learned way of life shared by a group of people. It is through common values and world views that these communities stayed strong.

Citizenship and Identity

People of various ethnic origins helped each other in the West. You saw in Chapter 11 how a First Nations farmer, Jim Grey-Eyes, helped a group of Doukhobors. In another example, Father Albert Lacombe brought priests to Canada who spoke various languages so they could minister to European immigrants. These are two strong

demonstrations of active citizenship.

Immigrants from Eastern Europe took advantage of their new freedoms to get involved in Canadian politics. It was not long before they were winning election to public office. For example, in 1913, Andrew Shandro was elected to the Alberta Legislature. He was the first Canadian of Ukrainian heritage to do so. Many more Canadians of Eastern European descent were elected to office in the years following Shandro's election.

Today more than three million Canadians are of Eastern European heritage. Many of these people are descended from those first immigrants to the West.

Figure 12.10 *The Ukrainian Voice* newspaper, 1914. How can having a newspaper help a community strengthen its identity? The *Voice* is still published today. What is the value of newspapers to historians?

Figure 12.9 Dozynki celebration, Tide Lake, Alberta, 1915. Dozynki is a Polish harvest festival. If you weren't sure when this photograph was taken, what information in it could help you estimate a date? (You may want to refer to Skill Check: Interpret Images on page 6 for guidance.)

Think It Through Discuss with a partner how you would use the primary sources in this section to give a talk on the contributions of Eastern European immigrants to Western Canada. Consider the Millie Melnyk quotation; the lesson book; the Ukrainian newspaper; and the photographs of the school children, the festival, and the church (see the Voices feature on the previous page and Figures 12.6 to 12.10). How do these documents help you see multiple perspectives?

Chinese Immigration to the West

People from China were among the earliest immigrants to Western Canada. The first Chinese came in 1858 with the gold rush in British Columbia. Later, thousands of Chinese men worked on the construction of the Canadian Pacific Railway (CPR). (You may recall reading about their experiences in Chapter 9.) In this section you can read about some of the other ways Chinese newcomers helped build Canadian society. You will also discover how their lives were affected by Canada's immigration policies.

Focus

How did Chinese immigrants contribute to the development of Canada?

Choosing to Stay

After the railway was finished in 1885, some Chinese returned to China. Others found jobs as cooks, storekeepers, and farmers. In British Columbia, many Chinese went to work in the salmon canneries.

Chinese people also settled on the prairies, usually in towns along the rail line. Many opened businesses such as laundries and restaurants or sold vegetables from their gardens. There was a great need for these kinds of businesses in the growing communities. In the East, Chinese immigrants settled in Montréal, Toronto, Hamilton, and Ottawa. Very few settled in the Maritime provinces or Newfoundland.

Of the Prairie provinces, Alberta had the largest number of Chinese immigrants. As well as starting businesses, Chinese people worked in the coal mines, on sugar beet farms, and as cooks on cattle ranches.

A Change in Policies

Male Chinese immigrants were welcome to work on the CPR. After the railway was finished, though, the federal government

Biography

Wong Yet

In 1895, Wong Yet came to Canada from China to work for the CPR. After a couple of years, he had saved enough to start up a laundry and restaurant. In 1903, his son Wong Pond came from China to help with the business. When the restaurant burned down in 1912, they put up another one called the Public Lunch. During the Depression, they provided food and shelter to homeless men looking for work doing chores. The Wongs became well known for their role in charity and sports projects in the community. Wong Pond owned and ran the Public Lunch for many years, and then his son took over and ran it until 1972.

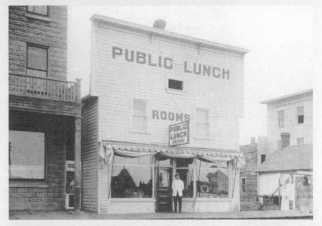

Figure 12.11 Public Lunch, Olds, Alberta, about 1912. This restaurant and rooming house was just one of the businesses the Wong family owned in Olds. What businesses in your community existed at that time? How do long-lasting businesses help a community?

started passing laws to keep Asian immigrants out. Many non-Asians believed that people from Japan, China, and India would not fit in to Canadian society. They feared the different customs of the Asian newcomers. Some non-Asians were also afraid that Asian immigrants, who were paid lower wages, would take any available jobs.

Tech Link

To see a photograph of one of the few early female Chinese immigrants, open Chapter 12 on your *Voices and Visions* CD-ROM.

One law to keep Asians out was the Chinese head tax. This was a fee that every person from China had to pay to enter Canada. The tax started in 1885 at $50 per person. Over the years it rose to $500. In 1923, a new policy stopped Chinese from coming to Canada at all. People could not even bring their family members to Canada. It was not until the late 1940s that attitudes started to change. Only then did Canadians of Chinese heritage begin to enjoy the same rights as other Canadians.

WEB LINK

Figure 12.12 Head tax certificate for Yip Sai Kai, issued in 1922. How much did his parents have to pay for it?

Chinatowns

Like many other immigrant groups, Chinese people who came to Canada wanted to live near family and friends. As a result, they moved to certain neighbourhoods, which came to be called Chinatowns. These can be quite distinctive neighbourhoods, with many crowded shops and bustling streets.

In Alberta, the largest Chinatown was in Calgary. In Saskatchewan, the biggest was in Moose Jaw. Over the years, Chinese communities have built cultural centres in many cities, including Vancouver, Winnipeg, and Toronto.

Figure 12.13 Chinese Cultural Centre, Calgary. The centre is a vibrant place where different aspects of Chinese culture can be enjoyed. Find out about some types of events put on at one such centre. Share them with your classmates. How do these centres help build Canadian society?

Think It Through ▶ Make a poster that shows some of the contributions of Chinese immigrants to the development of Canada.

From Majority to Minority: Francophones in the West

Think of Western Canada in the beginning as a movie theatre before the show starts. At first there are groups of First Nations people sitting at different places around the theatre. They are joined by Canadien and Scottish fur traders, Métis, and a few homesteaders from Ontario and Québec. Then, not long before the curtain rises, the theatre begins to fill up with newcomers. They come from many different countries. All around are people dressed in different styles of clothing, speaking different languages, and eating different foods. But everyone is there for the same movie.

That is the kind of place Western Canada became as a result of immigration. It meant big changes for Francophone communities in the West.

Focus

How did the arrival of so many immigrants affect Francophone peoples in Western Canada?

A Storm Brewing

In the years after Confederation, Francophone communities existed all across the prairies. Francophone Métis and Canadiens had been at home there for many years. As you learned in earlier chapters, some Canadien migrants joined them. So did Francophone immigrants from France and Belgium. They believed in the promise of Confederation—they hoped that the West would be a bilingual society.

Francophone culture and language were strong in the West. Until the late 1800s, French was the most common European language in use in the West. Then the great numbers of non-Francophone immigrants arrived. French soon became just one of many languages spoken on the prairies. As you saw in Chapter 11, the government had a policy of advertising in non-Francophone

Figure 12.14 Street corner in St. Albert, Alberta, 1912. This community was named to honour Father Albert Lacombe. In 1861, he had started a mission there for the Cree and Métis. It later grew into the largest agricultural centre west of Winnipeg. It was largely a Francophone community. What evidence in the photograph supports this fact?

countries. The government presented Canada as a country where English was the norm. Therefore, the new immigrants were expected to learn English, not French. Over the decades, they and their children became Anglophones. Anglophones became a bigger and bigger majority. As you will see, the provincial governments didn't want to pay for education and services in two languages.

Using French in Government

When Canada was created in 1867, the Constitution Act guaranteed several things. It said that politicians speaking in the federal Parliament, or in the Assembly in Québec, could use either French or English. The Act also said that laws should be printed in both languages. It said that people could use either language in the courts. In other words, French and English were equal in government and the law.

In 1870, the Manitoba Act made French and English equal in the Manitoba government. This meant that provincial government business took place in French or English. People could speak either

language in provincial courts. The Act began to fulfill the promise of Confederation. Most Francophones were pleased.

Hopes faded in 1890. In that year, the government of Manitoba made English the only **official language** in the province. (A language is "official" when the right to use it is protected by law.) Franco-Manitobans could no longer use French in the Manitoba Assembly, nor could they use it in provincial courts. This situation lasted for 90 years. Then, in 1979, the Supreme Court of Canada overturned the 1890 law. Today, the Manitoba government offers services in both official languages. This matches the spirit of the Manitoba Act.

Next door, the North-West Territories (which included the areas that are now Alberta and Saskatchewan) had been officially bilingual since 1877. Then, in 1892, the Assembly passed the Haultain Resolution. This motion made English the only language of government. For almost 100 years, the provinces of Alberta and Saskatchewan gave no official status to the French language. Then, in 1988, the Supreme Court ruled that the 1892 motion was not valid. The lieutenant-governor of the time had never proclaimed the law. This means it never was a real law. In response, both provinces quickly made real laws. They made English their only official language.

The Manitoba Schools Question

Francophones in the West struggled hard to protect their language rights. The right to separate schools was a major issue. (See the text box in Chapter 10 on page 234 for types of schools.)

As the West filled with new arrivals, people set up schools for their children.

Canada Today

French and English have been the official languages of the federal Parliament since 1867. In 1969, Members of Parliament voted in the Official Languages Act. It ensures that every citizen has the right to federal government services in either official language. Other laws have made Canada even more bilingual. For example, one law affects the items you buy every day. It says that all product packages must give information in both French and English. Canada's official languages are protected in sections 16 to 22 of Canada's Charter of Rights and Freedoms.

Since most of the first newcomers were Roman Catholic, most of the schools were Catholic schools. As we have seen in Chapter 10, the rights to schooling in a Catholic school system were guaranteed by the 1870 Manitoba Act. Since these newcomers were Francophone, the language of instruction was French. The teachers and students spoke French, and the students learned to read and write in French. Then newcomers of the Protestant faith started arriving. They set up their own schools. Even though the students spoke a variety of languages, the language of instruction was English.

Soon there were far more Protestant schools than there were Catholic schools. In 1890, the government of Manitoba voted to stop funding Catholic schools. It did not want the expense. Instead, it wanted a single system of schools. Protestants and Catholics would go to the same schools. Instruction would be in English.

Francophone Catholics were outraged. They knew that Confederation and the Manitoba Act had guaranteed the right to separate schools. They demanded their schools back. Francophones in Manitoba had the support of Francophones in Québec. The legislation became a national debate! The arguments dragged on for years. The Manitoba government tried to hold on to its English-language-only policy. The Francophones tried to stop it. The federal government had the right to enforce the constitutional guarantee of a French, Catholic school system in the West. It chose not to. Many Francophone Catholics felt betrayed, both in Manitoba and in Québec.

Finally, in 1896, Prime Minister Wilfrid Laurier and Manitoba premier Thomas Greenway reached a compromise. Catholics did receive the right to have some religious teaching in the schools. Also, if there were ten or more Francophone students, they would be taught in French. However, Catholics did not get their separate school system back. This was not the case in Québec. There, the provincial government had always funded a separate school system for the Protestant minority. For Francophones all over the country, the outcome of the Manitoba Schools question was a great disappointment. It dealt a terrible blow to French and Catholic rights in Canada.

Using French in Schools in the Northwest

As you learned in Chapter 10, Francophones in the West had a similar experience. First they enjoyed their rights as a minority. Then, in 1892, the territorial government made English the language of instruction in all schools. This situation continued after Alberta and Saskatchewan were created in 1905.

It wasn't until the Charter of Rights and Freedoms became law in 1982 that Francophones in the West had a chance to have their education rights recognized once again. In the meantime, they were left to try

Figure 12.15 First stopping place and separate school, Trochu, Alberta, 1910. When Francophone newcomers to the area first arrived, they visited the stopping place, at centre. Here they could rest before going out on the land. A building addition can be seen at left. The separate school is on the right. It would have been a Francophone, Catholic school.

to preserve their language without assistance. They published their own newspapers, built hospitals and churches, and organized social clubs. Community members also worked hard to start French radio stations in all three Prairie provinces. This included CHFA in Alberta, for which they raised funds. Volunteers also built the needed transmission tower.

Opening private schools was another strategy. Members of Catholic religious orders founded many schools and colleges. Collège Mathieu, for example, was founded in 1918 in Gravelbourg, Saskatchewan. It is still operating—the only private Francophone high school in Western Canada. All of these actions helped keep French in use. They helped keep alive the cultures of the Franco-Albertans, Franco-Saskatchewans, Franco-Manitobans, and Métis.

Franco-Albertan Citizens in Action

In 1982, the Charter of Rights and Freedoms became law. Section 23 states that all Anglophone and Francophone Canadians who live as minorities have education rights.

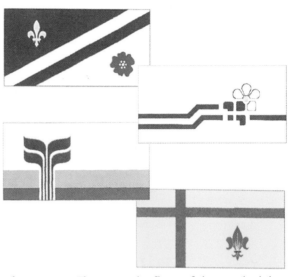

Figure 12.17 These are the flags of the provincial Francophone organizations in the Western provinces. What do flags have to do with group identity?

They are entitled to have their children educated in the minority language.

Some provinces did not take action right away, even though they had signed the Constitution. But Franco-Albertans did not give up. They lobbied. They protested. Within two years, they convinced two school boards to open Francophone schools. The efforts of the *Comité ad hoc pour l'école française catholique* resulted in the opening of École Maurice-Lavallée, in Edmonton. Franco-Albertans in Calgary successfully campaigned to open École Saint-Antoine in that city.

In 1988, the Alberta government saw that it needed to change the Alberta School Act to bring it in line with the Charter. The Act was changed twice, in 1988 and 1993. It now recognizes Section 23 rights, including the right of the minority to govern its schools through Francophone school boards. This educational right stems from the promise of Confederation—that Canada would be a bilingual nation in which the French and English languages would enjoy equal status. It helps fulfill the promise that Francophones and Anglophones would be equal partners.

Figure 12.16 This welcome sign appeared on a wall in Edmonton's first publicly funded Francophone school. In what ways can a Francophone school influence the identity of its Francophone students?

VOICES AND VISIONS

Think It Through

1. Make a cause-and-effect chart to show how Francophones became a minority in the West. Consider government policies, actions, and lack of action. (You may want to refer to Skill Check: Analyze Causes and Effects on page 76.)

2. In 1889, a group of Franco-Albertan citizens campaigned on behalf of a Catholic school district in Edmonton. You read about this action in Chapter 10 (page 234).

About a century later, another generation of Franco-Albertan citizens took action that involved the same school board. (You read about it in Franco-Albertan Citizens in Action on the previous page.) Research these two examples of active citizenship. Make up a chart on paper or on computer to compare the two efforts and find parallels. Did both groups have lasting positive impacts on the face of Alberta?

Building an Economy

B y the 1920s, Canadians had been living with the ideas of the National Policy for many years. The federal government and most people in Eastern Canada were happy with the way the economy was going— businesses were prospering, and trade with the other regions of Canada was good. The Canadian Pacific Railway was carrying goods, farm produce, and people from coast to coast. All across the prairies, small communities along the rail lines were growing into busy towns and cities.

Focus

How did government policy affect the growth of Western Canada?

This section begins with information on how Canada grew under the National Policy. You will see how the West was affected by other government policies, too.

Reading STRATEGY

To analyze information in charts, begin by reading the title and the caption. Next, note the column headings and any units of measurement used.

Year	Manitoba	Saskatchewan	Alberta	Total	Total as % of Canadian Population
1871	25 288	48 000		73 288	2%
1881	62 260	56 446		118 260	3%
1891	152 506	98 967		250 500	5%
1901	255 211	91 279	73 022	419 000	8%
1911	461 394	492 432	374 295	1 327 000	18%
1921	610 118	757 510	588 454	1 956 000	22%

Source: Statistics Canada, Censuses of Population, 1871–1921.

Figure 12.18 Population of the Prairie West, 1871–1921. The population of the Prairie provinces doubled almost five times within five decades. Make a bar graph to show how the *percentage* of Canadians living in the Prairie West changed from 1871 to 1921. Then, in point-form, explain how government policies worked to cause this change.

CASE STUDY

Ranching in Alberta

It was the North-West Mounted Police working in southern Alberta who first pointed out that cattle did well on the grasslands of this area. There was plenty for the cattle to eat, streams for water, and low hills to provide shelter.

The federal government wanted to stop American cattle companies from buying up all the land in the Canadian West. It wanted to give a boost to the Canadian cattle industry. It said that Canadian ranchers could lease 100 000 acres (about 40 000 hectares) for up to 21 years. It would cost only one cent an acre per year. The federal government also made sure there was a railway to transport the cattle to markets.

As ranches developed, they contributed to the Alberta economy in many ways. Ranching led to businesses that processed the cattle. It led to transportation businesses that moved cattle and meat products to larger communities to be sold. Cities such as Calgary grew up as centres of meat packing and cattle shipping.

The profits were good in the cattle industry. Ranchers could afford to pay shipping costs and buy any equipment they needed. Grain farming and the oil industry developed in the twentieth century. Nonetheless, cattle ranching remained an important part of the economy of the West. Today, southern Alberta is home to many large and thriving cattle ranches.

Respond

How did government policy help ranching develop in the West? How did ranching help the economy in the West?

Tech Link

To see a photograph of early mechanization on a turn-of-the-century Alberta farm, open Chapter 12 on your *Voices and Visions* CD-ROM.

Figure 12.19 *A Ranch in the Rockies*, painted by Edward Roper about 1887–1909. What view of ranch life does this painting give? What different kinds of information do you think you would get from a photograph of the same place? (For guidance, you may want to refer to the Skill Check on page 6.)

Figure 12.20 A view of 8th Avenue SE, Calgary, 1905. Speculate on how ranching contributed to the growth of Calgary.

An Unfair Policy?

As you read in Chapter 9, many Western wheat farmers believed that the federal government's economic policies benefited Eastern Canada more than the West. The tariffs the Canadian government had put on foreign goods meant that farmers had to pay high prices for farm equipment. Some felt that shipping their grain could end up costing more than they were getting paid for it.

In response to this situation, Western farmers took several actions. In 1901, they formed the Territorial Grain Growers Association, at Indian Head, Saskatchewan. This led to other associations, including the United Farmers of Alberta, formed in 1909. Western farmers also formed their own marketing outfit, and began publishing their own newspaper, the *Grain Growers' Guide*, in 1908.

Canada's Prosperity—and Its Foundation

Figure 12.21 Editorial cartoon, *Grain Growers' Guide*, 1910. The United Farmers of Alberta published this cartoon in their association newsletter. How is it useful historical evidence for the way wheat farmers felt about the National Policy?

> ## Tech Link
>
> Watch the "Schools of Agriculture" video on the *Voices and Visions* CD-ROM. It will show you how the government of Alberta promoted "new" farming technology in the West.

Think It Through ▶ Form an opinion about whether or not the West benefited from government policies in the late nineteenth and early twentieth centuries. Think about the perspectives of the various people you met in the opening of this chapter. Refer to other chapters to help inform your opinion. Use facts to back up your opinion. Express your opinion in a format of your choice.

Translations of Comments from Page 267

Francophone Doctor (in French):	I worry about losing our language and culture. There are so many newcomers, and not many speak French.
Métis Grandmother (in Michif):	We keep moving west to find land, but there is no place left to go now.
Ukrainian Girl (in Ukrainian):	I'm excited to be in this new country because Father says we'll soon have a farm of our own. I wonder, what will that be like?
Chinese Store Owner (in Mandarin):	Working on the railway was hard. Now I hope I can bring the rest of my family from China and start a small business.
Nehiyaw Elder (in Woodlands Cree):	It is being told that there are many different peoples coming to move into our land. I wonder what will happen now?

Chapter 12 PROJECT Television Talk Show

Imagine that a Doukhobor farmer, a Chinese restaurant owner, a Siksika hunter, a Franco-Albertan shop owner, a federal government official, and a rancher who immigrated from the United States all got together in 1900. What kind of conversation would they have about how government policies were affecting their lives? In this chapter project you can work as a group to role-play a television talk-show discussion among characters such as these.

Focus

1. As a class, decide which specific policy your panel will discuss. For example, it could be an immigration policy such as the head tax.
2. As a class, decide on the different characters you might invite as guests to your talk show. Think of six or seven guests who could have a lively discussion showing different points of view on federal government policies of the time. Give each character a name. Remember that not all people from one group will have exactly the same opinion—you might choose to have two different Francophone participants with two different views, for example.
3. Form one group for each character, including the talk-show host. Group members can work to locate information to help their character come alive. One person from each group will represent the character on the panel.

Groundwork for Various Characters

4. Research the specific policy that will be the topic of the talk show. Try to find out as many facts about the policy as you can: When was it announced and by whom? What was its aim? Who opposed it, who supported it, and why?

5. Decide what you need to know about your group's character. Divide the research work among group members.
6. After you have gathered information, work together to decide what information is most important to present during the discussion.
7. As a group, help the person who will be role-playing your character. Make notes on the facts of the situation, the character's perspective, and how the character feels and acts.

Groundwork for the Talk-Show Host

In your group, you will assist one person to serve as the talk-show host. This person will open the talk show by introducing the guests, describing the policy that will be discussed, and asking questions of the panel. Complete step 4, above. Then write an introduction and prepare questions.

Prepare to Present

Help the presenter from your group practise by giving feedback.

Present and Reflect

Stage the talk show. Afterward, meet with your group to ask how you might have changed things to present your character's point of view better.

Research Tip

Use a word processor to make a file on your character. Copy and paste information you find on the Internet. Then add your own comments and ideas. Don't forget to credit all your sources of information.

Chapter 13 A New Canada

Key CONCEPT

Society and Technology

Take a moment to think about some of the things you've done today. Did you begin by brushing your teeth and combing your hair? Perhaps you made toast for breakfast, or cut some fruit while you listened to the radio. Maybe you checked your email. How did you get to school? By bicycle? By bus? Think about all the tools, machines, and appliances you used. All of them—the toothbrush, comb, toaster, knife, radio, bicycle, bus, and computer—are examples of technology.

Technology is everything that we use to carry out tasks. It can be as big as a spaceship, or as small as a watch. It can be as complicated as a television, or as simple as a pencil. Some of the best technology is the simplest, like the wheel. But technology is more than the tools we use. It is also the way that we use tools.

Technology has a huge impact on society. Take the automobile. The invention of this machine let Canadians travel farther and faster than ever before. It also changed us. We now organize our cities and neighbourhoods around the car. Many of us work in the automotive industry. We use gasoline more than any other fuel, so we create a lot of air pollution by driving cars. Every technology affects society in both good ways and bad ways.

Honing Your Skills

Would you like to master effective Internet searching? The Skill Check feature in this chapter shows you how to **Do a Keyword Search.** This skill is important to your studies because it will enable you to find good information fast. The project at the end of the chapter will ask you to research a great Canadian of your choosing.

Technology and Canadians

In this chapter, you will learn about technologies that we started using about a century ago. These include the light bulb, the telephone, the automobile, the airplane, new farm equipment, radios, and machine guns. Together, they turned our world upside down. You will see how these inventions created a new Canada.

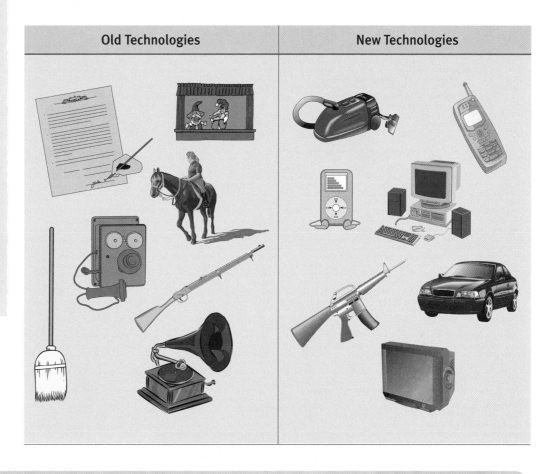

Old Technologies	New Technologies

Think ► AHEAD

1. a) For every old technology shown above left, identify the new technology shown above right that replaced it.
   b) Discuss the positive and negative effects of each one.

2. Sometimes graphics can help us think of more ideas.
   a) As a class, choose one of the examples of new technology shown above.
   b) Think about its positive and negative effects. Organize your ideas in a doughnut chart like this.
   c) Did the new technology benefit Canadians? Did it benefit you? Explain.

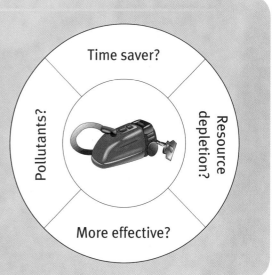

SKILL CHECK:
Do a Keyword Search

The library has a wealth of information about the many changes that took place in the twentieth century. So does the Internet. How do you sift through all the masses of material to find a few useful sites? A good keyword search on an effective search engine can do the trick. Choose your keywords carefully. That way, you'll have several useful sites to look through instead of thousands of useless ones.

Generating Your Keywords

1. Decide what subject or topic you are researching (for example, *Canadian inventions*).
2. Brainstorm keywords. These can be single words or phrases (for example, *technology, Canadian inventors, industry, inventions, famous, discoveries*).
3. Weed out unimportant, general, or very similar words (such as *inventions* and *famous*).
4. Put your words in order of importance (for example, *Canadian inventors, technology, discoveries, industry*).
5. Check your spellings.

Do Your Keyword Search

Do your search. Just list the words with no commas. Put phrases within quotation marks (for example, *"Canadian inventors" technology discoveries industry*).

1. If the number of hits you get is large, be more specific or reduce the number of keywords.
2. If you don't get any hits, change or add keywords.
   - A thesaurus can help you find synonyms for your keywords. Synonyms are words that mean the same thing. Synonyms for *invention* include *creation* and *discovery*.
   - Think of words related to the subject that are not synonyms, such as *tool, mechanical, medicine*, and *weapon*.

   Keyword searches get better results when you use multiple words or phrases related to the subject. First you'll see hits with all the keywords in order. Then you'll see hits with all the keywords but not in order. Finally, you'll see hits with some of the keywords.

Figure 13.1 Why waste your time with worthless searches? Perfect your keyword searches, and you'll become a pro surfer.

Try It!

Generate some keywords you could use to research these topics: industrialization, urbanization, and technological change.

The Rise of Industry

Before the twentieth century, most Canadians had jobs related to fishing, logging, or farming. We harvested the natural resources and sold them around the world. Then a great change took place after Confederation. It was the start of **industrialization**. This is an economic system based on large industries. It was a big change—so big that we called it a revolution. This section tells how the **Industrial Revolution** changed the Canadian identity.

Focus

How did the rise of industrialization help develop Canada's economy?

A Global Revolution

When you hear the word *revolution*, you probably think of politics. When a government is overthrown and replaced with another, we call it a **revolution**. But the word *revolution* can describe any major change in the world. For example, when people started using computers instead of typewriters, we called it a **computer revolution**.

Tech Link

Look on the *Voices and Visions* CD-ROM to see how "modern" manufacturing techniques were applied to the dairy industry in Alberta.

The Industrial Revolution began when people started using **mechanical power**. The steam engine gave people a way to harness energy. It burned coal. This heated water and turned it to steam. The energy in pressurized steam could pull a train, twirl a merry-go-round, or run a power loom.

The Industrial Revolution did not begin in Canada. It began in Great Britain in the mid-1700s. From there it spread to other countries. Three factors made the revolution possible in Canada: new technologies, business investors, and a large workforce.

The Rise of the Factory

Before industrialization, most goods were made by hand. A dressmaker sewed a dress by hand. A logger laboured with saw and axe. Most goods were made by skilled craftspeople using hand tools. These were called **cottage industries** because the workplace was a home or small shop.

The introduction of machines changed where people worked. Steam engines, water power, and electric motors could power big, new machines. But a single worker could

Figure 13.2 Two photos showing the changes brought by industrialization. On the left, a shoemaker works in his Ontario workshop. On the right, workers make shoes in an Alberta factory. Make two lists of words and phrases to compare the workdays of the shoemaker and the factory workers.

not afford one. Machines were expensive. Instead, business investors bought the machinery and hired people to run it. A new type of workplace emerged: the **factory**. Here, many workers worked together to run the new machines. They could produce many more goods than they could have produced on their own.

Working in the Factory

Factories changed the *way* people worked, too. In a cottage industry, a shoemaker might make three pairs of shoes in a day. In a shoe factory, a worker did just one step. For example, he or she might cut out shoe

soles for 200 shoes. Other workers would do the other steps. This was called the **division of labour**. Work became repetitious. As a result, workers lost many of their skills.

To become even more efficient, factories introduced the **assembly line**. An incomplete product was placed on a conveyor belt. As the product moved down the line, each worker did one task on it. By the end of the line, the product was complete.

Early factories were organized with machines in mind, not people. They were hot, airless, dusty, and dangerous. The managers who ran the factories were very strict. Workers—some of whom were children—spent ten to twelve hours a day on the job, six days a week. No wonder factories were compared to jails. Workers who got sick or injured lost their pay or their jobs. There was no employment or health insurance.

Figure 13.3 Young girls collecting waste coal beside the train tracks in Toronto in 1900. Some children took the coal to heat their homes. Others sold it to earn money. What would be the pros and cons of children collecting coal on train tracks? Think about health and safety concerns as well as earning potential.

Canada Today

What jobs are Canadian 14-year-olds allowed to do today? Make a list, and then discuss why young people are allowed to work at some jobs but not others.

Several laws protect children today. For example, Alberta teenagers must go to school full-time until they are 16 years of age. Also, a provincial **minimum wage** law states the lowest hourly rate an employer can pay you. **WEB LINK**

CASE STUDY

Child Labour in Canada

Is it acceptable for children to work? Children in Canada's new industrial society were expected to work. They helped buy food and pay bills because their parents' wages were so low. Many children worked on farms.

In the 1880s, Théophile Charron worked in a cigar factory. He was 14 years old. In 1888, he answered questions about his job.

Q. *When you call yourself a cigar-maker, you mean that you have served your apprenticeship, do you not?*

A. *Yes, sir.*

Q. *How long?*

A. *Three years.*

Q. *You began working at 11 years?*

A. *Yes, sir.*

Q. *What wages did you get during your apprenticeship?*

A. *One dollar a week for the first year, $1.50 for the second year, and $2 for the third year. When I worked extra, I got more.*

Q. *Did you have any fines to pay during your apprenticeship?*

A. *Yes, sir.*

Q. *Many?*

A. *A good number.*

Q. *How many hours did you work a day?*

A. *Sometimes 10 hours, other times eight hours. It was just as they wanted it.*

Q. *Do you remember why you paid these fines?*

A. *Sometimes for talking too much; mostly for that.*

Q. *You were never licked* [struck; hit]?

A. *Yes; not licked so as any harm was done me, but sometimes they would come along, and if we happened to be cutting tobacco wrong, they would give us a crack across the head with a fist.*

Q. *Was it usual to beat children like that?*

A. *Often.*

Source: *Royal Commission on the Relations of Capital and Labor in Canada*
(Ottawa: Queen's Printer and Controller of Stationery, 1889).

As the years passed, the government made laws to ban child labour. In 1891, one in four Canadian boys between the ages of 10 and 14 worked full-time. By 1911, that number had dropped to one in twenty. In the same year, two out of every hundred Canadian girls had a job.

Reading STRATEGY

When you read and view primary sources like this interview, remember that they show the perspectives and values of society at the time.

Respond

Many children around the world live in very poor families. Should they be allowed to leave school to put food on the table? What are the short-term and long-term results of such a decision?

Global Connections ■

At the age of 12, Canadian Craig Kielburger learned about a Pakistani boy who was murdered for speaking out about child labour. In response, he started Free the Children. Find out more about this organization of young people by doing a keyword search. How does it help children? As an active citizen, what could you do to help this organization? SKILLS WEB LINK

An Expanding Economy

The growth of industry made the Canadian economy grow by leaps and bounds. Three new railways sped up the transport of goods. In turn, the building of railways created a need for steel and iron. New factories made many types of products. Alberta, for example, began to see meatpacking plants, dairies, lumber mills, grain mills, wool factories, glass factories, sugar factories, cigar factories, and brick factories, among others.

Preventing Aboriginal Participation

Many First Nations and Métis people were prevented from taking part in the economy. Often the government was involved in limiting their activities. For example, the West Coast First Nations had fished for salmon on the coast and rivers for as long as they could remember. During the 1870s, newcomers began fishing, too. They built industrial canneries to process the fish. Competition for fish grew, so the government said that First Nations could only catch fish to eat. For many years, they could not sell their catch.

	1867	1900	1910
Number of people in the workforce	170 000	443 000	500 000
Dollar value of manufactured goods*	$170 000 000	$556 000 000	$1 152 000 000
Dollar value of goods exported*	$34 000 000	$100 000 000	$136 000 000

* In dollars of the day

Figure 13.4 Data for measuring the Canadian economy. An efficient economy gets the most out of the resources it has. By how much did the workforce grow from 1900 to 1910? What happened to the value of goods produced during that time? Would you say the economy became more efficient, less efficient, or stayed about the same? Explain.

Think It ▶ Through

1. Railways were crucial in Canada's early industrial society. Building and running railways created a lot of economic activity. Draw a tree diagram with a railway engine as the trunk. On the branches, show how the railway encouraged spinoff businesses. Alternatively, write about the spinoff businesses.

2. Create a similar tree diagram or paragraph showing the impact of the computer.

Technology and Identity

The new technologies of the early twentieth century changed people's lives. The 1910s and 1920s brought new ways to travel and communicate. In this section you will learn about a few key technologies.

Focus

In what ways did new technology contribute to the development of Canada?

The Horseless Carriage

Canadians began driving cars in the years before the First World War.

Electricity or steam powered the earliest cars. Within a few years, gasoline engines became the norm. They were more reliable and easier to use.

Not everyone was happy about the new technology. Farmers didn't like cars because they frightened the horses. So the government made a law. When a car met up with a horse and carriage on the road, the car had to stop while the horse passed by.

The assembly line made the price of cars low. In 1924, a Model T Ford cost only $395. (At that time, the minimum weekly wage was about $14.) By 1929, 1.2 million motor vehicles were on Canadian roads.

More automobiles created the need for better roads. Before the First World War, most roads were dirt tracks. In 1912, a journalist named Thomas Wilby set out to drive across the country from Halifax to Vancouver. At times he had to hitch a ride on a ferry or the railway. He made it, but it took him 48 days and many flat tires. It was 1942 before it was possible to drive on a continuous road all across the country.

Figure 13.5 A Canadian car factory, about 1930. Other factories made car parts and tires. What other businesses spin off from the auto industry?

VOICES

The *Telescope* newspaper voiced people's fear of the car in this editorial. What is the writer worried about? Compare this to modern Canadians' gripes about traffic.

> **Gradually the nuisance is becoming more general. Every town in Ontario has its automobile and some have more than one. It will not be long before the automobiles will drive the farmers off the roads altogether, unless something is done to restrain them. The farmers built these highways in the first place and are straining themselves to keep them in repair.**
>
> **What they ought to do is pledge every candidate for Parliament to vote in favour of a law banning automobiles from using the public high-ways altogether, or at least under conditions that will not interfere with traffic.**

Source: Editorial, *Telescope* newspaper, Walkerton, Ont., 1908.

Up, Up, and Away

A second revolution in transportation arrived with the airplane. The first aircraft flew in Kittyhawk, North Carolina, in 1903. Canada wasn't far behind. J.A.D. McCurdy designed the *Silver Dart* in Baddeck, Nova Scotia. He flew it for almost a kilometre on its first flight, in 1909.

During the First World War, airplanes were used as weapons of war. Afterward, hundreds of Canadian pilots returned home. They were eager to fly for a living, but there were no passenger aircraft. The technology wasn't reliable yet. Former war pilots such as Wop May got jobs flying bush planes to remote locations to transport people, spot forest fires, haul the mail, take photographs from the air, do rescue work, and conduct surveys for new mineral resources. The first passenger planes began flying in the 1920s.

Tech Link

Open Chapter 13 on your *Voices and Visions* CD-ROM to see a few of the airplanes produced in Canada.

The Age of Radio

Canadians want to keep in touch with each other. It helps us know what is going on in our communities. We like to hear about other parts of the country. It strengthens our feeling of being Canadian.

We use the **mass media** to find out about each other. Newspapers have been around for a long time. The first issue of the *Edmonton Bulletin*, for example, came out in 1880. Radio came later. In 1920, a station in Montréal aired the first radio broadcast in Canada. By 1930, there were 60 stations across the country. Virtually every household had a radio. Even later came televisions and television stations. Global TV, for example, began in Calgary as CHCT-TV in 1954.

Figure 13.6 Fred McCall, one of the pilots who put on flying exhibitions after the First World War. He is shown here at the Calgary Exhibition in 1919, standing in front of his Curtiss Jenny aircraft wearing a scarf and goggles. Once, McCall crashed onto a merry-go-round! Why do you suppose the public considered pilots to be dashing heroes in the 1920s?

Figure 13.7 A boy tuning in to his favourite program in 1935. Before television, radio was the most important form of mass media. It was the way most people stayed in touch with the world. How do you get information about your community? about the world?

VOICES ■

Max Ward, bush pilot and founder of Wardair (Canada's largest charter airline, operating from 1953 to 1989), comments about the legendary bush pilots:

66 If you were born and brought up in Edmonton during the 1920s and 1930s, the most exciting people around were the bush pilots, who were always in the news with stories of their exploits. My whole idea of adventure, of living, was tied up in the notion of joining their ranks some day in a magnificent flying machine. 99

Source: Max Ward, *The Max Ward Story: A Bush Pilot in the Bureaucratic Jungle* (Toronto: McClelland & Stewart, 1991). Found on http://www.exn.ca/FlightDeck/Aviators/ward.cfm.

Identity

Media and Identity

Why are the mass media so important to identity? Let's think about some examples.

Radio signals cross borders. The early programs that Canadians listened to came from the United States. Canadians worried. Would there be room for Canadian ideas and stories? In 1936, the government founded the Canadian Broadcasting Corporation and its French-language counterpart, together known as CBC/Radio-Canada. The goal was to bring a Canadian voice all across the nation. By the next year, new transmitters allowed English radio to reach 76 per cent of listeners.

This was not the case for Francophone radio. Canada's first publicly funded French radio station, Canada Broadcasting French (CBF), went on the air in Montréal in 1936. But it was not broadcast all across the nation. Francophones in Alberta were not permitted to have a French radio station, even if they funded it themselves. The Association canadienne-française de l'Alberta (ACFA) kept trying, though. Volunteers raised $140 000. Finally, they got a permit to start the privately owned CHFA in 1949. What do you think the Francophone community missed during those early radio-free years?

Currently, CBC/Radio-Canada has stations all across the nation broadcasting in both French and English.

Respond

In a small group, debate this statement: "Radio and television are good for Canada."

Figure 13.8 A camera operator at work at the Inuit Broadcasting Corporation. The IBC is publicly funded. How does it benefit the Inuit community and Canada as a whole?

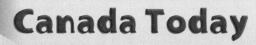

Canada Today

How do you keep your cultural identity in a multimedia age? Embrace it, says Buffy Sainte-Marie. "The reality of the situation is that we [the First Nations] are not all dead and stuffed in some museum with the dinosaurs: we are Here in this digital age." A Cree, Sainte-Marie was born on the Piapot Reserve in Saskatchewan. She has had a long and successful career as a musician. Now she is an educator and multimedia artist. She uses new technology to link communities. Check out her online presence by developing a keyword search. **SKILLS**

Think It ▶ Through

1. Research one of the following Alberta inventions: the hay bale booster, fairy phonograph, rubber curling hack, Jaycopter, and bear-proof bin. How did the new technology affect people's lives? **SKILLS**

2. a) Draw up a list of your own mass media habits. How much Canadian content do you absorb in a day?
   b) Should mass media in Canada have Canadian content? Write a letter to the editor or a poem in which you communicate your opinion.

3. Identify the dates of important technological advances in Canada, such as the first airplane flight or the introduction of the motorized tractor. Build on what you find in this section by searching the Internet. Then make a timeline of your findings. **SKILLS**

An Industrial Society

Focus

What strains did industrialization place on Canadian society?

Rapid growth seldom occurs without growing pains. The expanding economy brought prosperity. It also brought social problems. As cities grew, parts of them became overcrowded, dirty, and unhealthy. Some people grew wealthier. Others were trapped in low-paying jobs. Competition for wealth led to the most destructive wars the world had ever seen. This section looks at Canada's growing pains.

The First World War (1914-1918)

At the end of the century, the winds of war were blowing. Germany had built up the biggest army in the world. In response, Great Britain, France, and Russia had built up big armies, too. National pride spurred on nations to use their arms.

In June 1914, an assassination was used as an excuse to set in motion a train of events that led to the First World War. The war was fought mainly in Europe but had an impact all over the world. Canada went to war as part of the British Empire.

Factories can make inexpensive clothes, but they can also make guns. All through the war, Canada's factories made deadly technology. They made guns, tanks, aircraft, battleships, submarines, and poisonous gases. Technology gave armies the ability to kill many people quickly. Technology did not cause the war, but it made the fighting far more deadly.

The war finally ended in 1918, when Germany surrendered. It didn't feel like a victory. Nine million soldiers had been killed. Canada had 60 661 dead. Many thousands more were injured and maimed.

More than 4000 of Canada's volunteer soldiers in the First World War were Aboriginal. Many were heroes, such as Private David Kisek, a soldier from the Shoal Lake Band in Ontario. Private Kisek leaped into the open to take on four enemy machine guns. Why do we honour this act of bravery?

Figure 13.9 A recruitment poster for the Canadian Armed Forces. The war began in a spirit of adventure. Farmhands wanted to see the world. Young men wanted excitement. How does this poster try to interest young men?

Identity

Vimy Ridge and the Canadian Identity

Is fighting for one's country the supreme act of citizenship?

For Canadians, the most important battle of the war took place at Vimy Ridge in France. Both French and British soldiers had failed to capture this height of land from the enemy. Capturing it, however, was crucial. So in April 1917, the Canadians stepped up to the plate.

Canadian soldiers fought and died on the ridge over five long days. They finally drove the Germans back. The cost was heavy: 3598 Canadians were killed and another 7000 were wounded. The whole world saw the remarkable accomplishment. This was not the feat of a mere colony.

Canada's efforts during the war helped Canadians feel proud. They also won us the respect of nations around the world.

Remembering

Every November 11, Canadians mark Remembrance Day. We honour those who have died defending our country, including the heroes at Vimy Ridge.

There are many ways of remembering. Some people visit the Canadian Battlefields Memorial in Vimy, France. Other Canadians visit Ottawa for the National Remembrance Day Ceremony. Some communities create their own way of remembering. For example, in Edmonton in 2004, the community honoured Aboriginal veterans with a Tribute Jamboree. The White Buffalo Dance Society drummed, danced, and sang a traditional honour song for the veterans.

Respond

How can an event such as a battle affect a nation's identity? Does remembering the past help you feel more Canadian?

Life in the Industrial City

The end of the war in 1918 brought more change to Canadian society. The factories no longer needed to produce war goods, so they began to make consumer goods again. More factories were built in urban areas. Returning soldiers came to live in cities. So did farm workers, who were being replaced with farm machinery. Mohawk ironworkers came to build the new office buildings.

The cities got bigger and bigger. During the 1920s, more Canadians began to live in cities than in the country. The complex Canadian identity slowly changed.

Growth of the Suburbs

Originally, cities were a jumble of shops, factories, and houses for rich and poor alike. People lived close to where they worked and where they shopped. For the most part, they walked everywhere.

During the Industrial Revolution, the city changed. It reorganized itself into neighbourhoods. The key to this change was the street railway. Streetcars ran on tracks down the middle of the street. They were powered by electricity. They were the first technology for moving large numbers of people quickly through a city at low cost.

The street railway allowed people to live far from where they worked. People moved to the **suburbs**, residential neighbourhoods at the city's edge.

Workers Organize

Early factories were not nice places to work. There were few rules to protect workers from management. Employers could hire or fire them whenever they wanted. Wages could be reduced. The workers had no say.

Workers began to form **unions**. Unions speak for the workers who belong to them. They tried to improve the conditions under which people worked. They argued for fair wages, shorter workdays, and safe working conditions.

Figure 13.11 Stephen Avenue in downtown Calgary in 1892 (top) and Eighth Avenue looking East from First Street in 1930 (bottom). What technological changes can you spot? Speculate on how these changed life. Do a keyword search for images to see other historical photographs of Canadian cities. [SKILLS]

City	1891	1911	1921	2004
Montréal	219 616	490 000	618 506	3 606 700
Toronto	181 215	380 000	521 000	5 203 600
Vancouver	13 700	120 000	163 220	2 160 000
Winnipeg	25 639	136 000	179 087	702 400

Figure 13.10 Population of four Canadian cities, 1891–2004. Which city grew the most during each period? Make a graph showing how much each city grew in each period. Why would this help you "see" it better?

Strike in Winnipeg

In a **strike**, unionized workers refuse to work until their employer agrees to give them what they want. It is an active citizen's way to fight for workers' rights.

After the First World War, Canada saw many strikes. The biggest strike of all took place in Winnipeg in 1919. Workers from many unions all went on strike at the same time to support one another. This was a **general strike**. There was no telephone; the mail stopped coming; streetcars stopped running. Even the police voted to support the strikers. The city was paralyzed.

The workers went on strike for higher wages and union recognition. Employers refused to negotiate. They wanted the government to force everyone back to work. They argued that the strikers were troublemakers. The mayor called in the Royal North West Mounted Police (RNWMP). Before long, two strikers were dead and thirty were injured.

After the strike failed, people elected politicians to speak for them. Farmers helped form the National Progressive Party in 1921. The Progressives opposed tariffs. They opposed the influence of business people on government. In 1921, the Progressives became the official opposition in Ottawa. Other farmers' parties won victories in Alberta, Ontario, and Manitoba.

People empowered themselves in other ways. For example, farmers formed wheat pools in the 1920s. They used these to buy and sell wheat on world markets.

Sharing the Wealth

Not everyone benefited from industrialization. First Nations peoples still suffer from problems that started in these times. For example, miners did not realize that chemical waste damages the land for generations, including First Nations lands. Gradually, though, the lives of most working people did improve. Working conditions became safer and healthier. People got help when they were sick or lost their jobs. Farmers gained some control over their livelihoods. Ordinary people began to share in the benefits of change.

Figure 13.12 Chaos in the streets of Winnipeg in June 1919. The RNWMP are on horseback. Government officials met with Winnipeg business leaders but not with strike leaders. Was this fair?

Think It Through

1. Scan the section.
   a) Identify problems that Canadians faced because of industrialization.
   b) Which was the worst? Why?
   c) Did some groups of people suffer from these problems more than others? Explain your thoughts.

2. Here are some words that describe a liveable city: *safe*, *clean*, *healthy*, and *beautiful*. Think of other words to add to the list. Next to each word, describe or draw one or more things your class could do to help your community fit the description.

Canadian Women Step Up

The industrial era saw many women entering the workforce. As they took on a wider role outside the home, women began to demand the same rights as men. This section looks at the changing role of women in industrial society.

Focus

What were the social and economic effects of the changing role of women in Canadian society?

Women and the Workplace

New labour-saving technologies gave women more free time. Many wanted to work. Some worked as maids or nannies. Others found work in the new factories. New inventions such as the telephone and typewriter created other jobs for women. Offices, department stores, banks, laundries, and restaurants employed thousands of women. Even so, few of these jobs paid well.

During the First World War, many men left their jobs to fight overseas. This gave women a chance to show that they could do these jobs, too. After the war, though, women had to go back to domestic life.

Women Speaking Out

Women started to speak up more about the issues of the day. Some of them wrote articles, published books, or spoke at gatherings. Canada has benefited by the added voice of women on all issues.

Tekahionwake (Pauline Johnson) was one of the most popular speakers in Canada in the years leading to the First World War. She was a Haudenosaunee [hah-duh-nuh-SAH-nee] woman from the Six Nations Reserve in Ontario. Because of her charisma, Tekahionwake got people's attention.

Women Get the Vote

As women moved into the workplace, more and more of them wanted to have all the rights of citizenship. Before the First World War, women in Canada could not vote in elections. They could not run for election, either. Politics was considered "man's work."

Women began to organize. They wanted **suffrage**—the right to vote. They put pressure on the government. They collected

VOICES ■

Tekahionwake (Pauline Johnson) wrote poems, stories, and articles. Here she criticizes novel writers for using stereotypes of First Nations women. A **stereotype** is an overgeneralized portrayal of people from one group. Stereotypes can reflect people's prejudices.

66 [The First Nations heroine] is always desperately in love with the young white hero .... She is so much wrapped up in him that she is treacherous to her own people, tells falsehoods to her father and the other chiefs of her tribe, and otherwise makes herself detestable and dishonourable. Of course, this white hero never marries her! 99

Respond

Why is the use of stereotypes in fiction harmful?

Source: Pauline Johnson, "A Strong Race Opinion: On the Indian Girl in Modern Fiction," Toronto, 22 May 1892. Available online at http://www.humanities.mcmaster.ca/~pjohnson/writings.html.

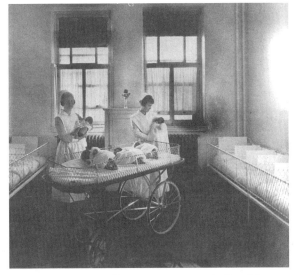

WEB LINK

Figure 13.13 Canadian nurses at work. Teaching and nursing careers had long been open to women. Why do you think these professions welcomed women, while others did not?

petitions, held rallies, and lobbied the government. But the elected politicians were all men, and they would not budge.

Finally, during the First World War, Canadian women won the vote at two levels of government. Provincially, the three Prairie provinces were first. Here, women won the right to take part in provincial elections in 1916. In 1918, women across Canada won the right to vote in federal elections.

One battle was won. Women could now vote for a person to represent them in government. Did women automatically get the right to run for Parliament? No, that was another battle. In July 1920, the Dominion Elections Act was changed to allow women

VOICES ■

Perspectives on Women and the Vote

❝ Women who believe in woman suffrage seem to think that we men want to deprive them of their liberties; but we wish to do no such thing. All men ... place women on a very high pedestal ... and we want her to remain there, where she can command our respect and esteem .... Why should she besmear herself with the rottenness of politics? ❞

—A letter to the editor
Source: Toronto *Globe*, 1912.

❝ Let it be known that it is the opinion of the Roblin government that woman suffrage is illogical and absurd as far as Manitoba is concerned. Placing women on a political equality with men would ... break up the home; ... it will throw the children into the arms of servant girls .... The majority of women are emotional and very often guided by misdirected enthusiasms, and if they had the franchise they would be a menace rather than an aid. ❞

—Manitoba premier Rodmond Roblin
Source: *The Grain Growers' Guide*, 4 February 1914.

❝ We are not here to ask for a reform, or a gift, or a favour, but for a right—not for mercy, but for justice. ❞

—Nellie McClung, activist for women's suffrage
Source: *The Grain Growers' Guide*, 4 February 1914.

❝ Women's place is in the home, I hear, but do you think it is part of a mother's mission to sit quietly by and see her sons and daughters growing up under conditions which she knows are bad but, through lack of power, is unable to remedy? ❞

—A.V. Thomas, suffrage activist
Source: Cited in R. Craig Brown and Ramsay Cook, *Canada 1896–1921: A Nation Transformed* (Toronto: McClelland & Stewart, 1974), p. 299.

 **Respond**

Create a point-of-view organizer. In the first column, summarize the arguments expressed in this feature. In the second column, explain why you agree or disagree with each argument.

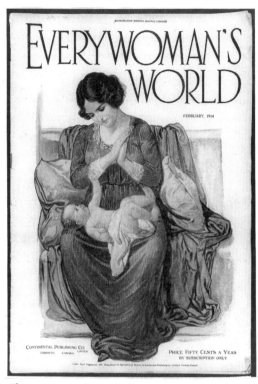

Figure 13.14 A magazine cover from 1914. How does it present the role of women in society? Is this "every woman's" world today? How does it compare with magazine covers today? [SKILLS]

Nellie McClung once said, "Never retreat, never explain, never apologize. Get the thing done and let them howl." What do you think she meant? Think of a situation where a strategy like this is justified.

Figure 13.15 Statue of the Famous Five, 1999, in Calgary. The artist is Barbara Paterson of Edmonton. Think of a possible reason why the federal government built a replica in 2000 to stand on Parliament Hill.

to sit in the House of Commons. Even so, many people still believed that government was a man's job, so they wouldn't vote for women. Beliefs are much harder to change than laws. However, one by one, women began to be elected. The first female member of Parliament, Agnes Macphail of Ontario, was elected in 1921.

Alberta women formed organizations such as the United Farmers Women of Alberta (UFWA) to fight for women's property rights as well as voting rights.

The "Persons" Case

Are you a person? Is the girl sitting next to you a person? Believe it or not, the government of Canada did not always regard women and girls as persons.

Emily Murphy was the magistrate of a newly created Women's Court in Edmonton. In 1919, she thought it was time that a woman was named to the Canadian Senate. When she asked the prime minister, however, she was told that it was impossible. Under the law, only "qualified persons" could be senators, and women were not "persons."

Murphy would not accept this answer. She and four other Alberta women brought the question to the Supreme Court of Canada. The other women were Nellie McClung, Louise McKinney, Irene Parlby, and Henrietta Muir Edwards. They became known as the "Famous Five."

The court ruled against the women. Then they took the case to the highest court, in England. In 1929, this court ruled that Canadian women were indeed persons. Four months later, Prime Minister Mackenzie King made Cairine Wilson the first female senator.

In 2005, 33 women were serving in the 105-member Canadian Senate.

CASE STUDY

Other Groups Gaining a Voice

Did all citizens now have equal democratic rights? No. Many Canadians still could not vote. Before the Second World War, no Chinese, South Asian, or Japanese Canadians could vote. After the war, attitudes changed. Here are the dates when various groups of Canadians won the right to vote.

- 1947: Canadians of Chinese and South Asian background
- 1948: Japanese Canadians
- 1950: The Inuit
- 1960: First Nations
- 1970: Citizens 18 to 20 years of age

Before 1960, the government did not let First Nations vote unless they gave up their treaty Indian status. That explains why most of them refused to vote until the policy was changed.

Respond

Comment on this statement: "Voting in a democracy is a responsibility as well as a right." Should the voting age be lowered again?

Figure 13.16 Won Alexander Cumyow, the first person of Chinese descent born in Canada. He was born in British Columbia in 1861. This Canadian citizen worked as an interpreter in the law courts. However, he was not eligible to vote until he was 86 years old, in 1947. In this photo, Won casts his first vote in a federal election. What would it have felt like to work for a government that wouldn't allow you to vote?

Think It Through

1. a) Today, what jobs are done largely by women? by men? by both? Brainstorm some ideas in order to come up with three lists. Sort your findings in a Venn diagram (see page 21).
   b) Discuss this situation in class. Ask these questions:
      - Why are certain jobs held mostly by one gender?
      - Is it possible for both men and women to do any of these jobs? If not, what prevents them?
      - Is there discrimination in the workplace today?
      - What is your bias on this topic?

2. All adult citizens in Canada now hold the vote, and all are considered persons. Are women and men therefore equal? Debate this question in a small group.

3. After reading this section, have your ideas about women's rights changed? If so, how have they changed? Write a journal entry or poem to answer this question.

Bad Times, Good Times

The 1920s had brought a decade of good times for many people. Then, in 1930, Canada, along with much of the rest of the world, plunged into the Great Depression. In this section, you will learn how the Depression and the world war that followed threw Canada into turmoil.

Focus

What were the impacts of the Great Depression and the Second World War on Canadian society?

The Depression

In the 1930s, the economy slowed almost to a halt. Factories closed. Wages fell. Workers lost their jobs. Others lost their life savings. The resulting financial crisis affected nearly the whole world. Nothing

Reading
STRATEGY

Scan the titles in this section. Think of one question you hope to have answered by the time you've finished learning about these topics.

like it had been seen before. Men, young and old, drifted to the cities looking for work. Many families were left with no income at all.

The Depression hit the West particularly hard because of a terrible drought. In the farm districts, incomes fell. Some people lost their farms. Others left their farms to search for work. During the 1930s, more people left the Prairie provinces than arrived.

Aboriginals Coping in Hard Times

First Nations people continued to make a living as they had in previous decades. Most were already poor. Many didn't have jobs to lose. The Depression made an already difficult situation worse, but they continued to cope. They kept on hunting, trapping, selling their handiwork to tourists, growing produce, and keeping livestock. Marlene Brant of Tyendinaga, Ontario, tells how her family coped.

The most influential person in my life, of course, was my mother, who was a real Mohawk Matriarch. A very strong and intelligent person who brought up ten children in the midst of the depression and was a real partner and co-worker with my father. She always had a little business going on, on the side. She believed really strongly in education …. My father was a quieter person …. He did farming for our own food supply, so we were never hungry.

Source: Quoted in Bernadette Wabie, "Aboriginal Women and Community Development: Consistency Across Time" (Master's Thesis, Trent University, 1999), p. 55.

Figure 13.17 A prairie-wide dust storm pictured at Fort Macleod, Alberta, in the 1930s. For years, little rain fell. Crops withered in the fields. The soil turned to a fine dust and blew in great clouds across the prairie. Did any of your relatives live through those years? Why are times of great trial sometimes very memorable?

VOICES ■

Voices of the Depression

"I am so worried on account of the children as we never have any vegetables except potatoes and almost no fruit and the baby hasn't any shoes."

—Letter to Prime Minister R.B. Bennett
from a farmer in Benton, Alberta, 1935

Source: From Michiel Horn, ed., *The Dirty Thirties: Canadians in the Great Depression* (Toronto: Copp, Clark Publishing, 1972), p. 236.

"We tried to sell our ranch, and it was a good one, but nobody would buy it. Who would in those days when cows were selling for about six dollars each?... So we just loaded up the wagon and drove away from it."

—Anonymous

Source: Barry Broadfoot, *Ten Lost Years: 1929-1939* (Toronto: Doubleday Canada Ltd., 1973), p. 51.

"If you could see what I saw. People hungry and dying down on the beach. Three stakes and a sack, that was home for them ....

And then the trouble in [Vancouver] started. People had iron bars, they broke windows at Woodward's and everyone went in and helped themselves. You see, they had no jobs and no food....

And the garbage cans: on Hastings Street, Granville Street, people ate from them. I saw a mother with a baby pull out some chicken bones, set them on the garbage lid and right away three, four kids were standing around eating chicken bones."

—Shinichi Hara

Source: Quoted in Daphne Marlatt and Carole Itter, eds., *Opening Doors: Vancouver's East End* (Victoria: Aural History Program, Province of British Columbia, 1979), p. 123.

Respond

Imagine you are a teenager living in the 1930s. Your family has left the farm in search of work. Be an active citizen: write a letter to the prime minister. What would you say?

Figure 13.18 Men at a Montréal soup kitchen in 1931. Unemployed men and women could find a free meal at a soup kitchen. These were run by churches and other charities. What similar acts of citizenship go on in your community?

Figure 13.19 Young Canadian, painted in 1932 by Charles Comfort. The artist lived in Winnipeg when he was young. What elements in the painting tell of the hard times of the 1930s?

Making Change

On to Ottawa!

By 1933, about one quarter of the workforce was jobless. The government created work camps for unmarried, unemployed men. Here the men did hard labour. They cleared roads and cut firewood for 20 cents a day.

The camps seemed like prisons to the men who lived in them. They wanted real work at a decent wage. In 1935, they went on strike in Vancouver. The men climbed on freight trains heading east. They were going "on to Ottawa" to meet the prime minister face to face.

Figure 13.20 "On to Ottawa" trekkers arrive in Regina, Saskatchewan, in June 1935. What modern protest treks do you know of?

As the trains crossed the country, more trekkers jumped on. When they reached Regina, police received orders to stop the men. Prime Minister Bennett refused their demands. In Regina, police and protestors clashed in a bloody riot. A police officer died, and many protestors were injured or arrested.

Politics during the Depression

The old political parties did not seem to be helping people, so several new parties appeared. In Alberta, "Bible Bill" Aberhart

captured the ears of the people. Every Sunday, he spoke to Canadians on his religious radio program. People liked his new ideas. He started a political party called Social Credit. Among other things, the party wanted to give $25 a month to every citizen. It would do this by printing its own "prosperity certificates." Aberhart believed this would get the economy moving again. Albertans elected the Social Credit Party in 1935. The federal government stopped the certificate program because provinces do not have the right to print money. Nonetheless, Social Credit stayed in power for more than 35 years.

Another new party was the Cooperative Commonwealth Federation (CCF). Its roots were grassroots prairie farmers' organizations. The CCF argued that the government should have programs such as employment insurance, workers' compensation, and public ownership of key industries. Then it could prevent downturns such as the Depression. The CCF eventually became the New Democratic Party.

Social Services in Canada

The poverty and suffering of the Depression made Canadians think. Couldn't government do more to protect citizens from hard times?

- The **old-age pension** began in 1927. It gave elderly people an income.
- **Employment insurance** came after the Depression. It was short-term financial help for people who lost their jobs.
- **Family allowance** came next. A small sum was paid monthly to every family with children.
- **Public health care** was the idea of Tommy Douglas, the CCF premier of Saskatchewan. His government started paying for hospital care in 1947. This led to a Canadian health care system.

Figure 13.21 A "prosperity certificate" printed by the Alberta Social Credit party in the 1930s. To maintain the value of this "money," people had to put a one-cent stamp on it every week. How might this make the certificates unpopular?

Canada Today

Today, private citizens, companies, and governments all pitch in when disaster strikes. Drought hit the prairies in 2001 and 2002. By the second year, Western farmers were desperate. They had no feed for their cattle and horses. So farmers in Ontario started the Hay West campaign. Individuals across Eastern Canada donated 30 000 tonnes of hay to 1000 Alberta farm families. What does this tell you about Canadian citizenship?

Figure 13.22 Workers at the VMD Shipyard in Victoria, BC. Women produced weapons and ammunition in war factories. They operated farms and ran businesses. Others served as nurses, radio operators, and ambulance drivers. By 1945, more than 43 000 women were in the armed forces (though not in armed combat roles). How can a time of war be both exciting and boring?

The Return of War

The Depression did not really end until 1939 when, once again, the world went to war. The army gave a job to anyone who wanted one. The sudden demand for arms and supplies got the wheels of Canadian industry turning again.

The war started when Nazi Germany invaded its neighbours. The Axis countries were Germany, Italy, and Japan. The Allies were Britain, the countries in its empire, France, and China. In 1941, the Soviet Union and then the United States joined the Allies after being attacked by Germany and Japan respectively. For the first time, Canada entered a war as an independent nation.

The fighting lasted six years. Canadian troops saw action in western Europe, Italy, and Asia. As in the First World War, new technology was put to use with horrible results. Aircraft dropped bombs on enemy cities. They killed many civilians. Luckily, Canada was not bombed. Warships bombarded each other with heavy artillery. Submarines used torpedoes. By the war's end, the United States had the atomic bomb. This piece of technology was the most destructive weapon of all.

During the war, more than a million Canadians served their country. Of these, 42 042 gave their lives. Another 54 414 were wounded.

In both the First and Second World Wars, Canada experienced a conscription crisis. Many Francophones were opposed to what they viewed as Britain's wars. They did not like the idea of compulsory military duty. This strained relations between them and Canadians who favoured supporting Britain.

VOICES ■

Mervin Wolfe, from Brandon, Manitoba, was 19 when he joined the Canadian Army. Here he tells about his experience in the D-Day invasion to free Europe from Nazi (German) occupation. Make a list of the technologies he mentions.

66 There were snipers firing at us from this big, old house right at the edge of the beach. There must have been half a dozen guys dead on the beach when I went in. As I ran up the beach, I was loaded up pretty heavily with my packsack, wireless set, a Sten gun, six rounds of ammunition and six hand grenades. One of the British commandos was running faster than me, probably because I was weighed down. He crossed in front of me and the moment he did he got hit. 99

Source: Quoted in Luke Fisher, D'Arcy Jenish, and Barbara Wickens, "Tale of War," *Maclean's*, 6 June 1994, vol. 107, no. 23, pp. 44–45.

Figure 13.23 The Feser family of Rockyford, Alberta, in the 1950s. Many 1950s families had four or five children. Do you know many families like that today?

Postwar Prosperity

After the war, prosperity continued. The West's oil and coal continued to be in demand around the world. Factories went back to producing consumer goods. Canadians had the money to spend on cars, housing, and other goods.

After the soldiers came home, many Canadian men and women got married and started families. A huge number of children were born in the years following the war. This group came to be known as the **baby boomers**. In the early 1950s, the first baby boomers reached school age. Governments had to scramble to build more classrooms. Between 1945 and 1961, enrolment in Canadian schools almost doubled.

Think It ▶ Through

1. Think about changes in technology that have occurred since the First World War. One example is the invention of television. There are many others. Make a list of five changes that have affected the complex Canadian identity. Rank them by importance. For each one, list the positive and negative effects on society or the environment.

2. Our society tends to label each generation as it comes along. There are the baby boomers and the GenXers. What would you call your generation? Think about your biggest problems and greatest assets.

3. How did industrialization, urbanization, and technological change affect the identities of Canadians both positively and negatively? Write an opinion piece or create a collage to answer this question.

SKILLS Chapter 13 PROJECT   Great Canadian Citizens

Canada has a wealth of great Canadian citizens. We have inventors and athletes, explorers and humanitarians, medical doctors and politicians. Canadians from all walks of life have made an impact on Canada. We have made an impact on the world, too. This textbook has introduced you to many outstanding Canadians.

This chapter project challenges you to find a "Great Canadian Citizen." You will make a poster, bulletin-board display, or computer presentation about this person. It will show how he or she has changed Canada and the world.

Plan Your Search

Work with a partner. Together, plan a search to choose your great Canadian citizen.

- First, limit your search. Choose a specific period of time in Canada's history. Or choose a particular area of excellence. For example, you might want to focus on war heroes. First Nations leaders or Canadian inventors of space technology would be good choices, too.
- Working with your partner, create a list of keywords and phrases. Use Skill Check: Do a Keyword Search on page 288 to help you.

Tech Link

During the First and Second World Wars, many Canadian women did their part on the "home front" by working in the war factories. To see images of a few of them, open Chapter 13 on your *Voices and Visions* CD-ROM.

Search for Possible Candidates

Conduct your search. Make a list of Canadians you and your partner think make great citizens. Then choose.

Find Out about Your Great Canadian Citizen

Plan and conduct a search to find out about your great Canadian citizen. Find out who, where, when, what, why, and how he or she changed Canada or the world.

Make Your Poster, Display, or Report

After you have completed your research, design a poster, bulletin-board display, or a computer presentation with your partner. It should present your information in an eye-catching manner. Include both text and graphics.

Share

In small groups, exchange information about your great Canadians. Discuss their accomplishments. How did their impact on Canada and the world compare and differ?

Thinking about It

- What could you add to your poster, display, or report that would show the connection to the world?
- Has your vision of Canada's identity changed as a result of this project? How?
- What personal qualities made the person you researched a great citizen? Could you become a great citizen, too?

WEB LINK

How have citizens reacted to the social and political changes that have been taking place in Canada since the 1960s?

Key CONCEPT

Active Citizenship

As you have learned in previous chapters, citizenship means membership in a community. The community could be as small as a village or as large as a planet. No matter what the size of the community, every citizen has a role to play. Think of your school. Everyone at school plays a part in making it a success. Teachers lead the classes; librarians help you find the books that you need; custodians keep the school clean. Every student also has a role to play, such as attending class, respecting others, taking part in activities, and following the rules.

In the same way, every citizen of a country plays a part in making it a better place to live. We all come from different backgrounds, and we all have different talents. What we all share is a common citizenship and an interest in improving our country.

People Who Make a Difference

Citizenship in a country brings certain rights. For example, Canadian citizens have the right to obtain a passport and run as a candidate in an election. We also have a right to a fair trial if we are accused of a crime. Citizenship also brings responsibilities. Canadians are expected to participate fully in society. This is called being an active citizen. One way to be active is to vote in elections. Another is to volunteer to help a charity. Active citizens are people who try to improve life in their community, their country, and even the world.

This chapter explores examples of active citizenship in Alberta since the 1960s. You will investigate the ways in which Albertans and other Canadians have brought about positive change on issues that are important to them.

Honing Your Skills

Most people know of problems and issues in their societies. The next step for every responsible citizen is to act on those concerns. The Skill Check feature in this chapter will show you how to **Become an Active Citizen**. In the project at the end of this chapter, you will be asked to take an active role in improving your community.

Think ▶ AHEAD

What does active citizenship mean to you? Why is it important?

a) Using a word web, write down words or phrases that you think describe active citizenship.

b) As you read this chapter, your understanding of this concept may change or deepen. Return to your web diagram and add new words and ideas after completing the chapter.

SKILL CHECK:
Become an Active Citizen

Making a difference in your community takes planning. This Skill Check will help you through the process step by step.

1. **Identify the issue.** Pick a problem or issue that really matters to you. Describe it. How would you like things to be instead? What is stopping this from happening?

2. **Brainstorm actions.** Make a list of all the possible things you could do to make a change for the better.

3. **Choose an idea.** Look at all your ideas, and cross out the ones that present obstacles you can't overcome right now. From the rest, pick the one you think you can do best.

4. **Think it through.** Consider the following before you go any further with your plan.
   - Who will be affected by what you do?
   - Who can help you?
   - What resources will you need? How will you get them?
   - What do you need to find out about?

5. **Plan and act.** Make a project plan. Describe what needs to happen, who will do it, and when it will be done. Then carry out your plan!

6. **Reflect.** Afterward, ask yourself:
   - Did I make a difference?
   - What worked well?
   - What might have worked better?

Try It!

Find an example of an active citizen. Read the local or national newspapers and monitor the other media to find someone you feel has made a difference in his or her community or country, or in the world. Clip the article or summarize the news report, and explain why you chose this person.

A Diverse Society

Focus

How have we created greater diversity in Canada through our immigration policies?

The world is not a static place. Every day, millions of people around the globe move from country to country. A person who moves to a new country from his or her home country is called an **immigrant**. The First Nations and Inuit have always existed in the land we call Canada. Over the centuries, though, French, British, German, Chinese, Ukrainian, and many other peoples have immigrated to this land. This section investigates the kind of society we have created together.

Early Cultural Diversity

As you learned in Chapter 1, First Nations and Inuit cultures are very diverse. When newcomers started arriving from around the world, they added to this diversity.

From colonization until the Second World War, the majority of the people living here were of either French or British descent. These two groups saw themselves as the founding peoples of Canada. They did not think of the Aboriginal peoples as a founding people at that time. As a result, they considered the country **bicultural**. This means it is built on two cultures.

A New Immigration Policy

The idea of Canada having two main cultures began to change during the 1960s. In the decades following the Second World War, fewer and fewer immigrants from Western Europe were moving here. Canada's economy would fail if the government didn't find other immigrants to take their place. Therefore, the government changed its immigration policy. It stopped favouring immigrants from Britain and the United States. Instead, Canada began to open its doors to other countries.

People who had not been allowed to move to Canada in the past were now welcome. However, Canada was still choosy about who it let in. The government introduced a **points system** to rate each person who wanted to move here. All potential new Canadians received points for their education, skills, age, and wealth. If they had 50 points or more out of 100, they could enter the country. This system was an attempt to be fair to everyone, no matter what country a person was from. The

Even though Canada is not bicultural (a nation of just two cultures), the idea of Canada as a *bilingual* nation is one of the country's fundamental characteristics.

number of immigrants from Asia, Africa, and the Caribbean began to rise.

Immigration Act of 1978

In the 1960s and 1970s, Canada's economy was booming. The country needed even more immigrants to fill all the new jobs that had been created. Therefore, the government introduced the **Immigration Act of 1978**. (An act is a major law.) The Act had four main aims:

- attract skilled, educated immigrants from around the world; if these immigrants were rich and wanted to invest in Canada, even better
- reunite families that had been separated
- accept **refugees** (people who were in danger in their home country)
- allow them all to become citizens

Figure 14.1 These Caribbean immigrants arrived in Montréal in 1958. After living in Canada for three years, immigrants may become citizens. Why might people from Asia, Africa, and the Caribbean be interested in moving to Canada?

Reading
STRATEGY

When asked to analyze a graph, start by noting its title and reading the rest of the caption. Next, note the units of measurement used. If there is a legend, make sure you understand what the colours and symbols represent.

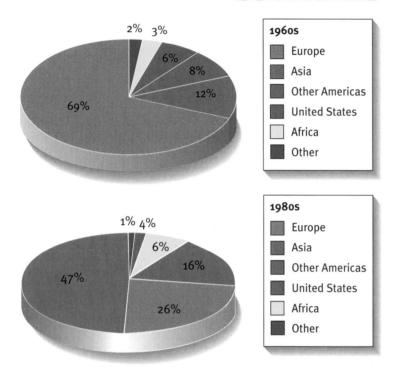

1960s	
▓	Europe
▓	Asia
▓	Other Americas
▓	United States
▓	Africa
▓	Other

2% 3%
6%
8%
12%
69%

1980s	
▓	Europe
▓	Asia
▓	Other Americas
▓	United States
▓	Africa
▓	Other

1% 4%
6%
16%
47%
26%

Source: *Time*, 31 May 1999, p. 39 and Statistics Canada.

Figure 14.2 Origins of Canadian immigrants in the 1960s and 1980s. Analyze the differences between these two pie graphs. What effect do you think the Immigration Act of 1978 had on Canada's cultural diversity?

Figure 14.3 Immigration to Canada since 1900. Each line running across the graph stands for 100 000 immigrants. In what year did the most immigrants enter Canada? Do some research to find out the reason. What accounts for the steep decline in immigrants before 1920, in the 1930s, and in the early 1940s?

Multiculturalism

These new immigration polices made it possible for people from many different countries to move to Canada. Canada became more and more diverse. As a result, no one could consider it bicultural anymore. Canadians needed a new way of defining their society. Prime Minister Pierre Trudeau introduced the policy of **multiculturalism** in 1971. It had three main ideas:

1. Canada must recognize that it is made up of people from many different cultures. Each of these groups makes an important contribution to society.
2. The government should help Canadian citizens protect and enhance their cultures. This might include supporting a festival, or helping a group of people keep their first language.
3. The government should promote respect and equality for all Canadians, no matter where they come from.

This act was preceded by the Official Languages Act of 1969. Through bilingualism, Canadians had begun to respect peoples of different cultures and languages. Bilingualism, therefore, opened the door for multiculturalism.

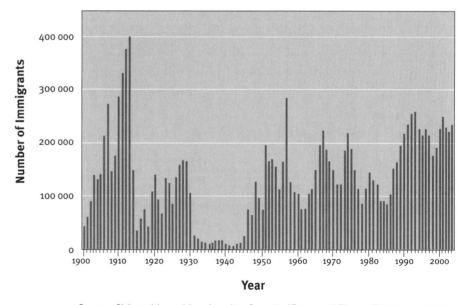

Source: Citizenship and Immigration Canada, "Facts and Figures," 2002 and 2004.

VOICES ■

Points of View on Multiculturalism

" Although there are two official languages, there is no official culture, nor does any ethnic group take precedence over any other. No citizen or group of citizens is other than Canadian, and all should be treated fairly ... "

—Prime Minister Pierre Trudeau to the House of Commons, 1971

" Multiculturalism is not about songs and dances, not about special interest groups. It is an affirmation of the right of those Canadians whose heritage is neither French nor English— 40 percent of our population—to be participants in the mainstream of Canadian life. "

—Lilian To, Director of a Chinese community group in Vancouver

Source: "Does Official Multiculturalism Unite Canada?" *Vancouver Sun*, 10 April 1997.

" Multiculturalism ... heightens our differences rather than diminish them. It has preached tolerance rather than encouraging acceptance .... "

—Neil Bissoondath, Canadian author from the Caribbean

Source: Neil Bissoondath, *Selling Illusions* (Toronto: Penguin, 1994).

" ... Multiculturalism is complete nonsense.... Immigrants come in, hang on for a few generations to whatever identity they brought .... While this is going on, they can be a very enriching influence on the host culture. But eventually, like fertilizer in the soil, they are bound to disappear into the host culture. "

—René Lévesque, former premier of Québec, 1973

Source: Alf Chaiton and Neil McDonald. *Canadian Schools and Canadian Identity* (Toronto: Gage Educational Publishing, 1977), p. 178.

Respond

Is each of these people in favour of or against the policy of multiculturalism? In an organizer, explain each of these quotations in your own words. Add a space to your organizer where you give your own opinion of multiculturalism.

Figure 14.4 At left, Canadians of Caribbean heritage dance during a multicultural celebration in Calgary. At right, Thai Canadians preparing to perform during the Lethbridge Heritage Day festival. What impact might these performances have on the sense of identity of Caribbean or Thai Canadians?

Source of Immigrants	Percentage of Immigrants
Asia and Pacific	49%
Africa and the Middle East	21%
Europe and United Kingdom	18%
South and Central America	9%
United States	3%

Source: Citizenship and Immigration Canada, "Facts and Figures," 2004.

Figure 14.5 The five main areas of the world from which Canada attracted immigrants in 2004. Present this information in a pie graph. (You may want to refer to Skill Check: Use Statistics to Create Graphs on page 124 before beginning.) From what area did most immigrants come? Why do you think Canada attracts so many immigrants from this region? If you were making a similar graph for 1900, how do you think the percentages would differ?

Biography

Norman Kwong

In the 1950s, Norman Kwong was a star football player for the Edmonton Eskimos and the Calgary Stampeders. He was known as the "China Clipper." Today everyone calls him "Your Honour" because he became lieutenant-governor of Alberta in 2005.

When Kwong was born, in 1929, his parents named him Lim Kwong Yew. They were immigrants from China. The family settled in Calgary and opened a grocery store.

Kwong began playing in the Canadian Football League in 1948. He was the first Chinese Canadian to play football for a living. During his career, he was the league's outstanding player twice. His team won the Grey Cup six times. To honour his achievements, he was made a member of the Canadian Sports Hall of Fame. In 1998, his work in sports and in the community earned him acceptance into the Order of Canada, Canada's highest honour.

Kwong is a great supporter of multiculturalism and once chaired a national committee to promote it. In his role as lieutenant-governor he stated:

Growing up as a member of a visible minority, I understand the challenges faced by immigrants, particularly immigrant youth. Therefore, I intend to devote some of my time to Alberta's young immigrants and their families by encouraging and supporting their academic and athletic pursuits. In this way, I hope to help them in their journey to becoming successful, involved citizens.

Figure 14.6 Norman Kwong, once a Canadian football star, became the lieutenant-governor of Alberta in 2005. How has Kwong benefited from being an active citizen? How has his active citizenship benefited other Canadians? SKILLS

Citizens' Rights

One of the main ideas of Canadian citizenship is that every citizen has the same individual rights. In 1982, a document called the **Canadian Charter of Rights and Freedoms** became law. The Charter lists the basic rights that belong to every citizen. No one can take away these rights, not even the government.

These are some of the individual rights protected by the Charter:

- the right to vote in elections
- the right to belong to any organization, such as a political party
- the right to a fair trial if accused of a crime
- the right to practise any religion
- the right to run for political office
- the right to move freely from place to place in Canada

The Charter guarantees collective rights as well. The rights of Aboriginal people are listed in Section 82 of the Charter. As you learned in Chapter 12 (page 281), Section 23 protects the education rights of the official language minority.

Tech Link

Open the *Voices and Visions* CD-ROM to see the entire Charter.

CASE STUDY

Wartime Injustice

The stories of Japanese and Ukrainian Canadians shows how citizens' rights have changed over time. During the Second World War, about 23 000 people of Japanese descent were living in British Columbia. Most of them were Canadian citizens.

Japan was one of Canada's enemies during the war. The government suspected that the Japanese might attack Canada from the Pacific Ocean. The government did not trust Japanese Canadians to be loyal. Japanese Canadians never gave Canada any reason to believe this. Nevertheless, the government forced them to move from their homes on the coast. Most were sent to camps in the interior of British Columbia, Alberta, and Ontario. The government told them their property would be safe until after the war. However, after the Japanese Canadians left for the camps, the government sold all of their property.

Tech Link

To read the letter nine-year-old Ukrainian Katie Domytyk wrote to her imprisoned father, open Chapter 14 on the *Voices and Visions* CD-ROM.

It was a terrible shock when we learned that this safekeeping business meant nothing. All of our stuff had been sold at auction .... [It] *caused a lot of bitterness. People would say, "That's all we had and now we have nothing."... First they take us from our homes and stick us in a dump, and now this.*

Source: Barry Broadfoot, *Years of Sorrow Years of Shame* (Toronto: Doubleday, 1977).

A very similar thing had happened to the Ukrainian Canadians during the First World War. They were viewed with suspicion because part of Ukraine was under Austro-Hungarian control at that time, and Austria-Hungary was one of Canada's enemies during the war. Some had their homes destroyed. Ukrainian newspapers and magazines were banned. About 5000 people were taken from their homes on the prairies.

They were moved to camps all across the country. Once there, they were poorly fed and forced to work long hours. They worked in the logging industry, in steel mills, and in mines. They even worked to develop Banff National Park! They received no pay for this work.

Today, Canadians view the wartime treatment of the Japanese and the Ukrainians as a terrible wrong. In 1988, the federal government apologized to Japanese Canadians. A fund was set up to repay those who had had their property sold or damaged. In 2005, the federal government apologized to Ukrainians. It set up a fund to sponsor projects that recognize Ukrainian contributions to Canada.

Figure 14.7 Japanese Canadians were forced from their homes and onto trucks. They could take with them only what they could carry. What was unfair about all of this?

Respond

The government took and sold these peoples' property, took away their communications, moved them against their will, and forced them to work. Do you think any of these things could happen in Canada today? Explain.

Think It Through

You have learned that the term *multiculturalism* means that all cultures are accepted and supported. While we all hope that all people are treated fairly in Canadian society, this is not the case. Prejudice and racism still exist in Canada.

a) Read your local and national newspaper or the CBC website (www.cbc.ca) every day for a week. Look for examples of Canadians who have been treated differently because of their cultural background. Clip or print the articles and bring them to class.

b) Make a list of possible reasons why these people were discriminated against. Did stereotyping play a role?

c) As a class, brainstorm things that could be done to make sure that all Canadians are treated fairly, whatever their background. **SKILLS**

First Nations and Métis in Western Canada

Focus

How have the First Nations and Métis in Western Canada reacted to the challenges and opportunities of today?

You have read that the number of Aboriginal people in Canada decreased for many years. The main reasons for this were warfare, disease, and poverty. Then, during the 1920s, the Aboriginal population began to rise. Today, the population is growing faster than the non-Aboriginal population. In this section, you will investigate some of the challenges and opportunities facing this growing population in the West.

Aboriginal Baby Boom

In the last chapter, you read about the baby boom. This refers to the generation of children born in Canada after the Second World War. Today, another baby boom is happening—among Aboriginal peoples. Aboriginal youth make up the fastest growing population group in Canada.

Tech Link

Artistic expression is a way of expressing one's identity. To see images of Aboriginal artists and their works of art, open Chapter 14 on your *Voices and Visions* CD-ROM.

This boom has given Aboriginal peoples a chance to strengthen their cultures. For example, First Nations have renewed interest in traditional arts. Adults in the communities now have many children to whom they can teach these arts. Also, many Aboriginal students are learning their original languages. The energy of youth can bring strength and vitality to a community.

The large number of young people also presents challenges to Aboriginal communities:

WEB LINK

- More schools and houses are needed for the growing number of families.
- Better health care is needed.
- More jobs will be needed as young people enter the workforce.

Self-Government

Until the 1950s, the federal government kept tight control over the running of many Aboriginal communities. First Nations and Inuit wanted to choose their own solutions to the challenges facing them. They wanted to make decisions on such things as their education, health care, and local economy. The ability of First Nations and Inuit to make the decisions that affect their lives is called **self-government**.

In 1951, First Nations leaders went to the federal government and argued for self-government. They regained at least some control over their own communities. By the end of the 1960s, many Aboriginal communities had their own police forces and ran their own social services.

The Assembly of First Nations was founded in the 1980s. It is an organization of leaders from First Nations across the country. The Assembly played an important role in fighting for the right of Aboriginal people to self-government.

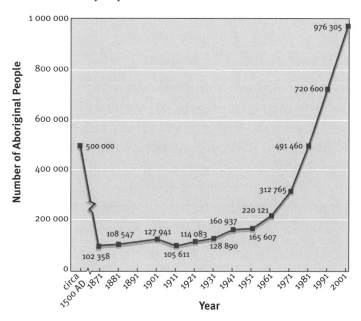

Source: Report on the Royal Commission on Aboriginal Peoples, vol. 1, p. 14.

Figure 14.8 Aboriginal population in Canada from 1500 to 2001. Analyze this line graph. Apply your learning from previous chapters to explain the main reasons for the sharpest decrease and increase in the Aboriginal population.

Figure 14.9 First Nations youth taking part in a cultural festival in Banff. According to the most recent census (2001), there are 976 305 Aboriginal people living in Canada, more than 150 000 of whom live in Alberta. How might a young person benefit from belonging to a large cultural community?

VOICES AND VISIONS

CASE STUDY

The Issue of Aboriginal Health

The Challenge

In 2003, a team of First Nations people surveyed 238 communities across the country. They found that the health and living conditions of First Nations people were much worse than those of other Canadians.

For example, the study found that obesity rates in First Nations are twice as high as for Canadians in general. This in turn leads to high rates of diabetes. First Nations adults between the ages of 35 and 54 are six times more likely to have diabetes than the average Canadian of the same age.

Diabetes can be prevented by eating healthy foods and staying active. Individual First Nations communities are working on finding solutions. Sandy Lake First Nation, for example, created safe walking trails.

The study identified other health problems resulting from an unsafe environment. Jane Gray, the coordinator of the survey, stated:

Too many families live in … overcrowded homes in need of repairs. Too many homes have mold. Too many First Nations people do not have safe drinking water. Too many people don't have the basic level of health and living conditions that most Canadians take for granted."

Source: First Nations Centre, National Aboriginal Health Organization, First Nations Regional Longitudinal Health Survey, 2002–2003.

Respond

Why is it important that Aboriginal people find their own solutions to the challenges facing their communities? **SKILLS**

One Solution

Aboriginal people created the National Aboriginal Health Organization to promote healthy living in their communities. They set up a program called "Lead Your Way!" Every year, 12 Aboriginal youths are selected to be role models for their peers. These role models visit Aboriginal schools and attend community events. They try to inspire other young people to make healthy choices and achieve their goals.

Levi McAteer, 15, from Manning, Alberta, was the youngest role model chosen for 2004–2005. In addition to being an excellent student, McAteer works part-time in a family business. He is an active volunteer in community projects. For example, he is helping to establish a skateboard park for youth in his community.

McAteer has a strong knowledge of his Métis heritage. His family has passed on their traditional teachings to him. He follows their traditional ways by hunting, camping, and making moccasins. McAteer plans to study mechanical engineering or computer technology after graduating from high school.

Figure 14.10 Explain why Levi McAteer could be called an active citizen. How can active citizenship strengthen a person's identity? How can a strong sense of identity affect a person's health? **SKILLS**

Today, First Nations and Inuit communities have different forms of self-government. Some are run at the community level. In these, the people might run their own schools and health clinics. Other groups have wider control. In Nunavut, for example, the Inuit own 18 per cent of the land and have designed a government to suit the needs of their scattered community.

Self-government is not something that First Nations and Inuit want the government to give them. They believe it is a right that already belongs to them. They just want other Canadians to recognize it and respect their decisions.

Identity

Aboriginal Art

Art has always played an important role in Aboriginal societies. Before the arrival of Europeans, every object in the First Nations and Inuit cultures was handmade. Many were decorated with designs that told of family history or the spiritual world. Haida [HY-duh] artist Robert Davidson explains:

Art was one with the culture. Art was our only written language. It documented our progress as a people. It documented the histories of the families. Throughout our history, it has been the art that has kept our spirit alive.

Source: Ian M. Thom, ed., *Robert Davidson: Eagle of the Dawn*, (Vancouver: Vancouver Art Gallery and Douglas & McIntyre, 1993), p. 8.

As you have read, the arrival of Europeans brought many hardships to the First Nations and Inuit. As a result, fewer and fewer Aboriginal people created traditional art during the first half of the 1900s.

However, as Aboriginal populations began to grow, so too did the people's interest in their art. They began to practise their traditional ceremonies again. They created more masks, robes, and drums in order to do so. Since the 1950s, there has been a big increase in Aboriginal arts in Alberta and across the country.

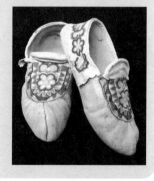

Figure 14.11 Mrs. Gray of Onoway, Alberta, made these moccasins in the Dene [DEN-ay] style. She made them from moose and caribou hide. She sewed the artwork with embroidery silk. Why is the decoration of everyday objects important to a people's cultural identity?

Think It Through

1. Do you have a role model? If so, explain how he or she helps you make good choices. If not, choose someone you have read or heard about. Explain why he or she would make a good role model for you.

2. Invite an Aboriginal person from a local community to talk to your class about what he or she believes to be the greatest challenges and opportunities facing his or her people today.

Francophones in Alberta and Canada

Francophones live in communities all across Canada. No matter which province you visit, you will find French place names on the local map. You can watch French-language television and go to a Francophone school if you meet the criteria. This is because Canada is officially a **bilingual** country.

However, outside of Québec, many of these Francophone communities are small in comparison to the English-speaking population around them.

Focus

How do Franco-Albertans keep their language alive and their identity strong?

In this section, you will explore the meaning and origins of bilingualism. You will also investigate how Franco-Albertans counter assimilation in their province.

Bi means two. So if you can speak two languages, you're bilingual. A country is bilingual if its government operates in two official languages.

French and English in Canada

As you read in earlier chapters, Canada developed as a country in which two languages, French and English, both played important roles. The beginning of this relationship goes all the way back to New France, the homeland of the Canadiens. As you will recall, the British took control of New France in the 1700s. Nonetheless, the Canadiens remained, becoming the first citizens of the new British colony. Francophone communities grew as part of the new country.

Today, one Canadian in five is of Canadien descent. One in four people speaks French as his or her first language. Many study in **Francophone schools**, which are exclusively for Francophone students. Many non-Francophone Canadians study French as a second language in **French immersion schools**.

Language Spoken	Canada	Alberta
English only	20 014 645	2 704 895
French only	3 946 525	1 895
Both English and French	5 231 575	202 905
Neither English nor French	446 290	31 455

Source: Statistics Canada, "Population by knowledge of official language, by provinces and territories (2001 Census)."

Figure 14.12 Knowledge of official languages, 2001. Make two graphs to compare these statistics. Which figure is most striking? Why?

Figure 14.13 Herman Poulin is a Francophone artist from St. Paul, Alberta. Here, he stands beside a scale model of the monument he is creating to stand on the grounds of the Alberta Legislature. It is intended to recognize the contributions of the Franco-Albertan community to the development of their province.

Official Languages Act

In the 1960s, Francophone and Anglophone Canada did not seem to be getting along. The government asked a group of prominent Canadians to study the problem. The group was called the **Royal Commission on Bilingualism and Biculturalism**. It discovered that Francophones had second-rate status in Canada. For the size of the population, Francophones were under-represented in the civil service and in business. They did not have enough decision-making power in the federal government. Nor did they have enough educational opportunities outside Québec. The tensions these injustices were causing had created a terrible crisis.

How did the government respond? It acted quickly to reinforce bilingualism. Canada had been officially bilingual since Confederation. Now the country's leaders wanted to ensure that the federal government would provide all services to citizens in both official languages. So, in 1969, they passed the **Official Languages Act**. This law restates that French and English are Canada's official languages. An **official language** is one that the federal government uses to serve its citizens. When dealing with the federal government, citizens across the country would now have the right to use either French or English. The law was meant to give both official languages equal status. It also commits the government to supporting linguistic minority Francophone and Anglophone communities. Official bilingualism is now protected permanently by the Constitution.

Bilingual and Unilingual Provinces

Canada is bilingual at the federal level. New Brunswick is bilingual at the provincial level as well. This means that, in New Brunswick, local and provincial services are offered in both French and English. New Brunswick became bilingual because of its large Acadian population.

Except for New Brunswick, all other provinces are **unilingual**. This means that they do not have to provide services in both English and French. Examples of provincial services include libraries, licensing offices, health and family services, provincial courts, and information on provincial government programs. Although the provinces do not *have* to offer services in both languages, they may still choose to do so. For example, the Québec provincial government has provided services to the Anglophone community in English since 1867.

Alberta has been acting as a unilingual province since the Haultain Resolution in 1892. In 1988, it passed Bill 60 to make English its only official language.

Figure 14.14 In 1987, Alberta MLA Léo Piquette exercised his legal right to speak French in the Legislature. When he did so, however, he was told he could only speak English. Franco-Albertans and other Canadians supported Piquette. This photograph shows protesters cheering on Piquette outside the Alberta legislature. The Supreme Court of Canada told the Alberta government that Piquette was right. (See page 279.) In 1988, both Alberta and Saskatchewan then made English their only official language. Why do you think it is important to Francophone politicians to be able to speak French freely during government debates?

French in Alberta

In 2001, nearly 60 000 people whose first language is French lived in Alberta. Some of these people call themselves Franco-Albertans, especially if they have been born into a Francophone family in Alberta. Others may identify more strongly with the province or the country where they were born. Over the years, Franco-Albertans have had to struggle with attempts to assimilate Francophones. They worry that their language and culture will be swallowed up by the English majority.

Figure 14.15 Crystal Plamondon hails from the town of Plamondon, north of Edmonton. This successful Franco-Albertan singer, songwriter, and percussionist grew up on ranch life, Canadien songs, and Acadian rhythms. She sings in French, English, and Cree. In this way, she is carrying on her grandfather's dream of keeping the family's heritage alive. In 2004, she received the Prix Sylvie Van Brabant for Excellence in Artistic Creation in Alberta.

Some Albertans have learned French as a second language. For example, in 2005, 318 000 students were enrolled in French immersion programs across Canada. This included students in 41 towns and cities in Alberta.

Countering Assimilation

Franco-Albertans believe they can best fight assimilation by keeping their community vital. The most important tool for making this happen is the Francophone school. These are run by Francophones for Francophones. When Francophone students walk through the doors of the school, they feel at home. By identifying with the community of the school, students also bond with the larger Francophone community. When a community stays vital, so does its language. In 2006, Alberta had 28 Francophone schools across the province.

Schools are not the only way to keep a language and culture alive. Franco-Albertans also started a radio station, television programs, a newspaper, bookstores, arts groups, and more than 60 other different Francophone organizations. Over time, the community has created various youth organizations to engage young people.

Think It Through

1. Do you agree with Alberta's 1988 decision to make the province unilingual? Debate this issue with a partner. One of you will support unilingualism, the other bilingualism. (You may want to refer to the Skill Check on page 170.)

2. Local and provincial governments offer some services in many languages. What services do you know of that are offered in languages other than French or English? In which languages are they offered? Do you think this is a good idea? Explain.

3. a) Should all Albertans, not just Francophones, be concerned with countering the assimilation of French communities? Explain your answer.

   b) What can you do to show support for the French language and culture in Alberta? As a class, work together to come up with a list of suggestions. **SKILLS**

Identity

Francophonie Jeunesse de l'Alberta (FJA)

Currently, the association that brings together youth aged 14 to 25 is Francophonie Jeunesse de l'Alberta. It aims to represent Alberta's Francophone youth and promote their well-being. It also establishes and maintains contact with the Francophone community.

Every year, 2000 people take part in FJA local, provincial, and national celebrations, gatherings, and events. Sophie Nolette is one of those young Francophones. She is a 15-year-old from the Francophone community of Girouxville in northern Alberta.

Tech Link

Sophie Nolette is a young active citizen. To find out about other active Canadian citizens, open Chapter 14 on your *Voices and Visions* CD-ROM.

Sophie, does where you live make it difficult for you to keep your French language and culture alive?
I live in a small French community, which is within a bigger [Anglophone] culture. Without help, it's hard to find yourself and keep your identity strong.

French is the main [language] in Canada, along with English. French is really strong in Québec, but it is in every other province as well. In our province, it is not as noticeable as it is in Québec, so we have to celebrate it and remind everybody that French is here.

Is that why you got involved in FJA?
FJA events bring together lots of people from communities all across the province. It's a great way to meet other kids your own age who also speak French. Also, just because it's fun!

What kinds of events does FJA host?
They have le Raje [short for le Rassemblement Jeunesse], which means youth gathering. These are dances where different bands come to play. Most bands are from Québec, but sometimes school bands are the opening act. They also have ateliers [workshops], where they teach us all kinds of different things like music and arts. Of course, all of this happens in French.

Do you think organizations like FJA are important?
Yes, it is important because it helps us not to be afraid of our French background. No one who goes to the events is afraid to express their culture, and they can just be who they are.

Source: Oxford interview, June 2005.

Respond

With a partner, discuss how Sophie's involvement in this youth organization could have a positive effect on her and on her community. SKILLS

Urban and Rural Canada

Do you live in a rural area or in an urban area? If you live in an urban area, you are in the majority. However, this was not always the case. Before the 1930s, most Canadians lived in small rural communities. They were mainly farming families, who needed lots of room for their crops and animals.

Focus

How has movement from the country to the cities affected rural communities in Canada?

Since then, there has been a steady stream of people moving from the countryside to the cities. This process is called **urbanization**. In this section, you will examine the reasons for this change. You will also investigate some of the impacts on rural Canada.

New Resources

After the Second World War, Canada really began to prosper. Valuable resources were discovered, and many of these were in the West. The most dramatic discovery happened on 13 February 1947. A drilling crew struck oil at Leduc, Alberta, south of Edmonton. Never before had anyone found such a huge amount of oil! Overnight, Canada became one of the world's leading producers of this valuable fuel.

These finds changed the economy of the Prairie provinces. Wheat was still an important resource. However, it was no longer the only major resource.

Growing Cities

The last half of the twentieth century brought other changes to Alberta. For example, farmers and farm workers started to move from the country to the cities. By 1980, there were only half as many farmers in Western Canada as there had been in 1940.

Figure 14.16 Leduc was followed by other oil finds around Edmonton and farther north. At the same time, natural gas was discovered elsewhere in Alberta. Use a natural resources map in your atlas to find out what other resources were found.

Year	Rural	Urban
1901	63%	37%
1931	46%	54%
1961	30%	70%
2001	20%	80%

Source: Statistics Canada, "Population urban and rural, by province and territory (Canada)."

Figure 14.17 The percentage of Canadians living in rural and urban areas over the years. Choose the type of graph you feel best suits this information, and draw it. What do you predict the percentages will be in 2031? Explain your prediction.

Global Connections ■

The growth of cities has happened all over the world, not just in Canada. More people everywhere are drawn to the opportunities that cities offer. One hundred years ago, about 14 per cent of the world's population lived in cities. Today that figure has grown to about 50 per cent.

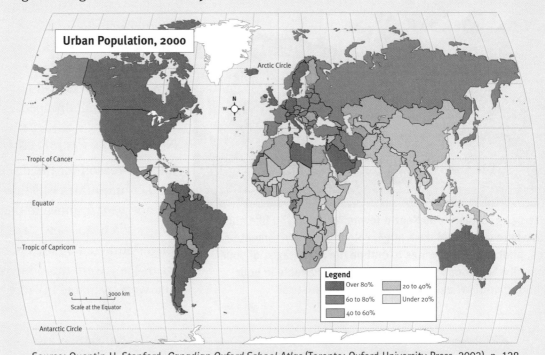

Source: Quentin H. Stanford, *Canadian Oxford School Atlas* (Toronto: Oxford University Press, 2003), p. 128.

Figure 14.18 This map shows the percentage of a country's population that live in urban areas. Analyze the map. Make a list of the most highly urbanized countries. Make another list of the least urbanized. What characteristics do most of the countries on each list seem to have in common? How might these characteristics explain their level of urbanization?

Reasons for the Move to the City

Why did so many people migrate away from the countryside?

Jobs

After the Second World War, more jobs were available in the cities where the factories were located. Running a farm is like any business. It involves risk. Some people preferred receiving a weekly paycheque.

Larger, but Fewer, Farms

Meanwhile, on the farms, new machinery came into use. These machines made it possible for fewer people to farm more land. The machines were expensive, though. Small, family-run farms could not afford the equipment and so couldn't compete with large commercial farms.

As farms became much larger, there were fewer of them. Farmers and farm workers who were no longer needed moved to the cities. Today, farming is a very expensive business to start. Few people can afford to move back to the country to farm.

Rural Towns Shrinking

The movement of farmers out of the countryside meant the dwindling of rural towns. Without farming families to shop in their stores, visit their banks, and attend schools, some of these small towns had little reason to exist. The town of Winnifred, for example, was once located in southwestern Alberta. It became a ghost town.

As farming towns became smaller, a few new "instant" towns popped up. These instant towns were built wherever valuable new resources were found. Thompson, Manitoba, and Uranium City, Saskatchewan, are two examples. These towns provided homes and services for the mineworkers and their families. However, even with these new towns, the overall population of the countryside still dropped.

Newcomers Preferred Cities

Another reason for the disappearance of rural communities was that new immigrants did not want to move to them. Land was no longer so cheap. New Canadians were no longer attracted by the chance to own a farm. They were more interested in jobs that were available in cities.

Figure 14.19 Calgary's McKenzie Towne. What do you like about living where you do? Make a large, colourful advertisement using words, photos, and drawings to outline the advantages of your community. For example, what services are available in your neighbourhood? What are its unique characteristics?

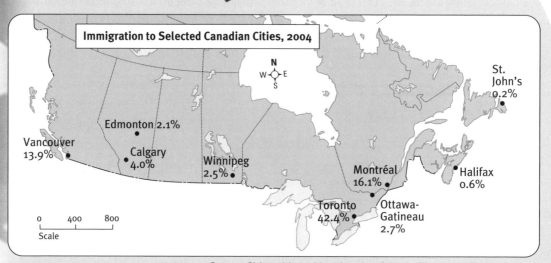

Source: Citizenship and Immigration Canada, "Facts and Figures," 2004.

Figure 14.20 This map shows the percentage of immigrants who settled in some Canadian cities in 2004. Most immigrants to Canada do not settle in the countryside. Calculate what percentage of immigrants settled in smaller towns and rural communities not shown on the map. How does this figure compare with the percentage who settled in the cities shown? Do you think this settlement pattern is likely to change in the future? Why or why not?

CASE STUDY

Rowley: The Town that Refused to Die

How can active citizenship save a town? As you read this case study, make a list of ways the citizens of one small town did just that. **SKILLS**

It was 1911 when the town of Rowley was born in central-east Alberta, just north of Drumheller. That was the year the railway reached the area and brought with it many farmers and cattle ranchers. By the 1920s, the population of the town had grown to 500. Rowley thrived. Schools, shops, and a community hall sprang up. The future looked bright for everyone in the rural town. Then things started to change.

Rowley slowly began to die in the 1950s. One reason was that new highways made it easier to get to places like Calgary and Edmonton. So, young people began leaving Rowley for the big cities. Also, rising transportation costs and dropping grain prices forced many small family farms to close. The farmers had to move to the cities to find work. By the 1970s, only a few dozen people were left in Rowley. It looked like the town would soon disappear.

Respond

Create a timeline that shows the major points in the history of Rowley. Add an entry for a decade from now. Use it to predict the future of the town.

The residents wanted to save Rowley from becoming a prairie ghost town. They raised money to fix up the pioneer homes. They opened an old-fashioned saloon and turned the railway station into a museum. Soon the town was attracting tourists.

Would the good times last? In the late 1980s, wooden grain elevators were replaced with modern steel elevators in larger centres. The government wanted to close Rowley's elevators for good. Again, the town residents came together. They decided to buy two of the old elevators and keep them as a tourist attraction.

Their troubles were not over. In 1999, the train stopped coming to Rowley. One older resident said, "That is really going to hurt our cash flow." Nevertheless, the people of Rowley have not given up on their town. Today, the 12 permanent residents who remain are hopeful that word of mouth will continue to bring tourists to Rowley and keep the town alive. Perhaps you will go there.

Figure 14.21 Rowley, Alberta. This photo shows the boarded-up main street in about 1999. The pioneer storefronts, including Sam's Saloon, used to be a big tourist attraction. Why would tourists be interested in visiting Rowley?

CASE STUDY

Does the Family Farm Have a Future?

Family farms are just that—farms run by the members of one family. Usually, the same family has owned the farm for generations. This used to be the pattern for most of the farms in Canada.

After the Second World War, technology allowed farms to become much bigger. Companies, rather than families, owned some of the biggest farms. These commercial farms could produce very large amounts of crops and raise large numbers of animals. The family farms could not compete. When family farms went out of business, the commercial farms bought them and became even bigger. Family farms still exist, but not in the same numbers as before. Many farming families have left the countryside and moved to the city.

Some people feel that family farms promote important values, such as self-reliance and community spirit. The disappearance of the family farm could mean these values become less important in Canada.

Respond

What impact do you think the disappearance of the family farm would have on rural Alberta? You may present your answer in a form of your choice. Do you believe it is important that the family farm continues? Explain your opinion.

Figure 14.22 A family farm (left) and a commercial farm (right) in rural Alberta. Create a chart to outline some of the differences between these two types of farms.

Conclusion

With rights come responsibilities. A family responsibility, for example, is something you are expected to do to support your family. Citizens also have responsibilities. Sometimes this can be as serious as going to war to defend your country. At other times, it is as simple as voting in an election or obeying the law. Citizenship means accepting that not all Canadians share the same group identity. It also means accepting the bilingual nature of our country.

In this chapter, you have studied several important issues that affect Canadians today. There is an important role for active citizenship in all of these issues.

Think It ▶
Through

1. You have read that the town of Rowley has managed to stay alive. However, many other rural towns have disappeared. Write an opinion piece on why you believe it is or isn't important that small rural towns survive in Alberta. (You may want to refer to Skill Check: Develop an Opinion on page 170 before beginning.)

2. Use examples from this chapter to make a pamphlet showing how active citizens can bring positive change to their communities. SKILLS

SKILLS Chapter 14 PROJECT Improve Your Community

Every citizen needs to participate in some way in Canadian society. It is the price we pay for the opportunity to enjoy the rights and freedoms that come with living in Canada. It is the responsibility of every citizen to try to make Canada a better place to live.

Your mission in this chapter project is to improve some aspect of your school or community. Working as a class, you will choose a local problem or issue and then act on it!

Brainstorm Problems or Issues

Take a critical look at your school and the local community. What things about it would you like to see changed or improved? What are your concerns?

As a class, make a list of all the local problems or issues you might like to address. For example, you might think of problems similar to these:

- A stream near the school is littered with trash.
- Equipment in a local playground is broken and dangerous.
- People are not cleaning up after their pets on the sidewalks around your school.
- A local organization supports a good cause but doesn't have enough volunteers.
- The local food bank is running short of donations.

- The cafeteria at your school does not offer healthy food choices.

Make Your Choice Candidates

Consider each of the problems and issues carefully. Some of them may be too big or complicated to address in the time you have. Others may be too expensive. Cross possibilities off your list until you have only a few good choices remaining. As a class, vote on these to choose your project.

Plan Your Project and Act On It

Review Skill Check: Become an Active Citizen on page 312. Since you have already chosen your project, begin at step 2, Brainstorm Actions.

When you reach step 5, Plan and Act, you may want to divide the class into groups. Each group could be responsible for a different task.

Reflect

Make sure you talk about the project as a class after you have completed it. Did you accomplish the goal you set out? Why or why not? Discuss any problems you encountered and think of ways you could do better next time.

Glossary

Aboriginal The descendants of the original inhabitants of North America. First Nations, Inuit and Métis peoples have unique heritages, languages, cultural practices, and spiritual beliefs. "Aboriginal" is also used in other parts of the world to refer to the first inhabitants of a given area.

Acadian A Francophone citizen of Acadia

alliance A union in which groups agree to trade and help each other resolve disputes

assembly line A production method used in factories whereby an incomplete product is placed on a conveyor belt and, as the product moves down the line, each worker does one task on it; by the end of the line, the product is complete

assimilation A process by which culture or individual is absorbed into a more dominant culture because of its overwhelming influence

authentic Trustworthy and reliable; original, not a copy

baby boomer One of the huge number of children born in the years following the Second World War (1945 to about 1960)

barter The exchange of goods for other goods rather than for money

bias A personal like or dislike of something or someone that is not necessarily based on fact

bicultural Built on two cultures

bilingual Fluent in two languages (of a person); officially recognizing two languages (of a country)

bilingualism A policy of recognizing two official languages

Bill of Rights A document created by the Métis Provisional Government and presented to the government of Canada that requested that Métis receive the rights enjoyed by other Canadians

bishop A high-ranking cleric; the head of the church in New France

Les Bleus A group of conservative, business-oriented Canadiens in the Canadian Assembly in the 1850s who were in favour of co-operating with the English

The Blues English name for Les Bleus

bribery A way for politicians to influence voters by making promises or paying money

Canadian Charter of Rights and Freedoms A legal document created in 1982 that lists the basic rights that belong to every Canadian citizen

Canadien(ne) A Francophone descendant of the settlers of New France living anywhere in North America, including the West (in use until about the First World War)

Catholic school A school for Catholic students

cause Something that makes an event happen

Château Clique The Anglophone friends and relatives of the governor of Lower Canada who were also Executive or Legislative Council members

citizen A member of a society

Clan Mother The head of a Haudenosaunee longhouse

clan A small village of extended families who lived together, co-operated, and shared resources

Clear Grit Party A group of radical reformers in the Canadian Assembly in the 1850s who wanted a more democratic government

colony A territory controlled by another country

communal Something done or owned collectively

communal lifestyle A means of living whereby a group has no private property and shares both possessions and responsibilities

competition The act of competing with others for profit or a prize

compromise A method of resolving a disagreement whereby everyone gives up a little to get an agreement they can all live with

computer revolution A major change that occurred when people started using computers for everyday tasks such as typing

consensus An agreement reached by a group as a whole

core value An important idea or belief about how people should live

cottage industry A workplace in a home or small shop where a skilled craftsperson makes goods using hand tools

Country Born Métis The children of First Nations women and British traders from the Hudson's Bay Company

coureur de bois A Canadien trader ("runner of the woods" in English) who paddled on long journeys into the wilderness to trade for furs with the First Nations

culture A way of life or a way of being shared by a group of people; culture includes the knowledge, experiences, and values a group shares and that shape the way its members see the world

deadlock A situation where no progress can be made

decision making by consensus A debate in which people discuss an issue until they can all agree on one outcome

democracy A system of government in which the people of a nation are involved in decision making

demographics The characteristics of the people of a particular place

discrimination Unfair treatment of a person or group based on prejudice

diverse economy An economy with many types of industry

division of labour A production method that breaks work into small pieces; each worker specializes in only one step of the production process

economics Financial considerations

economy The way in which people meet their basic needs, such as food, clothing, and shelter

effect The result of an event, sometimes called a consequence

Elder A respected member of an Aboriginal community who uses Traditional Teachings, experience, and wisdom to help people in his or her community make good decisions

emigrant A person who leaves his or her homeland permanently

empire A network of colonies controlled by a single country

employment insurance A social program in which people receive an income when they lose their jobs

ethnocentric A viewpoint that judges other global cultures and ideas according to personal values and standards; believing one's own ethnic group is superior

factor A trader in charge of a Hudson's Bay Company fort

factory Another name for a Hudson's Bay Company fort

factory A workplace where workers run machines to produce goods

false advertising Using ads to mislead people

family allowance A social program that provides financial aid to people with children

Family Compact Anglophone friends and relatives of the governor of Upper Canada who became Executive or Legislative Council members

federalism/federal system A system of government in which a central government has power over matters affecting the whole country and provincial governments have power over local and regional matters

First Nations Aboriginal Peoples of Canada who are not Métis or Inuit; groups of the same. There are more than 600 First Nations across Canada, with 46 First Nations in Alberta.

fortress A permanent military stronghold that often includes a town

Francophone A person for whom French is the first language learned and still in use; a person of French language and culture

Francophone school A school exclusively for Francophone students and run by Francophones

La Francophonie An organization of regions and countries around the world in which French is many people's first language or an official language

free trade Tax-free trade between countries (no tarrifs on imported or exported goods)

French immersion school A school where non-Francophone students study French as a second language by taking their core subjects in French

general strike Occurs when workers from many unions all go on strike at the same time to support one another

government The way people organize themselves to choose their leaders and make decisions

governor A powerful official; in New France, the most powerful member of the Sovereign Council and the King's personal representative

habitant A Francophone farmer of New France

haven A place of refuge

historical perspective A viewpoint that uses history to understand why things are the way they are

identity A set of characteristics and values that describes the essence of a person or group

immigrant A person who moves to a new country

Immigration Act of 1978 A Canadian law meant to attract skilled, educated immigrants from around the world, to reunite families that had been separated, to accept refugees, and to allow all new immigrants to become citizens

imperialism A country extending its control over other countries, often using economic or military means

Independents Individuals in the Canadian Assembly in the 1850s who did not join any governmental party

Indigenous people The original inhabitants of a given area

Industrial Revolution The shift from home-based hand manufacturing to large-scale factory production

industrialization Transformation to an economy based on large industries

intendant In New France, the second-most important figure of the Sovereign Council; he was in charge of the day-to-day affairs of the colony

internal migrant A person who moves from one region to another within one country

Inuit Aboriginal people in northern Canada mostly living above the tree line in the Northwest Territories, northern Québec and Labrador.

Iroquois Confederacy An alliance including the five Haudenosaunee nations living south of the Great Lakes: the Seneca, Cayuga, Onondaga, Oneida, and Mohawk; the Tuscarora later joined the alliance

Jesuits An order of missionaries who came to North America to convert First Nations peoples to the Catholic religion

Legislative Assembly A government group elected by voters in British North America or in a province of Canada

Liberal-Conservatives Conservative, business-oriented English Canadians in the Canadian Assembly in the 1850s who were in favour of co-operating with the Québécois

liberator Someone who releases people from oppression, confinement, or foreign control

magistrate A judge

Manifest Destiny An American belief that it is the natural right of the United States to control all of North America

Manitoba Act A law that was passed in July 1870 in response to the Métis Bill of Rights; it created the province of Manitoba

manufacturing To make or process goods, especially in large quantities and by means of industrial machines

mass media A variety of public communication tools, including newspapers, radio, and television, used to share information with a large number of people

matrilineal ancestral descent through the maternal line

mechanical power A force that accomplishes tasks via machine

mercantilism An economic system that allowed an imperial country to become rich by selling the resources taken from its colonies

merchant In the fur trade, a financier and organizer

Métis People of mixed First Nations and European ancestry who identify themselves as Métis people. They are distinct from First Nations, Inuit and non-Aboriginal peoples. The Métis history and culture draws on diverse ancestral origins such as Scottish, Irish, French, Ojibway and Cree.

Métis Provisional Government A temporary government established by the Métis in 1864

migration movement of people within a country

minimum wage The lowest hourly rate an employer is allowed to pay an employee according to provincial law

monopoly When only one company or group is allowed to sell or trade a product in a certain area

Multiculturalism government policy designed to promote cultural understanding and harmony in a society made up of people from varied cultural, racial, and ethnic backgrounds

municipal government Local government

natural resource A part of nature that people can use

natural world The land, water, mountains, forests, plants, wildlife, and climate

Ninety-Two Resolutions A widely supported document prepared by the Patriotes in 1834 calling for sweeping governmental reforms

Nor'Wester A North West Company employee

Numbered Treaties A group of 11 treaties signed by the Canadian government and various First Nations living between the Great Lakes and the Rocky Mountains

official language The two languages the federal government must, by law, use to serve its citizens

Official Languages Act A law passed in 1969 that restates that French and English are Canada's official languages at the federal level

old-age pension A social program that provides an income for elderly people

opinion A person's thoughts or beliefs about something

oral culture A way of life in which language, teachings, and traditional stories are memorized and passed down orally from one generation to the next

pacifist A person opposed to violence as a means of settling disputes

Patriotes A group of Canadien radicals led by Louis-Joseph Papineau who wanted governmental reform leading up to the rebellions of 1837

pemmican Dried, shredded buffalo meat mixed with fat and berries

Pemmican Proclamation A government law created in 1814 that banned the Métis from exporting any meat, fish, or vegetables from the Red River settlement

persecuted Subjected to poor treatment because of one's beliefs

personal identity A complex combination of characteristics that together describe a unique person

Perspective the generally shared pont of view of a group. It can reflect the outlook of people from a cultural group, faith, age category, economic group, and so on.

petroglyph A drawing on a rock recording events or information

pluralistic society A society made up of many different groups of people, each with its own unique identities, ideas, perspectives, and culture; the resulting society has a sense of respect for all cultures

point of view An individual's personal viewpoint

points system A component of the immigration policy that rated each person who wanted to move to Canada; potential new Canadians received points for their education, skills, age, and wealth

policy A formal plan of action to achieve a specific goal

political persecution Treating a person cruelly because of his or her political beliefs

polling station Location where people vote in an election

population growth An increase in population

portage A path connecting two waterways; carrying boats or goods over land between waterways

primary source image An image of an event created by a witness

private school A school that is funded by parents or guardians through tuition fees

prospector A person who searches for precious metals

protective tariff A tax placed on a product crossing a border

Protestant school A school for Protestant students

Province The major political subdivision within Canada that shares power with the federal government

public health care A social program to provide for the public's medical needs

public school A school for all students

pull factor A factor that influences people to migrate to a certain country

push factor A factor that pushes people to leave their homelands

quarantine station A building or area where people suspected of carrying a contagious illness are kept so that they will not infect a population

Reciprocity Treaty A trade agreement between the United States and Canada by which natural resources could flow both ways across the border free of any import taxes

Red River cart A form of transportation invented by the Métis that hauled goods such as buffalo meat on land and water

The Reds English name for Les Rouges

referendum A public vote on an issue

Reformers A group of radicals in Upper Canada who wanted governmental reform leading up to the rebellions of 1837

refugee A person who flees to a country because he or she can no longer live in safety in his or her own country because of war, torture, famine, or persecution

religion A personal or institutionalized belief system

religious persecution Treating a person cruelly because of his or her religious beliefs

representation by population A system (also referred to as "rep by pop") in which elected members all represent the same number of people; the greater the number of people, the more power a region has

representative democracy A form of government in which citizens elect people to make decisions for them; the representatives make laws that are in the best interest of the people

reserve A parcel of land that the government agreed to set aside for the exclusive use of a First Nation

residential schools Boarding schools where Aboriginal children were sent and forced to adopt English ways

residual powers In Canada, the legal power over things that no one knew about in 1867

responsible government In Canada, a government (cabinet) that must answer to elected representatives

revolution An event whereby a government is overthrown and replaced with another; a fundamental change in the world

Roman Catholic missionary A Roman Catholic priest who travels for the purpose of religious charity work and promotion of the religion

Les Rouges A group of radical Canadiens in the Canadian Assembly in the 1850s that wanted independence for Québec

Royal Commission on Bilingualism and Biculturalism A group of prominent Canadians appointed in the 1960s by the Canadian government to assess why Francophone and Anglophone Canada did not seem to be getting along; this group concluded that Canada was having a language crisis and that Canada also had to consider the multicultural nature of Canadian society

Rupert's Land A vast territory named after Prince Rupert, the first head of the Hudson's Bay Company, consisting of most of what is now Western and Northern Canada

secondary source image An image created from memory, imagination, or a pre-existing image

secret ballot A method used in elections whereby an individual citizen's vote is kept confidential

seigneurial system A social system based on nobles (or seigneurs) who rented land to farmers (or habitants); the habitants had to give seigneurs a portion of their annual crop and pay other fees, and the seigneurs had to build a mill and a church on their land for the farmers

self-government A form of government in which a group is able to make the decisions that affect their lives directly

separate school A public school meant for a particular group, such as Catholic students

settlement pattern The way farms and human dwellings are arranged in a community or region

Seventh Report on Grievances A document prepared by Reformers led by William Lyon

Mackenzie in Upper Canada in 1834 requesting governmental reforms from the British

sovereign Self-governing and independent of external powers

Sovereign Council A government with three officials: a governor, an intendant, and a bishop, set up by King Louis XIV to govern the colony of New France

sovereignty Supreme governing authority

stereotype An overgeneralized portrayal of people from one group; stereotypes can reflect people's prejudices

stockade A wooden barrier of upright posts

strike An organized work stoppage by unionized employees who want to influence their employer

suburb A residential neighbourhood at a city's outskirts

suffrage The right to vote

superficial characteristic A noticeable rather than meaningful feature

superpower A country that is more powerful than almost all other countries

technology Everything that we use to carry out our tasks; the tools we use and the way we use them

territory In Canada, a major political subdivision that does not have the powers of a province

Three Sisters Haudenosaunee name for corn, beans, and squash

Traditional Teaching A unique belief of the First Nations passed down orally from generation to generation that explains how the earth was created,

how people came to exist, or the relationships among the plants, animals, land, people, and the spirit world

traitor One who betrays one's country, a cause, or a trust

transcontinental railway A railway that extends across a continent

treaty A formal agreement between nations

turning point An event that causes a significant change

Underground Railroad A secret network that transported enslaved African American escapees to the British colonies where they could be free

unilingual Use of one language

union An organization that speaks for the workers who belong to it, the purpose of which is to improve the conditions under which people work

United Empire Loyalist An inhabitant of the Thirteen Colonies who remained loyal to Britain during the American Revolution and fled to the British North American colonies after 1776

urbanization The process of people moving from the countryside to towns and cities, causing an area to become more urban

voyageur A Canadien or Métis employee of the North West Company who paddled back and forth from Montréal to the trading forts in the West

world view A way of looking at the world that reflects one's core values

York boat A boat used by the Métis to transport furs; it replaced the canoe as the main means of transportation on western rivers and lakes

Index

A **boldfaced** page number tells you where to find a related photo or diagram.

Text Credits

All text credits appear within the pages of this textbook except the following: **74 l** The journal of Father Tomás de la Peña, quoted in Donald Cutter, ed., *The California Coast* (Norman, Oklahoma: University of Oklahoma Press, 1969), p. 157, **r** Winifred David, quoted in "The Contact Period as Recorded by Indian Oral Traditions" in Barbara S. Efrat and W.J. Langois, eds., *Nu-tka: Captain Cook and the Spanish Explorers on the Coast*, (Victoria: Aural History, Provincial Archives of British Columbia, 1978), p. 54.

Photo Credits

top = t; bottom = b; centre = c; left = l; right = r

Canadian Museum of Civilization = CMC; Glenbow Archives = Glenbow; Granger Collection, New York = Granger; National Archives of Canada = NAC

Cover (clockwise from top right) Raymond Gehman/Corbis, Manitoba Archives, Glenbow/NA-3091-8, CP/Jonathan Hayward, NAC/C-002774, Background image: Jim Reed/Digital Vision/Getty Images; **4-5** Warren Gordon/Gordon Photographic; **6** NAC/C-001994; **8** Arnold Jacobs; **10** Harvey Feit; **12** NAC/C-085137; **15** © Roger Simon, 1994; **16** © Roger Simon, 1994; **18 t** Carnegie Museum of Natural History, **b** Permission of the artist, Lewis Parker; **19** Courtesy of Brenda Chambers; **21** CP/AP/Itsuo Inouye; **24 l** NAC/PA-084721, **r** Dick Hemingway; **26** Wabuno Fish Farms; **27** Spectrum Stock/Ivy Images; **30-31** History Section, Nova Scotia Museum; **36** History Collection, Nova Scotia Museum, Halifax, P179/59.60.3/N-14,501; **37** NAC/C-013938; **38** NAC/C-011226; **39** Barrett & MacKay Photography Inc.; **41** NAC/C-0057570; **42** NAC/C-005746; **43** Buffalo Bill Historical Center; **45** Réunion des Musées Nationaux/Art Resource, NY; **46** National Assembly of Quebec; **48** Congrégation de Notre-Dame, Montreal; **49** NAC/C-010688; **50** Ron Garnett/AirScapes; **52-53** NAC/C002482; **59** CP/Andrew Vaughan; **60** NAC/C-036288; **61** NAC/C-028544; **62** Parks Canada/H.03.32.09.01(01); **64** Granger; **66** D. Tanaka/Ivy Images; **67** Confederation Life/Rogers Communication; **69** Hudson's Bay Company Archives, Provincial Archives of Manitoba, G.2/27; **71** Kennan Ward/Corbis; **75** North Wind Picture Archives; **77** Kevin Fleming/Corbis; **78** Anna Clopet/Corbis; **81** NAC/C-011013; **82** NAC/C-075209; **84** NAC/C-019041; **87** Hudson's Bay Company Archives/Archives of Manitoba/P-118; **89** Spectrum Stock/Ivy Images; **90** NAC/C-002774; **91** With permission of the Royal Ontario Museum © ROM; **93 t** Derek Hayes, First Crossing: Alexander Mackenzie, His Expedition Across North America, and the Opening of a Continent, Douglas & McIntyre, Vancouver: 2001, p. 221; **93 b** NAC/C-001854; **95** Archives, McCord Museum of Canadian History, Montreal; **96** © The Field Museum/GN90633_264d/Photographer: John Weinstein; **97** Glenbow/NA-3694-1; **98-99** Granger; **103 c** NAC/C-004696, **b** Barrett & MacKay Photography Inc.; **104 t** Soldier, Drummer, Compagnies franches de la Marine, by Michel Pétard, © Parks Canada, **b** Permission of the artist, Lewis Parker; **105 l** G. Daigle/Ivy Images, **r** Barrett & MacKay Photography Inc.; **107** Permission of the artist, Lewis Parker, Courtesy of Parks Canada, N.H.S.; **108** CP/Andrew Vaughan; **109** G. Daigle/Ivy Images; **110** NAC/C-005907; **112 t** The Art Archive/General Wolfe Museum Quebec House/Eileen Tweedy, **b** NAC/C-027665; **113** CP/Le Soleil/Clement Thibeault; **115** Mackinac State Historical Parks; **116** NAC/C-000357; **119** CP/Jacques Boissinot; **123** Granger; **125** Reader's Digest; **127** Nova Scotia Archives and Records Management/1979-147/56; **128 t** CP/Andrew Vaughan, **b** Granger; **129** © National Gallery of Canada, Ottawa, 5777; **130** CP/Brantford Expositor/Brian Thompson; **132 t** NAC/C-000276, **b** Toronto Public Library/J. Ross Robertson Collection/T16600; **133 t** © Canada Post Corporation (1992). Reproduced with Permission, **b** NAC/C-003297; **135** David Tanaka; **136 t** Bettmann/Corbis, **bl** NAC/C-011811, **br** Nova Scotia Museum/79.149.3/N-9411; **138** Cincinnati Art Museum; **140** CP/Aaron Harris; **141** NAC/C-000396; **142** NAC/C-001242; **143** Toronto Public Library/Baldwin Room/Broadsides, 1841; **144** D. Tanaka/Ivy Images; **147** NAC/C-008541; **150** Royalty-Free/Corbis; **151** Granger; **152** Toronto Public Library/J. Ross Robertson Collection/1456TIB; **154 t** North Wind Picture Archives, **b** NAC/C-000773; **156** New Brunswick Museum, John Lars Johnson, painting: Marco Polo, c. 1930, oil on canvas, overall: 68.6 x 91.4 cm, Gift of the artist, 1933, 20898; **157** NAC/C-022002; **158** © National Gallery of Canada, Ottawa, 26955; **161** NAC/C-008007; **162** Al Harvey/The Slide Farm; **164** NAC/C-078864; **168-169** NAC/C-041273; **172** Glenbow/NA-4868-175; **173 t** Archives of Manitoba, **b** CP/Brandon Sun/Colin Corneau; **174 t** Courtesy Métis Nation of Ontario, **b** NAC/C-001926; **175** NAC/C081787; **176 t** With permission of the Royal

Ontario Museum © ROM, c © Library and Archives Canada. Reproduced with the permission of the Minister of Public Works and Government Services Canada (2005); **178** Hudson's Bay Company Archives, Archives of Manitoba, P-378; **179** With permission of the Royal Ontario Museum © ROM; **180** NAC/C-004572; **181 l** Glenbow/NA-293-2, **r** NAC/C-006165, **b** NAC/PA-028853; **183** NAC/C-006692; **186** NAC/C-002775; **188** Glenbow/NA-250-15; **189** Glenbow/NA-1063-1; **190** NAC/C-017430; **191 t** NAC/C-002424, **b** NAC/C-022249; **192** NAC/C-001879; **194-195** NAC/C-011033; **197** Glenbow/NA-218-1; **198** Glenbow/NA-52-1; **199 c** Parks Canada/H.08.83.02.06(52), **b** CP/Brandon Sun/Colin Corneau; **200** Glenbow/NA-1406-165; **201** Glenbow/NA-1237-1; **203 l** Al Harvey/The Slide Farm, **c** Clarence Norris/Lone Pine Photo, **r** Bill Ivy/Ivy Images; **204** CP/Rene Johnston; **205 tr** Glenbow/NA-1654-1, **bl** Canadian Pacific Railway Archives/NS.960A, **br** NAC/C-014115; **207** NAC/C-011030; **208** Glenbow/NA-978-4; **209 t** O. Bierwagen/Ivy Images, **b** Archives of Manitoba; **210** The New Iceland Heritage Museum; **211** Glenbow/M-1837-22a; **213** NAC/C-095466; **215** Steve and Mary Skjold/Index Stock Imagery; **218** Centre For Newfoundland Studies/Memorial University of Newfoundland; **219** British Colulmbia Archives PDP02612; **220** NAC/C-008077; **221** British Archives A-03081; **222 t** NAC/PA-011629, **b** NAC/C-065097; **225** City of Vancouver Archives/MAP 547; **226** Neil Rabinowitz/Corbis; **227** Confederation Arts Centre; **228** Public Archives and Records Office of Prince Edward Island/2320/12-14; **229** Collection Centre de recherche acadien de l'Î.-P.-É./1.145; **230** Public Archives and Records Office of Prince Edward Island/2602/29; **231 t** NAC/PA-027027, **b** Ron Garnett/AirScapes; **232** Glenbow/NA-488-11; **234** Provincial Archives of Alberta, B.4134; **235** Glenbow/NA-3696-11; **237** Glenbow/NA-2676-6; **238** Centre For Newfoundland Studies/Memorial University of Newfoundland; **240** NAC/PA-128080; **243** NAC/C-004745; **245** NAC/C-000932; **247** NAC/PA-025940; **248 l** NAC/C-030620, **c** NAC/C-085854, **r** NAC/C-063256; **250 t** Glenbow/NA-2507-26, **c** http://www1.travelalberta.com; **251** NAC/PA-010226; **253** NAC/C-014974; **254** D. Tanaka/Ivy Images; **255** NAC/PA-041785; **257** D. Trask/Ivy Images; **258** Craig Popoff/Take Stock; **259** CP; **261** NAC/C-081314; **262 l** NAC/PA-038567, **r** NAC/PA-021207; **264 tl** CMC/S93-1658, **bl** CMC/S94-22779, **r** CMC/S93-332; **266-267** NAC/C-011024; **270** Glenbow Museum/"Crowfoot Speaking at the Treaty 7 Negotiations" by A. Bruce Stapleton/75.10.9; **271** NAC/C-145227; **273** B. Lowry/Ivy Images; **274 t** Glenbow/NA-1584-1, **b** NAC/R6795-0-4-E, MG 30 D212 vol. 9 file 31; **275 l** Glenbow/NA-3091-8, **r** Ukrainian Voice Newspaper/Oseredok Ukrainian Cultural and Educational Centre; **276** Glenbow/NA-1926-1; **277 l** Courtesy of the Family of Yip Sai Gai, **r** Chinese Cultural Centre Calgary; **278** Glenbow/NC-6-436; **280** Glenbow/NA-332-11; **281 b** Edmonton Journal/Michael Dean; **283 l** NAC/C-011024, **r** Glenbow/NA-468-6; **284** Glenbow/NA-789-25; **286** Glenbow/NA-3267-58; **288** Jose Luis Pelaez, Inc./Corbis; **289 l** NAC/C-008827, **r** Glenbow/ND-3-3578b; **290 l** NAC/PA-181961, **r** David Young-Wolff/Photo Edit; **292** Free The Children; **293** NAC/C-036184; **294 l** Glenbow/NA-1258-22, **r** NAC/C-080917; **295** Inuit Broadcasting Corporation; **297** NAC/C-095377; **299 tl** NAC/C-024225, **tr** NAC/C-029462, **c** NAC/C-034020; **301** Notman Photographic Archives, McCord Museum of Canadian History, Montreal; **302 t** Toronto Public Library, **b** David Tanaka; **303** University of British Columbia Archives, Chung Collection [UBC 1848.9]; **304** Glenbow/NA-7928-26; **305 l** NAC/PA-168131, **r** "Young Canadian" by Charles Comfort, JM Barnicke Art Gallery, Hart House, University of Toronto; **306** NAC/C-024840; **307 t** Glenbow/NA-1170-4, **b** British Columbia Archives F-09694; **308** Glenbow/NA-3652-6; **310** Mary Kate Denny/Photo Edit; **311 tl** CP/Calgary Herald/Mikael Kjellstrom, **tr** CP/David Lucas, **c** CP/Jacques Boissinot, **bl** CP/Edmonton Sun/ Tyler Brownbridge, **br** Michael Newman/Photo Edit; **313** © Library and Archives Canada. Reproduced with the permission of the Minister of Public Works and Government Services Canada (2005), NAC C-045104; **315 l** Mach 2 Stock Photography/David Schaefer, **r** CP/Lethbridge Herald/ Ian Martens; **316** Canadian Football Hall of Fame; **318** NAC/C046350; **319** Lyle Korytar/Take Stock Inc; **320** National Aboriginal Role Model Program; **321** Native Cultural Arts Museum/H-84-397-01; **322** Larry Wong/Edmonton Journal; **323** CP/Edmonton Journal/Mike Pinder; **324** Crystal Plamondon; **326** Lyle Korytar/Take Stock Inc.; **328** Dave Elphinstone/Lone Pine Photo; **329** Johnnie Bachusky; **330 l** Mach 2 Stock Photography/Helga Pattison, **r** CP/Jeff McIntosh.